COSMIC WOMB

"Beginning in the 1960s, Chandra Wickramasinghe, Ph.D., together with Fred Hoyle systematically founded the new science of astrobiology. Their discoveries and explanations—reported in numerous scientific papers and eloquently written books—put them in a class of their own, in the same pantheon of scientific immortals as Nicolas Copernicus, Galileo Galilei, Johannes Kepler, Isaac Newton, and Charles Darwin. And now, the brilliant astrophysicist and astrobiologist Chandra Wickramasinghe, Ph.D., has joined with Robert Bauval in bringing *Cosmic Womb* to a new early 21st-century audience. *Cosmic Womb* is required reading for all those who want to understand the origins of life on Earth and throughout the cosmos. It is that important."

EDWARD J. STEELE, PH.D., MOLECULAR IMMUNOLOGIST
WITH INTEREST IN VIROLOGY AND EVOLUTION

"A fascinating book based on cutting-edge science that gives us twofold, compelling evidence—first that life (as molecules or bacteria) seeded in the whole cosmos via comets and hence there is a high probability of advanced intelligent civilizations all around us, and second, the embedding of pi, phi, geodetic units, the circumference of Earth, and the speed of light in the Great Pyramid leaves us no alternative but to admit that such a highly scientific civilization has indeed left its imprint on our planet."

CHRIS H. HARDY, PH.D., SYSTEMS SCIENTIST
AND AUTHOR OF *DNA OF THE GODS*,
WARS OF THE ANUNNAKI, AND *COSMIC DNA AT THE ORIGIN*

"*Cosmic Womb* is a book that ties together much of the cutting-edge science and theories that are defining a new paradigm of human origin and self-discovery. It is a masterpiece of investigative research that speaks to a cosmic foundation for the development and evolution of human consciousness, technology, and civilization."

GLENN KREISBERG, AUTHOR OF *SPIRITS IN STONE*
AND EDITOR OF *MYSTERIES OF THE ANCIENT PAST*
AND *LOST KNOWLEDGE OF THE ANCIENTS*

"What a team! This one is really going to make you think!"

DAVID ROHL, EGYPTOLOGIST AND
AUTHOR OF *A TEST OF TIME*

"Chandra Wickramasinghe, Ph.D., starts off by inviting us to join him on his journey as a scientist searching for the origins of life on our planet. His passion for the topic and his joy with each new discovery are contagious and spellbinding. Then Robert Bauval continues the journey by bringing fresh insights into the Giza pyramid complex as he did in his bestselling book *The Orion Mystery*."

WILL HART, AUTHOR OF *ANCIENT ALIEN ANCESTORS*
AND *THE GENESIS RACE*

COSMIC WOMB
THE SEEDING OF PLANET EARTH

CHANDRA WICKRAMASINGHE, Ph.D.,
AND ROBERT BAUVAL

Bear & Company
Rochester, Vermont • Toronto, Canada

Bear & Company
One Park Street
Rochester, Vermont 05767
www.BearandCompanyBooks.com

Text stock is SFI certified

Bear & Company is a division of Inner Traditions International

Library of Congress Cataloging-in-Publication Data
Names: Wickramasinghe, Chandra, 1939– | Bauval, Robert, 1948–
Title: Cosmic womb : the seeding of planet Earth / Chandra Wickramasinghe,
  Ph.D., and Robert Bauval.
Description: Rochester, Vermont : Bear & Company, [2017] | Includes
  bibliographical references and index.
Identifiers: LCCN 2017015057 (print) | LCCN 2017015864 (e-book) |
  ISBN 9781591433071 (pbk.) | ISBN 9781591433088 (e-book)
Subjects: LCSH: Exobiology. | Life—Origin. | Life (Biology) | Life on other
  planets.
Classification: LCC QH326 (e-book) | LCC QH326 .W5338 2017 (print) |
  DDC 576.8/39—dc23
LC record available at https://lccn.loc.gov/2017015057

Printed and bound in the United States by Lake Book Manufacturing, Inc.
The text stock is SFI certified. The Sustainable Forestry Initiative® program
promotes sustainable forest management.

10 9 8 7 6 5 4 3 2 1

Text design and layout by Debbie Glogover
This book was typeset in Garamond Premier Pro with Aquawax and Gill Sans
MT Pro for display fonts

To send correspondence to the authors of this book, mail a first-class letter to
the authors c/o Inner Traditions • Bear & Company, One Park Street, Rochester,
VT 05767, and we will forward the communication, or you may contact
Chandra Wickramasinghe at **www.profchandra.org** and Robert Bauval at
www.robertbauval.co.uk.

Contents

PART II

Intelligent Speculation Based on Cutting-Edge Science
By Robert Bauval

All truths are easy to understand once they are discovered. The point is to discover them.

GALILEO

The two greatest mysteries in all nature are the mind and the universe.

MICHIO KAKU

As a science writer, I am constantly amazed at how much stranger science is than science fiction; how much weirder the Universe we find ourselves in is than anything we could possibly have invented.

MARCUS SHOW, INSTITUTE OF PHYSICS, LONDON

If we value the pursuit of knowledge, we must be free to search wherever that search may lead us.

ADLAI E. STEVENSON II

A Mystery of the Third Kind

"Space. The final frontier . . ." These words, spoken at the beginning of each *Star Trek* episode, shaped the imaginations of a generation of baby boomers who dreamed of becoming astronauts, scientists, engineers, and explorers. Suddenly, the idea that there were other worlds and other beings out there became a real possibility. President John F. Kennedy included space exploration in his vision of the "new frontier." Our ancestors had crossed oceans, prairies, mountains, and deserts in search of better places. A rocket became the replacement transportation for the ships and covered wagons of earlier times. We humans saw ourselves as the pioneers who would be the first to explore the universe.

But are we the first "superior" beings who are here on Earth reaching toward space, or were there advanced civilizations from far away who made contact with this planet and brought knowledge so advanced that we are just beginning to grasp the magnitude of such a possibility?

In this book the renowned mathematician, astronomer, and astrobiologist Chandra Wickramasinghe, Ph.D., and the author, lecturer, and Egyptology researcher Robert Bauval have joined forces to provide compelling arguments and possibly even evidence that in ancient times an advanced civilization from somewhere in the cosmos brought life and knowledge to Earth. One important piece of physical evidence that reflects this use of advanced mathematical, geodetic, and astronomical knowledge is the Great Pyramid of Giza, built with the clear intention to have it and its two neighbors aligned with and mirroring the pattern of the stars of Orion's belt.

Throughout his life, Wickramasinghe has been consumed with the indomitable desire to know the reason why things are the way they are. As a young boy he asked the questions What is life? What are we here for? What makes the world tick? These are questions that have been asked by our ancestors from time immemorial. Attempts to answer these questions can be thought to define the progress of science.

He was born in tropical Sri Lanka—Ceylon, as it was then called—an island that was tucked away in a remote corner of the British Empire. His father was a Cambridge-educated mathematician who, in the 1930s, had attended lectures by astronomer and physicist Sir Arthur Eddington and University of Cambridge mathematician Godfrey H. Hardy, among others, and had graduated from Cambridge with the highest distinction of "B star wrangler" in the Mathematical Tripos. It was this background, combined with the fact that Sri Lanka is a country dominated by Buddhist rather than Judeo-Christian traditions, that shaped Wickramasinghe's somewhat idiosyncratic scientific and spiritual development.

In 1960 at Cambridge, Wickramasinghe, under the supervision of iconic astronomer and astrophysicist Sir Fred Hoyle, started research with the ultimate goal and dream of understanding how life started on Earth and in the universe. Hoyle made monumental contributions over a wide range of fields within astronomy and changed the way we think about the universe more than anyone had done in more than a hundred years. By 1962, Hoyle and Wickramasinghe were convinced that interstellar dust provided the chemical fabric from which life must have originated, and he collaborated on the theory of panspermia, which postulates that life originated in the cosmos long before the formation of our solar system and that it was carried to our planet by comets. Wickramasinghe learned from Hoyle that scientific opinions held by scientists, no matter how eminent they might be, should always be questioned. Hypotheses and theories are there to be continuously challenged and rigorously tested against the data that emerges from the real world. The history of science makes it amply clear that in all past ages authority stifled and strangled the progress to science. It is no different today. Blind adherence to authority must therefore be condemned.

Robert Bauval was born in Egypt in 1948. He has been haunted by the mystery of the Great Pyramid of Giza since the 1960s, and as a young boy his head was full of questions regarding this greatest of mysteries from the remote past.

Who created it? When and, more pertinently, why? The pondering of this "mystery of the third kind" has been a lifelong involvement, and now Bauval feels it is time for him to step up and expose what he has come to believe. It is a bold step, because he is aware that by doing so he is putting himself in the firing line of his critics and detractors. But so be it. Noblesse oblige.

Bauval is no stranger to criticism from his peers, and his Orion correlation theory (OCT)* has met with heated debates since it was put into the public domain in 1989. Like so many other innovative ideas, the OCT threatened the established consensus. This is especially now the case given the origins and significance of the Great Pyramid.

For the past five thousand years, and perhaps even much longer, this gigantic structure has stood on a small promontory at the eastern edge of the Sahara, a few kilometers from the Nile River and almost spot-on at the thirtieth parallel. It is a perfect geometrical assembly of two 2.6 million stone blocks, some as heavy as a modern locomotive. It has a total mass of six million tons, towering like a man-made mountain a staggering 146 meters above the ground. It was originally intentionally sealed, ostensibly made impenetrable to a nonadvanced intelligence. Only when iron tools were available was it finally broken in to, only to find its interior totally bare and bereft of any signs of human presence. Its strange and elaborate system of corridors, chambers, and shafts to this very day baffles everyone. Why was nothing found in it other than an empty and uninscribed coffer made of a single block of granite? Why

---

*See Bauval and Gilbert, *Orion Mystery*.

Fig. PP.1. The Great Pyramid of Giza in Egypt

not even one single official inscription in the pyramid or outside of it? Why this stark nakedness?* Despite the many theories proposed, the blatant truth is that no one—no scholar, no scientist, no dilettante—knows who conceived it, who designed it, and, more intriguingly, why? It is the mother of all ancient mysteries. *And what is the explanation?*

Late in 2014 the Swiss author Erich von Däniken invited Bauval and Wickramasinghe to speak at his eightieth birthday party in Stuttgart, Germany.

Bauval and Wickramasinghe had first met in late 1999, when they had participated in a conference at the Thor Heyerdahl Museum on Tenerife Island in Spain, but they had lost touch since then. The gathering at Stuttgart gave them the opportunity to rehash an old idea to do a book together on the possibility that an extraterrestrial contact had occurred in

---

*Three tiny artifacts were found in 1872, two of which, a bronze hook and a granite ball, are displayed in the British Museum (since 1994). The third artifact, a small wooden rod, has been misplaced at the Glasgow Museum. See Bauval, *Secret Chamber Revisited,* for more information.

Fig. PP.2. A meeting in Germany with (from left) Robert Bauval,
Chandra Wickramasinghe, Dominique Görlitz, and Erich von Däniken

Fig. PP.3. Robert Bauval (left) and Jean-Paul Bauval (right)
with Chandra Wickramasinghe, England, 2016

remote antiquity. It was then that Bauval told Wickramasinghe about the recent findings of his architect brother, Jean-Paul Bauval, and of intuitive mathematician Gary Osborn (appendices 1, 2, and 3) and how these dedicated researchers, among others, had convinced Bauval that the geometry of the Great Pyramid encoded a high knowledge of mathematics, geodesy, and physics that strongly implied a contact with an advanced civilization, perhaps even an extraterrestrial one.

Wickramasinghe was refreshingly open to this possibility. He had himself long suspected that such a contact might have taken place in ancient times and had no problem discussing this issue openly in a coauthored book, as long as all speculation was based on science. It was then that the phrase "intelligent speculation based on cutting-edge science" was coined, which, both authors agreed, would be the hallmark of the book project. This book presents, in two distinct parts, two different approaches on the issue that converges toward the common conclusion that perhaps a highly advanced system of knowledge, and perhaps even life itself, was brought to Earth from an alien civilization. Wickramasinghe's task was to present his findings and views on the origins of life in the cosmos and how we, as humans, evolved from it. Bauval's job was to update readers on the "new science" entailing advances in physics, cosmology, neurology, computers, virtual reality, artificial intelligence, and also what visionary scientists predict for the future. Armed with this update, Bauval would then explore the geometrical design of the Great Pyramid and give conclusions as to what this monument might really be and who or what could be behind its conception and design. Let us be clear from the outset that both authors strongly suspect extraterrestrial contact or, at the very least, an influence.

Both authors are aware, of course, how high and precarious the stakes are in the undertaking of this intellectual adventure. Both have faced the wrath of the academic and scientific communities with their theories, and now a joint collaboration between them will surely stir the controversies even further. But it was not as if they had decided to throw all caution to the wind by tackling the vexed extraterrestrial, or "ET," topic, but more that they now felt that it was high time to present with honesty and without peer intimidation the idea that the seed of life on Earth originated long ago in the cosmos, that it was carried to our planet by comets, that an ET contact might have taken place in the past, and that the various anomalistic features of the Great Pyramid should be tackled in the light of these latest discoveries in science. The authors decided to follow the argument wherever it may lead, regardless of how controversial or counterintuitive it might appear and, above all, regardless of the consensus of Egyptologists.

Alea jacta est. The proverbial die was cast.

Acknowledgments

I wish to express my gratitude to my wife, Priya, for her unstinting support at all times and her encouragement, without which my part of the book would not have become a reality.

CHANDRA WICKRAMASINGHE

This has not been an easy project for me. There was a huge learning curve to update myself on various cutting-edge scientific topics and new ideas. But the effort has been truly worthwhile, because it has forced me to reflect on the universe, on our planet, on myself, and, more importantly, on the ancient past in a completely new and exciting manner. As always, my lovely wife, Michele, has had to endure the creation of a book that, in this case, has required her to hear of very unusual topics not normal in this household. I owe Michele an immense debt for having stood by me through thick and thin for nearly forty years. I also give thanks to our two children, Candice and Jonathan, for having finally accepted that their father is not, to say the very least, the paragon of the typical dad. I would like to give special thanks to my beautiful daughter for the concept of the artwork for this book. I am, of course, also grateful to many others, far too many to name here. But the following deserve to be mentioned for their friendship and support: my brother Jean-Paul, Gary Osborn, Robert Dakota, Roberta Comuni, Maria Salabasheva, Dominique Gorlitz, and Richard Fusniak. I also want to express my appreciation to Bethany Brandon, Roberta Comuni, and Anouk Zarbhanelian for having proofread the draft and giving me their useful commentaries. Last but not least I must thank profusely my favorite editor, Mindy Branstetter, as well as all the staff at Inner Traditions • Bear & Company for making this book an item to be proud of. Finally a big "thank you" to my readers around the world: it is because of you that all this effort has been meaningful for me.

Robert Bauval

PART I

ORIGINS OF LIFE
IN THE COSMOS

BY CHANDRA WICKRAMASINGHE, PH.D.

Prologue

By Chandra Wickramasinghe

In part 1 of this book I will discuss the dilemmas and contradictions faced by conventional models in considering a vast body of evidence relating to life and its origins in the cosmos. Although a new scientific discipline has emerged by the name astrobiology (a name in fact coined by Fred Hoyle and me in 1980 but now forgotten), I shall show that a correct understanding of all the relevant facts that demand relinquishing a suite of antiquated ideas is something that the scientific community is loathe to do. It insists on following the straight and narrow path of orthodoxy. In part 2 Robert Bauval will indicate that ancient mysteries connected with archaeology require new scientific paradigms to be explored. One such case refers to the alignment of the Giza pyramids.

In modern times the involvement of the state or of large organizations in the conduct of science has become necessary to varying degrees. This is due mainly to the requirement of funds to set up laboratories, which are often expensive and beyond the reach of individual scientists. Moreover, the so-called big projects require large teams of scientists using expensive equipment, so organization and central control become imperative. Examples of ongoing big projects include the space exploration of planets by NASA, the Hadron Collider operated by CERN, Laser Interferometer Gravitational-Wave Observatory (LIGO), the observatory that recently detected gravitational waves, and several major genome sequencing projects in several countries—to name but a few.

In its earliest beginnings science arose as the solitary pursuit of individual philosophers whose ideas were often opposed to the status quo. The pre-Socratic philosopher Anaxoragas in the fifth century BC declared that the sun was a red-hot stone and the moon was made of earth, and for his heresy he was banished from Athens.

There are many aspects of the conduct of twenty-first-century science that are uncannily similar to the behavior of a totalitarian state. A totalitarian regime in politics sets out a rigid framework of rules to govern society and a system of law for punishing those who disobey. Transgressions being met with severe penalties implied that there was always a firm motive for citizens to conform. Communist regimes, such as existed in the Soviet Union in the twentieth century, fit well into this general pattern.

While in the spheres of politics and economics such state control may have a justification as a prerequisite for firm and effective government. A similar control extending to other areas of creativity including art, music, and science is less desirable and may act in a way that impedes progress. The justification of eugenics in Nazi Germany with its grotesque and inhumane consequences and the enforcement of obscurantist biological theories including Lamarckism in the Soviet Union, provide examples of such conduct. Biology under Marxism also vigorously defended the principle of spontaneous generation despite the fact that this principle was essentially disproved by the experimental work of Louis Pasteur in the 1860s.

Ideas of the Russian biologist Aleksandr Oparin, which led to the theory of the origin of life in a primordial soup, were undoubtedly inspired by the tenets of dialectical materialism. Oparin and the Soviet scientists drew their inspiration from the German philosopher Freidrich Engels, who had proposed that new qualities of "being" arose at each new stage of organic evolution. Engels noted that higher levels of existence resulted from lower levels, and this progression was deemed part of the natural order of things. The primordial soup paradigm of the origin of life derived from this philosophy still remains the reigning dogma

Fig. P.1. Aristarchus of Samos, first Western philosopher to propose the idea of panspermia

in science although its political and philosophical antecedents are now largely forgotten. We shall discuss this paradigm in a later chapter.

As we already mentioned, science in the earliest days arose from the initiative of a few, often rebellious, individuals who did not require support or sponsorship from the state. Aristarchus of Samos (310–230 BC) and Hipparcus of Niceae (190–120 BC), who estimated the sizes of the Earth, moon, sun, and the distances of stars by methods of parallax, did not need any expensive equipment. Their work could not therefore have been stopped or prevented by state intervention, if the state happened to be hostile to the outcome.

Modern science has taken on a totally different turn, where progress depends crucially on expensive equipment, large teams of workers, and the support, direct or indirect, of large organizations sponsored by the State. If ideas ran counter to those of an influential majority or a powerful establishment, progress will be severely hampered. This is true both in a capitalist system as well as under Communism, such as prevailed in the old Soviet Union. In either case the control of new ideas is what one would expect within a totalitarian political system. Dissent from a majority position in science is quickly and effectively quelled by starvation of funds or the chastisement of those attempting to promote contrary views.

If all this is true, how, one might ask, is scientific progress still taking place, seemingly at an astounding pace? To answer this question it is useful to divide science into several types. The type of empirical/

predictive science that informs us how matter—living or nonliving—behaves is the kind of science that we routinely learn at school and university. The mechanics of Newton, atomic and nuclear physics, the well-attested properties of matter and radiation do not offer themselves as subjects of political dispute of any kind. It is upon this kind of science that the entire structure of modern technology depends. It is this type of science that was involved in the recent launch of the Rosetta Mission to a comet and the amazingly successful landing of spacecraft *Philae* on a 1-kilometer-size target, which was 317 million miles away! Although biology at a molecular level (for example, DNA sequencing) is in the same category, the bigger organizational and inferential structures of biology (for example, theories of the origin and evolution of life) lend themselves to manipulation by political and scientific authorities. This is the reason why paradigm shifts in these areas are so difficult to accomplish and their execution fraught with such bitterness and strife, as we shall see in this section.

1
Definite Knowledge vs. Speculation

The stars that yon great firmament adorn
Have birth and death, and yet again are born
And in the skirt of Heaven, the womb of Earth
And they whom God will yet bring to the morn.

THE RUBAYYAT OF OMAR KHAYYAM
TRANSLATED BY EDWARD FITZGERALD

Fig. 1.1. Earth from the moon

Fig. 1.2. Sun, planets, and dwarf planets

We now compare aspects of the external world that constitute definite knowledge with others that still occupy the realm of speculation or hypothesis. In some instances a speculative idea eventually comes to be supported by an overwhelming weight of evidence that transports it across the boundary into the realm of fact.

In all past ages people have suffered from wrong ideas about the nature of the world often mistaking speculation for fact. The wrong ideas were often passionately defended until eventually with the arrival of new facts they came to be overturned and replaced. The idea of an Earth-centerd universe was the order of the day for the astronomer-poet Omar Khayyam in eleventh-century Persia. Geocentric cosmology so placing Earth at the center of things prevailed throughout Europe from the time of the Rubayyat well into the Elizabethan era. The slow process of demoting the Earth from the center of things began at the beginning of the sixteenth century. The Copernican revolution, beginning with publication by Copernicus of *De revolutionibus orbium Celestium* in 1543, progressing through the trial of Galileo Galilei, and culminating in the efforts of Tycho Brahe, Kepler, and Newton, finally

Fig. 1.3. Our solar system's placement in a galaxy similar to our Milky Way

removed the Earth from its privileged position of centrality in the solar system. This trend in which our place in the cosmos became diminished continued with advances in astronomy through the nineteenth, twentieth, and twenty-first centuries. Newer and more powerful telescopes and equipment combined with deployment of spacecraft continue to contribute to this process. We now know that our solar system is one of hundreds of billions of similar planetary systems in our Milky Way galaxy, which itself is one of countless billions of galaxies in the observable universe.

The material of all earthly life, including ourselves, is derived from atoms that owe their existence to cosmic processes. The carbon, oxygen, nitrogen, phosphorus, and metals in our bodies were all synthesized in the deep interiors of stars and were scattered into our midst by massive stars that exploded at the end of their lives—supernovae.

Regarding current ideas about the grand structure of the universe, cosmology favors a unique origin of the entire universe that is supposed to have taken place 13.8 billion years ago—the big bang theory. This theory owes its origins to Edwin Hubble's discovery in the 1940s of an expanding universe—distant galaxies moving away from one another. From this discovery the idea developed that the entire universe started

Some look like our galaxy, the Milky Way

Fig. I.4. Deep Hubble field of distant galaxies highlighting one spiral galaxy

as a "point" at some instant of time in the past. After the lapse of 10^{-36} seconds following this big bang event 13.8 billion years ago, the universe, which was then still smaller than a single atom, is supposed to have undergone an episode of inflation lasting for some 10^{-33} seconds. Quantum fluctuations in this submicroscopic universe are next posited to be amplified along with the expansion of the universe, so accounting for everything we observe—subatomic particles, atoms, clusters of galaxies, galaxies, stars, planets, and ourselves. And what was there before the big bang event 13.8 billion years ago? Of course nothing, and this is the question that is reckoned by some to be meaningless—because nothing existed before: not even time! Even the very concept of time may not have a meaning.

This is the so-called standard cosmological theory, elegantly crafted in mathematical formulation and widely supported by a vast and powerful scientific establishment. But for sure it is not cast in stone. It has to be admitted that a sizeable chunk of relevant ideas still occupy the realm of speculation, and societal and cultural constraints play a crucial role in defense of this model. Other, less popular but equally elegant, formulations involve models of the universe that are oscillating, with expansion successively followed by contraction, and possessing an essentially infinite age. It is interesting to note that some of these models are strikingly reminiscent of Vedantic cosmologies and the philosophies of India that predated the Christian era by many centuries. Likewise it must be admitted that the standard big bang cosmology does indeed look very much like a modern rendering of the Judeo-Christian story of creation.[1]

The modern trend to support the currently fashionable big bang cosmology is likely to be as transient as were earlier arguments favoring a long sequence of other cosmologies. The medieval cosmology famously describing the world as a globe carried on the back of a white elephant standing on top of an infinite stack of turtles comes to mind. As mentioned at the outset, all earlier models of the world, including the pre-Copernican Earth-centered cosmology, were passionately defended, but they all turned out to be wrong. It seems likely that the currently favored big bang cosmology will require serious revision in the fullness of time. Modern astronomical data on galaxies forming some four hundred million years (a twinkling of an eye!) after the big bang are beginning to strain the credibility of standard cosmologies. Moreover, we cannot but remain slightly uneasy with the current status quo where the age of the entire universe is scarcely three times the age of the Earth. But let's not tarry on such inconsequential details.

Let us next turn our attention to Earth, planets, and smaller things, knowledge about which is more certain. Recent studies have shown that the earliest evidence of microbial life on the Earth dates to a time some 4.1 billion years ago.[2] Signatures of this early life are to be found as carbon isotope signatures in grains trapped within zircons that condensed when the Earth's surface was still molten hot and when comet and meteorite impacts were still frequent. This episode of intense meteorite bombardment, representing the last stages in the accumulation of the Earth's crust, was followed by a period of bombardment by cometary bolides from the outer solar system that would have lasted for a third of a billion years. It is such icy bodies that brought most of the water that went to form the Earth's oceans. Evaporation of water from the oceans led to an atmosphere and a cloud cover beneath which microbial life that also came with the comets was able to thrive.

In addition to the eight planets in the solar system there are tens of thousands of minor planets, planetoids, or asteroids, and surrounding this entire system at a distance of a tenth of a light-year from the sun is a gigantic shell of comets—the so-called Oort cloud. Most of the asteroids orbit around the sun in a plane between the orbits of Mars and Jupiter in the solar system, but an important class of objects known as Trans-Neptunian, or Kuiper-Belt, objects have orbits that take them far beyond the orbit of Neptune. Over the past decade several comets and minor planets (e.g., Ceres and Pluto) have been examined at close range using instruments carried by spacecraft. We are finding that the distinction between comets and large-class minor planets—typified by Pluto and Ceres—is fast disappearing. Most of the comets that we see from time to time in the sky come from this cloud of comets when they get pushed by passing stars into highly elliptical orbits that bring them into the inner solar system. We shall have much more to say about comets later in this part of our book.

There is also in our vicinity a vast number of small fragments of rock and ice that orbits the sun. When these objects enter the Earth's atmosphere they are heated to incandescence; and the visible streak in the sky is recognized as a meteor. If such a piece survives to reach the Earth's surface it is recognized as a meteorite.

Most of the Earth's early history as a planet from 2.4 billion years ago to 0.6 billion years ago was marked by an alternation of intense cold leading to almost total glaciation and greenhouse/hothouse conditions when tropical temperatures would have prevailed from pole to pole. The so-called Huronian glaciation, which is possibly the severest of ice ages on record, straddled the period from 2.4 to 2.3 billion years ago, and the last major glaciation event, the Cryogenian snowball Earth, persisted from 850 to 630 million years ago. In both these instances the Earth was plunged into the deepest cold.

LIFE ON EARTH

Bacteria and other unicellular life-forms are the only life that existed on the Earth for the first 2 billion years of its history. The record of such early life is found in accumulations of carbonate mineral including calcite and dolomite that are pointers to biology. From evidence of this kind, and more directly from the existence of stromatolites—layered sedimentary grains cemented by biofilm—it can be inferred that microorganisms existed throughout the first 3.5 billion years of the Earth's history. Such single-celled life-forms were followed by a dramatic explosion of an extraordinarily wide range of multicelled life-forms between 530 and 520 million years ago—the so-called Cambrian explosion. The fact that this happened with extreme suddenness, leaving no trace of any intermediate forms or stages of development leading to multicellularity, presents a continuing enigma for Earth-bound evolutionary theories.

Recent studies on the DNA sequencing of many life-forms have shown that regulatory genes that determine cell function as well as morphology span a wide range of phyla, but why a particular set of genes conducive to cooperative behavior and multicellurality took 3.5 billion years to switch on remains a puzzle. The neo-Darwinian idea that a succession of small changes caused by mutations and consequent innovations derived in situ and followed by natural selection—survival of the fittest—explains such sudden jumps is not supported by the available data.

Some 40 million years after the Cambrian explosion of life, much of the newly evolved species fizzled out from the geological record and were replaced by an exceedingly rich assortment of brand-new flora during another sudden event known as the Great Ordovician biodiversification event. This moment in time can arguably be regarded as the starting point of all the radiations of modern flora and fauna on the Earth. Recent studies have thrown light on the likely extraterrestrial origin of the Ordovician event. In 2014 a group of Swedish scientists discovered a new class of meteorite that appears to have resulted from a gigantic collision in the asteroid belt precisely 470 million years ago, coinciding exactly with the timing of the Ordovician event. Similar events involving cometary and meteoritic interactions with the Earth may, in our view, be responsible for later episodes of biodiversification as well as for a series of mass extinction events that punctuate the long history of terrestrial life.

EMERGENCE OF HOMINIDS

Our own immediate line of descent, the hominids, are thought to have inhabited Eastern Africa five to seven million years ago. The first modern humans walked out of the jungles of Africa as hunter-gatherers 300,000 years ago, when the total population may have been less than 1 million. By about 15,000 years ago we have evidence from cave paintings showing animal shapes linked with constellations in the sky bearing testimony to a burgeoning interest in the cosmos. Artists in more recent times have further pursued our links with the cosmos, as for instance in Paul Gaugin's famous nineteenth-century painting with the title *Where do we come from? What are we? Where are we going?* These questions epitomize an unending human quest to understand our ultimate origins, a quest that continues to the present day. In 2017 we have perhaps a little more than a glimmer of the correct answers; but their fullest significance could well continue to elude us for centuries or millennia to come.

Fig. 1.5. Where do we come from? What are we? Where are we going?
Painting by Paul Gauguin (see also color plate 1)

The nature of our existence as sentient humans was mostly shrouded in magic, mystery, and religion until the intervention of Charles Darwin in 1859. The publication in that year of Darwin's *On the Origin of Species* met with violent opposition, particularly from the church. In a debate that took place at the Oxford University Museum a few months after the Darwin book was published, Bishop Samuel Wilberforce is said to have famously asked Huxley, geologist and Darwin's friend, whether he claimed his descent from a monkey on his grandfather's or grandmother's side! Whether this exchange really took place is largely irrelevant. But it cannot be denied that removing God from the story of creation caused great consternation. Many people felt at the time that they were robbed of the comforting sense of security they had enjoyed for so long in the illusory belief in an omniscient, all-powerful God.

Darwin's theory of 1859 still remains the cornerstone of modern biology. The most recent studies on genome sequencing have established a genetic and biochemical unity of all life, with our own links traced back to simpler life-forms extending all the way down to the humblest bacterium.

At the most rudimentary chemical level, life in all its varied shapes and forms involves the interaction between two groups of biochemicals— nucleic acids and proteins. Each of these constitutes linked chains of simpler molecules, the arrangements of which carry information crucial for life. The nucleic acids (which are double stranded) are themselves constructed from a sugar (ribose) and a phosphate wrapped into a heliacal structure, with pairs of bases (adenine, guanine, thymine, and cytosine) straddling the double helix. The proteins contain about twenty-one separate amino acids linked in folded chains of several hundred molecules in length. The myriad possible arrangements of these twenty-seven or so basic chemical structures make for the enormously wide diversity of life.

IMPROBABILITY OF LIFE

The blueprint for all life from bacteria to plants and animals was discovered in the 1950s by Watson and Crick to reside in DNA—in

Fig. 1.6. Chandra Wickramasinghe and Fred Hoyle at the blackboard in 1979

particular in the precise arrangements of the nucleotides A, G, T, C that effectively code for proteins that in turn control cell function. In a series of books and articles published in collaboration with the late Sir Fred Hoyle, I have argued that the highly specific arrangements needed for the operation of living cells cannot be understood as arising from random processes.[3] For the simplest bacterium (*Mycoplasma genitalium*) the probability that its few hundred genes will be discovered by random shuffling of their amino-acid components gives a figure of 1 in 10^{1000} or smaller. Hoyle and I have compared such horrendous improbabilities to the odds against a "tornado blowing through a junk yard leading to self-assembly of a BOEING 707 airplane."

But how, when, and where did the first bacterial cell originate? With the successful completion of the Copernican revolution at the end of the sixteenth century the importance of the Earth as regards its physical placement in the cosmos diminished. However, the Earth's supremacy in regard to life and our own existence lingered well in to the twentieth century. The idea of life originating on Earth in a primordial soup was first proposed by Haldane and Oparin in the early part of the twentieth century, and this point of view gained support throughout the latter part of the century.

The idea of an Earth-based primordial soup is now beginning to wear exceedingly thin with the arrival of new evidece from many directions. We have already mentioned that the oldest evidence of life on Earth dates back to 4.1 billion years ago, which is perhaps the first moment in Earth's history when life could have survived.[4] The window of opportunity for a primordial soup, therefore, appears to be pretty well squeezed out of the geological record. The emerging paradigm is of comets and meteorites that predated Earth introducing life in a full-fledged genetic form from 4.1 billion years ago. We shall argue in a later chapter that the blueprint for all life embracing every future contingency and possibility may have predated the solar system by billions of years and may even be in some way an intrinsic property of the universe. This implies an element of teleology—meaning that the shape of life and things to come are in some way already predetermined. Some readers may find this point of view culturally or philosophically unacceptable. But the universe is the way it is and cannot be constrained by social or cultural prejudice.

Once the first life took root on Earth its later development involving the incorporation of new cosmically derived genes was dictated largely by the ever-changing conditions at the Earth's surface.[5] New bacterial and viral genes as well as minor mutations of existing genes manifested themselves in emerging phenotypes subject to their fitness for survival in the context of ever-changing habitats.

While evidence for life originating on Earth is fast vanishing, there still remains a mystery as to *where* the first self-replicable and evolvable living cell arose. Extending the canvas of life's origin to embrace ever-larger cosmic dimensions is of course a help, but the ultimate mystery of overcoming a superastronomical improbability hurdle does not entirely vanish.

We can argue that such essentially impossible odds provide the most compelling evidence of a form of intelligence at work—a cosmic intelligence or even an intelligent universe. Crick and Orguel, in their article "Directed Panspermia,"[6] skirted around a similar idea based on the high degree of specificity in the arrangement of nucleotides in DNA. The possibility that the Earth was deliberately seeded with life designed by a superintelligent civilization thus remains a logical possibility. But that still begs the question of how and where the superintelligent civilization emerged. Perhaps we are witnessing a convergence of some abstract concept of God.

At the present time the transfer of genes (DNA) between diverse life-forms is being discussed, and some such transfers are routinely carried out for practical purposes—for example, developing pest-resistant or better yielding genetically modified crops.[7] A thousand years from now it is entirely conceivable that our descendants will have developed biotechnology to the stage of actually being able to engineer the construction of new life-forms and distributing their genetic seeds throughout the galaxy. Then there is the even more radical possibility that a superhuman civilization became sufficiently advanced technologically to travel between neighboring stars and perhaps directly influenced the course of evolution on alien planets. As far out an idea as this might seem, the prospect has come closer to reality in recent years following the discovery of exoplanets (alien planets like Earth) in our own neighborhood. On the basis of a small sample of our galaxy that has thus far been searched, the current estimate for the total number of habitable exoplanets in the galaxy exceeds 140 billion, with an average separation between neighbors being only some five light-years. The discovery of an Earth-like planet orbiting our nearest neighboring star Proxima Centauri 4.1 light-years away is of particular interest in this context. The prospects for alien life and alien intelligence have soared.

2
Unraveling of a Controversy

We mentioned earlier that the oldest evidence of microbial life on Earth now goes back to 4.1 billion years. At this time the surface of the Earth would have been relentlessly pounded by comet and meteorite impacts leading to surface temperatures that would have been too high for any incoming life to take root. What is found as evidence of life at this time is most likely microbes falling from space that become instantly carbonized on reaching a molten lava field on the Earth. The rocks containing this evidence are found in an outcrop in western Australia and another outcrop in Quebec, Canada.

A somewhat mysterious fact we touched on earlier is that once life is indeed established on Earth in the form of single-celled microbes, it remains in this form for the next 3.5 billion years. Suddenly, 540 million years ago, multicellular life turns up. No one really understands why it took so long to appear, but it remains a fact that every life-form existing today—plant, animal, insect—can trace a direct link genetically to the panorama of life that came to be suddenly established 540 million years ago. It may not be a coincidence that the solar system at this time was brushing against a giant molecular cloud as it was pursuing its 240-million-year-long orbit around the center of our Milky Way galaxy.

From this time forward living forms began to evolve, not continuously but in fits and starts, until at the end of a long line of descent a

18

life-form emerged that that can look back on the processes that created it. This is the stage we have reached today—*Homo sapiens sapiens* endowed with a brain and intellect capable of unraveling the mysteries of the universe, so say.

A PERSONAL BACKGROUND

My own interest in astronomy and thinking about our place in the universe started at a very early age.[1] I think I was fortunate to grow up as I did outside Colombo, Sri Lanka, at a time when there was almost no light pollution to speak of. Night after night the magnificent spectacle of the Milky Way arching across the sky greeted me. By the age of thirteen I vividly remember many evenings of animated discussion about the universe I had with my father, who was himself a gifted mathematician. How did the universe come into existence? How many stars and planets are there? Are there other beings on other planets? Is there life like ours outside the Earth? All these questions had a resonance with my Buddhist upbringing, and I noticed quite early that answers from science and Buddhism often converged.

As a child I was passionate to find answers to these questions, but I soon realized that to make progress one had to acquire a strong background in physics and mathematics. After my schooling I went on to study mathematics at the University of Ceylon and after three years obtained a First Class Honors degree in mathematics. I next found myself, in September 1960, proceeding to Cambridge on a British Commonwealth Scholarship. My plan was to work for a Ph.D. in astrophysics under the direction of Fred Hoyle—the iconic astronomer and astrophysicist of the twentieth century. My first research project was on a somewhat mundane astrophysical problem. It was to understand how the sun's magnetic field reversed every eleven years. This could not have been more distant from my ultimate goal and dream of understanding how life started on Earth and in the universe. That goal came to be approached more cautiously and in slow stages occupying the next fifty years.

INTERSTELLAR DUST THEORIES

The first tentative steps in this direction were taken in the summer of 1961.[2] Fred Hoyle invited me to join him on a walking trip in the Lake District, and it was on this occasion, in the lounge of the hotel where we stayed, that the beginnings of my intellectual journey properly began. I told Fred quite directly that I would like to work on problems that related to the origin of life in the universe. Fred Hoyle could not immediately see how such a goal could be achieved in practical terms, but he led me in a direction that showed some sign of a connection. It was fortuitous that he himself had skirted around this subject in the 1950s and had an intuition that the galaxy must be chockablock with organic molecules.

On dark, clear, moonless nights the whitish band of light arching across the sky is the Milky Way, comprised of billions of individual stars more or less similar to the sun. The Milky Way is splattered with dark clouds and striations, which are actually gigantic clouds of microscopic dust particles that are so dense as to blot out the light of background

Fig. 2.1. Fred Hoyle in the Lake District, 1961

Fig. 2.2. Eagle's nest nebula showing dense clouds of dust in the galaxy (see also color plate 2)

stars. What is this dust made of, and where does it originate? In 1960 the fashionable answer was that they were comprised of microscopic ice grains, very similar to the ice particles that exist in the cumulous clouds of the Earth's atmosphere.

After less than a year of study in Cambridge, I was able to debunk this hallowed ice grain theory, proposing instead that the particles were made mostly of the element carbon. This radical new theory was published in 1962 and immediately led to a ferocious debate among astronomers who wished to maintain the status quo and not let go of the old ice grain idea that had become the holy grail of astronomy for twenty years. After a decade and a half of bitter struggle I won my first scientific battle: the carbon dust theory replaced the ice grain theory, and that was that, or so it seemed to me at the time.[3] But in science it is never that easy. One thing often leads to another, and sometimes new and unexpected connections emerge.

LIFE MOLECULES IN SPACE

In 1974 the carbon dust theory took a new turn. I published a compelling argument in the journal *Nature* that the carbon in interstellar dust was not in the form of inorganic soot or graphite but existed as complex organic polymers.[4] Although Fred Hoyle did not himself coauthor the first paper on organic polymers, he fully endorsed the idea and felt impelled to take the matter even further. After many exchanges of letters and phone calls Fred Hoyle became convinced that the interstellar dust to which he introduced me in 1961 provided the chemical fabric from which life must have originated and that the Earth-bound primordial soup idea had to be challenged.

In 1977, I came to the conclusion that the chemical composition of interstellar dust (judged by certain features in astronomical spectra) was unequivocally organic, and the best types of organics that matched all the data were similar to biochemicals—that is to say, molecules or chemical substances associated with life.[5] However, there were several problems to be resolved. Just as when we see a streetlamp through a fog its light is dimmed and reddened due to scattering by microscopic droplets on the way, a star shining through clouds of cosmic dust is also made to look dimmer and redder. Over the visible wavelength range from 7,000 to 3,000Å, the extinction or dimming of starlight was observed by astronomers to show an invariable pattern, and this behavior was exactly the same in whatever direction one looked. Such a constancy and invariance of behavior was difficult to reconcile with the dust grain models that were being discussed within the framework of orthodox astronomy involving mixtures of inorganic dust particles.

BACTERIAL DUST IN SPACE

Unraveling the composition of interstellar dust had led us in slow stages through a sequence of options: carbon (graphite) particles, organic polymers, and then to complex biopolymers such as cellulose. These organic polymeric particles that had to be present everywhere in the galaxy

possessed an average size of a typical bacterium and scattering properties for starlight that exactly matched a freeze-dried hollow bacterium.
Good fits to all the available astronomical data became possible on
this single assumption—bacteria-like particles in space. Could this be
a coincidence? A fluke? Could all this be somehow explained without
invoking biology? Of course these questions continued to plague us for
many months but had to be explored.

DAWN OF LIFE AS
A COSMIC PHENOMENON

After weeks of fumbling through a long sequence of ideas, all of which
were proving to be woefully inadequate, we alighted on the most promising, if not utterly outrageous, question. In the gigantic clouds of
interstellar dust could we be witnessing nothing other than the dissemi-
nation of biology? Could interstellar space be chockablock, not simply
with the chemical building blocks of life but with the end products of
the living process as well? Living cells and their degradation products!
And this would then be required to happen on an unimaginably vast
scale. At the end of a long run of frenzied telephone calls between my
home in Cardiff and Cockley Moor in the Lake District where Fred
Hoyle then lived, we decided that was it! Interstellar grains must surely
be bacteria—albeit freeze-dried—but not all dead![6]

SERENDIPITY

Here next was an example of the intervention of serendipity in help-
ing our case. My brother D. T. Wickramasinghe (Dayal), professor of
mathematics at the Australian National University in Canberra, was
also an astronomer and frequently used the 3.9-meter Anglo-Australian
Telescope, which happened to be equipped with just the right instruments to look for a spectroscopic signature of interstellar bacteria we
could predict on the basis of our bacterial model.

Shortly after our calculations on the scattering properties of bacterial
dust was published in 1979, Dayal visited Cardiff to spend some time

with our family. Dayal's visit happened to coincide with a time when Fred Hoyle was also in Cardiff. We naturally got talking about matters relating to interstellar bacteria. Dayal asked, "What do you think can be done at the telescope to prove or disprove your theory?" to which we promptly replied that he could use the infrared spectrometers on the AAT to look at infrared sources near the wavelength of 3.4 micrometers in greater detail than before. A very long path length through the galaxy was needed to have any hope of detecting such an effect unambiguously. The longest feasible path length through interstellar dust that existed within our own galaxy was defined by the distance from the Earth to the center of the galaxy. There were several sources of infrared radiation located near the galactic center that could serve as searchlights for interstellar bacteria. Dayal was doubtful that he would be allocated observing time if he applied for such time specifically to do this project. The general consensus then was that searching for life in space was not regarded as respectable science! Dayal overcame this difficulty however. Although honesty is the best policy it often pays handsomely to be economical with the truth in a world of dubious morality. The deceit involved applying for telescope time to do a quite different project and then illicitly using part of the time to look for the signature of organic matter.[7]

The observations that were to mark a crucial turning point in our story were carried out in this way by Dayal and D. A. Allen at the AAT in May 1981 *after* an experimental prediction of what we might expect from bacterial dust had been made. Dayal sent us his raw data by fax to compare with our laboratory spectra, and after an hour or so of straightforward calculations we were able to overlay the astronomical spectrum over the detailed predictions of the bacterial model to find a staggering fit. This was the best possible confirmation of our model that we could hope for, particularly because the experimental data was obtained *before* the astronomical observations became available. A precise agreement between a set of data points and a predicted curve is normally regarded as a consistency check and validation of the model. The closeness of this fit would normally have been hailed as a triumph of the model. But in our case, because the model of bacterial grains runs counter to a major paradigm in science, the situation was otherwise. All hell broke loose!

REPLICATION OF BACTERIA
IN A COSMIC CONTEXT

We all know that given the right conditions, which include liquid water and nutrients, bacteria can grow exponentially. A typical doubling time for bacteria would be two to three hours. Continuing to supply nutrients, a single initial bacterium would generate some 2^{40} offspring in four days, yielding a culture with the size of a cube of sugar. Continuing for an additional four days and the culture, now containing 2^{80} bacteria, would have the size of a village pond. Another four days and the resulting 2^{120} bacteria would have the scale of the Pacific Ocean. Yet another four days and the 2^{160} bacteria would be comparable in mass to a molecular cloud like the Orion Nebula. And four days more still for a total time since the beginning of twenty days, and the bacterial mass would be that of a million galaxies. No nonbiological process remotely matches this replication power of a biological cell. Once the immense quantity of organic material in the interstellar material is appreciated, a biological origin for it becomes an absolutely necessary conclusion. This was the position we had arrived at in 1980, and it continues to constitute one of the most compelling arguments in favor of cosmic biology.

But where are astronomical locations where conditions for replication of bacteria can be found? Certainly not in the cold depths of space, where microbes could merely remain in a freeze-dried, dormant state. Planets like the Earth provide too small a total mass of carbonaceous material in the right physical state to make any impact. It is therefore to comets we turned, arguing that comets are the main sources of biological particles in interstellar clouds. An individual comet is a rather small and insubstantial object. But our solar system possesses more than a hundred billion comets that in total mass equal the combined masses of the outer planets Uranus and Neptune, about 10^{29} grams. If all the dwarf stars (sunlike stars) in our galaxy are similarly endowed with comets, then the total mass of all the comets in our galaxy, with its 10^{11} dwarf stars, turns out to be some 10^{40} grams, which is just the amount of all the interstellar organic particles that are found to be present in the dust clouds within the galaxy.

How would microorganisms be generated within comets, and then how could they get out of comets? We know as a matter of fact that comets do eject organic particles, typically at a rate of a million or more tons a day when they visit the inner regions of the solar system. Hoyle and I argued that comets, when they are formed, incorporate interstellar bacterial particles from which only the minutest fraction (10^{-22}) needs to retain viability for a cosmic regeneration process to operate.[8] For at least a million years, at the time of their origin, comets would have possessed liquid cores due to the release of energy from radioactive materials which were incorporated within them. Within a very brief period sequential doublings of viable microorganisms would lead to an entire cometary core being converted into biomaterial. When the comets refreeze this amplified microbial material is also frozen in, only to be released when they become periodically warmed in the inner solar system. Some of this bacterial matter may reach planets, which they can seed with life; some of it is expelled back into interstellar space.

DISEASES FROM SPACE?

The next development in our story also came as a surprise and led to further clashes with orthodox science.[9] June of 1977 was a particularly inclement month in Wales, and I had succumbed to one of the worst bouts of flu that I could remember. Fred Hoyle and I were in a phase of brisk telephone and fax communication at the time trying to fit a swathe of new astronomical data to our biological dust models.

All this was to change dramatically when, delirious with high fever, I telephoned Fred Hoyle in Cockley Moor in June 1977. I was prompted to pose the question, "Could this flu bug I am suffering from have possibly come from space? Could the old myth that influenza is connected with rain and drizzle be right after all? Could viruses and bacteria be carried in comet dust and actually be entering Earth to infect us at the present time? I recalled that the connection between diseases like the common cold and influenza and inclement weather was well entrenched in Sri Lankan folklore. My mother always told us, 'Don't go out in the rain, you'll catch the cold.'"

My question to Fred brought down a pall of silence on the phone line. Fred Hoyle had listened to all that was said and replied, "I shall think about it and phone you back." He did in fact telephone back only to agree that this could well be so! Fred was reminded of conversations he had many years back with Australian physicist E. G. (Taffy) Bowen, who had pointed out that an amazing connection existed between freezing nuclei in rain clouds and meteor showers.[10] So the evidence we needed may have already been in place two decades earlier.

As a natural consequence of this line of thinking I guessed that patterns of viral diseases over the centuries may reflect the changing environment of cometary meteor showers—the Earth crossing the orbits of debris from different life-bearing comets. Could the common cold and influenza, which are so common today, have been absent in the portfolio of diseases in past times? I remember asking Fred another question that took him aback. Did he know of any Shakespearean character with a common cold? Surely Shakespeare, who dealt with almost every human condition, may have thought fit to have a character sniffling with a heavy cold? After combing through Shakespeare's plays the answer was that there were none.

This prompted us to study a variety of books on medical history, including the writings of Hippocrates and Galen and the classic Indian medical treatise *Charaka Samhita,* all of which confirmed that there was certainly clear evidence of a changing pattern of infectious diseases over time. The twentieth-century belief that all pathogens must necessarily have a purely terrestrial origin had no basis in fact. We had argued earlier that comets carried the first life to the Earth 4.1 billion years ago, and this process of bringing new viruses and bacteria could not be assumed to have stopped at some distant time in the past. Comets are with us still and so must continue to have an effect.

Our ancestors of bygone ages were unanimous in believing that comets were the cause of disease and pestilence. All ancient civilizations, including the Indians and Chinese, subscribed to this point of view. We tend nowadays to dismiss these ancient ideas as primitive superstition born out of ignorance. But was this really so? They were perhaps more civilized in many ways than the societies that strut the stage today.

Fig. 2.3. Diseases raining down from space—
The Triumph of Death; *painting by Pieter Bruegel, circa 1562*

They were certainly not bound by adherence to dogma. Nor were they constrained by the authority of institutions that decided what was respectable and proper to believe and what was not. They observed and reported what they saw and experienced.

RED FLU PANDEMIC AND ANTECEDENTS

The incident of June 1977 was followed by another serendipitous event. A variety of flu (H1N1) that had not been in circulation for many decades was causing an epidemic that apparently started in Russia (Red Flu Pandemic). This was a godsend for testing the hypothesis of flu from space. Schoolchildren younger than twenty-one years of age would not have encountered this virus and would in principle all be equally susceptible. It was Fred's idea to use such children as "detectors" of the virus; so we set about the mammoth task to conduct a survey of schools in Wales and England.

The outcome of the survey amply confirmed our suspicions. The way in which cases of influenza were distributed among the boarding-houses at Howell's School Cardiff and Eton College could not be explained on the basis of person-to-person spread. The indications were clear: that a component at least of the causative agent fell from the skies and was distributed at ground level in accord with the vagaries of swirling air currents.

The success of our studies of the epidemiology of the 1977/1978 influenza pandemic followed by investigations of the history of past epidemics amply confirmed our conviction that viral and bacterial agents of external origin are involved. One particular case was the influenza pandemic of 1918/1919 that claimed more than thirty million deaths worldwide. In 1974, Louis Weinstein, reviewing data from the archives, reported on several aspects of the pandemic that did not fit a simple person-to-person spread. For example, the first outbreaks of the lethal second wave of this pandemic were reported on the same day in Boston and Bombay. This was of course several decades before air travel and so was a clear indication that the virus or a component of it was an incident from space.

VIRUSES IN OUR GENES

In 2001 the genetic code for the entire human genome was first deciphered. One immediate surprise was that there were far fewer genes actually coding for proteins than we had thought—perhaps under 25,000. It is remarkable that sequences of nucleotides in our DNA, which lie outside the genes responsible for coding proteins, appear to be involved in our evolution. A surprisingly large fraction of our DNA, perhaps as high as 10 percent, is in the form of sequences that are ultimately derived from viruses. And a subset of this is in the form of what we now recognize to be related to "retroviruses," of a type of which the AIDS virus is just one example.[11]

Some years ago Hoyle and I were ridiculed for suggesting in *Lancet* that the SARS and AIDS viruses may have originated in space. From what is now emerging it can be seen that this is most likely to be true. Our ancestral line, which led through primates and anthropoids to *Homo sapiens* over hundreds of millions of years, shows clearly the relics of repeated viral or retroviral attacks presumably similar to AIDS. At each such viral attack the evolving line was almost completely culled, leaving only a small, surviving immune-breeding group to carry through with a relic form of this virus tucked away in its genome.

Viral sequences so added as a result of pandemics, in our view, provide evolutionary potential that could lead to new genotypes and new species at one end of the scale and to new traits and the capacity to express our genes in novel ways at the other. It is becoming clear that our entire existence on this planet is contingent on the continuing ingress of cosmic viruses.

Viruses occupy a gray area in biology between living and nonliving states. Its essential components involve a protein coat or capsid enveloping a genome comprised of either DNA or RNA that codes for function. A virus can replicate only within the cell of a host it infects, and such infections are known to cause a large number of diseases in plants and animals. Examples of human diseases caused by viruses include the common cold, influenza, SARS, smallpox, polio, and AIDS. On our model of cosmic life the genes of eukaryotic cells, as well as their dependent viruses, must coexist and be carried in comets.

While the unlikely combination of epidemiology and astrochemistry continued to give us confidence in the concept of life being a cosmic phenomenon, our critics were vocal with an alleged one-line disproof of the theory of diseases from space. It was asked, "How could a virus that evolved outside the Earth possess the capacity to attack terrestrially evolved plants and animals?" The correct answer of course is that this is possible only if life itself originated and evolved on a vast cosmic scale— a scale enormously exceeding the scale of our minuscule Earth. We shall elaborate on this statement later, but for now let it suffice to say that this is the point of view that is today overwhelmingly supported by hard facts and evidence. To ignore this would be to our peril.

ZIKA VIRUS

It is generally agreed that a virus or bacterium that has been resident on Earth for some time could acquire new characteristics, not only from random mutations but also by incorporating new genetic information from incoming viruses (virions). The Zika virus, which is much in the news, appears to have recently undergone precisely such a change.[12] Before the year 2000 the Zika virus was in circulation, but it did not cause microencephaly—the smaller skull size and brains—in newborn babies, and this does indeed suggest a major change in the virus. The altered Zika virus that is now spreading in many countries via a mosquito vector has been found to affect fetuses in pregnant women, causing babies to be born with reduced brain and skull size. It has also been shown that a transfer of the virus to gametes (sex cells) can take place in an infected male. The isolation of the virus in semen is an indication of the soma-to-germline feedback process already occurring in this instance. This might lead to a situation similar to the sexual transmission mode of HIV when it exploded worldwide in 1981.

The Zika epidemic, if it proceeds unchecked, will eventually lead to the emergence of a new human phenotype with reduced brain size and diminished cognitive capacity. It is to be hoped, however, that modern medical science, including the development of an effective vaccine, will intervene in time to prevent such a tragic outcome.

It is interesting to note in this connection that the human brain has seen dramatic changes of volume in the past. Between 2 million and 500,000 years ago, skull volumes in hominid skeletons appear to have doubled, possibly in several discrete steps. Over the same period it seems likely that our cognitive abilities including the development of speech with the acquisition of the FOXP2 genes had grown. Many investigators have shown that viral footprints can be identified in human brain tissue to mark important steps that led up to its present condition. The possibility that Zika virus–induced microencephalitis might represent a retrogression of this trend is an alarming prospect that medical science will have to avert before it is too late.

In the 1980s Fred Hoyle and I suggested that it would be prudent to maintain a microbiological surveillance of the stratosphere in a search for incoming pathogens (such as the Zika virus and new strains of flu) so that vaccines may be developed, if necessary, to avert the danger of a future devastating pandemic. It might be predicted that, in general, weeks to months would elapse between the arrival of viral particles at the top of the stratosphere and their descent to ground level. This would give enough time for action in the event that a potentially lethal pathogen is discovered. The time may well be ripe for instituting such protection protocols before a devastating pandemic provides macabre proof of the theory of cometary panspermia.

COMET HALLEY TO THE RESCUE

Historically, another crucial development in the theory of cosmic life was connected with the return to perihelion of Halley's Comet in 1986. This was the first time that a comet was being studied by scientists since the beginning of the space age. From as early as 1982 a program of international cooperation to investigate this comet came into full swing, the aim being to coordinate ground-based observations, satellite-based studies, and space-probe analysis on a worldwide basis. No fewer than five spacecrafts dedicated to the study of Comet Halley were launched during 1985, the rendezvous dates being all clustered around early March 1986, about one month after the comet's closest approach to the sun.

In the immediate run-up to these events Fred Hoyle and I had met

Fig. 2.4. First image of a comet's nucleus—Comet Halley from the Giotto spacecraft in 1986

to discuss what observations might be likely according to our present point of view. What predictions might we possibly make? Our deliberations led us to conclude that organic/biologic comets of the kind we envisage would have exceedingly black surfaces. This is due to the development of a highly porous crust of polymerized organic particles that can permit vigorous outgassing only when the crust comes to be ruptured. We put all our arguments in the form of a scientific paper, which came to be published much later in *Earth, Moon and Planets*.[13] This was only twelve days before the encounter, and our priority would have gone unrecorded had it not been for the fortunate circumstance that the *London Times* picked up on it and reported its contents.[14]

On the night of March 13, 1986, we watched our television screens with nervous anticipation as Giotto's cameras began to approach within 500km of the comet's nucleus. The fears that the spacecraft might be badly damaged and even destroyed by impacts with cometary dust were proved to be wrong, and the equipment functioned well throughout the encounter. The cameras were expecting to photograph a bright snow-field scene on the nucleus consistent with the then fashionable Whipple dirty snowball model of comets. In the event the television pictures transmitted worldwide on March 13 proved to be a disappointment. The cameras had their apertures shut down to a minimum and trained to find the brightest spot in the field. As a consequence, very little of any interest was immediately captured on camera—the scene was far too dark. The much publicized Giotto images of the nucleus of Comet Halley were obtained only after a great deal of image processing. The stark conclusion to be drawn from the Giotto imaging was the revelation of a cometary nucleus that was amazingly black. It was described at the time as being "blacker than the blackest coal . . . the lowest albedo of any surface in the solar system. . . ." Naturally we jumped for joy! As far as we were aware at the time we were the only scientists who made a prediction of this kind, a prediction that was a natural consequence of our organic/biologic model of comets. Fred and I regarded this development as yet another decisive triumph of our point of view. More triumphs were soon to follow.

A few days after the Giotto rendezvous, infrared observations of the comet were made by Dayal Wickramasinghe and David Allen using the 40-meter Anglo-Australian Telescope.[15] March 31, 1986, they discovered a strong emission from heated organic dust over the 2 to 4 micrometer waveband. As noted earlier basic structures of organic molecules involving CH linkages absorb and emit radiation over the 3.3 to 3.5 micrometer infrared waveband, and for any assembly of complex organic molecules as in a bacterium, this absorption is broad and takes on a highly distinctive profile. The Comet Halley observations by Dayal Wickramasinghe and David Allen were found to be identical to the expected behavior of desiccated bacteria heated to 320 K. Another triumph for our model! Later analysis of data obtained from mass spectrometers aboard Giotto also showed a composition of the breakup fragments of dust as they struck the detector to be similar to bacterial degradation products.

The Halley observations, in our view, clearly disproved the fashionable Whipple's "dirty snowball" theory of comets. The theory dies hard, however, with variants of it still in vogue with the claim that Whipple was still mostly right, except that there was more dirt (organic dirt) than snow! It could not be denied that water existed in comets in the form of ice, but great quantities of organic particles indistinguishable from bacteria are embedded within the ice. This conclusion was unavoidable unless one chose to ignore the new facts.[16]

CLUES FROM METEORITES

Because meteorites continue to play a key role in the story of life in the cosmos, I must briefly refer to our contact with Hans D. Pflug, a geologist from the University of Giese. Pflug contacted me in 1980 offering information that he claimed to be compelling evidence for bacterial microfossils in carbonaceous meteorites. The historical background to this work is worth recalling before describing Pflug's new finds.

As the name implies, the carbonaceous meteorites contain carbon in concentrations upward of 2 percent by mass. In a fraction of such meteorites the carbon is known to be present in the form of large organic molecules.

*Fig. 2.5. Hans D. Pflug,
paeleontologist from
Giesen University*

It is generally believed that at least one class of carbonaceous meteorite is of cometary origin. If one thinks of a comet containing an abundance of frozen microorganisms, repeated perihelion passages close to the sun could lead to the selective boiling off of volatiles, admitting the possibility of sedimentary accumulations of bacteria within a fast-shrinking cometary body. We can thus regard carbonaceous chondrites (a type of meteorite) as being relic comets after their volatiles have been stripped.

Microfossils of bacteria in meteorites have been claimed as early as the 1930s, but the very earliest claims were quickly dismissed as being contaminants. The story did not end there, however, and the whole argument was revived in the early 1960s. The actors in the new drama included Harold Urey, who was one of the greatest geologists of the century. Urey, together with G. Claus, B. Nagy, and D. L. Europe, examined the Orguel carbonaceous meteorite, which fell in France in 1864, microscopically as well as spectroscopically.[17] They claimed to find evidence of organic structures that were similar to fossilized microorganisms, algae in particular. The evidence included electron micrograph pictures, which even showed substructure within these so-called cells. Some of these structures resembled cell walls, cell nuclei, flagella-like structures, as well as constrictions in some elongated objects that suggested a process of cell division. These investigators, like their colleagues before them, became immediately vulnerable to attack by orthodox scientists.

With a powerful attack being launched by the most influential meteorite experts of the day, the meteorite fossil claims of the 1960s became quickly silenced. One of the more serious criticisms that was made against these claims was that the meteorite structures included some clearly recognizable terrestrial contaminants such as ragweed pollen. But the vast majority of structures ("organized elements") that were catalogued and described were clearly not contaminants. Intimidated by the ferocious attack that was launched against them, Claus reneged under pressure, and Nagy retreated while continuing to hint in his writings that it *might be so,* rather in the style of Galileo's whispered *"E pur si muove."*

In 1980, Pflug reopened the whole issue of microbial fossils in carbonaceous meteorites. Pflug used techniques that were distinctly

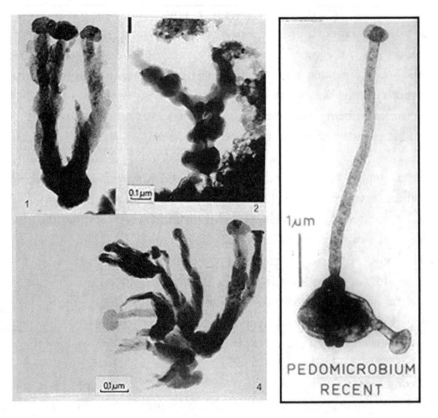

Fig. 2.6. Microfossils in the Murchison meteorite imaged by Hans D. Pflug

superior to those of Claus and his colleagues and found a profusion of cell-like structures comprised of organic matter in thin sections prepared from a sample of the Murchison meteorite, which fell in Australia about a hundred miles north of Melbourne on 28 September 1969. He showed these images to Fred Hoyle and me, and we were immediately convinced of their biological provenance. Pflug himself was a little nervous to publish these results, fearing for his career and anticipating the kind of reaction that was seen in the 1960s.[18] We convinced him to present his work at the out-of-town meeting of the Royal Astronomical Society, held in 1980 in Cardiff, to which I have already referred.

The method adopted by Pflug was to dissolve out the bulk of the minerals present in a thin section of the meteorite using hydrofluoric acid, doing so in a way that permits the insoluble carbonaceous residue to settle with its original structures intact. It was then possible to examine the residue in an electron microscope without disturbing the system from outside. The patterns that emerged were stunningly similar to certain types of terrestrial microorganisms. Scores of different morphologies turned up within the residues, many resembling known microbial species. It would seem that contamination was excluded by virtue of the techniques used, so the skeptic has to turn to other explanations as disproof. No convincing nonbiological alternative to explain all the features was to be readily found.

EVOLUTION AND DISEASE

As we saw earlier our views on cosmic evolution must connect also with the idea of disease-causing viruses coming from space. One might thus legitimately ask: If virus infections are bad for us why did the evolution of higher life not develop a strategy for excluding their ingress into our cells? Logically it seems easy enough for the greater information content of our cells to devise a way of blocking the effects of the much smaller information carried by a virus, and yet this has not happened in the long course of evolution. Could it be, we wondered, that this "invitation" to viruses was retained for the explicit purpose of future evolution? It is only many years later that an affirmative answer to this question was provided by data from the human genome project. A large fraction of the human genome contains viral sequences that are copied faithfully generation to generation, and this could be the potential for future evolution. Moreover, there is further evidence from genome studies that our ancestral line was attacked periodically with bacterial or viral infections that nearly culled the evolving line save for a small breeding group that came through to modern times. We were now, by the early 1980s, firmly committed to the view that an immensely powerful cosmic biology came to be overlaid on the Earth from the outside some 4 billion years ago, through the agency of comets. Other planetary bodies, within the solar system and elsewhere, must also be exposed to the same process. Wherever the broad range of the cosmic life system contains a form of life (genotype) that matches a local niche of a recipient planet, that form would succeed in establishing itself. In our view the entire spectrum of life on Earth, ranging from the humblest single-celled life-forms to the higher animals, must have been introduced from the external cosmos and must, with minor variations, be all-pervasive in the cosmos.

RED RAIN AND METEORITES

Descriptions of a rain of blood falling from the sky have been recorded in diverse cultures from very ancient times. Early literary allusions are to be found in Homer's *Iliad,* where Zeus twice caused blood to rain from the sky and on one occasion did so to warn of imminent slaughter in battle. In Book 16 of *The Illiad* it is recorded that in the midst of an episode of meteoric activity there was a shower of bloody rain. "Zeus noticing that his son Sarpendon would die sent a shower of bloody raindrops to the Earth in tribute." The Greek historian Plutarch (AD 47–120) refers to rain of blood during the reign of Romulus, founder of Rome. Similar ideas persisted through the Middle Ages and into the seventeenth and eighteenth centuries.

In classical Greece events such as a shower of blood were interpreted as a demonstration of divine power, while in Christendom in medieval Europe people were less inclined to attribute such phenomenon to supernatural causes, and natural explanations were often sought. Indian mythology also records similar events and likewise considers them to be omens and portents of the end of the world. In the classic epic *Mahabharata* the following account is given.

> The air was filled with the shouting of men, the roaring of elephants, the blasts of trumpets, and the beating of drums: the rattling of chariots was like to thunder rolling in heaven. The Gods and Gandharvas assembled in the clouds and saw the hosts which had gathered for mutual slaughter. As both armies waited for sunrise, a tempest arose and the dawn was darkened by dust clouds, so that men could scarce behold one another. Evil were the omens. Blood dropped like rain out of heaven, while jackals howled impatiently, and kites and vultures screamed hungrily for human flesh. The earth shook, peals of thunder were heard, although there were no clouds, and angry lightning rent the horrid gloom; flaming thunderbolts struck the rising sun and broke in fragments with loud noise.

Patrick McCafferty, in a scholarly review of many historical sources,[19] collates many noteworthy allusions to the conjuction of meteoritic events and rain-type descriptions. Although caution has to be exercised in assessing ancient documents, the sheer weight of evidence is impressive and cannot be ignored, in the author's view.

Two impressive records cited by McCafferty are worthy of note: the strongest link between red rain and a meteor fall is probably the following example, from Egypt, 30 BCE:

> Not only did rain fall in places where no drop had ever been seen before, but blood besides, and the flash of weapons appeared from the clouds, as the showers of blood mingled with water poured down. In other places the clash of drums and cymbals and the notes of flutes and trumpets were heard, and a serpent of enormous size suddenly appeared and uttered a hiss of incredible volume. Meanwhile comets were observed in the heavens . . . (Dio, Book 51, xvii)

Chinese mythology also recounts a similar correspondence:

The three Miao tribes were in great disorder and Heaven decreed their destruction. The sun came out at night and for *three days it rained blood* [author's emphasis]. A dragon appeared in the ancestral temple and dogs howled in the market place. Ice formed in summertime, the earth split open until springs gushed forth, the [cereal crops] grew differently, and the people were filled with a great terror . . .

In the nineteenth century there was a trend for examining these events more scientifically. Christian Gottfried Ehrenberg (1795–1876), German naturalist and professor of medicine at Berlin University, conducted experiments at the Berlin Academy to re-create "blood rain" with a mixture of red dust and water. He showed that many of the red rain incidents in the past hundred years may have been caused by red dust possibly from the Sahara; Ehrenberg was on the right track. But many red rain episodes in modern times may have had other causes, of which red biological cells—perhaps algae—were common. It is possible that red rain–type events are relatively common even in the present day but go unnoticed and unrecorded except on occasions when the redness was particularly strong.

Popular as well as scientific interest in the red rain phenomenon was revived in a dramatic way following events that took place on the morning of July 25, 2001, over a large area around the state of Kerala in India.[20] A sonic boom heard over the area was followed by a fall of red rain, just as was described in many historical accounts. The redness of the rain was said to be intense enough to stain the light-colored clothes of people walking on the streets. The first red rainfall lasted for about twenty minutes, and this was repeated throughout the day and also over a longer time intermittently and episodically for nearly eight weeks. My friend Godfrey Louis, a physicist (currently pro-vice chancellor of Kochin University) who collected and examined samples of the red rain in 2001, was quickly able to dispose of the possibility of red dust being the cause of the redness.

From estimates of the total rainfall the mass fraction of red cells in a typical red rain sample, and the area over which it fell, we can estimate the total mass of red cell material that was deposited to be 50,000 kg (5 metric tons). Assuming the red rain material is 1 percent of the mass of a porous cometary bolide in which this material was most likely dispersed we can calculate that its radius is some 10 meters. If this object is assumed to be a loose fragile structure it can easily disintegrate in the high atmosphere releasing the red rain cells that eventually seeds rain clouds in the troposphere. In this connection it is interesting to note that McCafferty[21] cites a documented red rain event in October 1846 in France where the total mass of red particles of more than 300 metric tons was recorded. It is interesting in this instance that ⅛th of the mass was said to be in the form of microscopically identified diatoms—microscopic plant cells, of a kind that was recently discovered by Russian scientists on the windows of the international space station.

With the strong influence of an Earth-centerd viewpoint in biology that still prevails it is not surprising to find any suggestion that the red rain cells were extraterrestrial to be vigorously challenged. An official investigation by a team of botanists in India asserted with very little evidence that the red rain cells were none other than microscopic algae belonging to the genus *Trentepohlia,* a full 50,000 metric tons of this being supposedly lofted to the clouds from trees on Earth. This claim has not been substantiated, although it has been widely repeated in the electronic media (fake news!) as a refutation of a cosmic connection. Such is the stranglehold that conservative authoritarianism has over science.

To counter such wrong criticisms Professor Louis and his student Santhosh Kumar showed that the cells in the red rain are morphologically different from both ordinary algae and red blood cells, and this result has been independently verified by my student as well as by a group of scientists led by Professor Gehan Amaratunga at the Sri Lanka Institute of Nanotechnology. It has also been demonstrated that the red rain cells have a range of extraordinary properties that all point in the direction of an extraterrestrial origin. When subjected to certain harsh physical and chemical conditions, such as high concentration of

H_2SO_4 (sulphuric acid), high temperature (300°C), and low pressure (0.01 millibar), the cells remained intact and viable. Moreover, Louis and Kumar have shown that under very high pressure and temperatures as high as 450 degrees they can even replicate, thus making them the most extreme of known terrestrial extremophiles—if indeed they are terrestrial in their origin against all the odds.

Based on the available laboratory findings to date, together with the observation that the first red rain event was preceded by a sonic boom presumably caused by the explosion of a meteoroid, an extraterrestrial origin of the 2001 red rain event seems most likely. The geographical pattern of incidence and the distribution in time of the red rain cases do not fit readily with any terrestrial-origin hypothesis and appears to be more consistent with an origin from fragile cometary fragments that disintegrated in the upper atmosphere. The prolonged period of settling of small particles to be expected following an initial deposition in the upper atmosphere can explain the protracted episodes of red rain events over several weeks. Alternatively it is possible that the terrestrial clouds provided a local habitat in which an initial injection of red rain cells on June 25 came to be episodically replicated and amplified in several discrete bursts.

Godfrey Louis supplied me with samples of the Kerala red rain, and these were investigated in various ways by three Ph.D. students: Kani Rauf, Nori Miyake, and Rajkumar Gangappa. The results of their studies formed a major component of three separate doctoral theses. The extensive investigations of the Kerala red rain carried out by these investigators led to results that were in accord with those obtained by Louis and Kumar. The cells show variations in shape, size, and internal structure depending on the plane through which the cells were sectioned. All cells show an exceptionally thick cell wall outlined by two darkly stained membranes—one internal and one external. The cell wall has an average thickness of some 6,000Å. Many cells also have additionally a 2,000 to 3,000Å thick protective exterior coat. Rauf's and Miyake's dissertations are lodged with Cardiff University[22] and that of Gangappa is with Glamorgan University (now the University

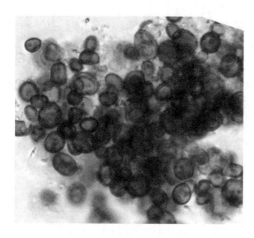

Fig. 2.7. Red rain cells from Sri Lanka under an optical microscope (see also color plate 3)

of South Wales). The situation that the red rain cells have defied identification after work that led to three academic dissertations speaks for itself. If it were indeed a well-known algal cell such as *Trentepohlia* it would have been long since discovered, and it has not. Thus, although the elusive Kerala red rain cell has yet to yield all its secrets, its space origin cannot be easily challenged.

If the red rain cells have an astronomical origin we would expect them to have spectral properties common to interstellar material. These have remarkably been found. Fluorescence studies on the Kerala red rain carried out by Kani Rauf have shown that over a wide range of excitation wavelengths from 4,120Å to 6,000Å three prominent fluorescence emission features appear at 6,700Å, 7,630Å, and 8,230Å. These features coincide remarkably well with the range of wavelengths over which a phenomenon known as extended red emission (ERE) has been observed in astronomical sources.

Perhaps the single most contentious claim by Professor Louis in relation to the properties of the Kerala red rain cells is that they replicate in a high pressure chamber at a temperature of 450°C. At this temperature DNA is expected to break down, and other complex biomolecules may also be denatured. Although elemental analysis of the red rain cells showed 50 percent carbon, Louis and Kumar found no phosphorous in the cells. Phosphate groups form an important part of the DNA double helix, so the absence of phosphorous, if real, would imply that no DNA is present in the cells. This is what Godfrey Louis has maintained, and continues to do so. Because DNA is the genetic material that carries the information content of life in all terrestrial cells, it would provide arguably the strongest case for an extraterrestrial origin. One might speculate on the presence of a non-DNA-based genetic template of some kind. The challenge then would be to identify a DNA precursor that does not contain phosphorous or some other template to hold the information content of the cells. Otherwise, replication and reproduction will be impossible.

Several investigators, including Kani Rauf and Milton Wainwright, have found conflicting results with regard to DNA in red rain cells. Biologists use a stain called DAPI applied to cells to detect the presence of DNA. DNA binds to the DAPI stain and can be observed to fluoresce, by which effect a positive DNA content is inferred. These tests, when applied to the red rain cells, have on some occasions shown a positive result for DNA, but then the conflict with no phosphorus result has to be resolved. The fact remains, however, that although several attempts have been made to isolate DNA from the red cells and sequence it, so far they have all proved unsuccessful. The mystery therefore deepens.

By the end of 2012 our investigations on the red rain of Kerala had come to a dead end, at least as far as identifying the precise nature of the organisms was concerned. The original claim that the organisms are algae belonging to the genus *Trentopohia* could not have been substantiated, and the difference between such algal cells and the red rain cells have been emphasised in later studies by by Santhosh Kumar and his colleagues.

We have referred to Serendipitous interventions earlier, particularly in relation to the Red Flu pandemic in 1976 and also the visit of my brother Dayal to begin the spectroscopic search of interstellar bacteria. *Serendipity* is a word first introduced into the English language by Horace Walpole in a letter to Horace Mann in which he refers to a Persian fairy tale, "The Three Princes of Serendip." The heroes in this story were making discoveries by accidents and sagacity. The name

Serendip refers to the old name for Sri Lanka, and the word *serendipity* has come to mean the combination of sagacity and luck in making discoveries, which in science is well recognized. It is a curious fact that serendipity played a role in the developments now to be discussed with the source material for further discussions of extraterrestrial life turning up in no place other than Serendip—Sri Lanka—the country of my birth!

On the morning of November 14, 2012, the skies darkened over the ancient city of Polonnaruwa in Sri Lanka, and in the surrounding district red rain fell intermittently for several hours.[23] The red rain of Kerala, which we discussed earlier, finally showed up on the island of Serendip. At earlier dates in November as well as in December there were also numerous reports of fireball sightings in the same area. Meteor activity generally tends to peak during this period with the Taurids, Geminids, and Leonids being among the prominent regular showers. Such meteor showers result when the Earth in its orbit crosses the orbits of debris released from a particular comet—Comet Encke in this case for the Taruids. Astronomer David Ascher predicted that the Taurids would peak in intensity during this time in 2012 with the dominance of larger fragments, in a sixty-one-year cycle. It is not surprising, therefore, that fireball sightings were more frequent during this particular Taurid shower of November 2012 and December 2013. The connection between meteors, freezing nuclei, and rain would be expected, and it can be surmised that red rain cells dispersed by meteoroids seeded the red rain events in Sri Lanka.

Just as in Kerala there was a succession of similar but less heavy red rain episodes that were distributed spatially over a few thousand square kilometers. The heaviest rains took place in a smaller area and were centered around the original site of incidence on November 14. Through the good offices of the director of the Medical Research Institute in Sri Lanka, I secured samples of the red rain material for study in the United Kingdom. These were analysed by my student Nori Miyake, who found the red cells to be very similar to the Kerala red rain cells. Elemental analysis by Professor Gehan Amaratunga and his team confirmed the claim made earlier for the Kerala red rain: that there was no phosphorous in the cells. Miyake also found that the outer layer of the cell wall contained Uranium, which appears strange for an organism that evolved on Earth. Uranium is a rare element on Earth, so to find an organism that can actually concentrate uranium, and for kilotons of it to be lifted into the stratosphere, appears to stretch credulity to the limit.

As with the Kerala red rain the jury is still out as to the origin of these cells, but there are tantalizing clues that point to their alien origin. If phosphorous is really absent in these cells there is a good chance that the biology carried with the red rain cannot interact with DNA-based living cells. It may be an alien life-form that fell from the sky but did not take root on our planet.

The real serendipity that emerged in Sri Lanka was not so much the red rain but the meteorite falls that occurred in two separate events on December 29, 2012, and January 4, 2013.[24] It was serendipitous, moreover, that I happened to be visiting the island in both December and again in January and was able to secure samples of the meteorite and also to interview eyewitnesses on the ground.

Fig. 2.8. Location of meteorite fall in December 2012 near
Polonnaruwa, Sri Lanka

The first meteorite event took place at 6:30 p.m. local time in a rice paddy in the village of Aralaganwila a few kilometers away from the historic ancient city of Polonnaruwa. Farmer Tikiri Banda was finishing the day's task of watering his newly planted field when he saw a fireball light up the darkening sky in the southwest. Moments later the fireball broke up into what Tikiri Banda described as a "swarm of fireflies." Overcome with shock and fear he ran home, put down the shutters in his windows, and retired for the night. When he returned to his field the following morning he found to his utter astonishment the rice paddy splattered with fist-size lumps of stone of a kind he had not seen before. He carried a bagful of the stones to the local police station to report the incident. The police had already had other similar reports, including that of a woman burning her hands upon picking up a rock after it fell from the sky. Other reports described pungent odors emanating from the rocks. All this is consistent with meteorites falling at high speed through the upper atmosphere, the surfaces being heated by friction, and frozen organic gases fizzing out. I visited the site and spoke to witnesses and the police, who confirmed these statements. There appears to be no doubt whatsoever that these rocks did fall from the skies, and if so they are meteorites. To add to the mystery surrounding these events, five days later at 9:30 p.m. on January 4, 2013, a second fireball event and accompanying meteorite falls were reported in two villages known as Rakkinda and Girandanakotte (7.5 km apart) and some 70 kilometers south of the location of the first event on December 29, 2012. The structure and appearance of the meteorites collected in Aralaganwila and Rakkinda were virtually indistinguishable—characterized in particular by their high degree of porosity and low density—but those collected in Girandanakotte were far less porous and much more dense.

I received the first samples of this meteorite also through the good offices of Keerthi Wickramaratne of the Medical Research Institute in Sri Lanka. When these meteorites were received in Cardiff, a new student I had taken on, Jamie Wallis, set about the task of conducting a series of laboratory experiments, first to examine their content and second to establish by means of independent analysis that these stones were indeed meteorites that actually fell from the skies. The former was the easier of the two tasks; the latter more challenging. In the eventual outcome we found the necessary evidence to confirm eyewitness reports that these stones really did come from space. However, the Aralaganwila-Rakkinda stones were untypical of most known meteorites in that they had a low density (less than 0.8 g cm^{-3}) and were dominated by the mineral silica although certain rare minerals that are found only in meteorites were discovered in much smaller quantity. The exact type of the parent body from which the meteorite was derived remains unresolved, but a comet—probably Comet P-Encke—is the most likely source.

Aralaganwila-Rakkinda stones when examined under a light microscope displayed a highly porous structure and a morphology similar to cometary particles that were collected from the stratosphere. A small percentive of carbon, as revealed by elemental analysis of these meteorites, places them tentatively in the category of an unknown type of carbonaceous meteorite.

At the time of entry into the Earth's atmosphere on December 29, 2012, and January 4, 2013, the parent body of the Sri Lankan meteorites would have had most of its interior porous volume filled with water, volatile organics, and possibly also a component of viable living cells, in accord with the ideas of cometary panspermia. A remarkable coincidence to be noted is that within several days of the meteorite fall, an extensive region around the site of the fall experienced an episode of red rain.

We now turn to the most dramatic discoveries from our meteorite studies that could essentially prove the theory of cometary panspermia. Jamie Wallis took a sample from a freshly cleaved interior surface of the Polonnaruwa meteorite under sterile conditions and mounted them on aluminium stubs for examination under an environmental scanning electron microscope. Images of the sample at low magnification displayed a wide range of structures that were distributed and enmeshed within a fine-grained matrix. The most startling discovery made by Wallis at the scanning electron microscope was to find a range of diatom types securely lodged within the meteorite matrix. Diatoms are unicellular phytoplankton characterized by elaborately sculptured frus-

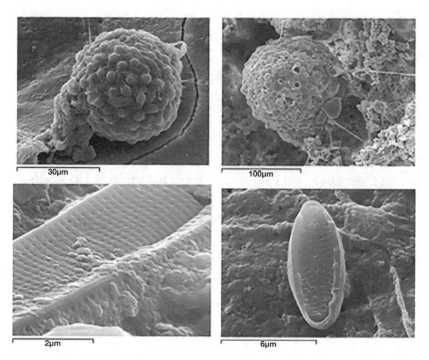

Fig. 2.9. Electron microscope images of diatoms fossilized within the meteorite

tules comprised of a hydrated silicon dioxide polymer. The intricately woven microstructure of these frustules would be impossible to generate abiotically, so the presence of structures of this kind in any extraterrestrial setting could be construed as unequivocal proof of biology. Diatom fossils of a wide range of types are found in marine sediments dating back to the Cretaceous Tertiary boundary 65 million years ago.

As with earlier microfossil discoveries, contamination is always the main objection to be raised and has to be addressed. We argue that the extraordinarily wide range of genera/species found in meteorite militates against local contamination from the surrounding sand. Moreover, in many instances diatom frustules appear to merge with the rock matrix, making postimpact introduction virtually impossible.

There is no doubt that the majority of meteoroids that enter the Earth's atmosphere, particularly around the time of regular meteor showers, are derived from comets. They consist mainly of

~1–10 μm-radius dust from normal outgassing, which forms cometary meteor streams, as well as larger fragments that result from sporadic breakup, as has been observed recently in several comets, particularly the comet 73P Schwassmann-Wachmann3, in which subfragments were seen to separate from the main comet nucleus. It is possible that Comet P/Encke behaved in a very similar way and the Polonnaruwa meteorites resulted from fragments of this comet reaching Earth as part of an extended meteor storm. Frequent fireball events are common in storm years of the Taurids, although so far no one has succeeded in "catching" the debris from such a "falling star."

The stream of debris, which gives rise to the Taurid meteor showers, is thought to be comprised of remnants of a giant comet that disintegrated some 20,000 to 30,000 years ago according to theories developed by Victor Clube and Bill Napier. The resulting fragments, ranging from 10μm-radius dust to fragments possibly larger than the Polonnaruwa bollide or even Tunguska bolide, are distributed in the stream, being released both by normal cometary activity and occasionally by tidal interactions with planets. The Earth takes several weeks to pass through this rather wide stream and so results in extended periods of meteor activity as we found in the case of the Sri Lankan events.

In view of the groundbreaking nature of the discovery of alien life-forms in these meteorites it is natural to find that skepticism and opposition will come to the fore. Many ways of refutation can be attempted, but what cannot be denied is that the biological structures found within the meteorites were indeed diatoms. These were similar to diatoms recently discovered by Russian scientists on the windows of the International Space Station orbiting at 400km above the Earth. If these diatoms somehow crept into the meteorite after it landed on the ground we have to explain both the wide range of species in one piece of stone, frustules evidently fused into the rock, and a few instances of acritarchs, a fossilized extinct class of microbes that have not been around for more than 2 billion years.

The critic might be eager to assert the modern contaminant hypothesis on the ground that the species of diatoms found in the meteorites are indistinguishable from modern contemporary species, and the argument goes that diatoms evolving in an extraterrestrial habitat are unlikely to follow exactly the same patterns of evolution. This argument fails, however, if, as we have mentioned many times earlier, the genes for all life, including diatoms, came from space and still continue to come from space. The argument of nonconvergent evolution can only be supported in terms of an incorrect "closed box" theory of biological evolution that is long overdue for abandonment.

A last-ditch desperate attempt to discredit all these discoveries is to assert that what we have recovered in Sri Lanka is not a meteorite of any type notwithstanding the weight of all the anecdotal and documentary evidence. True enough the structure of the Aralaganwila and Rakkinda meteorites would be unfamiliar to those who have dealt with other meteorites. But these are not run-of-the-mill meteorites by any means. They are most probably recently cleaved fragments from the surface of a comet, probably Comet Encke, that was added to the Taurid stream relatively recently.

For many years space scientists have used isotope studies to infer the cosmic, nonterrestrial origin of meteorites. One particular element used in this connection is oxygen, which comes in the form of three stable isotopes ^{16}O, ^{17}O, ^{18}O, the proportions of which are different for Earth-derived material from those of extraterrestrial material. To establish the extraterrestrial origin of these meteorites Jamie Wallis sent a sample to the Isotope Laboratory at Gottingen University, Germany, for determining the ratios of the three oxygen isotopes ^{16}O, ^{17}O, ^{18}O—which would be significantly different for extraterrestrial material compared with terrestrial material. The results that came back were decisive—the data did not match terrestrial material. The same result was confirmed by a team of geologists in Tokyo, Japan. The rocks can therefore be assumed to be nonterrestrial and therefore of cosmic or meteoritic origin.

3
History of Panspermia

I have already described how my own ideas relating to panspermia and to life as a cosmic phenomenon came to evolve. They followed from investigations on the properties of cosmic dust that I began in Cambridge in 1962 in collaboration with my mentor and friend Sir Fred Hoyle. Our conclusions were, however, more-or-less independent of a past history of related ideas that extended over many centuries.

EARLIEST HISTORY—REVIVAL OF
AN ANCIENT IDEA

Perhaps the earliest philosophical ideas about the distribution of life in the universe is found in the Vedic traditions of ancient India (Vedanta) that go back to at least the third millennium BCE. According to these traditions life, including consciousness, is regarded as an essential component of the cosmos, and its seeds are distributed throughout the material universe. These traditions, which were transmitted orally at the outset, appear in written form at a much later date.

In the Western world we see analogous ideas emerging in Classical Greece of the third century BC in the writings of Aristarchus of Samos (ca. 310–230 BC), which come to be recognized by the name Panspermia (pan = everywhere, spermata = seeds). Aristarchus's ideas did not last long, however, being replaced by Aristotle's Earth-centered cosmology. The Aristotelian doctrine of "fireflies emerging from a mixture of warm earth and morning dew" was the dominant philosophical paradigm in regard to life that persisted throughout Europe until the middle of the nineteenth century.

PASTEUR AND PANSPERMIA

In 1856, Louis Pasteur (1822–1895) was responsible for effectively disproving the prevailing doctrine of spontaneous generation. He demonstrated that in sterilized and sealed flasks microbes did not grow, but in flasks open to the air microbial cultures were always found. His experiments showed clearly that in the absence of contamination, microorganisms could not develop. He inferred accordingly that microbes are always generated by reproduction of microbes that existed before. This led to his famous dictum "all life from life" and his premature pronouncement that "never will the doctrine of spontaneous generation recover from the mortal blow of this simple experiment."

Pasteur's classic life-from-life discovery is easily extended to higher life as well: each generation of every plant or animal is preceded by a generation of the same plant or animal. This view was taken up enthusiastically by several prominent scientists in the late nineteenth century, among whom the physicist John Tyndall was one. A lecture delivered by Tyndall at the Royal Institution in London on January 21, 1870, was ruthlessly criticized in the newly established journal *Nature*. Underlying the criticism was the realization that if Pasteur's paradigm was taken to be rigorously true, the origin of life would need to be external to the Earth. So the reigning Aristotelean dogma of Earth-centered biology would be instantly threatened. For if life had no spontaneous origin it would be possible to follow every species of life generation by generation back to a time before the Earth itself existed, the origin being therefore required to have taken place outside the Earth in the wider cosmos.

PANSPERMIA CATCHES ON

This logical conclusion was expressed in a most succinct form by the German physicist Hermann von Helmholtz in *Handbuch der Theoretische Physik*.

It appears to me to be a fully correct scientific procedure, if all our attempts fail to cause the production of organisms from non-living matter, to raise the question whether life has ever arisen, whether it is not just as old as matter itself and whether seeds have not been carried from one planet to another and have developed everywhere where they have fallen on fertile soil. . . .[1]

Not long afterward the physicist Lord Kelvin joined the fray and further endorsed Pasteur's paradigm.

Dead matter cannot become living without coming under the influence of matter previously alive. This seems to me as sure a teaching of science as the law of gravitation. . . .

So if life had preceded the Earth, how had it arrived here and where had it come from? In his presidential address to the 1881 meeting of the British Association, Lord Kelvin offered an answer that inaugurated an idea that is now recognized by the term *lithopanspermia*.

When two great masses come into collision in space, it is certain that a large part of each is melted, but it seems also quite certain that in many cases a large quantity of debris must be shot forth in all directions, much of which may have experienced no greater violence than individual pieces of rock experience in a landslip or in blasting by gunpowder. Should the time when this earth comes into collision with another body, comparable in dimensions to itself when it is still clothed as at present with vegetation, many great and small fragments carrying seeds of living plants and animals would undoubtedly be scattered through space. Hence, and because we all confidently believe that there are at present, and have been from time immemorial, many worlds of life besides our own, we must regard it as probable in the highest degree that there are countless seed-bearing meteoric stones moving about through space. If at the present instant no life existed upon the earth, one such stone falling upon it might, by what we blindly call natural causes, lead to its becoming covered with vegetation.

With modern experiments showing that seeds of some flowering plants and even microscopic animals (tardigrades) can survive the space conditions described by Lord Kelvin, it is likely that this was exactly the way the Earth came to be clothed with life.

Historically the next development in relation to panspermia is associated with the Nobel Prize–winning chemist Svante Arrhenius,[2] whose book *Worlds in the Making* appeared in English in 1908. In this book Arrhenius developed Kelvin's thesis further and argued that bacteria in freeze-dried form would easily be propelled and spread across the galaxy by the pressure force exerted on them by starlight. Neither Kelvin's or Arrhenius ideas caught on, however. Arguments such as survivability of microbes in space were used by many to discard these ideas for the time being at least. All these arguments were much later found to be wrong.

ULTIMATE COPERNICAN REVOLUTION

Turning to space for the origins of life would have been considered an outrageous heresy even as recently as fifty years ago. Every textbook on biology began with the statement that life on Earth *must* have started on Earth, in some form of "primordial soup," a few billion years ago. The sole argument that could be used to defend this position was that the only life we know of is located here on the Earth, and so it must be inferred that life started here. This position is logically flawed, however, and many counterarguments can be sited to prove this point. For example the Celtic languages are spoken in certain parts of the British Isles, but they certainly did not originate here. These languages originated in Europe more than three thousand years ago and eventually found their way into Britain. The presumption that life must have originated on the Earth for the sole reason that it is here now is without any logical foundation. Nevertheless scientists have accepted this myopic point of view uncritically for many decades, and the result in my view has been disastrous for science. The Earth-centered view of life has led to many contradictions in present-day biological thought.

As we saw in an earlier chapter, nearly half a millennium ago

Nicholas Copernicus dethroned the Earth from its privileged status as the physical center of the universe. Our planet, however, has continued to be regarded as the supreme center of life almost to the present day. Throughout the past six decades scientists have entertained the futile hope that they would one day create life from nonlife in the laboratory. In 1954, Harold Urey and Stanley Miller were able to produce in the laboratory organic materials that may have served as very simple chemical building blocks of life[3], but this was of course a far cry indeed from making life. A few years ago Craig Venter "engineered" a new bacterium starting from an already existing bacterium by inserting an artificially assembled segment of DNA. The fact that this "new" organism was able to reproduce using the already complex machinery present in the cell merely shows that a feat of genetic engineering was performed. It was not success in an attempt to start life anew as has sometimes been claimed.

As we mentioned in the previous chapter, once the amino acids and nucleotides are all supplied, the most difficult step is the arrangement of these building blocks into the highly specific order that is needed for life. That step requires the prior generation of a genetic blueprint carrying "building instructions," information that is exceedingly specific in kind and unimaginably vast in quantity. Attempts to quantify this information lead to numbers that can only be described as superastronomical.

In view of the insuperable difficulties evident in starting life on Earth, it would seem natural to turn to the biggest available setting for the first emergence of life, and that is by definition the cosmos as a whole. One might think that the totality of material available in all the star systems in the entire universe, acting somehow cooperatively, might perhaps solve the insuperable problem of starting the first living system. However, in the standard big-bang cosmology, with a finite mass and with limited material and probabilistic resources, a life-origin event would still need to be understood as a unique and miraculous cosmic event. Once it has happened, however, possibly at a very early stage in the universe, its spread might take place within deep frozen bodies—for example, comets—with the expansion of the universe. That at any rate is the theory that Fred Hoyle and I developed from the 1980s onward, and for which evidence continues to grow.

EXTREMOPHILES AND PANSPERMIA

Recent developments in microbiology have shown that many types of bacteria are endowed with properties that make them ideally suited to space travel and survival under extreme conditions. Thermophyllic, or heat-loving, bacteria are found to replicate in superheated water at temperatures about 100°C. Psychrophyllic, or cold-loving, bacteria thrive in permafrost deposits of the Antarctic, and a vast undiscovered microbial ecosystem lies under tens of meters of ice in the frozen wastes of Lake Vostok in Antarctica. Some types of bacterial species are found to survive and even replicate in the intense radiation environment within a working nuclear reactor. Bacteria have been found at depths of some seven kilometers below the Earth's crust. Microbiologists now think that many millions of species of extremophiles (bacteria seeking extreme environments) lie dormant in surface soil and surface water, waiting perhaps for the right host to emerge.

Many of the properties associated with extremophiles are of a kind that one would not have expected to evolve on Earth. In addition to bacteria, viruses with enormous space survival attributes also exist in vast quantity on the Earth. A million virions exist in a single drop of ocean water, and some 10^{31} virions are estimated to be present throughout the oceans. Viruses may be even more important than bacteria in transmitting genetic information over cosmic scales.

We pointed out earlier that the first strong indications of life coming to Earth from space had surfaced when it was recently discovered that the earliest microbial life on Earth dated back to more than 4.1 billion years ago. At this time we know that the Earth was being severely pummeled by impacting comets and asteroids. So the relatively quiescent conditions that had once been thought to prevail throughout a billion-year initial time span in which a primordial soup might have brewed, have now all but disappeared. The facts from a wide range of scientific disciplines including astronomy, geology and biology all point in one direction—panspermia and the cosmic origin of life. Once the formation of the inner planets was complete viable, bacteria and viruses were delivered by comets to planetary surfaces, including the Earth.[4]

RESURGENCE OF PANSPERMIA

After many years of being in the doldrums, panspermia theories suddenly came to the fore in August 1996 following the announcement of a possible detection of microbial fossils in a Martian meteorite codenamed ALH84001. Although the Martian microbial fossil claim is still being disputed, the idea of microbial life being moved from one planetary body to another through impact ejection of life-bearing rocks is now rapidly coming into fashion. ALH84001 has demonstrated beyond any doubt that complex organic structures, and by inference even microbial cells, could be transferred from one planetary body to another— justifying panspermia albeit to a limited extent.

As far as deep-space bacteria is concerned, identifications made thus far had been done using only a variety of remote-sensing techniques— for instance by studying the way that cosmic dust absorbs starlight and making comparisons with the known behavior of microorganisms in the laboratory. This work has continued, covering a wide range of wavelengths from the infrared to the far ultraviolet. As of 2017 the most distant galaxies formed scarcely a few million years after the presumed big bang are displaying evidence of biological signatures in their spectra.

The first-ever direct studies of cosmic dust made at a distance of some 150 million miles from Earth were made with instruments aboard the NASA *Stardust* spacecraft. Between May and December 1999 this spacecraft captured dust from the deepest recesses of interstellar space. The analysis of five dust particles has led to dramatic results. The cosmic dust particles strike the detectors aboard *Stardust* at very high speeds of some eighteen miles per second. The impact shatters the impacting particle, and what survive are only the strongest structural units. A bacterium hitting a solid surface at this speed would be destroyed except for parts of its cell walls. Cell walls of bacteria are made of cross-linked

September 26, 1995

Fig. 3.1. Comet Hale-Bopp producing dust and becoming active beyond the orbit of Jupiter in the cold depths of space (see also color plate 4)

sugar molecules and proteins that render them stronger than reinforced concrete. What the stardust instruments discovered are precisely such cross-linked polymers.

Recent studies of comets have yielded data that are fully consistent with this point of view.[5] As we have already mentioned, infrared or heat emission properties of dust from Comet Halley obtained as far back as 1986 were found to be indistinguishable from heated bacterial particles, and spacecraft studies of the same comet showed the dust to be made of organic material that would be consistent with the detritus biology. Similar results were found for a host of other comets since 1986, notably Comets Hale-Bopp, Tempel 1, Wildt 2, and last of all 67P/C-G. Comet Hale-Bopp was the first comet to show unexpected activity in the cold depths of space (beyond the orbit of Jupiter), and the infrared spectrum of the material emanating from the comet was interpreted as being 90 percent organic and similar to the spectra of biomaterial.

Most recent investigations of Comet 67P/C-G in the ROSETTA mission showed evidence of biologic activity, which can only be reasonably understood on the basis of ongoing microbiology just below the

*Fig. 3.2. Comet 67P/C-G, the comet examined in the
ESA Rosetta mission (2015)*

surface ice. This includes the effusion of a combination of molecular oxygen and hydrocarbons from vents in the ice. Another Comet studied recently, comet Lovejoy, was found to produce jets of ethyl alcohol at the rate equivalent to 500 bottles of wine every second! Surely the result of microbial fermentation.

4
Cosmic Coincidences, God, Creationism, and Consciousness

A common-sense interpretation of the facts suggests that a super-intellect has monkeyed with physics, as well as with chemistry and biology, and that there are no blind forces worth speaking about in nature. The numbers one calculates from the facts seem to me so overwhelming as to put this conclusion almost beyond question.

FRED HOYLE

INTELLIGENT UNIVERSE

The idea of a universe endowed with an intelligent cause has long history. Perhaps the oldest discussion on record in Western culture goes back to Socrates in the fifth century BC. Later Hellenistic philosophers pursued the same theme in different ways, leading eventually to the elaborate construct of the Aristotlean universe. Such discussions eventually paved the way to theological discussion and to dogmatic assertions concerning the existence of an all-powerful and omniscient God.

Both Plato and Aristotle shared the view that the natural world is endowed with intrinsic values and final causes, which it would be our duty to discover. This effectively defines the philosophy of teleology in which the present state of the world is determined by conditions that would prevail at a future time. Science has generally shunned such teleological ideas on the grounds that they are beyond the bounds of direct experimental verification.

One of the most celebrated claims to use logic to infer the existence of God was due to William Paley (1743–1805). Paley's "design argument" appeared at the time to be based on impeccable logic. He cited evidence from anatomy and astronomy to support his claim. The absolute perfection of the human body and human anatomy on the one hand, and the precise regular clockwork like movements of the solar system on the other, gave rise to the famous watchmaker analogy. The intricate movements of a carefully engineered clock require the intelligence of a watchmaker and so it was contended would be the case for the solar system. The intelligent design argument was thus born.

Paley's thesis had a profound influence on political and theological thought from the late eighteenth to the middle of the nineteenth centuries. It is interesting to note that Paley's evidence was a text that was deemed essential reading for all University of Cambridge undergraduates almost to the end of the nineteenth century.[1] The quality and level of Paley's intellect and academic credentials were second to none. William Paley graduated from Christ's College Cambridge in 1763 as Senior Wrangler in the Mathematical Tripos, which is to say, he stood first in what is still regarded as the toughest of mathematical examinations the world over. This accolade was followed by his election to a fellowship at Christ's College; and after the publication of many philosophical and theological theses he ended his career as the subdean of Bishop of Lincoln Cathedral.

The arguments for a deliberately designed cosmos predates Western civilization by many centuries. According to Hindu and Vedantic philosophies, which date back longer than 2000 BC, the universe is posited to be of infinite age and goes through an endless sequence of cycles involving creation, maintenance, and destruction. It is said that Brahma causes the birth of the universe, Vishnu maintains its continuation over a timescale of some billions of years, and Shiva causes its destruction.

Brahma, Vishnu, and Shiva are by definition intelligent or superintelligent deities that define and control the universe. These deities are in my view to be treated as metaphors for creation, survival, and decay. Quite amazingly each complete cycle in such a cosmology is reckoned by Vedantic scholars to be within a factor 2 of the generally accepted big-bang age currently favored by astronomers. This assertion, considering uncertainties of interpreting an ancient numerology, must in my view be taken with a large pinch of salt.

In the present scientific and technological age there is a tide of opinion against any form of adherence to religious or metaphysical belief. In parts of Europe, which have been traditionally Christian for centuries, ancient cathedrals and churches are fast emptying, leaving their curators in dismay. Only curious visitors now linger to admire the architectural beauty of these magnificent edifices and to wonder about the cosmological and religious ideas that provoked their creation. This exodus of congregations appears to be encouraged by the most vocal modern prophets of "rationalism" who argue that religion and science are intrinsically incompatible. Yet the natural world is filled with mystery that the human mind is left to unravel.

When our cave-dwelling ancestors first looked up at the pristine splendor of the night sky the unending quest for our origins began. This was probably the first moment in our history—in the history of terrestrial life—when we began to ask the most difficult of questions that still elude us. How did life originate from nonlife? How did intelligence arise in the course of the development and evolution of life? Science still fails to provide convincing answers, and the most distinguished and honest of scientists have expressed a combination of ignorance and bafflement. The American biologist George Wald wrote thus:

> There are only two possibilities as to how life arose. One is spontaneous generation leading to evolution; the other is a supernatural creative act of God. There is no third possibility. Spontaneous generation, that life arose from non-living matter, was scientifically disproved 120 years ago by Louis Pasteur and others. That leaves us with only one possible conclusion that life arose as a supernatural

creative act of God. I will not accept that philosophically because I do not want to believe in God. Therefore, I choose to believe in that which I know is scientifically impossible; spontaneous generation arising to Evolution.[2]

For George Wald (as for many other practicing scientists) there was an inevitable clash between scientific rationality and reductionism on the one hand and a Judeo-Christian culture on the other. An offhand rejection of an unprovable God in favor of an apparently flawed scientific position was a futile attempt to resolve the conflict. However, what George Wald and others have failed to recognize is that what is considered supernatural or outside science in the present day may not always remain so in the future.

ANTHROPIC IDEAS

The idea of a universe that is fortuitously fit for life and indeed for our very existence goes back more than a century. In 1913 the chemist Joseph Henderson somewhat trivially discussed the importance of water and the environment in regard to the existence of living things on Earth. It is now becoming increasingly clear that for life (ourselves) and indeed the entire physical universe to exist certain parameters that define our universe have to be precisely tuned. This has come to be known as the anthropic principle by which our existence demands and determines certain physical parameters—the so-called coupling constants of physics—to be fixed.

The first example of this principle is connected with a contribution from Fred Hoyle, my mentor whose name has been mentioned often in this section of the book. In 1953, Fred Hoyle predicted the existence of a hitherto unknown excited state of the nucleus of carbon-12 (the ordinary carbon in coal and in our bodies), arguing that this state was an imperative requirement for the production of carbon in stars. We know of course that all the chemical elements heavier than helium are synthesized in the deep interiors of stars as stars evolve, eventually scattering this material into space by the explosions of supernovae. In the early 1950s Fred Hoyle, after predicting the existence of this state, tried hard to convince his friend William Fowler at the California Institute of Technology to search for this predicted energy level of carbon-12 in the laboratory. Fowler, however, remained skeptical and uninterested in performing the experiment for a long time. The excited state of carbon at energy level 7.68MeV calculated by Hoyle was a consequence of the precise strengths of the forces that held the carbon nucleus together. Eventually after much persuasion Fowler and his colleagues at Caltech carried out the relevant experiments and discovered the predicted state of the carbon nucleus, which is now called the Hoyle state.

The implication of this discovery was clear: we (life) can only exist because of the 7.68MeV carbon-12 resonance. If the Hoyle state was shown not to exist the implication would be that the element carbon will not have been produced in stars, and carbon-based life would be impossible. This is an example of what is now widely called the anthropic principle (a term introduced by John Barrow). W. A. Fowler was awarded the Nobel Prize for physics for this discovery and Fred Hoyle the Crafoord Prize of the Swedish Academy for the prediction and discovery respectively, of the Hoyle state of the carbon nucleus.

Besides the carbon-12 excited state there is a whole suite of other even more fundamental constants of nature that need to be arbitrarily tweaked to precise values so as to permit and enable our existence. These include the masses of quarks (fundamental particles) that in turn make up protons and neutrons. Other physical parameters that need to be fixed precisely include the weak and strong nuclear forces and gravitational and electromagnetic forces, to name but a few. The slightest departures from the values possessed by these physical constants lead to a universe that we would not remotely recognize and one where life will not exist.

The physicist Freeman Dyson wrote as follows: "The more I examine the Universe, and the details of its architecture, the more evidence I find that the Universe in some sense must have known we were coming."[3]

It is perhaps not surprising that fine-tuning arguments such as we have discussed have an unsettling effect on those who believe that the universe at every level must have a rational, naturalistic explanation. The fine-tuning results point to the possibility of an intelligence inherent in the universe, if not to an intelligent creator or omnipotent God.

A few rationalist responses to fine-tuning arguments go as follows: we exist and are able to pose these questions therefore the universe must be the way it is. Otherwise our existence will not be a fact. This in our reckoning is not a scientific response but a clever cop out.

MULTIVERSE IDEAS

There is an explanation offered contingent on the inflationary models of the universe we discussed earlier. In such cosmological models the early universe expanded exponentially fast for a minute fraction of a second after the big bang. Cosmologists introduced this idea in 1981 to solve several important problems in cosmology. Before this episode of inflation the whole universe could have been in causal contact at a common temperature. The manner in which inflation occurred so as to lead to the present universe requires the fixing of several parameters, so at least some of the fine-tuning we experience today is tucked away into the hypothesized inflation process, which has itself to be arbitrarily fine-tuned.

Another response to the fine-tuning problem involves the idea of a multiverse. The multiverse hypothesis posits that there are many other universes (an infinity) and that the universe we find ourselves in is just one of them. Each universe within this multiverse ensemble is endowed different properties and different values of the basic constants of physics. We just happen to live in the one where everything comes out just right for us to exist.

Fred Hoyle compared the chance of obtaining even a single functioning protein by random combination of amino acids to a star system full of blind men simultaneously attempting to solve the Rubik's Cube puzzle, thus arguing that even biology seems to have come into existence by intelligent, not blind, chance. If blind chance is deemed to be the only acceptable option then it would be necessary to have an infinity of universes, of which only the one we live in is fortuitously fit for life.

MOVE AWAY FROM COSMIC INTELLIGENCE

Since the publication of Darwin's book[4] in 1859 scientists have tended to veer away from intelligent design-type argument, perhaps fearing that this would be a shortcut back to God, and a reversal of a hard-won victory. Compared with discussions about the existence of God by Socrates or Paley that were carried out at the highest philosophical level, some modern manifestations of religious interpretation have turned out to be erroneous or even pernicious to varying degrees. Christian fundamentalism that insists upon a literal interpretation of the Bible gives the age of the Earth and the universe to be about 6,000 years. This figure comes evidently from a particular interpretation of the Bible due to Archbishop James Ussher (1581–1656). We know of course that the Earth is 4.5 billion years old from impeccable scientific analysis, and the universe is nearly 14 billion years old. So the fundamentalist position of "young Earth" creationists is manifestly wrong and antithetical to science.

Another set of fundamentalist religious stances that is causing concern stems from certain interpretations of the Qu'ran. Here we have a text that is open to a multitude of interpretations, and in one of these there appears to be an exhortation to eliminate nonbelievers or those who oppose their faith.

ARKANSAS TRIAL OF 1981

I will now describe a personal story of how I became personally involved in a religious debate. In 1981, Fred Hoyle and I had published our book *Evolution from Space,* which was receiving a great deal of media attention, particularly a chapter with the heading "Convergence to God?"[5] On March 19, 1981, the governor of Arkansas had signed into law an act that stated: "Public schools within this State shall give balanced treatment to creation-science and to evolution-science." The U.S. Federal Government challenged the constitutional validity of this act, and a case was pending between the state of Arkansas and the federal government. In view of our much publicized views on the inadequacy of neo-Darwinism to explain the origin of life and evolution, the events that were now to unfold were not entirely unexpected.

In late October of 1981 I received a phone call from Mr. David Williams, the state's attorney for Arkansas, to explain the nature of the forthcoming trial and to invite me to come as an expert witness for the state. As I understood the situation, State Education Act No. 590, which required a balanced treatment for "Evolution Science" and "Creation Science," was being challenged by the American Civil Liberties Union as infringing on the First Amendment of the Federal U.S. Constitution, an amendment that required a strict separation of church and state. Although I held no brief for any particular religion or ecclesiastical group, my sympathies instantly went out to Mr. Williams, both in regard to defending individual freedom of belief and also because I had come to acquire a dislike for the way that Darwinian evolution was being taught as though it explained *everything* about the nature of life. Whatever Darwinian ideas may have been able to explain in relation to the vast body of facts in biology itself, they certainly could not explain the origin of life from nonlife. This was the thrust of all our research that culminated in the publication of our book *Evolution from Space*. Any opportunity to challenge the established position in this regard seemed welcome to me at the time.

After talking at length on the telephone to the Arkansas state's attorney I became convinced that to defend the ideas Hoyle and I had published in our book *Evolution from Space* was an entirely worthwhile thing to do. To be their expert witness I had to rebut the claim of the American Civil Liberties Union that neo-Darwinian evolution was in every respect a proven fact. Even if it could be argued that neo-Darwinism may have been a process that took place after the beginning of life, there remained one point in the trajectory of life when Darwinian evolution simply could not have occurred. This was at the moment of life's presumed origin from nonliving inorganic chemicals, and there were no facts whatsoever to support the claim that pre-Darwinian evolution occurred in a primordial soup of chemicals.

Although I was a little apprehensive at the outset, after talking to my editor at my publishing house, J. M. Dent and Sons, I resolved to accept the invitation. I also had encouragement from Fred Hoyle, whose judgment I respected, and he urged me to go to Arkansas and present a testimony that we would agree upon beforehand.

The case I presented in Arkansas essentially summarized the scientific position that Fred Hoyle and I had reached in our researches in 1982. The following quotations are an extract of my testimony.

> The facts as we have them show clearly that life on Earth is derived from what appears to be an all pervasive galaxy-wide living system. . . . Life was derived from, and continues to be driven by, sources outside the Earth, in direct contradiction to the neo-Darwinian theory that everybody is supposed to believe. . . . It is stated according to the theory that the accumulation of copying errors, sorted out by the process of natural selection, the survival of the fittest, could account both for the rich diversity of life and for the steady upward progression from bacterium to Man. . . . We agree that successive copying would accumulate errors, but such errors *on the average* would lead to a steady degradation of information. . . . This conventional wisdom, as it is called, is similar to the proposition that the first page of Genesis copied billions upon billions of time would eventually accumulate enough copying errors and hence enough variety to produce not merely the entire Bible but all the holdings of all the major libraries of the world. . . . The processes of mutation and natural selection can only produce very minor effects in life as a kind of fine tuning of the whole evolutionary process. . . .
>
> In our view every crucial new inheritable property that appears in the course of the evolution of species must have an external cosmic origin. . . .We cannot accept that the genes for producing great works of art or literature or music, or developing skills in higher mathematics emerged from chance mutations of monkey genes. . . . If the Earth were sealed off from all sources of external genes: bugs could replicate till doomsday, but they would still only be bugs. . . .
>
> The notion of a creator placed outside the Universe poses logical difficulties, and is not one to which I can easily subscribe. My own philosophical preference is for an essentially eternal, boundless

Universe, wherein a creator of life (or creative intelligence) may somehow emerge in a natural way. My colleague, Sir Fred Hoyle, has also expressed a similar preference. In the present state of our knowledge about life and about the Universe, an emphatic denial of some form of creation or cosmic intelligence as an explanation for the origin of life implies a blindness to fact and an arrogance that cannot be condoned.

My testimony, which was consistent with my beliefs then as indeed they are now, is not a cause for regret in itself. The State of Arkansas Education Board, which I was representing, lost their case. In his summing up of the judgment on January 5, 1982, Judge William R. Overton made the following statement.

In efforts to establish "evidence" in support of creation science, the defendants (The State of Arkansas) relied upon the same false premise . . . i.e., all evidence which criticized evolutionary theory was proof in support of creation science. . . . While the statistical figures may be impressive evidence against the theory of chance chemical combinations as an explanation of origins, it requires a leap of faith to interpret those figures so as to support a complex doctrine, which includes a sudden creation from nothing, a worldwide flood, separate ancestry of man and apes, and a young earth. . . .

The defendants' argument would be more persuasive if, in fact, there were only two theories or ideas about the origins of life and the world. . . . Dr. Wickramasinghe testified at length in support of a theory that life on earth was "seeded" by comets which delivered genetic material and perhaps organisms to the earth's surface from interstellar dust far outside the solar system. . . . While Wickramasinghe's theory about the origins of life on earth has not received general acceptance within the scientific community, he has, at least, used scientific methodology to produce a theory of origins which meets the essential characteristics of science.

The Court is at a loss to understand why Dr. Wickramasinghe was called in on behalf of the defendants. Perhaps it was because he was generally critical of the theory of evolution and the scientific community, a tactic consistent with the strategy of the defense. Unfortunately for the defense, Dr. Wickramasinghe demonstrated that the simplistic approach of the two-model analysis of the origins of life is false. Furthermore, he corroborated the plaintiffs' witnesses by concluding that "no rational scientist" would believe the earth's geology could be explained by reference to a worldwide flood or that the earth was less than one million years old.

My appearance in the 1981 Arkansas trial held out a brief for some form of intelligent creation, and this angered many of my scientific colleagues. The repercussions of my court appearance unfortunately lasted for several years. Although I had not compromised my beliefs when cross-examined, I often had to agree with the plaintiffs' claims. Many scientists were angry at what they wrongly perceived as my attempt to give credibility to "creation science," which had come to be regarded as the antithesis to science. It was only after meeting "creation scientists" in Arkansas who believed in the literal truth of the Bible, including a belief in an Earth no older than 6,000 years, that I began to doubt the wisdom of my decision to testify.

RELIGION AND SCIENCE

Brought up as I was in a Buddhist tradition in Sri Lanka, my instinct is to lean toward atheism, and certainly to reject the idea of an interventionist God who is concerned with day-to-day affairs of individual creatures. This is not, however, to rule out an intelligence that is somehow intrinsic to the universe and intimately related to space, time, and matter.

CONSCIOUSNESS

What is the nature of consciousness? Despite major advances in neuroscience and psychology in recent years, concepts of mind and consciousness still pose the deepest of mysteries. The widespread use of noninvasive human brain imaging technologies has greatly transformed and extended the boundaries of cognitive neuroscience. These include magneto-encephalography (MEG), which images the actual function of neurons; magnetic resonance imaging (MRI); computer tomography (CT); and positron emission tomography (PET). Human brain imaging using such techniques allows scientists to derive a spatial picture of brain activity in normal subjects as they undertake a variety of different tasks. Recently single-cell and multiple single-unit recording technologies have progressed to the point where it is possible to record simultaneously from large ensembles of neurons, sometimes in different brain areas. In this way data is obtained on how the firing of individual cells could influence other cells. Experiments conducted on humans as well as other mammals have improved our knowledge of the detailed mechanics of brain function, but the most fundamental of questions in relation to brain activity remain unanswered. What is the connection between brain activity and consciousness and free will? Are they separate entities or manifestations of the same entity wholly confined to the ensemble of neurons in our brains?

In the year 2017 ideas relating to these matters, and particularly the understanding of consciousness, hover uneasily in a domain that straddles science, philosophy, and religion. The ultimate source of our instincts and behavior can in every detail be ultimately traced back to our brains and our nervous system and localized to precise locations on the role of left or right hemispheres. Although consciousness at the most rudimentary level—sleep or awake—is more or less understood. Mind and higher levels of consciousness remain as obscure as ever. Whether "mind" can be fully comprehended in terms of interactions between neurons in the brain is still far from clear.

Experimental studies using the latest technologies can show clearly that certain emotions like anger and love can be linked to increased activity in particular areas of the brain. It is also known that in cases of epilepsy electrical stimulation of parts of the brain can restore the most distant childhood memories. As an information holding and processing instrument the brain is turning out to be perhaps the most complex information processing and storage system in the entire universe. The use of vast batteries of modern digital computers to mimic the operation of the human brain in relation to information processing is proving to be almost impossible.

Many thoughtful scientists have reflected on the brain-mind problem over many decades. Nobel Prize–winning biologist John Eccles wrote thus: "The self is not a 'pure ego' that is a mere subject. Rather it is incredibly rich. Like a pilot, it observes and takes action at the same time."

The astronomer Sir Arthur Eddington wrote, "Mind is the first and most direct thing in our experience; all else is remote inference."

Many others have expressed very similar sentiments over many years, revealing a sense of utter bewilderment as to the precise definition of mind and its operation. Despite great strides of progress in science including the detailed biochemistry and physiology of the brain, the linked phenomena of "mind," "consciousness," and "self" continue to present a perpetual enigma within the scope of reductionist science.

The question remains as to whether the mind can be reduced to the collective actions of a network of nerve cells (neurons) and a variety of transmitter chemicals in the brain. The brain with all its 100 billion neurons represents the hardware within which mind, consciousness, innovation, and creativity find expression.

The brain is also the control center for learned behavior in humans as well as in other animals. In nonhuman life-forms, however, the ability to learn by experience is found to vary among different species and classes. Even single-celled life-forms like amoeba show signs of possessing a rudimentary level of consciousness, for example, by moving away from imminent danger. There is also evidence that whole colonies of bacteria show purposive and collective behavior. Thus rudimentary levels of consciousness and a degree of self-awareness may arguably straddle the whole spectrum of life.

Consciousness plays an important role in Vedantic physics—the science encapsulated in the Vedas of ancient India. The same ideas relating to cosmic consciousness and many levels of consciousness enter the cannon of Buddhist doctrine around the fifth century BC. Consciousness equates to subjective experience in Buddhist and Vedic philosophy. Reductionist science, on the other hand, takes a wholly objective approach to the world, and on the face of it the two viewpoints are divergent and contradictory. From a strictly scientific viewpoint, if there does indeed exist a reality beyond human awareness and experience, it will remain unknown to us. The resolution of this apparent contradiction could be to assert that consciousness is a property of the universe at a subatomic level occupying higher dimensional spaces that are not immediately accessible to our senses. The brain, however, might be presupposed to tap in to this information of consciousness in a way that is yet to be scientifically unraveled.

The birth of quantum mechanics in the 1930s offered a brand-new perspective for uniting objective and subjective worldviews at the atomic and subatomic levels. Schrödinger's wave formulation of quantum mechanics with its implied principle of uncertainty opened the door to an intersection between the subjective and objective universe. The apparent dilemma known by the phrase "collapse of the wave-function" called for a rational explanation. When we make an observation of an atomic system (e.g., a molecule of chlorophyll) we can determine its "state" precisely. Thereafter well-attested laws of physics can be used to describe the later progress of the system, but when we next make a conscious observation of the system we cannot predict what its state would be. The interaction with the observer's conscious mind at the time of the first observation apparently played a role in determining the subsequent fate of the atomic system. This interaction between human consciousness and inanimate matter has led many scientists to speculate on the possibility of a causal connection. Our own consciousness might be derived from a cosmic consciousness (perhaps localized in a higher dimension) that is all pervasive. Although such a proposition has been hinted at by some scientists, it is fair to say that it still exists only in the realm of pure speculation.

Physicist Sir Roger Penrose and medical scientist Stuart Hameroff have recently developed a model where conscious responses are linked to cooperative quantum events at the "microtubule" level in the brain.[6] Microtubules are information-holding structures within neurons in the brain that respond instantly to mental events. Their model presumes that the ultimate repository and source of consciousness is the universe at a quantum level, a model, as we remarked earlier, that is in good accord with both Vedantic and Buddhist thought.

This connection prompts me to recall a conversation I had in my early adolescence with a distinguished Buddhist monk and scholar in Sri Lanka—Ven Narada Thera. Talking about the Buddhist idea of rebirth led me to ask him how he would define a sentient human life. How is human life related to the levels of consciousness of which Buddhism had a lot to say? He told me that every new human life is comprised of three essential components. The sperm derived from the father; the ovum, or egg, derived from the mother; and most importantly a third component, which is a "packet of consciousness" derived from the cosmos. All three must come together to initiate a new sentient human being or human life.

Allegedly, according to Buddhist belief, it is this third component that is connected with rebirth. Rebirth, as I remarked earlier, is an unprovable hypothesis, but one that might be linked in some way to consciousness.

REBIRTH IN BUDDHISM

In support of rebirth one might cite anecdotal accounts, particularly in India and Sri Lanka, of young children seeking to make contact with an earlier home or earlier parents. Such children are said to have directed observers and reporters to distant places and to homes where it was discovered that a death had occurred roughly at the time of their own conception. Furthermore, it is said, they predict and identify many artifacts such as furniture and toys with remarkable accuracy. Such reports number in the hundreds at least, if not more. They have been compiled and allegedly verified by authors and reporters, but because of their essentially anecdotal character it is always possible to question their authenticity.

In my own view the most powerful support for the rebirth idea comes from well-documented accounts of exceptional genius. The logic of karma and rebirth is one that involves the accumulation of experience and knowledge from one birth to the next. In any case of an infant prodigy we therefore see not only the limited experience of a few early years but also the accumulated experience of many past lives. Let us look at two specific cases that it could be argued would be hard to explain from any other point of view. The first is the case of the composer Wolfgang Amadeus Mozart (1756–1791) and the second that of the Indian mathematical prodigy Srinivasan Ramanujan (1887–1920).

As a musical prodigy Mozart's early achievements were phenomenal. By the age of three he was playing tunefully on a clavier. By the age of five he was composing simple pieces, and by the age of eight he was composing prolifically in many different musical forms. In a short life span of only thirty-five years Mozart composed music that has been loved and admired by every generation that followed. Genetics alone can hardly explain this phenomenon.

Almost as puzzling is the case of Srinivasan Ramanujan, a mathematical genius born into poverty near Chennai (Madras) in India. Although he had no formal education, around the age of twenty he gained access to one single outdated book on mathematics. After studying this book he became determined to meet influential mathematicians in India to convince them that he had discovered new and startling results. For the most part they ignored his claims, but one of them, Ramachandra Rao, was so impressed with what he saw that he assisted Ramanujan in contacting the University of Cambridge mathematician G. H. Hardy (1877–1947). Hardy eventually invited Ramanujan to Cambridge, and it was from Trinity College Cambridge that the work of Ramanujan spread throughout the world. His notebooks kept in the Wren Library of Trinity College Cambridge are still being poured over by mathematical scholars. Some of his amazing insights and results have played a crucial role in the development of many areas of science, for example, the physics of black holes, theories of cell division, and cancer, as well as in the logic that goes into computers. Ramanujan was a pious Hindu belonging to the priestly Brahamin caste. His discoveries in mathematics were most extraordinary. Often he would discover a formula or a theorem for which he was unable (or could not be bothered) to supply a rigorous proof, and such proofs were only later to be discovered by other more orthodox mathematicians who had the benefit of a formal education in mathematics. According to Ramanujan the goddess Namagiri would appear in his dreams to convey important mathematical results. It could be argued that his intuition was the result of past experience of mathematics in an earlier incarnation.

If rebirth is indeed a fact, then it would seem likely that an amnesic barrier exists in our memories that prevents us from normally recalling events before we were born. It is interesting to note that there are some reported incidents of people recalling past lives through hypnotic regression. If these are confirmed it could be an indication that consciousness has a continuity that precedes birth and conception.

That said, I should emphasize that the Buddhist idea of rebirth presents a major challenge to our conventional understanding of life. At the moment one has to admit that it is neither proved nor disproved in rigorous scientific terms. It may be an idea in some way related to the nature of consciousness. We know of course that consciousness exists, but as yet we do not know if it could be reduced to its basic components or whether a stream of consciousness could ever be satisfactorily defined and tested by experiment.

5
Bacteria Entering Earth

We saw earlier that in view of the possibility that some bacteria and viruses entering the Earth might pose a threat to humanity, a regular monitoring of the stratosphere would be prudent to conduct. It is easy to calculate the time lapse between the arrival of a particle at the top of the stratosphere and its descent to ground level, and this can be shown to depend crucially on size. A small virus would take several years to reach the ground, whereas particles of bacterial size and larger particles would fall through relatively quickly in weeks or months. One might therefore wonder why a population of such incoming particles has not been, or could not be, detected using the space technologies that were available even as far back as the 1960s.

LESLIE HALE AND THE CONSPIRACY OF SILENCE

In 1978 after Hoyle and I had published our first book on the subject of diseases from space we had an unexpected visit from the atmospheric scientist Leslie Hale from Penn State University in the United States. What he announced at our meeting was shocking to say the least. There was in fact hard evidence for bacteria coming from space. In a series of balloon flights conducted by NASA between August 1962 and October 1965, bacteria were discovered in the high atmosphere between 20 and 40 kilometers.[1] The latter height was well above the level of the tropopause above which particles of bacterial size could not be lofted unless an exceptionally energetic event like a volcanic eruption was involved. Calculations showed that more than a metric ton of biological material actually enters the Earth every year, if this data is accepted.

Political expediency dictated that this data could not be admitted to be valid, so it was promptly dismissed as being all due to contamination, and consequently further funding for the project was stopped. Perhaps the fear that the entire space program, which was gathering momentum at the time, would be put in jeopardy if this result was admitted as real was almost certainly the underlying reason for this action.

There was at this time a U.S. vs U.S.S.R. political battle to conquer space, so it is likely that politics took precedence over science. It is therefore of interest that in 1976 a team of Russian scientists led by S. V. Lysenko published a paper claiming the positive detection of microorganisms from heights of 48 to 77 km.[2] The Russian scientists who used both sounding rockets and balloons categorically ruled out contamination, but they made the assertion that the microbes they had discovered may have been carried to these heights by air currents. The arguments that they must be of terrestrial origin because they are similar to Earth microbiota is of course not strictly valid, because all microbes on Earth, according to our point of view, must also have originated from space. The admission that space exploration could bring down alien microbes may well have threatened the space programs on either side of the iron curtain, so a stalemate of progress ensued.

Two other personal stories are worth recalling at this point. In 1982, I had invited Lysenko to present his results on stratospheric microbes at an international conference in Sri Lanka in December. Lysenko enthusiastically accepted my invitation, and I was looking forward to hearing his presentation. At the very last minute, however, he informed the conference organizers that he could not come. My suspicion is that his exit visa to attend the meeting was refused by the Soviet authorities.

ARTHUR C. CLARKE'S VISITOR

My second anecdote involves the late Sir Arthur C. Clarke, science-fiction writer and space visionary, who was my friend from 1961 until the time of his death. In December 1982, I visited Sir Arthur at his home in Colombo, Sri Lanka, and a most amazing conversation ensued. There was a copy of *Diseases from Space* (the book by Fred Hoyle and myself) clearly displayed on his bookshelf, and when I drew his attention to this he related a strange story. A few months earlier, Arthur reported, he had a visit from a high-ranking official of the CIA. This person, according to Arthur, walked up to his bookshelf and, picking up the copy of our book, remarked with a smile, "We have known that these guys have got things right for quite some time!" If this were really true, the question is why was it not announced to the scientific community, and even more importantly to the general public, whose taxes supported U.S. science? After a lapse of thirty-four years I am more convinced than ever that a conspiracy exists to deny or misconstrue all data that relates to the ingress of alien organisms from space.

SURVIVAL OF MICROBES ON EARTH

We have already seen that microorganisms inhabit the most unlikely places on the planet—the dry valleys of the Antarctic, deep-sea thermal vents—thousands of kilometers below the ocean surface and depths of some 8 kilometers beneath the Earth's crust. There is scarcely any niche, natural or man-made, that has not been colonized by some microbial species. Survival of microorganisms in the abdomens of insects trapped in amber for some forty million years appears to be well established. Direct proof of the survival of bacteria exposed for months to years to radiation in the near-Earth environment has also been demonstrated in NASA's Long Exposure Facility and more recently in experiments conducted in the International Space Station.[3]

It has been repeatedly stated by critics that viral or bacterial ingress to the Earth in a viable form is impossible, even if such viruses and bacteria actually did exist on a cosmic scale. The assertion has been that microorganisms would all be destroyed by heating as they plunge into the Earth's atmosphere. This can be shown to be untrue. Laboratory experiments on the survivability of bacteria with respect to flash heating on atmospheric entry, carried out in the 1980s, found that heating even to 1,000-degree temperatures above absolute zero for a few seconds under dry conditions does not lead to any significant loss of viability. It is true that spacecraft reentering the atmosphere would be heated to the point of sterilization at its surface, and certain types of cosmic particles—for example, meteoroids of sizes of the order of a millimeter—are destroyed by frictional heating. But this phenomenon is sensitively dependent on the angle of entry, size, composition, and the degree of fluffiness of the incoming particles. It is also noteworthy that viruses and bacteria stuck onto the outer surfaces of sounding rockets have been found to survive launch through the atmosphere as well as reentry. Transient heating to 1,000°C appears to have less effect on viability than had hitherto been believed.

According to all the available evidence individual bacteria, well as viral-size particles, survive atmospheric entry to a significant degree. Survival is also possible for even the most delicate biological structures if they are embedded within loosely compacted cometary fragments that are dispersed within the stratosphere, or even lower down in the atmosphere. In the latter case the deposition of biological material could be highly localized on the surface of the Earth. This could be relevant to the occurrence of highly localized outbreaks of bacterial and viral diseases.

Cometary microorganisms reaching the upper atmosphere—say a height of 100 kilometers—begin to fall under gravity, but they are quickly sifted according to size. Particles of bacterial size continue to fall under gravity and could reach ground level in a matter of a year or two. Viral-size particles become trapped at a height of 20 to 30 kilometers in a stratospheric trap, and further descent is largely controlled by global mixing circuits of the stratospheric air. These circuits have an essentially seasonal character with the potential of bringing down common viruses to ground level in seasonal cycles—as is indeed seen in the patterns of influenza.

The collection of particulate material in the lower atmosphere at heights below 25 kilometers have been carried out as far back as the 1950s and consistently turned up populations of particles that resemble bacteria and viruses to varying degrees. The Australian physicist

E. K. Bigg recovered particles that are similar in external characteristics to microorganisms.[4] More recently D. E. Brownlee has obtained a large collection of particle clumps of cometary origin from 15-kilometer altitude flights of U2 aircraft equipped with "fly paper" collectors for impacting dust. In collections of particles from altitudes less than 25 kilometers a major difficulty is to distinguish between particles of extraterrestrial origin and those lofted from the surface of the planet.

The most likely route to ground level for an extraterrestrial microorganism once it is dispersed in the stratosphere is via rain. For many years scientists have been baffled by the problem of how clouds saturated with water vapor come to be seeded so as to produce rain. An atmospheric cloud of saturated water vapor at 0 degrees C or slightly lower does not spontaneously turn into rain without either the formation within or the introduction from outside of what are called "freezing nuclei." The microorganisms would effectively serve as condensation nuclei around which particles of ice could grow.

More than half a century ago the Australian physicist E. G. Bowen discovered a remarkable connection between such freezing nuclei in rain clouds and extraterrestrial particles. He showed that there was an astounding link between the frequency of freezing nuclei detected within clouds and the occurrence of meteor showers. Meteor showers occur at regular times of the year as the Earth crosses the trails of debris evaporated from short period comets. Although larger particles that enter in this fashion would be evaporated quite high in the atmosphere, microorganisms could survive and so be able to act as freezing nuclei. Exceptionally heavy rain systematically occurred about thirty days after the peaks of meteor activity.

Bowen wrote in *Nature* thus:

> The hypothesis has therefore to be advanced that dust from meteor streams falls into the cloud systems of the lower atmosphere, nucleates them and causes exceptionally heavy falls of rain thirty days after the dust first entered the atmosphere.[5]

Although this hypothesis may have appeared far out in 1956, it has since been established that bacteria often serve as the most efficient nucleating agents for rain. The thirty-day time lapse between the disruption of a meteoroid in the upper atmosphere and rainfall observed by Bowen is easily understood as the time of descent of submicron particles through the atmosphere.

MODERN STRATOSPHERIC EXPERIMENTS TO TEST PANSPERMIA

As soon as we realized that discovering incoming cometary microbes in the stratosphere was a prediction of our panspermia theory we began to wonder how this could be achieved. In the early 1990s Fred Hoyle and I made approaches to various Western-based space agencies—including British Aerospace—but encountered a general lack of interest. We next approached the Indian Space authorities (ISRO) using the good offices of our colleague Professor Jayant Narlikar, but again their first response was negative, although more polite. A decade later in 2000, however, ISRO changed its mind and agreed to cooperate.

On January 21, 2001, air samples were collected from a balloon flight launched over Hyderabad, India, in four height ranges: 19–20 km, 24–28 km, 29–39 km, and 39–41 km. The collection involved the use of balloon-borne cryosamplers—a manifold of sixteen stainless-steel tubes, fully sterilized and evacuated to high vaccum levels. These steel tubes were placed in a liquid neon chamber to cool them to 10 degrees above absolute zero.

The entrance to each stainless-steel probe was fitted with a metallic valve, which was motor driven to open and shut on ground telecommand. Throughout the flight the probes remained immersed in liquid neon so as to create a cryopump effect, allowing ambient air to be admitted when the valves were open. Air including aerosols dispersed within it was collected into a sequence of probes during ascent, the highest altitude reached being 41 kilometers. The cryosampler manifold, once the probes were filled with stratospheric air and aerosol particles, was parachuted back to the ground.

Once the probes were brought down and taken to the laboratory for investigation the internal pressure within the cylinders was about two hundred times the atmospheric pressure. In the design of the probes care was taken to choose material that can safely withstand such high pressures, but decompression had to be carried out with due care to prevent accidents. The air from the exit valve of each probe was passed in a sterile system in a microflow cabinet sequentially through a 0.45 μm and a 0.22 μm micropore cellulose nitrate filters to trap the aerosol particles, including biological cells.[6] Clumps of cocci-shaped submicron-size particles, of overall average radius 3.0 μm were discovered from isolates of filters that trapped air collected at 41 kilometers. The clumps were identified first using a scanning electron microscope and subsequently by deployment of other techniques.

With instrumental and laboratory contamination excluded at all stages of the experiment, two options remain. First, one might think that the organisms obtained from the stratosphere were carried from the ground in a volcanic eruption or in some other exceptional or rare meteorological event. The other possibility is that they arrived from space. A volcanic origin is ruled out for the simple reason that there was no volcanic eruption recorded in a two-year run-up to the balloon launch date on January 20, 2001, and calculations show that steady fall through the atmosphere would drain out particles of 3 μm radius in a matter of weeks.

Statistical sampling analysis of cell populations collected from a height of 41 kilometers in the stratosphere implied that microorganisms of a presumed cometary origin were incident over the whole Earth at an average rate of 0.1 metric ton per day. Critics of panspermia may argue that 3 μm radius particles get burned through frictional heating and end up as meteors. Some fraction do, but others would not. Survival depends on many factors, such as angle of entry and mode of deposition in the very high stratosphere. Several modes of entry can be considered that permit intact injection into the stratosphere, possibly starting off as larger aggregates released from comets that disintegrate into a cascade of slow-moving smaller clumps at heights above 270 kilometers where frictional heating would be negligible. Evidence for such disintegrations available from studies of Brownlee particles collected in the 1990s using U2 aircraft have also shown the survivability of extremely fragile organic structures.

A few years after our cryoprobe experiment of 2001, a second stratospheric aerosol collection from 41 kilometers recovered three new bacterial species with exceptional ultraviolet resistance properties, and one of these was named in honor of Fred Hoyle—*Janibacter hoylei.*[7] Of the daily average input into the Earth of some 100 metric tons of cometary material, we can conclude that $^1/_{10}$ percent is in the form of viable bacteria that reach the stratosphere and ultimately fall to the surface of the Earth.

From 2012 onward the search for microbes in the stratosphere was continued in a project led by Professor Milton Wainwright of the Universities of Sheffield and Buckingham. Balloons, flown to heights of up to 30 kilometers, carried devices that could intercept and capture falling cometary particles directly onto "stubs" that go straight into an electron microscope once the payload is sealed and parachuted back to ground. By analyzing chemical composition and shapes, sizes, and structures of the material the results discussed earlier in this chapter have been dramatically confirmed.[8]

The most direct proof of the ideas in this book would be the recovery of alien life-forms located well outside Earth's immediate environs and its biosphere. Only then could the possibility of terrestrial contamination be decisively ruled out. The International Space Station (ISS) orbits at a height of 400 kilometers, and there is no conceivable way by which terrestrial microorganisms could reach to contaminate its outer surface. In 2015 a team of Russia cosmonauts reported the discovery of a range of microorganisms including diatoms on the outside of the ISS.[9] The organisms appear to have come within fragments of cometary dust that splashed onto the surface and survived. Understandably, perhaps, a pall of silence has fallen over this news. However, facts of this kind once obtained would be hard to deny.

OCTOPUS DNA

We have already seen that the most crucial genes relevant to the evolution of all species of plants and animals were almost certainly of extraterrestrial

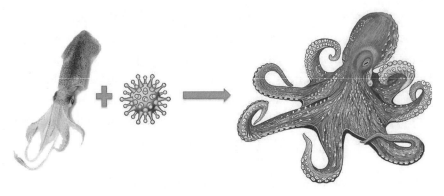

Fig. 5.1. The evolution from squid to octopus requires a suite of 33,000 genes inserted by extraterrestrial viruses.

origin, being transferred across the galaxy as virions. So far we have not been able to identify such biological entities in the material collected in the stratosphere.[10] It is to be hoped that with refined techniques that are planned for future experiments their presence will be established.

If a single development is to serve as a watershed on the journey to accepting the theory of cometary panspermia it is a recent discovery that concerns the genome of the octopus.[11] The octopus genome has recently been sequenced and revealed a staggering level of complexity with 33,000 protein-coding genes, more than in a human being. Octopus belongs to the coleoid subclass of mollusks that have an evolutionary history that stretches back over 500 million years. From the fossil record it appears that the octopus emerged suddenly from a squid lineage some 400 million years ago. Modern gene-sequencing techniques have recently been deployed to compare the DNA of the squid and the octopus.

The genetic divergence of octopus from its ancestral coleoid subclass is on a truly colossal scale. Its large brain and sophisticated nervous system, camera-like eyes, flexible bodies, and ability to switch color are just a few of the amazing features that appear suddenly on the scene. The transformative genes leading from squid to octopus are not to be found in any preexisting life-form—in a sense they seem to be borrowed from a far-distant "future" in terms of terrestrial evolution, or more realistically they came from the cosmos at large.

6
Alien Planets and Alien Intelligence

The history of assertions about alien planets goes back a long time. The pre-Socratic philosopher Metrodorus of Chios (ca. 400 BC) asserted that "it is unnatural in a large field to have only one shaft of wheat and in the infinite universe only one living world." The Roman poet Titus Lucretius Carus (ca. 99 BC–ca. 55 BC) wrote, "Nothing in the universe is unique and alone, and therefore in other regions there must be other Earths inhabited by different tribes of men and breeds of beasts." In Indian and Asian philosophy the many worlds interpretation extends even into prehistory. The Vedas, going back three thousand years, dwell on similar themes, and these ideas are encapsulated in Buddhist scriptures. In the comprehensive Buddhist Theravada text *Visuddhimagga,* by Buddhaghosa, written in circa AD 430 in Sri Lanka it is stated:

As far as these suns and moons revolve, shedding their light in space, so far extends the thousandfold world system. In it there are a thousand suns, a thousand moons, a thousand inhabited Earths, and a thousand heavenly bodies. This is called the thousandfold minor world system. . . .

Here a multiplicity of inhabited Earths and moons around other stars is clearly stated. The first similar assertion in western Europe had to await the successful completion of the Copernican revolution.

Giordano Bruno (1548–1600), an Italian monk, echoed closely the sentiments of the *Visuddhimagga,* being prompted by the Copernican revolution that was well under way. He went beyond the restricted Copernican model, however, by suggesting that stars were suns with planets orbiting around them, and moreover that they were inhabited by alien beings.

> Innumerable suns exist; innumerable earths revolve around these suns in a manner similar to the way the seven planets revolve around our sun. Living beings inhabit these worlds.[1]

While the pronouncements of the *Visuddhimagga* were well within the cultural constraints of Buddhism, Bruno's were not compatible with papal edicts. For his heresy he was tried at the Inquisition and burned at the stake.

SEARCH FOR ALIEN PLANETS

The actual search for alien planets was, however, to be a full four and a half centuries after Bruno's death. Hubble telescope images in the 1980s first revealed the presence of many protoplanetary discs that show edge-on views of planetary systems as they were being formed.

The first discovery of an alien extrasolar planet took place in October 1995. Michel Mayor and Didier Queloz were the first to interpret tiny wobbles in the position of stars in the sky to infer that planets orbiting the stars were rhythmically tugging at the parent stars. The first planet to be discovered in this way was a Jupiter-mass planet around the star 51 Peg in the constellation of Pegasus, fifty light-years away. This method of planet detection, known as the Doppler method, has a strong tendency to find large Jupiter-mass planets in relatively close proximity to the central star. On such planets life would not be possible.

Another method by which a planet can be detected is when it comes in front of a star and partially eclipses it in the course of its orbit. Measuring the minute dips in brightness of a star as a planet transits in front of it and partially obscures it can be used to detect the planet's existence. NASA's orbiting telescope, the Kepler telescope, dedicated to search for planets in this way, was launched in 2009. It has already provided an impressive roster of more than 3,300 confirmed exoplanets as of July 2016. Among the detections are several small Earth-like planets that are looking more likely now to be exceedingly common in the galaxy. The nearest such planet to be discovered in 2016 is Centauri b, an Earth-like planet orbiting the red dwarf star Proxima Centauri, which is the nearest star to the sun, at a distance of 4.1 light-years.

A habitable zone around a star is defined as the range of radial distance in which a planet can maintain the conditions needed for life. This includes the requirement for liquid water at or near the surface, and ideally also a planet that can retain an atmosphere for long enough timescales during which life can evolve. If the planet is too close to the star, surface temperatures would exceed the critical value for liquid water, and if it is too far away the water will be in the form of solid ice. Another condition for a stable, habitable planet is that it not be too close to a Jupiter-size planet, whose interactions could lead to it being perturbed inward or outward (away from the habitable zone) on timescales that are too short.

Water will remain liquid under a pressure of 1 bar (terrestrial sealevel pressure) between 0°C and 100°C. If complicating factors, such as the effect of an atmospheric greenhouse are ignored, a habitable zone for Earth-type life could be defined simply as the distance from a star where the effective temperature falls in the range 0 to 100°C.

However, such considerations are based only on the requirement of supporting life on the surface of a rocky planet like Earth, and they could turn out to be unnecessarily restrictive in our wider search for extraterrestrial life. Subsurface oceans, such as are almost certainly maintained in the Jovian satellite Europa through tidal heating, could define an additional class of habitable zone that lies well outside the limits that are generally considered. Likewise Saturn's cloud-covered moon, Titan, could also be warmed by a similar process, and the possibility of habitable zones cannot be ignored.

Using data from the Kepler telescope it has recently been estimated

*Fig. 6.1. NASA's Kepler orbiting telescope has so far detected
more than 3,000 exoplanets in a nearby sample of the galaxy.
The total for the whole galaxy is estimated at 140 billion!*

that the fraction of red dwarf stars that could host Earth-size habitable
planets may be upward of 10 percent. Ravi Kopparapu and his collaborators have further argued that upward of 140 billion habitable Earth-
size planets exist throughout the Milky Way, so the average distance
between such planets is only several light-years. This means that the
biospheres of planets like the Earth must seriously overlap with those
of neighboring planets, with exchanges of biomaterial via the agency
of comet and meteorite impacts being inevitable. The biosphere of the
Earth could therefore not be regarded as coming to a sharp end at the
top of the stratosphere—it must extend across much of the galaxy.

THE EARTH AS HOME OF LIFE

The Earth is home to many billions of species of microbes, plants, and
animals, and at the very summit of the evolutionary pile is *us,* the species
Homo sapiens sapiens. There are at the present time an estimated six thousand two hundred million individual members of this species grouped into

221 separate nation-states, with exceedingly diverse fortunes, and with more than 80 percent of the population living on the verge of starvation.

At the time of this writing (2017) there are several divergent world-views and religions in existence that divide our species even further. Different nations, different religions, are often seen to be at loggerheads, engaging in war, expressing what appears to be a primal instinct to gain territory and absolute control over the planet. Despite all these distractions what cannot be denied is that we have made enormous technological progress over the past few hundred years, and such advances have enhanced our capacity to exploit to the fullest the natural resources of the planet. Our noblest intellectual aspirations, however, are directed toward pushing forward the frontiers of knowledge and to exploring the universe to our fullest capacities. This includes our desire to communicate with other intelligent life-forms in the universe.

INTELLIGENCE OUTSIDE EARTH

On an alien planet, lying within the habitable zone of a sunlike star, the same genetic units that led to the evolution of life on Earth would also have been incident via comets. Under a reasonable set of assumptions self-similar patterns of convergent evolution would undoubtedly be repeated. It is hard to imagine that intelligence of the kind we associate with humans happened to evolve just on the Earth alone. Nor can we expect the level of intelligence we perceive in humans to be anywhere near the end of the road. Life, intelligent life included, must in my view be commonplace in the cosmos and span an enormous range of possibilities.

As early as 1896, Nikola Teska, a telephonic engineer who worked with Thomas Edison, made the first known suggestion that radio could be used to contact extraterrestrial civilizations. The technical feasibility of detecting extraterrestrial intelligence has been taken for granted for at least four decades. In a 1959 paper in the journal *Nature,* Philip Morrison and Giuseppe Cocconi first drew attention to the possibility of searching the microwave spectrum and suggested frequencies as well as a set of initial targets.

SETI (SEARCH FOR EXTRATERRESTRIAL INTELLIGENCE) PROGRAM

In 1960, Frank Drake conducted the first modern SETI experiment, named Project Ozma, using the 26-meter radio telescope at Green Bank, West Virginia. The target stars were two sunlike stars—tau Ceti and epsilon Eridani. Searches started over narrow wavebands around 21 centimeters, the famous neutral hydrogen line, but subsequently other wavelengths and multichannel detections have been attempted.

Historically there have been two episodes of alleged extraterrestrial intelligence detection that have been recorded in the past half a century. One was an error of judgment, the other still remains a mystery. In the winter of 1967, Anthony Hewish and Jocelyn Bell discovered a source of radio waves from a point source in the sky that was pulsing at the rate of once per minute. This source was later found to be a new type of astronomical object—a pulsar (PSR B1919+21), which was essentially a rapidly rotating neutron star. For some weeks after its discovery, before its natural cause was understood, there were serious discussions of the possibility that this was indeed the sign of an extraterrestrial intelligence. Further implications of such a contingency were also under discussion, albeit briefly—how to verify this conclusion, how to announce it, and whether such a discovery could be construed as dangerous.

The next more serious episode was one nicknamed the "Wow!" signal. This was a brief burst of radio waves detected on August 15, 1977, by Jerry Ehman, who was working on a SETI project at the Big Ear radio telescope in Ohio. The intensity of the signal coming from the direction of Sagittarius was observed to rise and fall over a period of seventy-two seconds. It would be nearly impossible for any earthbound object to match characteristics of the signal. If the signal did indeed originate in space, it was either a hitherto unknown astrophysical phenomenon, or it truly was an intercepted alien signal. The nearest star in the direction the telescope was pointing is 220 light-years (68 parsecs) away. The same star has been looked for since, but a signal was never repeated.

Nowadays, there is a growing trend to turn to the optical waveband in the belief that laser signaling may have been used more advantageously by some of our intelligent neighbors. The idea of optical SETI was suggested early by R. N. Schwartz and C. H. Townes and deployed to a limited extent, but so far there has been no success.

Whether using radio waves or light beams, a strong justification is needed if the search for extraterrestrial intelligence is to be conducted at great public expense. How can we be certain that extraterrestrial intelligence exists and that it is worthwhile or even wise to search for it? These are questions that need to be addressed.

A superficial defense for the existence of such intelligence of this position could go as follows: Intelligence and technology capable of SETI has arisen in only a span of a few thousand years out of a total history of terrestrial life that spans 4,000 million years. Superficially, at least, the probability of such intelligence comes out at one in a million, and that would at best give only a million stars with inhabited planets carrying the requisite level of intelligence throughout the galaxy. That may not be so damaging after all, but some critics would pursue the matter even further. They would say that intelligence on Earth has arisen at the very end of a long series of multiple contingencies, a succession of random events, each having a vanishingly small probability. If you multiply a few thousand such infinitessimal probabilities you may end up with a chance of ET intelligence to be vanishingly small. On that argument Earth will be the only planet with intelligence in the entire universe!

PANSPERMIC PERSPECTIVE

Panspermia, which has been described in this book, offers a totally different landscape on which the logic of SETI can be restored. We have argued that it is indeed the case that the emergence of the first life in the universe has a probability so vanishingly small that it could reasonably have occurred once and only once in the entire universe. The best condition of all would be for a spatially infinite universe, a universe that ranges far beyond the largest telescopes. Then the very small chance of obtaining a replicative primitive cell will bear fruit somewhere, and, when it does, replication in a suitable astronomical setting will cause an enormous number of copies of the first cells to be produced.

According to this model no great innovation in biology ever happened on the Earth. The Earth is merely a receiving station where cosmically determined genes were assembled. On this view of the origin of life there would be little variation in the forms to which the process gives rise, at least so far as basic genes are concerned, over the whole of our galaxy or even over all galaxies in the universe. On other planets around other stars the same processes of assembly of cosmic genes as happened on Earth would also operate. Life would thus inevitably develop on every habitable planet assembled from the same all-pervasive cosmic genes. Intelligence—leading up to at least the level found in humans—is part and parcel of the package of cosmic evolution and should show up inevitably in the evolutionary history of life on every inhabited planet. The improbability of repeating random evolutionary events converging on intelligence then disappears. Intelligence will show up sooner or later depending on particular circumstances, and it could last a short time or a very long time, again depending on local contingencies. But like the emergence of life, the emergence of intelligence would also be a cosmic imperative. The simple logic is that evolution, which involves assembly of a cosmically derived blueprint, must converge everywhere to the same result. This is evident, for example, in the emergence of the eye that occurred independently on at least three occasions in the development of life on Earth.

CURRENT PROSPECTS FOR PANASPERMIA AND SETI

In 1971 the U.S. space agency NASA funded a SETI program (Search for Extraterrestrial Intelligence) led by Frank Drake, but since then their support for this and other similar studies has fizzled out due to funding constraints and competing priorities. A report proposing construction of a radio telescope array with 1,500 dishes, known as Project Cyclops, has gone through many iterations since the 1970s, but its realization is still only a distant dream. A somewhat more modest modern successor to Project Cyclops is the Allen Telescope Array (ATA), formerly known as the One Hectare Telescope, currently located at the Hat Creek

Radio Observatory in northern California. The ATA is now a facility supported and managed by a private institute, the Stanford Research Institute. The ultimate plan is to have an array of 350 antennas scanning over a wide range of wavelengths and offering the best chance of detecting an intelligent signal. However, with just 42 antennas in operation since 2007, the project still limps along precariously, being passed on from one public institution to another.

The reluctance of any government institution or university to maintain an involvement is clear proof that this type of innovative science cannot be supported from public funds. Scientific authorities who decide on these matters may also have a subconscious fear of actually making a discovery that may forever change the face of science. It is clear from the way it has survived, however, that this ambitious project will not be stifled by such constraints. We can entertain an optimistic hope that with the advantages offered by ATA—its wide field and instantaneous frequency coverage from 0.5 to 11.2 GHz—a confirmed "Wow" signal will soon be received. If it finally happens it would surely be the most important development in the whole history of human civilization.

While radio SETI is the most favored way of searching for intelligence outside the Earth, an intriguing alternative can be described as biological SETI. Viral genomes, for instance, could carry coded information, if we can decipher them, and the transfer of viruses across astronomical distances appears to be a fully feasible proposition. Thus messages could in principle be carried in viral genomes, and both bacteria and viruses could serve as transmitters of intelligent signals.

Francis Crick, the discoverer of the DNA double helix, and Leslie Orguel had once proposed that the emergence of life on Earth was the result of directed panspermia—an artificially engineered bacterium or genome introduced to the Earth from outside. This would demand the existence of an intelligence or supeintelligence capable of genetic engineering to the extent of creating the blueprint of carbon-based life artificially. Such an intelligent "working out" of the blueprint of life might at first glance appear to be far-fetched, but it is certainly not a travesty of science. In 2017 biochemists can perform feats of genetic engineering, albeit in a limited way. Perhaps a few centuries from now human biochemists may be able to compute a genetic code and a set of crucial genes for any desired form of life and dissemminate them widely in the universe—within viruses or bacteria, for example. We have already seen that such particles would have sizes that make them easily dispersed by radiation pressure of stars and galaxies.

Frank Drake, the pioneer of SETI, has derived a simple equation for estimating the number (N) of extraterrestrial civilizations within the galaxy that we may hope to contact with sensitive enough equipment. The result given is the product of several factors.

We do not need to dwell on Drake's equation or go through all the relevant factors but only to say here that the factors all multiply to give a very simple result: N = L (years).

That is to say, the number of contactable extraterrestrial civilizations is roughly equal to the average lifetime (L) of such civilizations measured in years.

From our human experience our capacity to engage in SETI is ~100 years. Already at our present stage of technological advancement the nuclear arsenals throughout the world have grown to a stage that is evidently very unstable. Given the vageries of human behavior, the greed of our leaders to amass power, and the multitude of conflicts that plague the modern world, it cannot be denied that we face an imminent risk of destroying ourselves. The situation as far as the continuation of our own species is concerned is therefore balanced on a knife's edge. It would seem that in the case of humans moral progress has not kept pace with the advancement of scientific technology. Our most primitive instincts of competition, possession, and combat remain largely untamed.

If a typical advanced civilization inevitably destroys itself in a thousand years, then N = 1,000 and there will be only a thousand civilizations with whom we can communicate in the galaxy. On the other hand if this timespan is increased to ten million years, then the number rises to ten million. An enlightened civilization on a planet like Earth that develops a philosophy of peaceful coexistence could survive and for up to two billion years, before an unavoidable stellar or planetary catastrophe intervenes. If so their numbers within the galaxy may well run into billions. There may be a case for saying that those civilizations that have overcome their primal tendencies of conflict and developed enlightened pacifist philosophies dominate the cosmic scene by a process of natural selection.

But part of the reason for SETI not producing a result for more than fifty years may be a financial one—right from the start support for this program has been grudging at best and mean at worst. But perhaps this may be about to change. Russian billionaire Yuri Milner has offered some $100 million to give a boost to this seemingly ailing project and has recruited big names to promote a revamped SETI project. Milner has secured rights to use the world's two largest radio telescopes: the Green Bank Telescope in West Virginia and the CSIRO Parkes Telescope in Australia. He has also offered a million dollars to a person who can create the best message we could transmit were we to discover that another civilization was out there listening. Some are also thinking of transmitting modulated laser messages—for example, the whole of Wikipedia or the entire store of human literature and knowledge—to those planets that have the potential for bearing intelligent life; that is, confirmed exoplanets within a radius of twenty light-years from the Earth.

Fig. 6.2. The Parkes Radio Telescope that is to be used
to search for alien signals

It would be almost inevitable that a successful SETI contact would imply contact with a civilization at a much higher level of development than ours. If so there may be a great deal to learn. To begin with they may tell us how to avoid lethal and devastating conflict. They may even tell us the nature of God, if such exists, and thereby eliminate a major cause of strife and dissention on our planet. We may think of a world or cosmic religion in which petty squabbles such as we see on planet Earth today will have no place.

Should we fear contact? The answer in my view is of course NO. In this author's view our moment of first contact would arguably be the most important moment in the entire history of humanity. Humankind would instantly become enlightened to a degree that could scarcely be imagined. It would be like a Neanderthal man coming suddenly into contact with modern *Homo sapiens*—our horizons would expand immeasurably.

Our genetic links to ETs would of course be similar to our links with past life-forms on the Earth, for example to Neanderthal man. ETs would, according to the ideas discussed in this part of the book, also be made of the same cosmic genes—using of course the same genetic code. It is perhaps no wonder then that all depictions of ETs in fiction and on the screen have not departed much from the body plans of creatures we know on this planet.

If there is a humanlike civilization on a neighboring exoplanet within ten to twenty light-years from the sun, how would we know of its existence? We have already discussed in this chapter contact possibilities based on SETI-type projects as being the most promising. Radio emissions, traveling at the speed of light, as for instance emanate from our radio/TV-type broadcasts, would have certainly had ample time to reach these neighbouring exoplanets. Likewise, any similar emissions from the life-bearing exoplanets would have the potential for being picked up by our radio telescopes and interpreted as intelligent signals. The most promising prospect for detection would be if an alien civilization decides to beam a modulated radio "searchlight" that we can intercept. In a SETI-type program that scanned the skies in all directions we may have a chance of picking up such a modulated radio beam.

Perhaps the famous WOW signal of 1977 that lasted for a brief 72 seconds at 1,420 MHz (almost exactly the hydrogen wavelength) may have been such a fleeting event. This radio signal was detected in 1977 by Jerry Ehman, who was working on a SETI project at the Big Ear radio telescope in Ohio. Ehman had marked the signal with the letters WOW on the paper output, and this is the name by which the signal has come to be known. Despite a great deal of effort the WOW signal has defied identification to the present day. It is possible that it was due to a crossing of a modulated radio-seachlight beam lasting for the brief time when the Earth intercepted its path. Several astrophysical hypotheses to explain this phenomenon have been explored without success; and in the words of Sherlock Homes, when you have eliminated the impossible, whatever remains, however improbable, must be the truth! The prima facie case for an alien signal still remains strong. This gives us encouragement to continue our search for more.

Extrapolations from the Kepler telescope observations have yielded a grand total of about 140 billion exoplanets in the galaxy. Of these 40 percent may be expected to be Earth-size and occupying the habitable zones of their parent stars. The nearest red dwarf star to us around which an Earth-like planet was recently discovered is Proxima Centauri, 4.2 light-years away. Throughout our Milky Way the opportunities for the existence of planets capable of supporting intelligent life are vast, and at least one such planet could well be close!

SPACE TRAVEL PROSPECTS

How plausible is it to think of travel between neighboring planetary systems that may be just tens of light-years apart? In the brief fifty-plus years of our own technological space age humans have landed on the moon and will in a short time be heading for the planet Mars. The latter would surely be achieved on a timescale of decades. Although unmanned space exploration has extended as far as the outer planets and their moons, and one spacecraft in particular, *Voyager 1*, has actually left the planetary system, manned interstellar space travel still remains a distant dream.

The difficulties facing the prospect of manned exploration of nearby planetary systems appear at the moment to be insurmountable. To reach a target planet 10 light-years away in a spacecraft traveling at 1 percent of the speed of light (an extremely optimistic speed) will take a thousand years. Such a project, either manned or unmanned, will take more than thirty human generations. In terms of human psychology this will be very difficult to contemplate. There are also unsolved technical problems to contend with: the availability of fuels, the hazards of meteorite impacts, the energy requirements to maintain human life within the spacecraft, and most importantly the brevity of a human generation or lifetime. It would surely be necessary to think in terms of reproducing colonies to be maintained within the spacecraft with destinations being reached only after the lapse of several or many generations. These are now talked about glibly, but will our human psychology be able even to consider embarking on open-ended voyages?

Another option that is being exploited in science-fiction and space movies is the use of cosmic shortcuts called wormholes—tunnels through the fabric of space-time. Such tunnels are in fact a consequence of Einstein's general theory of relativity and so fall squarely within the realm of respecable science. Einstein and Nathan Rosen published a paper in 1935 describing such wormholes and bridges as real physical entities. Whether they really exist can still be disputed, but they certainly serve as ideas that are attractive to explore, at least in science fiction.

Ignoring the wormhole option for the time being, the considerations discussed earlier would seem at first sight to weigh heavily against the feasibility of space travel. The possibility of discovering ways of increasing the human life span dramatically or of transporting frozen embryos that wake up on arrival at a destination planet seems to be more in the realm of science fiction than plausible fact. At the present time the prospects for human travel to another planetary system do appear utterly remote. The prospect that an intelligent species on another planet may be far more advanced than humans and endowed with life spans in excess of a hundred thousand years opens up new vistas, however. Such creatures may well have the capability of travel to Earth from a planet located tens of light-years away.

We have seen in this chapter that in the light of the most recent detections of habitable planets in their billions the case for extraterrestrial intelligent life seems very strong. There is, however, one oft-repeated objection known as Fermi's paradox that argues against this. The paradox argues that if this is the case why have we not discovered it? Or it is sometimes put in the form of another question: "Where is everybody? Why have they not contacted us or even arrived here on our planet? There is also the argument that the other habitable planets in our vicinity orbit stars that are at a much more advanced stage of their evolution than the sun (white dwarfs, red dwarfs), and on such stars extraterrestrial intelligence, if it is a cosmic imperative, would have arisen long ago. Taking a cue from our own desire to colonize territory one may argue that they would have already located Earth as a suitable home of life and arrived at our planet. One might expect to see evidence of such invasions in the past record of the Earth.

For many reasons the objections implied in Fermi's paradox can all be answered satisfactorily. We already mentioned that interstellar travel is likely to be slow, and this would be a powerful limitation for prospective colonizers. Even if this limitation was somehow overcome, prospective colonizers may well have arrived here in the past and found the conditions, atmospheric properties, temperature, pressure, gravity, and so forth unsuitable for their particular form of biology—even if that biology was based as we think on the same basic genetic units.

Then the typical distance between a home planet and a destination planet being of the order of ten light-years, communication with any base station on the home planet might be deemed impractical—it taking twenty years for a reply to any message being received. In the seventeenth and eighteenth centuries slowness of communication was a major impediment to keeping empires sustainably together, and the same constraint may apply to the case of interstellar colonization.

There is also the possibility that a high level of technology and superintelligence would go with a lack of desire for colonization. But continuing reports of UFO sightings on Earth may actually belie this, if indeed even minute fractions are genuine sightings of extraterrestrial spacecraft. We can of course argue, justifiably in my view, that there is no conclusive proof of any genuine UFO sightings. But the fact remains that of the many "sightings" that are on record, most but not all are explained in terms of mundane terrestrial phenomena. A significant residue still presents an unsolved mystery and a rich ground for fantasy and speculation.

And finally there remains the possibility that intelligent aliens have indeed come here in past geological epochs, but the evidence has either been obliterated or become too fuzzy to perceive.

7
Earth's Continually
Changing Conditions

The truth lies betwixt and between. We have seen earlier that comets not only delivered the first forms of microbial life to Earth, but they also continued to bring new types of bacteria and new genes in the form of virions (viruses) that were added to the genomes of evolving life-forms. This process, we argue, played an overwhelmingly dominant role in life's evolution. Darwinian natural selection, survival of the fittest, served in the main to sort out newly emerging phenotypes in accordance with their fitness to survive under the continually changing physical conditions that prevailed on Earth.

The earliest geological history of the Earth from the time of its formation 4.5 billion years ago to 3.8 billion years ago was a tumultuous episode riddled with comet and asteroid impacts. From the first moment of life taking root on Earth, following its delivery by a life-bearing comet, later interactions with comets must have taken place both in the form of atmospheric dusting from disintegrating small fragments of comets as well as through direct cometary impacts. Impacts can leave evidence of craters, and, from the cratering record of both the Earth and its satellite neighbor, the moon, it can be inferred that comet/asteroid impacts have indeed been taking place at regular intervals. Some of these impact events appear to have contributed directly or indirectly to surges of biological evolution, as for instance in the Cambrian explosion of multicellular life that occurred between 570 and 450 million years ago. So far so good.

The last major comet impact occurred about 65 million years ago with a crater that resulted from it discovered in the seabed of the Yucatan peninsula. It seems likely that this crater-causing impact was also accompanied by a protracted episode of collisions with smaller cometary bodies that straddled the period 65 million years plus or minus 50,000 years. In my view it was this protracted cluster of smaller impacts that both introduced new genes and indirectly gave our mammalian ancestors a window of opportunity to emerge. At this point another personal anecdote would seem to be in order.

In September 1977, I was visiting the astronomy department of the University of Western Ontario, Canada, and my collaborator Fred Hoyle was visiting Caltech in the United States at the same time. Fred Hoyle and I began independently examining a volume titled *Cretaceous-Tertiary Extinctions and Possible Terrestrial and Extraterrestrial Causes* that was published in the previous year by the Canadian Museum of Natural History in Ottawa.

From these studies in 1977 it quickly became clear that the geological record shows clearly that there was a major extinction event in the history of terrestrial life 65 million years ago. The dinosaurs, and along with them a host of other animals with body weights above 25 kilograms, suddenly became extinct. Both Hoyle and I analyzed the data carefully and came to the conclusion that this could be due to the interaction of the Earth with a cloud of porous cometary dust derived from the extended coma of a comet that had just missed a direct hit of the Earth. When this happened the Earth's stratosphere would have been dusted over in a way that two-thirds of the light and incident energy from the sun was blocked for several years, while still permitting infrared (heat) radiation to leak out. The result would be semi-darkness for a decade, and this would have led to the withering of foliage in trees, causing a severe interruption of food chains.

Herbivorous creatures including dinosaurs would soon become extinct, and so also would carnivores that feed on the herbivores. With rivers still continuing to run and some lakes remaining unfrozen, fresh water organisms would survive—their food chains depending on decaying vegetable matter would take longer to be broken than marine organisms dependent on phytoplankton. The seeds and nuts of land plants would also survive so that small animals, including small mammals, living on nuts and seeds would also survive the dark and desolate years.

Although a direct hit by a comet also appears to have happened, as the seabed crater suggests, the dusting of the atmosphere by disintegrating fragments could be a more powerful process that explains the global extinction event. All these ideas were published by Fred Hoyle and myself in 1977 in the form of an article in the journal *Astrophysics and Space Science*.[1] Our ideas on the Cretaceous-Tertiary extinctions were similar (though not identical) to those of Alvarez and Alvarez that were published approximately two years after ours and which have now come to be more-or-less generally accepted and indeed most widely quoted. Such is the acquisitive nature of human behavior, it would seem.

In addition to causing extinctions of species we also argued in our 1977 paper that cometary dusting over a more protracted period could trigger the onset of an ice age. The last glacial period, generally called *the Ice Age*, occurred during the final 100,000 years of the so-called Pleistocene geological epoch, which lasted from about 110,000 to 12,000 years ago. During the past 2.6 million years or so in the Quaternary period, ice ages—times of extreme cooling of the Earth's climate when glaciers covered large areas of land—alternated with warmer interglacial periods. One hundred thousand years of ice-age conditions were followed by 10,000 year-long relatively warm interglacial periods, and this alternated with almost clockwork regularity.

We know that about 14,500 years ago the Earth's climate started to shift away from a very cold glacial condtion to a warmer interglacial state. Some 1,500 years later the temperatures in the Northern Hemisphere suddenly dropped again to near-glacial conditions, defining a period called the Younger Dryas. At this time more than three-fourths of the large ice-age animals, including woolly mammoths, saber-toothed tigers, and giant bears, died out. Simultaneously there was also a rapid disappearance of a long-established Stone Age population in North America, the so-called Clovis culture. Initial speculation on these post-ice-age animal extinctions was focused on a human overkill theory, which of course would have no impact on the disappearance of the Clovis culture. Recent research by Bill Napier and others has opened a new line of thought. It is becoming increasingly clear that the most likely cause of all the events of this period may indeed be a cometary body that exploded over southern Canada, causing environmental havoc on a scale that neither humans nor animals could endure.

Craters on the Earth's surface resulting from impacts by comets and asteroids do not persist indefinitely. They become eroded, buried, or disrupted by geological processes over many thousands of years. Some 170 known craters of various sizes have been discovered so far, and their ages range from thousands to millions of years. The Arizona Meteor Crater, which is perhaps the most famous crater, was caused by an impact some 50,000 years ago.

We already referred to the crater in the seabed of the Yucatan Peninsula caused by a 10-kilometer-size cometary body that led to the extinctions of a large number of species, including the dinosaurs, 65 million years ago. There is now growing evidence that interactions of the Earth with much smaller cometary fragments would have occurred much more frequently during historical times, but these are difficult to locate except through their effects on human populations.

The most recent event of a relatively minor nature that can be used as a standard for judging earlier impacts occurred in Siberia in 1918. This was the explosion of a comet fragment several hundred meters in size that took place in the skies of Tunguska, Siberia, leading to the destruction of thousands of square kilometers of forest. The fireball, which appeared to outshine the sun, was seen over a large part of Siberia and from a thousand miles away. The cometary fragment exploded at a height of 8 kilometers in the atmosphere, and the immense blast wave that resulted from it felled trees over a distance of some 40 to 50 kilometers; and the heat from the fireball charred tree trunks for up to 15 kilometers.

Estimates of the total energy of the impacting object range from 13 to 30 megatons of TNT, or the explosive power of 650 to 1,500 Hiroshima bombs. Although no human or animal extinctions occurred in the 1908

Tunguska event, on other past occasions, which may have involved not one isolated impact but a cluster of them, the situation would have been different.

Together with Bill Napier and Fred Hoyle, I have discussed the possibility that the history of civilization was marked by relatively recent episodes of such impacts by fragments of a large comet that disintegrated due to interacting with the giant planet Jupiter some 15,000 years ago. Fragments of this comet would have remained in an orbit around the sun, which was periodically crossed by the Earth. At each crossing a cluster of Tunguska-type collisions would have occurred. It is difficult to imagine how empires, kingdoms, and civilizations would have survived such protracted episodes of assaults from the skies, each of which may have lasted for decades.

According to this picture several otherwise mysterious facts of history might be explained, such as:

- The collapse of Mohenjo-daro
- The demise of the Akkhad culture of central Iraq
- The sudden disappearance of hundreds of early settlements in the Holy Land
- The collapse of the Roman Empire

Supportive evidence for one of these comes from an ancient account of the Deluge from the *Epic of Gilgamesh,* circa 2200 BC, which is an epic poem from ancient Mesopotamia written on clay tablets.

[A]nd the seven judges of hell . . . raised their torches, lighting the land with their livid flame. A stupor of despair went up to heaven when the god of the storm turned daylight into darkness, when he smashed the land like a cup.

At somewhat later dates the Old Testament is sprinkled with accounts of floods, rain, fire from the skies on the cities of Sodom and Gommorah, and all of these may have a rational explanation on the basis of cometary impacts.

When Joshua saw the sun stand still in the sky, we are naturally reminded of similar descriptions of the 1908 Tunguska event. When Jericho was attacked by the Israelites under Joshua (Joshua 2–6), its great walls collapsed, perhaps not by the sound of trumpets but by the enormous blast wave from a Tunguska-like cometary missile. The biblical archaeologist Bryant Wood has recently found evidence of a walled city that existed at Jericho until about 1400 BC when it was destroyed. All this is consistent with an episode involving a cluster of Tunguska-type assaults taking place over a timespan of a few years. According to this picture the Earth may have been passing through a cluster of debris from a shattered comet at this time.

The collapse of the Roman Empire in the sixth century AD may have had many contributory causes, but again impacts with cometary fragments could be argued as the main cause. The historian Edward Gibbon wrote thus:

> History will distinguish . . . periods in which calamitous events have been rare or frequent and will observe that this fever of the Earth raged with uncommon violence during the reign of Justinian (AD 527–565). Each year is marked by the repetition of earthquakes, of such duration that Constantinople has been shaken above forty days; of such an extent that the shock has been communicated to the whole surface of the globe. . . . An impulse of vibratory motion was felt . . . the sea alternately advanced and retreated beyond its ordinary bounds. . . . Two hundred and fifty thousand people are said to have perished . . . at Antioch.[2]

The type of prolonged and frequent earthquake activity described above is unusual in records of more recent times. An explanation exists in terms of Tunguska-type impacts that send pressure waves into the Earth's crust, thereby generating prolonged bursts of seismic activity.

The cometary impact idea has gained further support recently from studies of tree rings—the science of dendrochronology. Cross sections of ancient trees present a calendar of climatic fluctuations over thousands of years. The growth of a tree year by year is marked by the deposition of a tree ring that can be dated, and the thickness of the ring determines the extent of plant growth there had been. Plant growth requires sunlight, so when tree ring thicknesses diminish we can infer that sunlight was also reduced. It has been found that during critical moments in human history, for example around AD 500—the time of the collapse of Rome— tree ring thicknesses almost vanished. This effect has been interpreted by dendrochronologists to imply a darkening of summer skies with little sunlight reaching the surface. Here we have another strong indication of cometary dust blocking out sunlight.

CONCLUDING REMARKS

In this part of the book I have presented an overwhelming body of evidence that points inexorably to our cosmic origins. Nearly 4,200 million years ago microbial life was introduced to the Earth by comets and slowly came to be established on the planets. Comets have been shown to be the repositories, incubators, and distributors of all life in the universe. From the moment of its first inoculation onto the Earth the further evolution of life from single-celled organisms to the magnificent panorama of the living world required a continuing connection with comets—the injection of new genes in the form of bacteria and viruses. The Darwinian process of natural selection is then left to only a limited role of fine-tuning—involving the selection of the best possibilities that ensure survival in a given niche or environment

Recent studies by several groups of investigators have confirmed the presence of microorganisms from comets in the stratosphere at heights of 40 kilometers, and even entirely outside the atmosphere at a height of 400 kilometers on the surface of the International Space Station. All these facts combined with the discovery that inactivated viruses (retroviruses) lie buried in our DNA show the ideas discussed in earlier chapters are no longer speculation but fact. Our cosmic origin and genetic ancestry is now beyond dispute, although its acceptance by the wider community is fraught with problems mainly of a sociological nature. These ideas imply also that intelligence of the type we are well acquainted with is part and parcel of our cosmic genetic legacy. Such intelligence must show up not only on our planet but also on a large fraction of the hundred billion or more Earth-like planets that have been estimated to exist in the Milky Way. It is inconceivable that humans represent the end of the road in the development and evolution of intelligence. The odds must be high for levels of intelligence far higher than we are accustomed. This opens the door to superintelligent alien beings and even the possibility of alien invasions in the very distant past.

PART II

INTELLIGENT SPECULATION BASED ON CUTTING-EDGE SCIENCE

BY ROBERT BAUVAL

Prologue

By Robert Bauval

A BRIEF PREAMBLE

In part 1, Chandra Wickramasinghe has presented evidence that strongly supports the theory of panspermia with all its implications. These implications include the real possibility that life, quite possibly intelligent and conscious life, occurred long ago in the cosmos, well before the formation of our own solar system, and was imported to our planet by comets and meteorites. Another implication is that this form of cosmic "seeding" and thus evolution of intelligent and conscious life may have occurred on other planetary systems, perhaps on thousands or even millions of Earth-like planets within our own galactic system, the Milky Way. This, of course, raises several crucial questions, not least the possibility that more advanced intelligent and conscious life-forms exist in our galactic home and that "they" may have attempted, and perhaps succeeded, in making contact with humans in the past. Speculating on these lines merely a few decades ago would have been, at least for me, out of the question. This, however, is no more the case, now that I am compelled to take in to serious consideration the huge advances in science, some even taking place as I write these words, especially in physics, cosmology, neuroscience, biology, computer science, and artificial intelligence, not to mention the very recent archaeological findings pushing back in time the ascent of modern humans to three hundred thousand years ago. I have, albeit cautiously, become swayed in accepting that if a contact from an extraterrestrial super-advanced civilization has occurred in the past it should be detectable in the legacy left by our remote ancestors, specifically in the anomalistic geometrical design of their monuments and various possible clues within their written material. This approach, I am acutely aware, is fraught with intellectual danger, not least because of the excessive—not to say totally wild—speculation by some authors and television production companies. But so be it. It needs to be done. I only propose, however, to examine but one ancient monument that, in my opinion, is the most promising to yield some results: the Great Pyramid of Giza in Egypt.

Traditional Egyptologists, those self-appointed keepers of Egypt's ancient past, insist that there is no mystery surrounding the Great Pyramid. They say ad nauseam that it is just one pyramid among many others, so why single it out? They acknowledge, of course, that it is the largest and the most perfectly constructed and has a unique internal system, but to them it is another brazen "tomb and nothing but a tomb" for a megalomaniacal pharaoh called Khufu who reigned circa 2500 BC.[1] Never mind that no sign of a corpse was ever found inside the Great Pyramid—or even outside it. Never mind the pyramid's mind-boggling scale, its razor-sharp engineering, the precision of its astronomical alignments, the weirdness of its interior system of galleries and chambers, or the advanced mathematics—prime numbers, universal constants, geodetic units—encoded in its geometrical design. Never mind the narrow, protracted shafts that were directed to special star systems in the galaxy. Never mind the lack of official inscriptions inside or outside or that no iron tools or lifting machines were ever found near it. And never mind that no modern engineer, architect, or scientist can fully explain how it was built or, at best, propose unsatisfactory, incomplete, or contradictory theories. Egyptologists stubbornly cling to their "tomb only" consensus as if their livelihoods depend on it. Not one of them has offered—*dared* is perhaps a better word—to deviate from this established consensus. And so inevitably the attempts to solve this mystery are left to outsiders. But these too have not always been commendable in some of their conclusions. At any rate, for the past century or so Egyptologists have waged a sort of intellectual cold war against "pyramidologists" over a plethora of theories. But then, as the dispute abated in the 1980s, an uneasy truce began. It was around this time that I innocently broke that truce.

In the summer of 1984, I met Sir I. E. S. Edwards (1909–1996), the leading expert on Egyptian pyramids in the twentieth century. Edwards had been keeper of Egyptian antiquities at the British Museum from 1955 to 1974 and was regarded as the foremost authority on Egyptian pyramids. He was widely known for his book *The Pyramids of Egypt,* a classic in this field, and also for having masterminded the hugely successful Treasures of Tutankhamun exhibition at the British Museum in London in 1972. He was just the right scholar to consult on a theory I was developing on the Giza pyramids: the idea that the three pyramids on the Giza Plateau were constructed to directly mimic on land the three belt stars in the constellation of Orion. Refreshingly open-minded and clearly endowed with a sharp intellect and a critical mind, Edwards was sufficiently impressed with my theory to encourage me to publish a paper in the newly established Oxford-based journal *Discussions in Egyptology.* My paper, titled "A Master Plan for the Three Pyramids of Giza Based on the Configuration of the Three Stars of the Belt of Orion," appeared in 1989.[2] (Today my Orion correlation theory is generally known as the OCT.) In 1993, Edwards also participated with me in bringing to the attention of the world's media the discovery of a "door" in the shaft of the Queen's Chamber in the Great Pyramid by German engineer Rudolf Gantenbrink.

However, what had started as a positive and constructive movement in pyramid studies turned into an animated controversy in February 1994 after Edwards, Gantenbrink, and I were featured in the BBC documentary *The Great Pyramid: Gateway to the Stars,* based on my book (coauthored with Adrian Gilbert) *The Orion Mystery.*

The huge ratings of this documentary and the commercial success of the book were frowned upon by Egyptologists. Fuel was added to

Fig. RBP.1. The cover of
the February 3, 1994,
issue of the BBC's
Radio Times *magazine,*
announcing the documen-
tary The Great Pyramid:
Gateway to the Stars

Fig. RBP.2. Robert Bauval (right) with Sir I. E. S. Edwards at Oxford, April 1993

their academic rancor when Edwards also commented on the same BBC documentary, "I think that Mr. Bauval has performed an important service on giving this an airing."[3]

This was too much for Egyptologists to stomach. Edwards paying such a compliment on national television to me, an outsider who had proposed a controversial theory on the Giza pyramids, was regarded as a form of academic high treason in Egyptology (and to a lesser degree in other disciplines).

Unbeknown to me, in 1999 the crew of the BBC's *Horizon* series planned a big hatchet job on the OCT for their "Atlantis Reborn" documentary with the help of a heavyweight debunking society, the Committee for the Scientific Investigation of Claims of the Paranormal. Assigned as chief debunker was American astronomer Ed Krupp of the Griffith Observatory in Los Angeles. His silver bullet was to accuse me of "turning the map of Egypt upside down" in order to make my OCT work.[4] This, of course, caused an uproar with my readers and in the media. The BBC's ploy, however, badly backfired on them when several angry university scientists—themselves deeply shocked by such uncharacteristic debunking tactics by the BBC—offered to support me in remedying this unfair treatment I had received on national television.

But the battle with Egyptologists did not stop there. Chief among my critics was Zahi Hawass, the director general of the Giza pyramids and minister of antiquities in Egypt from 1994 to 2011. Using his growing media popularity, Hawass launched a smear campaign against me. But all this huffing and puffing by Hawass and his cronies, although quite unpleasant at times, did not bring down the OCT. In fact, the opposite eventually happened. In 2015 scientists at the department of physics and mathematics at the University of Salento in Italy put the OCT through rigorous "falsification" tests and had to admit in a peer-reviewed publication that *"our tests were not able to falsify the OCT."*[5] In science, this is where the buck stops for any theory, especially one that cannot be easily proved, even though the evidence is in its favor. In simple terms, the inability to falsify it means that it has to be seriously considered. To carry on attacking the OCT would be unscientific and disingenuous.

It was now time to raise the bar much higher.

8
The
"Coincidence Pigeons"

There are two mistakes one can make along the road to truth: not going all the way, and not starting.

SAYING FROM THE BUDDHA

THE KNOWLEDGE REVOLUTION

The new electronic era has brought us computers, color televisions, MRI scanners, the internet, smartphones, and a plethora of other hi-tech tools and gadgets. No one will deny that it has completely revolutionized the way we live, the way we communicate, and how we think of our existence in the world and the universe. The recent leaps and bounds in technology also opened the way for many exciting discoveries in physics, cosmology, and neuroscience and have made what were regarded as wild speculations a few decades ago into possibilities to be seriously considered.

Yet oblivious or insensitive to such exciting advances are the orthodox Egyptologists and archaeologists who carry on chugging with their "consensus" and remain unmoved by the new ways to view the mysteries of our distant past. To them the sophisticated mathematics, astronomy, metrology, cosmology, and even technology displayed in ancient monuments such as the Great Pyramid are but the product of coincidences. For a long time I tended to agree, but I finally had to concede that there

117

are limits to coincidence. For when coincidence upon coincidence pile up, as is the case with the Great Pyramid, any person who is not held back by his peers will relent and will seek other explanations.

During a talk I recently gave in a bookshop in Milan, Italy, near the Piazza del Duomo, I entertained the audience by asking what they would say if, hypothetically speaking, a pigeon from the piazza were to fly into the room and settle on the table in front of me. Nearly all said that it would just be a coincidence. But then I added another pigeon, then another, and yet another and so on. At the eighth pigeon only one person in the audience insisted that it was coincidence. The others, however, were struggling to find some other explanation. There was, of course, no explanation. I had made up the story as a thought experiment. I wanted to demonstrate that no matter how many pigeons were to fly into the room and settle on the table, there would always be someone who would attribute it to coincidence. This is because any alternative explanations would require people to consider what is psychologically uncomfortable to them. Retain this "coincidence pigeons" test, because I intend to use it when we later discuss the Great Pyramid.

There are strange happenings we sometimes experience that some of us brush away as *coincidence* while others feel they have *meaning*. One such phenomenon is *synchronicity*. This happens when a number, an image, a word, or even a sound keeps popping up in circumstances that appear "connected," even though no real connection exists. The number 11, a prime number, is often mentioned in connection with the Great Pyramid or, more specifically, with the King's Chamber containing the empty granite coffer, or "sarcophagus." Skeptics say that synchronicity is just a trick of the mind akin to wishful thinking and that it can be explained with statistics.* Even so, and because of the frequency of the synchronistic events in some cases, our mind refuses to accept any attempts at a rational explanation. At any rate, let us review

---

*Joseph Mazur, an emeritus professor at Marlboro College in Vermont, has written a book, *Fluke: The Maths and Myths of Coincidences,* arguing that all such phenomenon can be explained by "a rational order of the universe . . . called mathematics." But in my view this simply pushes the buck further up, because the questions then arise: Who or what created this "rational order," and what for?

some famous cases of synchronicity involving recognized geniuses in mathematics, some of whom were Nobel laureates.

THE GODDESS AND THE DREAMING

Godfrey H. Hardy (1877–1947) was a child prodigy with an amazing ability to do multiplication and division problems mentally while attending long and boring masses at church. Later, as a professor of mathematics at the University of Cambridge in the 1920s, Hardy introduced the study of pure mathematics (as opposed to Newtonian applied mathematics) in the university's curriculum and caused an academic sensation when he partially solved the Riemann hypothesis, a sort of super mathematical puzzle involving a series of prime numbers that, to this day, remains fully unsolved.* Hardy, however, is better known for having mentored mathematical genius Srinivasa Ramanujan, a young Indian man who was working as a clerk at the port of Madras.†

Fig. 8.1. Srinivasa Ramanujan, circa 1915

Fig. 8.2. Godfrey H. Hardy, circa 1915

---

*The Riemann hypothesis is one of the seven unsolved mathematical problems of the Millennium Prize, which offers one million dollars to anyone who can solve them.

†The story of Ramanujan has been made into the recently released movie *The Man Who Knew Infinity,* directed by Matthew Brown, with Jeremy Irons playing Hardy and Dev Patel playing Ramanujan.

This strange and inspiring story began in 1913, when Ramanujan mailed his mathematical theorems and formulae to Hardy and other scholars at Cambridge, boldly suggesting, among other things, that he had devised an equation to resolve the formidable Riemann hypothesis, which for years had dogged mathematicians around the world. Impressed by this young and audacious man and his obvious brilliance, Hardy arranged to have Ramanujan brought to England and became his mentor, friend, and even collaborator. But severe depression and chronic illness constantly plagued Ramanujan, and he was eventually interned in a sanatorium in London. It was during a visit to this sanatorium that Hardy casually remarked to Ramanujan that the taxi in which he had come had the number 1729. According to Hardy, this was a "rather dull number" with no significance whatsoever. "No," Ramanujan protested, "it is a very interesting number; it is the smallest number expressible as the sum of two cubes in two different ways." He was, of course, correct. The number 1729 is $1^3 + 12^3$, and also $9^3 + 10^3$; 1729 is also the product of three prime numbers: $7 \times 13 \times 19$. This anecdotal story has become folklore in the scientific community and is often used as a curious example of fateful synchronicity.[1] Ramanujan returned to India in February 1919 and died the following year.

What is particularly relevant here is that Ramanujan insisted that the mathematical ideas were put into his mind by the Hindu goddess Namagiri. In other words, he was convinced that he was the recipient of a higher knowledge that was expressed to him in a mathematical "language."[2] It was only recently that Ramanujan's mathematical discoveries, often left unproved by him, were confirmed, and they may even help modern physicists get a better understanding of black holes, those mysterious cosmic denizens that, incidentally, were virtually unknown in Ramanujan's time. According to Freeman Dyson, Ramanujan "had some sort of magic tricks that we don't understand."[3]

At any rate, Hardy outlived Ramanujan by twenty-seven years, and when asked what his greatest contribution to science was, he unhesitantly replied that it was Ramanujan, "the one romantic incident in my life." Like Ramanujan, Hardy also suffered from bouts of depression, and in his later years he even attempted suicide. Unkind colleagues jokingly attributed the depressions of Hardy and Ramanujan to the "curse of the Riemann hypothesis." But it is possible that such people with brilliant minds who are prone to depression may be "interpreters" of universal knowledge, and the source of why and how it "enters" the mind of certain gifted individuals like Ramanujan may be beyond human comprehension, at least at this present stage of evolution.

There is, however, a psychomedical term that may perhaps explain the mathematical genius of people like Ramanujan. . . .

ASPERGER SYNDROME AND SAVANTS

American theoretical physicist Michio Kaku spent many years interviewing more than two hundred scientists in many disciplines—among them neuroscientists, psychologists, and brain specialists, many of whom were Nobel Prize winners—to collate information on the latest cutting-edge research and compile ideas for his book *The Future of the Mind*.[4]

Fig. 8.3. Michio Kaku, at Interlaken, Switzerland, 2003; photo credit: Robert Bauval

He also interviewed Daniel Tammet, a young British man who is afflicted with the rare Asperger syndrome and savant syndrome. Asperger syndrome is thought to be a form of high-functioning autism—a not-so-well understood brain condition that causes mood disorders, depression, anxiety, and reclusion. The upshot, however, is that it can bring amazing photographic memory and a baffling ability in mathematics to the afflicted individuals, thus creating savants or, paradoxically, "idiot geniuses" that normally affects young children, instigating, among other things, severe impairments in social interaction, speech, and nonverbal communication, as well as repetitive interests and behavior. Its underlying cause is unknown, although it is suspected to be partly genetic.

Such a syndrome can be a serious social disability, but it can also be a blessing in disguise, such as in the case of Tammet, who also developed synesthesia, a neurological phenomenon in which stimulation of one sensory or cognitive pathway will produce an automatic experience in another sensory or cognitive pathway. In Tammet's case, he is endowed with prodigious abilities to solve mathematical problems mentally and with incredible speed, especially those involving prime numbers, as well as to learn languages in a matter of days and exhibit extraordinary feats of memory. For example, Tammet can memorize 22,514 decimal places of pi (π) by associating the numbers with colors. When Kaku asked him how he could remember such huge quantities of colors and convert them to numbers in his mind, Tammet replied that he didn't know; they just came to him, simply popped in to his mind. Tammet can also paint various shapes in different colors that represent numbers and also can factorize these numbers into primes. In his bestselling book *Born on a Blue Day,* Tammet explains:

> I have always been fascinated by prime numbers. I see each prime as a smooth texture shape . . . sometimes I close my eyes and imagine the first thirty, fifty, hundred numbers and I experience them spatially synaesthetically. Then I see in my mind's eye just how beautiful and special primes are . . . there are moments as I am falling asleep at night, that my mind fills suddenly with bright light and all

I can see are numbers—hundreds, thousands of them—swimming rapidly over my eyes . . . I never feel lost, because the prime number shapes act as signposts.[5]

There is also the case involving Orlando Serrell, a young boy who was hit in the left part of his head by a baseball and afterward discovered he "could do remarkable mathematical calculations, developed an amazing photographic memory, and could calculate dates thousands of years in the future."[6] Serrell's case is known as acquired savant syndrome, which is usually triggered by a head injury or severe blow to the head. This type of savant syndrome is rare, and apparently only 10 percent of savants fall into this category.[7] There is also the case of Stephen Wiltshire, the British autistic architectural artist who, after only a short helicopter flight over a city such as London or New York, can reproduce by memory the whole urban landscape with incredible detail by drawing it by hand.[8] Many moviegoers will also remember *Rain Man,* in which Dustin Hoffman played the role of an autistic savant based on the real megasavant Kim Peek (1951–2009), who had FG syndrome, a genetic condition caused by recessive genes on the X chromosome, so that it affects mostly men. Despite his related social disabilities, Peek was endowed with a supermemory. He could scan the left page of a book with his left eye and the right page with his right eye and remembered everything he had read. It is said that he could recall the content of twelve thousand books with stunning precision.[9]

The way we see things—their shapes, sizes, colors, motions, and even the way they make us feel—involves the photoreceptive cells in our eyes and our nerve cells and the neuron cells in our brain. With just a casual glance around a room full of objects, for example, your eyes will pick up some thirty thousand images and details—not merely their forms, shapes, and colors but also their dimensions, their distance from you, and the spatial distribution between them. Now think of the number of images you might see, consciously or unconsciously, in an average day of sixteen waking hours, perhaps moving about your home and your workplace, walking in busy streets, shopping in a mall or supermarket, visiting a museum or art gallery, watching television, reading a book, and so on. It would take dozens of computers working in tandem for several hours, perhaps even days, to calculate and tabulate the myriad images and details you saw, let alone the thoughts and feelings that they induced in you. A neurologist, however, will tell you that it is not your eyes that actually see, but your brain. The eyes receive reflected light— actually photons—from images and transmit them to special parts of the brain where the real work of seeing takes place. The brain then sorts out the images into different categories—vegetables and fruits, plants, animals, people, still objects, moving objects, words, and so on—for the purpose of archiving them in the parts of the brain where memory is stored. But that is just the initial activity of collecting, processing, and storing the images in memory banks. As impressive as this is, the real magic is how the images are then retrieved; that is, remembered.

Imagine visiting the British Museum with a female friend who is wearing a very expensive perfume, Joy de Patou, which has a very distinctive scent that is not commonly experienced. Indeed, this may be the only time you encounter this scent. Imagine then strolling together through the various sections, looking at the various objects displayed, at some casually, at others more carefully, and later having lunch in a busy restaurant near Coptic Street, discussing and chatting about various things while savoring a Greek salad and enjoying a glass of wine.

The vast number of images you have seen will not be stored in your memory in one big continuous "file," but instead in many "subfiles" sorted out in *categories*. Neurologists have, so far, identified more than twenty different categories of memories; namely, various objects, animals, plants, words, and so forth, which also include categories of emotions (fear, joy, worry, etc.), sounds, and scents related to the images. Now imagine that many years after that visit to the British Museum you find yourself in New York on Fifth Avenue and casually look at the display window of a *parfumerie* and see a small bottle with the label Joy de Patou or, alternatively, sit in the subway next to a woman wearing this particular perfume. Suddenly your mind is filled with images, colors, sounds, smells, words, moods, and emotions that merge to form one cohesive recollection of that day years ago when you visited the British Museum with that friend who wore that perfume. The manner in which memory works in this way is known as the "binding problem," so named because neurologists have little or no idea, at least not yet, of how the brain performs this supercomplex activity. It is possible, therefore, that genius savants like Ramanujan and Tammet can unconsciously express this process, or parts of it, with numbers and equations.

Dr. Darold Treffert, a psychiatrist and expert on savant syndrome, reported the case of a blind man who was asked how many corn kernels would be on the last, the sixty-fourth, square of a chessboard if you start with one corn kernel on the first square, then double the amount for the next square, and so on until you reach the end of the squares on the board. The blind man reflected for just forty-five seconds and then gave the correct answer: 18,446,744,073,709,616.

Some scientists think that there may be more people with a form of savant syndrome than previously predicted. This is because the degree of out-of-the-ordinary aptitudes may vary widely, ranging from what are considered normal abilities to extreme abnormal abilities. When I was a young boy in Egypt, I suffered a severe blow on the head when I tried to jump a wire fence and caught my foot in the wire, causing me to fall and bump my head on the stone pavement and lose consciousness for a few seconds or so. Although I fully recovered, I never felt quite the same again. I also began to ask myself questions about life and the universe, reading books about science in a manner I had not done before. It is possible that the knock on the head caused a mild form of savant syndrome in me, and this could explain why I see patterns and their connections when apparently no one else does until I point them out: the OCT, for example.[10] When I think of how the OCT came to me, I must admit that I am not sure at all if it *came into my mind* from "somewhere else." My wife will attest that in the autumn of 1983, when we lived in Saudi Arabia, she would find me in the garden in the middle of the night looking at the stars in Orion. I could not explain why I was doing this, except that something urged me to go out and look at the stars. *This was a few days before I noted in my mind the correlation between the three stars of Orion's belt and the three pyramids of Giza.*

Neurologists now think that savant syndrome (not the acquired variety) is linked to autism spectrum disorder, which, as I have already noted, can cause mood disorders, depression, anxiety, and reclusiveness. According to Kaku, "It may explain the strange, reclusive nature of physicists like Isaac Newton and Paul Dirac (one of the founders of the quantum theory)."[11] I cannot help wondering if milder forms of these syndromes cause the phenomenon of synchronicity with reoccurring numbers.

WOLFGANG PAULI AND 137

Another most bizarre story of a synchronicity with a special number that has also become part of scientific folklore is that of Swiss American physicist Wolfgang Pauli.

The story has its origins in 1915, when physicist Arnold Sommerfeld came across a number in his mathematical calculations of what are called fine structural lines in the spectrum of elements. This number is exactly 0.007297352566355. Today it is known as the fine-structure constant and given the Greek letter α (alpha). It is more commonly expressed in its reciprocal form, which is 137.035999139, rounded to 137. It mysteriously crops up in complex and exotic calculations involving universal constants such as π and e, although no one seems to know why it does so.[12] In vain have mathematicians and physicists tried to solve the mystery of 137. Many have been convinced that it might lead to the holy grail of physicists: *the theory of everything*. "What I like about Alpha is

Fig. 8.4. Wolfgang Pauli

that it combines three fundamental constants in a rather beautiful way," says physicist Laurence Eaves of the University of Nottingham.[13] These three constants are the charge of an electron, the speed of light, and Planck's constant. According to Eaves:

> If you decide you want to get in touch with aliens on some different planet orbiting a star perhaps like our own sun, it would be one of the numbers you would signal to these aliens to indicate that we have a scientific and technologically capable civilization on this planet . . . they would know that number as well if they made telescopes and got electronic equipment to send our radio waves and so on . . . if the value (of alpha) was a little bit different from the value it actually has, we would not be around here talking about it now. Atomic physics is the way it is because of the value of alpha. Cosmologists are now talking about universes in which alpha could be different, or the three constants that make up alpha could be different, then physics, chemistry, biochemistry would be totally different, and we might not be around to talk about it. So the value of alpha* is very, very special, but we still don't know why it has the value it has.[14]

The person most obsessed with 137 was Wolfgang Pauli, a founder of quantum physics and the Nobel laureate for physics in 1945. Somewhat like Ramanujan, Pauli claimed that his mathematical insights had come to him in dreams. Pauli also was prone to bouts of melancholia and entertained mystical ideas about the universe and his role in it. In his quest for esoteric knowledge, Pauli eventually collaborated with psychologist Carl Jung, who was also attracted to mysticism.[15]

The two men met in 1930, when Pauli, in a state of depression and despair, sought solace and direction for his emotional and psychological suffering. Although Jung was not Pauli's psychoanalyst as such, he nonetheless "reviewed some thirteen hundred of Pauli's dreams and studied a selection from the first four hundred. Over years of contact, the

---

*If alpha were just 4 percent bigger or smaller than it is, stars wouldn't be able to make carbon and oxygen, which would have made it impossible for life as we know it to exist.[16]

younger man's knowledge penetrated and influenced Jung's thoughts."[17] Jung and Pauli also corresponded from 1932 to 1958. The potent intellectual blend of a cutting-edge theoretical physicist and a progressive psychologist was to inspire both men, especially Jung, who formulated his theories of synchronicity and the collective unconscious after learning from Pauli the rudiments of quantum theory. (We will discuss quantum physics in greater detail in chapter 10.) In 1958, when Pauli was dying from cancer in a hospital in Zurich, he asked his colleague Charles Enz, who came to visit him, "Did you see the room number?" The number was 137.

Pauli, like Jung, seems to have been convinced that there was something about synchronicity that was real and that it had to do with a law of nature far too complex, chaotic, and weird for any human mind to comprehend. For example, in 1934, Pauli was to write to his friend Ralph Kronig, "After falling into depression during the winter of 1931–1932, I began slowly to recover. I met then the psychic events that I did not know before and I name here simply the proper activity of the soul. There is for me no doubt that there are things here that spontaneously developed and which be designated as symbols; something both psychic and objective that cannot be explained by material causes."[18]

The famous theoretical physicist Richard Feynman, who was also one of the founders of quantum physics, was to make a comment about 137 that is often quoted by mystics and researchers in esoteric studies. Following is a concise version of Feynman's musing about this enigmatic number.

It has been a mystery ever since it was discovered more than fifty years ago, and all good theoretical physicists put this number up on their wall and worry about it. Immediately you would like to know where this number . . . comes from. Is it related to pi (π) or perhaps to the base of natural logarithms (e)? Nobody knows. It's one of the greatest damn mysteries of physics: a magic number that comes to us with no understanding by man. You might say the "hand of God" wrote that number, and "we don't know how He

Fig. 8.5. Richard Feynman

pushed his pencil." We know what kind of a dance to do experimentally to measure this number very accurately, but we don't know
what kind of dance to do on the computer to make this number
come out,* without putting it in secretly![19]

Experimental physicist and Nobel Prize–winner Leon
M. Lederman reported how Feynman suggested, probably sardoni-
cally, that all physicists put a sign in their offices with the number 137
to "remind them of just how much they don't know." Lederman himself chose the address "137 Eola Road" for his home in the Fermilab
compound. He wrote, "It would be less unsettling if the relationship
between all these important concepts turned out to be one or three
or maybe a multiple of π. But 137? . . . It shows up naked all over the
place. This means that scientists on Mars, or on the fourteenth planet
of the star Sirius, using whatever god-awful units they may have for

---

*The number used by Feynman is also known as the coupling constant, -0.08542455,
the square of which is 0.0072973525 (the fine-structure constant), and, further more, the
reciprocal of its square is 137.0359.

charge, speed, and their version of Planck's constant, will also get 137. It is a pure number."[20]

Notwithstanding the potential importance of 137 in the study of physics and cosmology, it also happens to be the thirty-third prime number in the prime sequence, something that has not escaped the notice of mystics who point out that it is the age attributed traditionally to Jesus at the crucifixion and also the number of pearls in the traditional Muslim praying beads. The number 33 also happens to be the product of two primes, 3 and 11. (We shall later see how prime 11 was fundamental in the design of the Great Pyramid.) The number 137 also crops up in the Bible, where the age at death of three important patriarchs—Ishmael, son of Abraham and Hagar; Levi, son of Jacob; and Amram, father of Moses—is given as 137 years.[21]

As an aside, it was brought to my attention by my architect brother, Jean-Paul, that the more accurate value 137.03 is manifest in the design of the Second Pyramid at Giza, which allegedly belonged to the Fourth Dynasty pharaoh Khafre (ca. 2500 BC). The height of this pyramid is known to be precisely 143.5 meters, and its base side is 215.25 meters.[22] Jean-Paul pointed out that the height of this pyramid of 143.5 meters converts to 274.064 royal cubits (the unit used by the ancient builders), and if we divide this value by the *first prime number, 2,* we get 137.03. Also, the base side is 215.25 meters, or 411.096 royal cubits, and if we divide this value by the *second prime number, 3,* we also get 137.03. Interestingly, author and intuitive mathematician Gary Osborn has also found this mysterious number 137 in the design of the Great Pyramid. In fact, he obtained 137.035999, the value of the reciprocal of the fine-structure constant accurate to seven decimal places!*

This is our first coincidence pigeon.

---

*Osborn used the measure of the east base side of the Great Pyramid, 230.3649 meters, and divided it by half the height of the pyramid, 73.304 meters. He then divided the result by 100 and multiplied the result by the constant e. The square of the result was 0.007297367733037, which is the reciprocal of $1/137.035714326519$. This result is 99.9998 percent accurate when compared to 0.007297352566355, being the reciprocal of $1/137.035999139$ . . . the fine-structure constant.

MY OWN PRIME NUMBER,
THE SAINT, AND THE MYSTIC

We all have synchronistic numbers that crop up in our lives at meaningful moments and taunt our logical mind. One side of us wants to dismiss these happenings as coincidences playing tricks on our mind, while another side of us, perhaps the unconscious side, senses something—a sign, an omen—reaching us from God knows where. At any rate, my own synchronistic number is 503, a prime number that keeps manifesting itself with nagging regularity in the most unusual circumstances that to me seem meaningful. I have no rational or scientific explanation why this particular number does this. It just happens. For a long time I have tried to ignore it, but the high frequency at which it shows up eventually forced me to consider that I am dealing here with some law of nature so irrational, so counterintuitive, and so chaotic that it is well beyond human comprehension. I imagine an invisible flux or field, a sort of invisible and immaterial "library of knowledge" or "information matrix," to which we can occasionally connect to unconsciously.

One particular incident was when I immigrated with my family to Australia in 1986. My sister and her husband, who had already settled there in the 1970s, met us at the Sydney airport and drove us to their home. As we passed through the suburbs, I kept looking around for the number 503, hoping to see it on the license plate of a passing car or the signboard of a shop or a poster in the street. I wanted to be reassured by my "good omen" number that the decision to bring my family to a new life in Australia had been right. But this time 503 appeared nowhere, so I gave up looking. But when we crossed the Sydney Harbor Bridge, my brother-in-law casually turned to me and said, "Did you know that the bridge's longest free span is exactly 503 meters?"

It is when such things happen that no matter how rational you try to be and how hard you try to convince yourself that it can only be the work of coincidence, there is another part of you that rejects the rational and chooses instead to see it as "something else." I should add that it was only recently that I discovered, while looking at a table listing the first one hundred prime numbers, that prime 503 is the ninety-sixth prime

	2	3	5	7	11	13	17	19	23
29	31	37	41	43	47	53	59	61	67
71	73	79	83	89	97	101	103	107	109
113	127	131	137	139	149	151	157	163	167
173	179	181	191	193	197	199	211	223	227
229	233	239	241	251	257	263	269	271	277
281	283	293	307	311	313	317	331	337	347
349	353	359	367	373	379	383	389	397	401
409	419	421	431	433	439	443	449	457	461
463	467	479	487	491	499	503	509	521	523
541	547	557	563	569	571	577	587	593	599
601	607	613	617	619	631	641	643	647	653
659	661	673	677	683	691	701	709	719	727
733	739	743	751	757	761	769	773	787	797
809	811	821	823	827	829	839	853	857	859
863	877	881	883	887	907	911	919	929	937
941	947	953	967	971	977	983	991	997	

Fig. 8.6. Table of the sequence of the first 178 prime numbers

in the list. This is most bizarre, because I have always considered, for no reason at all I should add, that the number 96 is for me a "bad omen."

Prime 3, the second prime number, has also played a strange role in my life. The genesis of this story goes back to 1932, sixteen years before I was born. This was the year my father was hit by a car on a street of Alexandria, Egypt, and was taken unconscious to a hospital where the nurses were Catholic nuns. It was assumed that my father had suffered severe internal injuries and would probably not survive the night. A well-intentioned nun placed a photograph on his chest of Saint Thérèse of Lisieux, a Carmelite nun canonized by the Vatican in 1925. At almost exactly the time the nun did this, two hundred kilometers away in the district of Shoubra in Cairo, a newly built church (today a basilica) was being dedicated to Saint Thérèse by the apostolic vicarage of Alexandria.*

---

*Thérèse of Lisieux (1873–1897) is also popularly known with the epithets the Little Flower or Thérèse of the Child Jesus. She was a Carmelite nun who died of consumption at the young age of twenty-four, leaving behind a diary promising to do miracles after she died. The diary was published and became a huge bestseller, and people all over the world began to attribute miraculous cures to her. Thérèse was canonized on May 17, 1925, and in 1944 she was declared the co–patron saint of France, alongside Joan of Arc. She is one of the most popular saints in Christendom, next to Saint Francis of Assisi. In Egypt her fame is such that even Muslims believe in her miraculous powers. Dozens of churches, chapels, and basilicas all over the world are dedicated to her.

Fig. 8.7. Church of Saint Thérèse in Beaconsfield, England

The next morning my father made a miraculous recovery. Many years later, in 1989 to be more precise, which also happened to be the year I published my article on the OCT in *Discussions in Egyptology,* I resettled in England and purchased a house in the small English town of Beaconsfield. There, unbeknown to me at the time, was a small church dedicated to Saint Thérèse of Lisieux. The church is opposite the model village of Bekonscot on Warwick Road. I would often cycle past the church and wave at the little statue of the saint set in the back wall of the building. Several years later, in 1997, I fell into a deep depression that I could not shake off. After several months of this terrible affliction, I felt that my life was slowly ebbing away. In desperation, I asked my wife, Michele, to take me to the church of Saint Thérèse. I was so weak and tired that I had to be helped into the car. It was late evening when we got to the church, and we found it closed. But the rector, a kind man in his forties, opened the church for us. I had no idea what I wanted to do or expected to happen, so I went into the church and just sat in front of a small painted statue of the saint and prayed. A few days later I made a full recovery.

Confused as to what had happened, I decided to go to France to visit the house (today a museum) of Saint Thérèse in the town of Lisieux

Fig. 8.8. Saint Thérèse of Lisieux

in northern France. I did not know what I was looking for, really, but something urged me to go. While I strolled in the various rooms of the small house, I came upon a painting on a wall depicting Thérèse as a young girl wearing a large hat. She was holding her father's hand. It was nighttime, and she was pointing at something in the sky. As I looked more closely, I realized it was Orion's belt!*

There is another story running in parallel that also has its genesis in 1932, but this time in the American Midwest. A man called Edgar Cayce would go into deep trances and give "readings" about the pyramids and the Sphinx of Giza being a legacy of a highly advanced lost civilization that was in Egypt in 10,500 BC. Cayce's readings, some fourteen thousand of them, are now stored in the library of the Edgar Cayce Foundation in Virginia Beach, Virginia. Many of his followers around the world believe that he received his revelations by being able to plug into what are known as the Akashic Records, a sort of cosmic library in a nonphysical dimension, or astral plane. I am not one who believes in such things, so you can imagine my surprise when in 1995,

---

*Saint Thérèse used to say that her name was "written in these stars." Orion's Belt has since become the logo of the Carmelite nuns of Lisieux.

Fig. 8.9. Thérèse as a child, with her father, pointing at Orion's belt

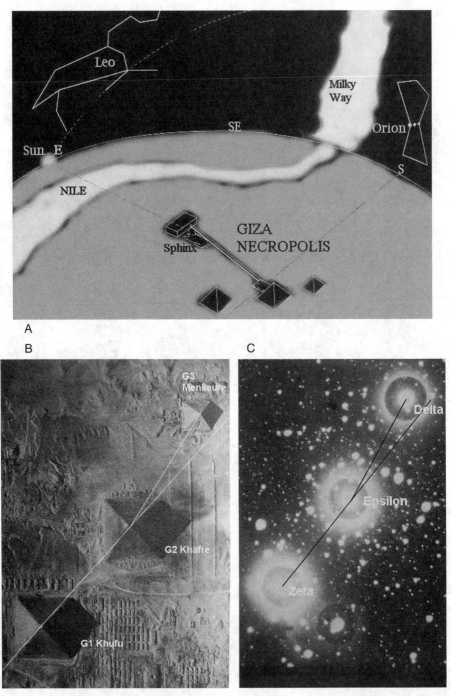

*Fig. 8.10. Artist's impression of (A) the Giza-sky correlation of 10,500 BC,
(B) plan of three main pyramids, and (C) pattern of three stars of Orion's belt*

Fig. 8.11. Montage showing the Giza/Orion and Nile/Milky Way correlations of 10,500 BC; courtesy of David Rohl

I made the discovery, using astronomical computer software, that the combined astronomical alignments of the pyramids and the Sphinx of Giza defined the date 10,500 BC.[23]

What are we to do with such things? Brush them aside as coincidences? Ignore them? Call them synchronicities and leave it at that? Or do we consider something else? But what else? There were no laws of nature that I could then think of to make any sense of this curious phenomenon.

Or were there?

9
Physics and Synchronicity

Science is a way of thinking much more than it is a body of knowledge.

CARL SAGAN

Science is fun. Science is curiosity. We all have natural curiosity. Science is a process of investigating. It's posing questions and coming up with a method. It's delving in.

SALLY RIDE

ANYONE CAN DO IT

I strongly believe that anyone with a balanced and healthy mind can learn anything, provided, of course, that enough time is given and the necessary effort is made. I therefore resolved to myself to find out if the current position of physics could help me make some sense of the phenomenon of synchronicity. I had a hunch that this was the way to progress in my investigation of the mysteries of the Great Pyramid.

Recently, my brother, Jean-Paul, and my friend, author Gary Osborn, finally got me interested in their solitary research concerning the geometrical design of the Great Pyramid. Throughout my writing

138

career I had refrained from doing so, concerned that their work would be seen as "pyramidology," and as such I wanted no part in it. But their persistence finally got me to take a closer look. I soon realized they were on to something. Coupled with his own findings, Jean-Paul also introduced me to the work of Miquel Pérez-Sánchez, Ph.D., a prominent Spanish architect who had devoted many years to researching the design of the Great Pyramid and had recently published his findings in a book based on his doctoral thesis at the University of Barcelona.[1] Being the skeptic that I am, I first thought that Pérez-Sánchez's book would turn out to be a rehash of the many theories related to the geometrical design of the Great Pyramid, but a scant look into his book soon caused me to change my mind. Pérez-Sánchez's research was detailed and meticulous, and many of his findings were difficult to ignore. There was one particular finding that especially grabbed my attention.

THE SPHERE

It is well known that the Great Pyramid has its top missing. Egyptologists assume that all pyramids were once capped with small pyramids called *pyramidions*. These objects were apparently inspired by the shape of a sacred stone called a *benben* that was once kept in the great temple of the sun at Heliopolis, located some twenty-five kilometers northeast of Giza. In the late 1980s, I carried out extensive research on the origins of the benben, which led me to conclude that it probably was a conical-shaped iron meteorite, which in the minds of the ancients symbolized a "star soul."[2]

Pérez-Sánchez, on the other hand, was convinced that the object that had crowned the Great Pyramid was not a pyramidion but a *sphere*. And based on his precise computer reconstruction of the pyramid, he estimated that this mysterious sphere had a diameter of 1.433 meters and was fixed on a small platform that had a perimeter of 1.643 meters. Pérez-Sánchez was quick to note that these values, when converted into royal cubits—the measuring unit of 0.5236 meters used by the pyramid builders (discussed in detail in chapter 11)—were 2.7183 royal cubits and 3.143 royal cubits, which he saw as good approximations of a universal constant known as Euler's number, 2.71828, denoted by the

Fig. 9.1. The "sphere" from Miquel Pérez-Sánchez, 2014

letter *e,* and the more familiar universal constant pi, 3.14159, denoted by the Greek letter π.

Assuming Pérez-Sánchez is correct in his deductions, the question is: Why was it necessary for the ancient designer to highlight these universal constants with a sphere on the summit of the Great Pyramid?

A PI IN THE SKY

We have seen how Daniel Tammet could memorize π to more than twenty-two thousand decimal places. But as impressive as this is, it is nowhere near the decimal places that π could have. In fact, no amount of decimal places ever will be enough, because the value of π is infinite. In other words, the decimal places will go on forever no matter how accurate you try to make the value of π.*

---

*Some mathematicians argue that the value of π lies between 3 and 4, and therefore it is not infinite but can be considered to be 3.14159. As such, they prefer to call it "irrational" because it cannot be fully expressed with decimal places. In other words, it is the decimal places that are infinite, but not π itself. But not all agree with this hairsplitting definition.

It is a number that fascinates many people. There are whole books written about pi, and there is even a Pi Day, celebrated by its devoted fans on March 14, a date chosen on account of 3, 1, and 4 being the first three numbers of pi. (It also happens to be the birthday of Albert Einstein.) The mathematician William L. Schaaf was quite right in saying that "probably no symbol in mathematics has evoked as much mystery, romanticism, misconception, and human interest as the number π."[3] Anyone with an elementary education has heard of π and how it is used to determine the dimensions of a circle or a sphere. Historians say that it was probably Archimedes who discovered π in the third century BC, but no one is really sure. At any rate, it is said that Archimedes calculated it down to three decimal places, 3.142, which can be expressed with the simple equation 22/7. Through the ages various mathematicians have tried to add more decimal places to pi, but it was only in the sixteenth century that French mathematician François Viete managed to calculate pi to nine decimal places. In 1961, John Wrench and Daniel Shanks added one hundred thousand decimals places, and in 1973, one million decimal places were reached. As far as I can make out, the current record is held by Nicholas Sze, a computer buff at Yahoo, who calculated pi to two quadrillion decimal places by running a thousand computers in tandem nonstop for twenty days![4]

Here is how π looks with only four hundred decimal places:

3.141592653589793238462643383279502884197169399375105820974944592307816406286208998628034825342117067982148086513282306647093844609550582231725359408128481117450284102701938521105559644622948954930381964428810975665933446128475648233786783165271201909145648566923460348610454326648213393607260249141273724587006606315588174881520920962829254091715364367892590360011330530548820466521384146951941511609....

To get the same result as Sze with a regular home computer would apparently take five hundred years! All this seems like great fun, but what is the use of such mind-boggling numbers of decimal places when only forty or so are more than sufficient, even in nanotechnology, the science and manufacture of microscopic things such as microchips?[5] Science writer Clifford H. Pickover, however, offers a futuristic application for π, which, on face value, seems totally wacky but, as it turns out, is not as improbable as it first seems. He suggested that because π has an infinite number of decimal places, then this means that these decimal places will create infinite numbers of combinations of "all of us—the atomic coordinates of all our atoms, our genetic code, a coding of our motions and all our thoughts through time, all our memories . . . π makes us live forever. We all lead virtual lives in π. We are immortal."[6]

A fascinating idea, for sure, but extremely difficult to digest, let alone prove. At any rate, an important universal constant, although less popularly known than π, is 2.71828, Euler's number, which also has decimal places extending toward infinity. Clearly, if Pérez-Sánchez is correct about the sphere on top of the Great Pyramid, this raises huge questions, not least because this constant was only discovered in the seventeenth century by Swiss mathematician Jacob Bernoulli (later allocated the letter *e* by Leonard Euler); that is, some four thousand years after the construction of the Great Pyramid!*

Euler's constant, *e,* is actually the base of *natural* logarithms, the latter discovered a century before Bernoulli's time, in 1614, by Scottish mathematician John Napier. "Rarely in the history of science," wrote mathematician Eli Maor, "has an abstract mathematical idea been received more enthusiastically by the entire scientific community than the invention of logarithms."[7]

Logarithms are very closely related to *exponential functions,* which are used to determine things such as the expansion of galaxies, radioactive decay, bacterial growth, population growth, and so forth. Although logarithms can be given different "bases"—for example, base 2 is used in information theory and computers, base 10 is used

---

*The first time the number 2.71828 was recognized "in its own right" was in 1690 in a letter from German polymath and philosopher Gottfried Wilhelm Leibniz to Dutch mathematician and scientist Christiaan Huygens, where it was given the letter *b,* later changed to *e* by Euler.

in chemistry—the *natural base* is 2.171828 and is used in calculus, an important branch of mathematics discovered by Isaac Newton (and also independently by Leibniz) that is fundamental for calculations in astronomy, physics, and cosmology. It is said that Newton *had to invent* calculus to derive his famous theory of gravity that explains the motion of planets!

It is not my intention here, of course, to review the various applications of e and π. I am not a mathematician, nor do I pretend to be one. Let us just note that without knowing these important constants (and many others as well), a technologically advanced civilization like ours would not have happened on this planet. So it is intriguing, to say the very least, that such universal constants pop out of the geometrical design of the Great Pyramid. But how could the ancient designer of this monument have known about these constants when they were not discovered until many centuries later? How is this possible?

10
The Next Frontier
of Knowledge

According to classical physics, particles are particles and waves are waves, and never the twain shall mix. . . . But the reality is different—particles turn out to exhibit wave-like properties, and waves exhibit particle-like properties as well. The idea that waves (like light) can act as particles (like electrons) and vice versa was the major revelation that ushered in quantum physics.

STEVEN HOLZNER

The point is no longer that quantum mechanics is an extraordinarily (and for Einstein, unacceptably) peculiar theory, but that the world is an extraordinarily peculiar place.

DAVID MERMIN

QUANTUM WEIRDNESS

Physicist Neil DeGrasse Tyson was once asked if he regretted destroying the power of myth and magic with the reality of physics. Tyson replied, "I don't mind the power of myth and magic, but take it to the *next frontier* and apply it there; don't apply it in places where we've long past (and) what we already know is going on" (italics added).[1]

So here I was, after having spent months to update myself to the "new frontier" of physics, wondering if I had not put myself in an awkward situation with this book project. After all, I was no scientist or mathematician. I only had passable grades in physics and math at school, enough to carry me to a Higher National Diploma in building engineering. But I reassured myself that most people are not physicists or mathematicians either and that in any case my objective was to get a "knowledge update" in science that would allow me, and thus my readers, to view ancient Egypt and, more specifically, the Great Pyramid from a new and fresh perspective. To put it another way, I wanted to take myself and my readers to the next frontier of science and from there review again the ancient past. This meant an initiation into the rudiments of cutting-edge science and especially the new and weird physics of quantum physics. Before we delve in to this scientific hotbed, I feel compelled to quote a few words by Carl Sagan from his book *The Demon-Haunted World*. According to Sagan, following is what lies in store for those wanting to seriously understand quantum physics.

> Imagine you seriously want to understand what quantum mechanics is about. There is a mathematical underpinning that you must first acquire, mastery of each mathematical sub-discipline leading you to the threshold of the next. In turn you must learn arithmetic, Euclidean geometry, high school algebra, differential and integral calculus, ordinary and partial differential equations, vector calculus, certain special functions of mathematical physics, matrix algebra, and group theory. For most physics students, this might occupy them from, say, third grade to early graduate school—roughly *fifteen years*. Such a course of study does not actually involve learning any quantum mechanics, but merely establishing the mathematical framework required to approach it deeply. . . . These mathematical complexities are compounded by the fact that *quantum theory is so resolutely counterintuitive. Common sense is almost useless in approaching it.*[2] (italics added)

Most people, like myself, do not have the time, the inkling, or the intellectual aptitude to go through fifteen grueling years of advanced and exotic mathematics. But there is no need to do that unless you are heading for a career in science. It is totally possible to learn the basics of quantum physics *without knowing the mathematics.* These days you will find all you need on the Internet on a "need-to-know" basis from popular books and articles and videos of presentations, lectures, debates, and discussions on YouTube channels. I have gone through this self-education process and now will outline it in this book for the benefit of the lay reader with a hunger for knowledge.

There comes a moment in everyone's life when we are prone to ask, as the 1960s popular jazz singer Peggy Lee did, "Is that all there is?"* Lee's answer was implying that we are born on this planet, endure the ups and downs of life, and finally die, and that's about it, so we may as well "keep dancing, . . . break out the booze and have a ball." But Peggy Lee was wrong. That is not all there is. Today, half a century after she sang this song, we know—or should know—that there is a lot more than that.

Take, for example, Max Tegmark, a theoretical physicist at the Massachusetts Institute of Technology. Tegmark once told an audience of friends that when he looked at them he also saw "a vast number of quarks and electrons."[3] Now, Tegmark did not mean he could *actually* see quarks and electrons, for these subatomic particles cannot be seen, even with the most powerful microscope.[†4] Tegmark, of course, was using his imagination, and what he saw in his mind was a fundamental truth of nature.

It is estimated that an average-size human is made from some forty trillion living cells, the smallest units of "life." There are some two hundred different types of cells of various shapes and sizes that make up the components of the human body—blood cells, cells for the various

---

*The song was originally sung by Georgia Brown in 1967. It was composed by songwriters Jerry Leiber and Mike Stoller.

†A team at École Polytechnique Fédérale de Lausanne in Switzerland, headed by Fabrizio Carbone, used electrons to image light and managed to photograph for the first time light behaving simultaneously as a wave and a flow of particles.

organs, skin cells, hair cells, bones cells, and so forth. You can see cells through a good optical microscope and see details inside them with more powerful means such as the transmission electron microscope.

It has long been known that each cell lodges tightly within itself, among other tiny structures called organelles, which have specific functions, a complete strand of DNA that is some three meters long, densely packed. The DNA contains the genetic information necessary for the cell to "know" when and how to replicate or repair itself, and to "communicate" with other cells elsewhere in the body. Cells run their own lives, so to speak, with very little help from you—the conscious "you," that is.

The most mysterious cells are, of course, the brain cells, more commonly known as neurons. Without the aid of a microscope, the human brain looks simply like a lump of grayish-pink flesh roughly the size and weight of a small cabbage. But magnified thousands of times, it can be seen to be made up of billions of neurons, passing signals to each other via a network of trillions of synapses. We will return to the wonders of the brain later on. But first let us see what Tegmark meant by seeing his audience as a vast number of quarks and electrons.

The forty trillion or so cells in an average-size human body are themselves made up of atoms, of which there are estimated to be 7×10^{27} (7 followed by 27 zeros), perpetually whizzing and vibrating at incredible speeds and frequencies. So Tegmark was perfectly correct in saying that his friends (and everyone and everything else on this planet and in the universe) are just "a vast number of quarks and electrons." But here's the thing: because quarks and electrons are so incredibly small and also so far apart from each other, relatively speaking, a human body is, in fact, 99.999 . . . percent *empty space*. If a human body could be magnified billions of times, a jumbo jet could easily fly through it without bumping into anything, much like a spacecraft can fly through empty space unhindered. Physicist Marcus Chow amused himself by working out that if all the empty space were removed from every living human being on the planet and their atoms compacted into one lump, *"you could fit the entire human race in the volume of a sugar cube."*[5] But that's not all that Tegmark had in mind. For he surely was also thinking of all those quarks and electrons spinning and vibrating at incredible speed and, strangest of all, behaving in the most irrational and counter-intuitive imaginable manner, as we shall see later on.

Meanwhile, let us imagine an atom being a small solar system with electrons orbiting around a nucleus made of protons and neutrons, which themselves are made of quarks. If this microscopic "sun" (the nucleus) were the size of a tennis ball, then a "planet" (electron) would be a pinhead orbiting one kilometer away. In real terms though, the sizes involved here are so incredibly small that they are measured in nanometers, a unit that is one-billionth of a meter. The smallest atom, hydrogen, has a nucleus of one proton and one neutron with only one electron orbiting around. The diameter of a hydrogen atom is roughly 0.1 of a nanometer, whereas that of an electron is thought to be about two-thousand times smaller (i.e., 0.00005 nanometer). Our planet, on the other hand, has a diameter of 12,742 kilometers and revolves around the sun, the latter having a diameter of 1,391,400 kilometers, thus 109 times larger than Earth. You could fit about 1.3 million Earths in the sun.*

You may well wonder if Earth is not just a giant electron in the cosmic scheme of things. The answer is no. This is because, inter alia, an electron is a fundamental particle and thus indestructible, whereas Earth is made of 118 atomic elements, which are in turn made of protons, neutrons, quarks, and electrons, all of which can be blown apart in one cataclysmic explosion if hit, for example, by another planet or if we humans develop sufficient megatons of nuclear bombs to do the job.†

Also, our sun is a supergiant thermonuclear cauldron, very unlike the nucleus of a stable atom. So although our solar system has a nucleus (the sun) with planets orbiting around it much like an atom

---

*Earth's orbit around the sun is not a perfect circle but a very gentle ellipse. The shortest distance to the sun is called the perihelion and is 149.6 million kilometers. The farthest distance is called the aphelion and is 152 million kilometers.
†It is estimated that there are some twenty-five thousand nuclear warheads in existence. If each averages 33,500 kilotons of destructive power, it would be enough to wipe out all the landmasses of the planet. Not a reassuring thought, to put it very mildly.

has a nucleus with electrons orbiting around it, the analogy is purely poetic. As we shall see in the course of this book, we exist in two distinct yet interconneced worlds: the world of the very small (atoms, electrons, and quarks), and the world of the big, starting with molecules and cells all the way to planets, stars, and galaxies, and, to boot, these two worlds are completely different and seemingly incompatible one with the other.*

ISLAND OF STARS

The sun is a star among one hundred billion other suns in our Milky Way galaxy.† So here is another interesting analogy: there are roughly as many stars in our galaxy as there are neurons in our brain.

Fig. 10.1. Artist's impression of the Milky Way galaxy

---

*Recently, however, professor Yasunori Nomura of the Berkeley Center for Theoretical Physics at UCLA, has argued that "everything in Nature obeys the laws of quantum mechanics, whether small or large."[6]

†All known suns have been given names or codes. Ours has the gentle name Sol. Our planet is named Terra. The number of stars in the Milky Way is given from 100 to 300 billion, depending on whose estimate you consider.

A galaxy can be imagined as being an island populated by billions of stars, floating in a vast ocean of empty space. Until the early part of the twentieth century, it was thought that our own galaxy, the Milky Way, was the whole universe. Then in 1920, Edwin Hubble came along, and suddenly the universe became much, much bigger; in fact, billions of time times bigger and filled with billions of other galaxies.*

Fig. 10.2. The Milky Way appears from Earth as a dense band of stars because we look into its flattened shape. Courtesy of Ken Holz.

---

*It is now thought that there are, in fact, more than one trillion galaxies in our universe. See *ASTRONOMY* magazine of June 2017, vol. 45, no. 6, p. 18.

Using the hundred-inch Hooker Telescope at the Mount Wilson Observatory in California, Hubble measured the redshift radiation from the light of these nebulas (faint, diffused patches of lights previously thought to be gaseous entities) and proved that they were, in fact, galaxies outside the Milky Way, some thousands, others millions, and others even billions of light-years away, each one of them the home of billions of stars.

But how many galaxies are there in the observable universe?

Fig. 10.3.
Edwin Hubble

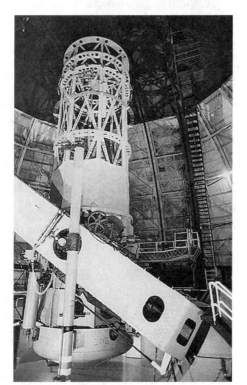

Fig. 10.4. The Hooker Telescope at the Mount Wilson Observatory, used by Edwin Hubble in the 1920s

The Hubble Space Telescope, which was launched into low Earth orbit in 1990 by NASA, has allowed astronomers to roughly estimate the number of galaxies. In 1995, when the Hubble deep field was observed, a reliable estimate could be made: one hundred to two hundred billion galaxies in the observable universe. But as if this was not a big enough mind-boggling number, in October 2016 an international team led by astronomer Christopher Conselice from the University of Nottingham in England, using data from the Hubble Space Telescope and other telescopes around the world, came up with an accurate census that stunned the scientific communities: *there are ten times more galaxies in the observable universe than previously thought.*[7]

This brings the number of galaxies to an astounding one trillion (1,000,000,000,000). If all of these galaxies contain on average as many stars as our own galaxy, then we are talking one hundred billion trillion stars!

How many of these stars have solar systems like ours, with some rocky planets orbiting around a stable star?

ENTER THE EXOPLANETS

Until the early 1990s no one was sure if planets existed outside our solar system. But in 1992, two planets orbiting pulsar PSR B1257+12 in the constellation of Virgo were discovered by astronomers Aleksander Wolszczan and Dale Frail, who were working at the Arecibo Observatory in Puerto Rico. From then on the term *exoplanet* entered the vocabulary of scientists, meaning planets that are in other solar systems. As noted previously, the first confirmation of an exoplanet orbiting a regular star was made in 1995, when a giant planet was detected orbiting the star 51 Pegasi in the constellation of Pegasus by Michel Major and Didier Queloz of the University of Geneva. Since then the hunt for exoplanets has progressed with a vengeance. In March 2009, NASA launched into Earth's orbit the Kepler spacecraft, equipped with a photometer Schmidt telescope with a focal plane of forty-two small-charge couple devices containing a total of ninety-five megapix-

Fig. 10.5. The Kepler
spacecraft, equipped
with a photometer
Schmidt telescope

els. The mission: to detect and measure the transit of planets, especially "terrestrial planets" (Earth-like planets) in "habitable zones" in a specific stellar region within our galaxy.

The first trial runs immediately produced a stunning result: an Earth-size exoplanet orbiting a star some 540 light-years away. Natalie Batalha, an astronomer at the Space Sciences Division of NASA's Ames Research Center, could hardly believe her eyes, exclaiming, "Oh my God! We're going to find lots of these things. We're going to find lots of Earth-size planets!"[8] And they soon did.

Earth-size planets are, quite simply, roughly the same size as our own, but not necessarily having life. For any to have life as we know it, they would have to be "planets for Goldilocks"; that is, not too hot and not too cold, but also not too big so as to have a crushing gravity and not too small so that the gravity cannot retain an atmosphere. These Goldilocks-zone planets also need to have the right elements to sustain life "as we know it." There are six main elements—carbon, hydrogen, nitrogen, oxygen, phosphorus, and sulfur, which are the six basic building blocks of life—although, of course, life may also exist in forms and

Fig. 10.6. Cygnus-Lyra region, investigated by the Kepler mission

conditions that are not "as we know it," such as, for example, the sulfur-based microorganisms recently discovered in Mono Lake, California, by a NASA team of astrobiologists.[9] At any rate, thanks to the Kepler mission, astronomers now have absolute proof that there are plentiful solar systems in our own galaxy with one or several planets orbiting around a star, many of which are of Earth size. The number of exoplanets so far confirmed is now about 3,500, though only thirty planets are thought to be rocky Earth-like planets (i.e., in the "Goldilocks zone").[10] This count, however, so far only covers a very small area of our galaxy in a single star field around the Cygnus-Lyra region.*

---

*During the editing of this book, on February 22, 2017, NASA announced the discovery of a small cold star, known as a dwarf star, some thirty-nine light-years away, that contains a system of seven planets, three of which are thought to be rocky Earth-like planets that could potentially have liquid water, and thus life. They called the star system Trappist-1, named after the Belgian-operated telescope in Chile that was used to discover two of the system's planets; the other five were discovered using NASA's Spitzer Space Telescope. It is hoped that NASA's James Webb Space Telescope, scheduled to be launched in 2018, will tell us more about the Trappist-1 system.

But looking only at that tiny patch of the galaxy is like looking at one square millimeter of Malibu Beach, where each sand grain is a star. By extrapolation, however, astronomers estimate that there could be billions of exoplanets in our galaxy alone. The estimates vary widely. The Harvard-Smithsonian Center for Astrophysics estimated seventeen billion planets in our Milky Way galaxy, but then in 2013 astronomers at the University of Auckland increased this estimate to one hundred billion planets in our galaxy and a staggering fifty sextillion planets in the whole observable universe.[11] Either way, at the very least, we can safely consider a very conservative figure of one hundred billion planets in our galaxy.

Let us use this conservative value to estimate the possible number of advanced civilizations in our galaxy—always bearing in mind, of course, that this figure could as easily be zero as it could be thousands or even millions! Most exoplanets will probably have weather and geological conditions far too hostile for life as we know it. So let us assume that only 0.1 percent is Earth-like with developed life-forms. The number is now reduced to 100 million planets. Now let us further assume that only 0.1 percent have an advanced civilization. Now the number is brought down to 100,000 planets. However, other estimates have been given; Michio Kaku is more concervative and estimated "ten thousand advanced civilizations in our own Milky Way Galaxy,"[12] while Carl Sagan in 1967, on the other hand, estimated one million advanced civilization in our galaxy! These estimates are only for our own galaxy, of course. Extrapolating for the (very conservative) one hundred billion galaxies in the observable universe, the number of possible Earth-like planets shoots up to one trillion potential planets that may harbor advanced civilizations. So far no proof of any exoplanet harboring life, let alone an advanced civilization, has been forthcoming. Yet given those huge numbers, it is very hard to imagine, knowing what we know today, that only our planet has life in a universe of such mind-boggling magnitude.

In the movie *Contact,* the SETI scientist Eleanor Arroway (played by Jodi Foster) was asked by a little boy, "Are there other people out there in the universe?" She replied, "The universe is a pretty big place;

it's bigger than anything anyone has dreamed of before. So if it is just us, it seems like an awful waste of space, right?"

So let us for a moment assume that there are indeed advanced civilizations on some of these exoplanets. Let us also assume that their technologies are ahead of ours by thousands or even millions of years. Could any of them have made contact with humans in the past? If these assumptions are correct, then the answer must be a tentative yes. And although many outside the scientific community—Egyptologists come to mind—balk at the very idea of a possible extraterrestrial contact, it should be a totally legitimate consideration these days. In fact, so legitimate is this consideration that since the 1960s very serious and costly efforts have been made to find out if extraterrestrial intelligences are trying to make contact with us.*

ET COMES HOME

It all began in an organized scientific way with the creation of SETI projects, the first of which was conducted in 1960 by astronomer Frank Drake using the radio telescope in Green Bank, West Virginia. Although the original idea was to listen for incoming signals, in 1971 the first coded radio message was transmitted from the Arecibo Observatory in Puerto Rico toward the global cluster M13.†

In 1995 the Phoenix Project was initiated in Mountain View, California, using much more sensitive technologies that were able to receive radio messages in the 1,200 to 3,000 megahertz range to study about one thousand stars similar to our sun that are promising candidates to have Earth-like planets. More recently, in 1999, an innovative approach in the search for extraterrestrial intelligence known as the SETI@home Project was initiated by astronomers at the University of California, Berkeley. SETI@home informally recruits computer buffs

---

*In the early part of his career Carl Sagan was very open to the notion that an extraterrestrial contact had taken place in the past.[13]
†A radio message would take twenty-six thousand years to reach M13, so the earliest possible reply would take fifty-two thousand years! So the first Arecibo message was merely symbolic.

Fig. 10.7. The Arecibo Observatory's radio telescope in Puerto Rico

to participate in the search for extraterrestrials using their home computers. The idea is to leave the screen savers on in order to scrutinize chunks of the massive amount of data from the Arecibo radio telescope in the hope that one of the five million participants may pick up a signal from an alien civilization. SETI@home is now one of the largest computer-based projects in the world, and the number of participants is growing by the day. Dan Werthimer, an astronomer and the director of SETI@home, is very optimistic that sooner or later a signal will be picked up, given the huge number of planets thought to exist in our galaxy. Seth Shostak, a senior astronomer at the SETI Institute, is even more optimistic now that the go-ahead has been given for projects such as the 350-antenna Allen Telescope Array in California, funded by multibillionaire Microsoft founder Paul Allen.

According to Shostak, "It is likely the new telescopes being built for SETI will trip across a signal by the year 2025."[14] His belief stems from the fact that the small number of stars currently being investigated for intelligent life—about one thousand so far—may be increased to a million in the coming years as more funding is raised to build more and larger radio telescopes, not just the Allen Telescope Array in the

Fig. 10.8. Allen Telescope Array in California

Fig. 10.9. The new Five-Hundred-Meter Aperture Spherical Radio Telescope (FAST) in China

United States, but also others around the world. The People's Republic of China has taken the lead by announcing in July 2016 the construction of the Five-Hundred-Meter Aperture Spherical Radio Telescope (FAST), the world's largest single-aperture telescope. The FAST will be able to detect low gravitational waves in the search for signals that may have been produced by alien civilizations, and it is slated to be fully operational in three years' time.

Many skeptics argue, however, that there is not much point in all this, because even if contact is made with an extraterrestrial civilization—and that is a huge *if*—the dialogue would be impossible because the distances are so large that radio waves would take dozens of thousands of years just one way. Indeed, so large are the distances that astronomers had to create a unit of measure called the light-year to define the distances between stars and galaxies. Light is known to travel in empty space (a vacuum) at the mind-boggling speed of 299,792 kilometers in one second. In the ten seconds it took me to write the last sentence, a beam of light would have had time to go around Earth seventy-five times. One light-year is 9.5 trillion kilometers. The nearest star to us, Proxima Centauri, is 4.2 light-years away, and the nearest galaxy to us is Andromeda M31 at 2.5 million light-years. Yet Andromeda M31 is our next-door neighbor in galactic terms. The farthest galaxy currently detected is GN-Z11 at 13.4 billion light-years from us. Our own Milky Way galaxy is about 100,000 light-years across, and the sun is just 0.0000158 light-years from Earth, but that is still a massive 149.6 million kilometers!

The closest rocky exoplanet so far detected that is similar to Earth is in orbit around Proxima Centauri some 4.2 light-years away. It was discovered in 2016 by the European Southern Observatory using the 3.6-meter telescope at the La Silla site in Chile and was named Proxima B. And although this star is practically at our doorstep, the distance involved is nearly 40 trillion kilometers, and it would take some seventy thousand years to reach this planet at the speed of current conventional space probes. But scientists working on the one-hundred-million-dollar Breakthrough Starshot Project (funded by billionaire Yuri Milner and supported by cosmologist Stephen Hawking) are planning on developing miniature "nanocraft" powered by solar radiation that could travel at 20 percent the speed of light. This would drastically cut down the journey time to Proxima B to twenty years. Also, NASA's Kepler mission is credited for discovering the first transit exoplanet—detected by measuring the "dimming" of its parent star when it transits across it—in the Goldilocks zone of a sunlike star in 2011, named Kepler-22B. But this planet is six hundred light-years away, thus much farther than Proxima B at 4.2 light-years. Also, as far as can be ascertained, it seems likely that Kepler-22B is a gaseous planet like Venus, and thus less likely as a habitable world. But Pete Worden, director of NASA's Ames Research Center, is optimistic that "we're getting closer and closer to discovering the so-called 'Goldilocks planet.'"[15]

So it is legitimate to ask the question: If we Earthlings will have the technology to undertake such interstellar trips after only ten thousand years of civilization, then it should be possible for intelligent beings in other worlds to do the same, and more so if they have had a head start of thousands, millions, or even—why not?—billions of years to develop their technologies. Skeptics, however, still evoke the Fermi paradox: *"Where is everybody?"*

The Fermi paradox sees a contradiction between the ten thousand possible advanced civilizations in our galaxy given by Drake (the Drake equation) and the lack of evidence of any contact with any of them so far. Surely, they say, we'd have heard something already if the galaxy was teeming with so many advanced civilizations. There may be, however, all sorts of good reasons why no contact has been made yet. Alien civilizations may not have developed a technology suited for interstellar communication or travel, or they may be so far advanced from us that we appear as slugs to them and therefore not worth noticing. According to Kaku, "More than likely, we are not on their radar screen. The galaxy could be teaming with intelligent life-forms, and we are so primitive that we are oblivious to them."[16] I go along with Kaku on this. But I would also add two other possibilities: a "contact" might have taken place long ago when humans either did not detect it, or, worse, they might have heard the "message" but misunderstood it as a divine revelation and turned it into religion. I know that this possibility will evoke the Erich von Däniken, ancient aliens, or paleo-SETI hypotheses that have vexed the scholarly and scientific communities. But this cannot be helped. For if we are to investigate the extraterrestrial issue with honesty and unhampered by fear of ridicule, then the possibility of contact in our distant past is a viable option.

DARKER THAN DARK

There is something else to consider in the multigalactic landscape: galaxies, stars, planets, and everything else that is physically known represent only 5 percent of the mass of the universe. The remaining 95 percent is thought to be "dark energy" and "dark matter." No one has seen these dark denizens or even knows what they are, yet they have to exist in order to explain why the expansion of the universe has been *accelerating* rather than slowing down since the big bang. There are many theoretical models that have been proposed to explain this mystery, but none seem to quite fit the bill. And so dark energy and dark matter remain so far the most important unsolved mysteries in astrophysics.

Well, I think I have covered it all, or most of it, to reply to Peggy Lee's question "Is that all there is?" And what does it all mean? you may ask. Well, your guess is as good as mine, as the old adage goes.

But maybe that is not all there is. Maybe, just maybe, there is something else, perhaps, that underpins everything else. Could the physical universe also have a nonphysical, nontangible aspect that, for lack of better words, we may call the *universal consciousness*? It comes as a pleasant surprise to know that some scientists today, especially physicists and cosmologists, are becoming open to this idea.

MANY WORLDS, MULTIVERSE, AND MANY DIMENSIONS

In post-Renaissance Europe discoveries such as the heliocentric theory of Copernicus, Kepler's laws of planetary motion, and Galileo's observations deeply disturbed and threatened the authority of the established orders—namely the church. The Vatican stubbornly insisted on the literal interpretation of holy scriptures, which placed Earth as the epicenter of the visible universe. It was a heresy punishable by death to even speak against this ecclesial authoritative stance. As noted before, one notable dissident in those very troubled and dangerous times was Giordano Bruno. Bruno not only endorsed the heliocentric theories of Copernicus and Kepler but also claimed that "there are innumerable suns and an infinite number of planets which circle around their suns as our seven planets circle around our Sun . . . innumerable suns exist. Innumerable Earths revolve around these. Living beings inhabit these worlds."*[17]

Bruno, not surprisingly, was arrested by the papal Inquisition and interrogated at length, thrown in the papal dungeons, and tortured physically and mentally for several months. Finally, after Bruno refused

---

*Some differences in the various English translations of Bruno's quotes are due to the old prose Italian in which he wrote (see citation for chapter 6).

Fig. 10.10. The statue of Giordano Bruno in Campo de' Fiori, Rome

to recant, the chief inquisitor pronounced on him the grisly sentence to be burned alive in a public square in Rome. The trial was witnessed by a German monk, Kaspar Schoppe, who reported that Bruno stared defiantly at his accusers and said, "You may be more afraid to bring this sentence against me than I am to accept it."[18] The entry in the Vatican's records for February 17, 1600, reads, "[Giordano Bruno] was led by officers of the law to Campo de' Fiori, and there, stripped naked and tied to the stake, he was burned alive, always accompanied by our company singing the litanies, and the comforters, up to the last, urging him to abandon his obstinacy, with which he ended his miserable and unhappy life."

Many centuries later, in 1930, the chief inquisitor at Bruno's trial, Cardinal Roberto Bellarmino, was made a saint by Pope Pius XI. In the tail end of this precarious epoch, especially for scientists, philosophers, and visionaries such as Bruno, came on the scene seventeenth-century French mathematician-cum-philosopher René Descartes, who uttered his famous edict, "Dubito, ergo cogito, ergo sum" (I doubt, therefore I think, therefore I am). But Descartes also wrote, inter alia, "Perhaps I am *something greater than I myself understand.* Perhaps all these perfections that I am attributing to God *are somehow in me potentially,* although they do not yet assert themselves and are not yet actualized. For now I observe that my knowledge is gradually being increased more and more to infinity. Moreover I see no reason why, with my knowledge thus increased, *I could not acquire all the remaining perfections of God*"[19] (italics added).

Descartes' mode of reasoning is known as Cartesian thinking. It has become, among other things, the modern rationalistic form of thinking that requires that all truths, or at least all *probable truths,* are derived from reason and logic. It was and still is the principal dogma of science, stamped, signed, and sealed, and taught in all schools and universities. It reassured everyone, especially hard-boiled rationalists, that the universe and everything in it behaves according to "laws" that can be logically explained by observation, reason, and, ultimately, by predictions that can be demonstrated with experiments. All this was good and fine. But then came the mother of all flies in the soup for the scientific community: quantum physics. Like in *Alice's Adventures in Wonderland,* suddenly things were not what they seemed to be anymore. But before we venture into the weird but supremely fascinating world of quantum physics, there is, however, one more nagging question that must be tackled: If all things are made of atoms, including us, then where did these atoms come from in first place?

FROM THE BOWELS OF STARS

Ninety-nine percent of the human body is composed of six basic elements: oxygen, carbon, hydrogen, nitrogen, calcium, and phosphorus. The remaining portion is made of small amounts of potassium, sodium, chlorine, magnesium, sulfur, and a few trace elements. All these elements, of course, are made of atoms and subatomic particles. Astrophysicists have proved that these elements came, quite literally, from the bowels of exploded stars. We are, quite literally, made of star stuff. As Carl Sagan once remarked, "Something in us recognizes the Cosmos as home. We are made of stellar ash."[20]

When a star reaches the end of its life by becoming too massive for its own good, it collapses under its own gravitational pull and then bursts in a cataclysmic explosion known as a supernova, the brightness of which can outshine even our sun in broad daylight. In doing so, the star spews into space the heavy elements cooked in its superhot interior. Everything on Earth is made from this disgorged stellar stuff. But how were the stars themselves made in the first place? Cosmologists tell us that it all happened some 13.8 billion years ago in an event they call the big bang. As noted previously, this was when an infinitesimally small and dense "singularity" that contained all the matter and energy that would become the universe, as well as being equipped with the fundamental laws of nature, blew up in one supercataclysmic explosion and expanded at superspeed, apparently lasting only from 10^{-36} seconds to 10^{-33} seconds—what is known as the cosmic expansion. At first protons, neutrons, electrons, and quarks whizzed loosely in space, but then some 380,000 years after the big bang, electrons were captured in the orbits around nuclei made from protons and neutrons, forming the first basic elements: hydrogen and helium, which floated as huge clouds of gas. This went on for another 1.5 million years, after which gravity—the most mysterious of the known forces of nature—began to pull together the gaseous matter to form stars and galaxies. The original atoms (hydrogen and helium) were cooked and soldered into heavier, more complex atoms (carbon, oxygen, iron, and so forth) in the inner thermodynamic cauldron of stars. Each time a star exploded in a supernova, these heavy atoms/elements were thrown out into space and eventually reached our planet, almost certainly carried here by comets and meteorites that bombarded the primordial boiling mantle of Earth, planting, as it were, the seeds that would spawn into living organisms.[21] The fantastic bombardment by these "cosmic carriers" has been going on throughout the formative period of our planet, bringing to us their wares and perhaps even ready-made organic compounds and microorganisms, constantly affecting the evolution of life on Earth.

In the past few decades astrobiologists have been studying certain microorganisms known as extremophiles and tardigrades, which thrive in the most extreme conditions. Studying such organisms helps scientists understand how life may exist on exoplanets, where climatic and geological conditions are far too extreme for life as we know it. One of the most robust of these tiny tardigrade creatures is prosaically known as a "water bear"; it is about one millimeter long and looks like a plump worm with four pairs of stumpy legs with claws (see plate 10). This minisuperhero of life is almost indestructible and can actually survive in outer space. It has even been suggested that it may have originally come from outer space. Recently I traveled to northern Andalusia, Spain, to have a look at metallotolerant organisms that can thrive in dissolved heavy metals, especially iron, in the reddish, thick waters of the Río Tinto. These organisms, known as *Ferroplasma acidiphilum,* have been investigated by NASA and the Madrid Astrobiology Laboratory.[22] (See color insert plates 2 and 3.)

GATECRASHERS OF EVOLUTION

For most of its 4.5 billion years, our Earth has existed without humans. You could say we are newcomers here, evolutionary gatecrashers in the natural scheme of things. If you compress these 4.5 billion years into one year of 365 days, then *Homo sapiens* (i.e., us) joined the party, probably uninvited, on the 364th day at 11:50 p.m.!

Newcomers, yes, but not the elements from which we are composed. These are as old as the stars and perhaps the cosmos itself. For these stable elements are indestructible in nature; only a nuclear interaction can change them fundamentally, something that can only happen artificially here on Earth with a nuclear explosion. Seeing it this way, the elements in our bodies have passed through all living and nonliving matter for millions of years before reaching us. We all are, in a sense, recycled elements that originated in the hearts of stars but somehow magically endowed with life and consciousness. As Carl Sagan aptly put it, "Our origin and evolution have been tied to distant cosmic events. The exploration of the Cosmos is a voyage of self-discovery."[23] And because the billions of neurons in our brains also have the same ancient cosmic pedigree, we may well wonder, What "information" could these living cells carry from Earth's past and even from other distant worlds in the cosmos?

MAPPING THE BRAIN

Today, neuroscientists use transmission electron microscopes, which allow them to see objects that are a million times smaller than the breadth of a human hair. They are powerful enough (magnification can be five hundred thousand times) to see the neurons in the human brain. Seeing is one thing, but trying to map their mind-bogglingly complex circuits is quite another. Tracking through the thick jumble of one hundred billion neurons and the one hundred trillion or more synapses that link them would seem like an impossible task.

Imagine a giant mush of overcooked spaghetti soaked in tomato sauce and tightly packed inside a pot the size of New York City and you get a rough idea of what is involved in trying to map the human brain. But even if it were possible (some think it is, as we shall see later), mapping would be the easy part of the problem. A mapped brain—all the "information" of a human brain, including all memories, emotions, thoughts, and so on—would have to be uploaded on an adequately sized

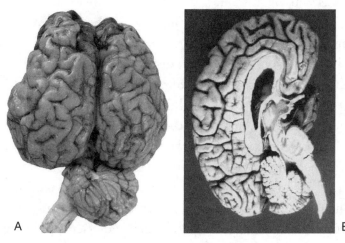

Fig. 10.11. (A) An adult human brain and
(B) a cross section of an adult human brain

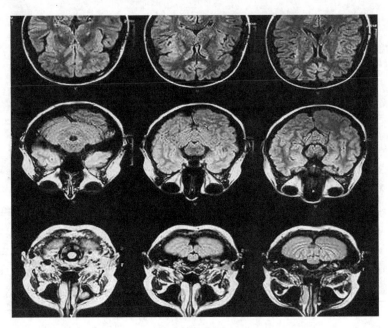

Fig. 10.12. MRI scan of the human brain

computer, requiring sufficient processing power and the software programmed to run it. No machine, at least none existing today, is anywhere near able to do this.

Let us consider the most magical function of the human brain:
memory. Neuroscientists today, with the help of powerful MRI scanners,
computers, and digital technology, have a fairly good idea in which parts
of the brain memory is processed, distributed, and stored. It is known
that sensory information collected via our five senses (sight, hearing,
touch, smell, taste) passes through the stem of the brain and into the
thalamus, located in the back of the brain. From there, information is
dispatched to various sections of the brain, where it is assessed and processed. It then enters the prefrontal cortex to be picked up by our "consciousness" as short-term memory, which may last from a few minutes to
a few hours. Long-term memory, however, is sensory information further processed in the hippocampus, a small seahorse-shaped lump in the
inner part of the brain, where it is organized into categories, zipped into
"files," and dispatched to those parts of the brain that act as archives.

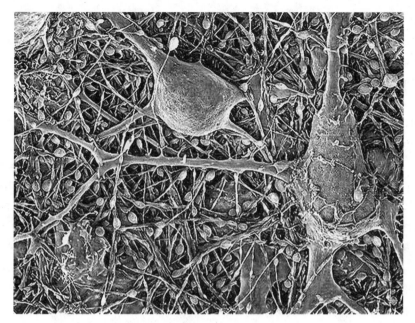

Fig. 10.13. Brain ganglia and neurons seen under an electron microscope

There, memories lie dormant, waiting to be retrieved when prompted by a thought or, more mysteriously, by an external sensory stimulus that is seen, heard, smelled, touched, or even tasted. These external stimuli can be so subliminal that we are generally unaware of their effects—making us often have this "Why did I remember this?" sensation, or déjà vu.

HELLO AND GOOD-BYE, MR. CHIPS

Neuroscientists concede that they are nowhere near fully understanding how this sophisticated organic "processor" that is our brain really works when it comes to memory. Perhaps better equipped for this task are computer experts or, more specifically, designers of microchips and processors. Today we can artificially store vast amounts of memory in microchips, which are smaller than a postage stamp and contain circuits of billions of microscopic switches called transistors that are made from silicon. The stored memory can then be retrieved at will. Although it's nowhere near the sophisticated memory mechanism of the human brain, computer technology can nonetheless give us some rough analog of how memory is processed and stored in the "biological computer" lodged in our skulls. So instead of a fleshy living binder on which the neurons are set, let us for a moment consider a silicon chip on which transistors are fixed.

Silicon is the seventh most abundant element in the universe, and in the compound form of silicon dioxide (common sand), it is the most abundant on Earth's crust. There is, quite literally, no shortage of it, unless, of course, we end up consuming the whole outer mantle of our planet. Silicon was discovered in 1824 by Swedish chemist Jöns Berzelius, and today it is produced by heating sand with carbon at temperatures just above 2,000°C. Crystals of crystalline silicon are grown by a process known as the Czochralski process, and when doped with boron, gallium, germanium, phosphorus, or arsenic, these crystals are used to make the microchips for processors that run the solid-state electronic gadgets that most of us use on a daily basis, such as calculators, computers, scanners, cell phones, smartphones, digital cameras, and so on.

A regular microchip these days is about the size of a fingernail and can contain millions, even billions of transistors in an integrated circuit. Transistors were first developed in 1947 at Bell Laboratories in New Jersey by physicists John Bardeen, Walter Brattain, and William Shockley, the latter considered by many as the Father of Silicon Valley. In 1958, Robert Noyce, one of Shockley's employees, left Bell Laboratories and, along with a group of engineers, founded Fairchild Semiconductor. It was there that Noyce invented the integrated circuit, better known as the microchip, the "brain" that runs the processor in a computer.*

In 1986, Noyce, along with Gordon Moore (of Moore's law, see page 173), went on to create the giant microchip manufacturer Intel.

---

*Noyce shares the invention with Jack Kilby, who also developed the microchip at Texas Instruments in 1958. Texas Instruments and Fairchild both filed for patents. Inevitably, a huge legal battle ensued. The patent was initially awarded to Kilby, but in 1966, after another legal wrangle, the decision was reversed and the patent went to Noyce. A happy arrangement, however, ensued between Texas Instruments and Fairchild, who shared the world market together based on royalties.

Today a regular Intel microchip contains billions of transistors that work by regulating the movements of individual electrons. These transistors are so small that they can only be seen with a powerful microscope.* Intel's vice president, Mooly Eden, boasts that by the year 2026 computer processors will have as many transistors as there are neurons in the human brain. This, of course, means anything between eighty to one hundred billion transistors crammed onto a wafer-thin silicon chip the size of the nail on your little finger.[24]

It is estimated that the memory capacity of a fully developed human brain is about one million gigabytes, compared with only five hundred gigabytes for the average laptop computer of today.[25] But it isn't just the capacity of the human brain for storing data that is impressive. The human brain can also memorize moods, ambiances, feelings, emotions, dreams, and even things that are imagined, none of which computers can do.

But electronic technology is experiencing exponential growth, leading some scientists to predict that within a few decades, perhaps just even a few years, there will be quantum computers that may match the capacity and processing abilities of the human brain, maybe even hugely exceed them. According to an article by science writer David Castelvecchi in the prestigious journal *Nature:*

> Quantum computers [are] ready to leap out of the lab in 2017. . . . Google, Microsoft, and a host of other labs and start-ups are racing to turn scientific curiosity into working machines. . . . Google started working on a form of quantum computing that harnesses superconductivity in 2014, [and] it hopes this year [2017], or shortly after, to perform a computation that is beyond even the most powerful "classical" supercomputers—an elusive milestone known as quantum supremacy. Its rival, Microsoft, is betting on an intriguing but unproven concept, topological quantum computing, and hopes to perform a first demonstration of the technology.[26]

---

*As of 2015 the highest transistor count in a commercially available central processing unit of a computer is more than 5.5 billion, in Intel's eighteen-core Xeon Haswell-EP.

There is even serious speculation in the scientific community that a human brain could eventually be "uploaded" into a quantum super-computer and thus be able to process information thousands, perhaps even millions, of times faster and more efficiently. Indeed, according to Kaku nothing is impossible as long as it is consistent with the "laws of physics." He wrote, "My own personal philosophy is that if something is consistent with the laws of physics, then it becomes an engineering and economics problem to build it. The engineering and economic hurdles may be formidable, of course, making it impractical for the present, but nonetheless it is still possible."[27]

MIND UPLOAD

Whole brain emulation, or mind uploading, is the theoretical process of copying the mental state and memory of a biological brain onto a computer with an analogous artificial neural network. This artificial mind could then be attached to an anatomical 3D-simulation model and placed within a virtual reality world or even connected to another biological body. Some futurists even speculate that this would be one way to preserve "who we are" (i.e., our "self" or "consciousness") in a nondecaying artificial body. In other words, the mental "you" would become eternal. Another use of mind uploading would be to make a complete backup of our brain to be used by others after we die. Although much of this is still in the realm of science fiction, there is nonetheless ongoing research being done on animal brains, as well as in creating supercomputers and near-real virtual reality. Apparently, much of the science and technology already exists to achieve mind uploading, and it is within engineering possibility given enough funds and time. In 2004 the Israeli neuroscientist Henry Markram, professor at the École Polytechnique Fédérale de Lausanne in Switzerland and lead researcher of the Blue Brain Project, was at first somewhat pessimistic that power-ful and large enough computers could be developed for brain upload, because "in the brain, every molecule is a powerful computer, and we would need to simulate the structure and function of trillions upon tril-lions of molecules as well as all the rules that govern how they interact.

You would literally need computers that are trillions of times bigger and faster than anything existing today."[28]

In 2009, after he had successfully simulated part of a rat's brain, Markram, now director of the Blue Brain Project, was much less pessimistic. He went as far as claiming that "a detailed, functional artificial human brain can be built within the next 10 years."[29] A very recent breakthrough by the Blue Brain Project team is the finding that the human brain may be functioning in several dimensions, perhaps up to eleven dimensions, apprently operated, as it were, by clusters of neurons that form a clique. According to Markram, "We found a world that we had never imagined. . . . There are tens of millions of these objects [clique] even in a small speck of the brain, up through seven dimensions. In some networks, we even found structures with up to eleven dimensions. . . . The mathematics usually applied to study networks cannot detect the high-dimensional structures and spaces that we now see clearly."[30] Also recently a director at Google, Ray Kurzweil, has postulated that by the year 2045 people will be able to "upload" their entire minds to computers and thus become "digitally immortal."[31]

Moore's law, postulated by Gordon Moore, stipulates that computer power doubles every eighteen months. This is evident when you compare the state of computers forty years ago with today's devices. And although there may be a limit to Moore's law (which is not really a law but a statistical prediction) because of the realities of particle physics, it is nonetheless often evoked by futurists, who revel in telling us how there will be machines a thousand, perhaps even a million times faster, smarter, and more efficient than humans.

In the 1960s, there was much hype on the future possibilities of artificial intelligence (AI) when one its founders, Herbert Simon, claimed that by the 1980s intelligent machines will match human mental and mechanical abilities. But it did not happen, mostly due to the underestimation of the huge technical problems involved. In the 1980s, however, another AI founder, Marvin Minsky, assured the world that all problems with AI will be solved within a generation. It still hasn't happened. The real obstacle for AI is that most of human intelligence is subconscious, while only "the tiniest portion of the computations of the brain is from our conscious part," says Kaku.[32] True, there exist today computers that can do computations and process data a billion times faster than the human brain, but, notes Kaku, such computers are "totally lacking in self-awareness or common sense."[33] Take the supercomputer Watson, developed by IBM in 2011, which was able to process information at the astonishing rate of five hundred gigabytes per second, with sixteen trillion bytes of RAM memory. Watson could read the equivalent of one million books in one second and could store two million pages as well as all the data in Wikipedia. But as impressive as this is, Watson had no idea what it was doing. True, Watson could analyze mountains of data at superspeed, but it could not think at all or even recognize an object as simple as a cup of coffee, let alone feel any emotions or use imagination.*

Take also ASIMO, a robot developed by Honda Corporation in Japan that looks like a mechanized boy. ASIMO thrilled television audiences with its ability to speak in many languages, run around, and even dance. When its developers were asked how "intelligent" ASIMO was, they had to admit that its intelligence was no greater than that of a flea.[34] Still, it may well be that in the future quantum or molecular or DNA computers will be able to match or even exceed the abilities of the human mind, but I personally doubt if such machines will ever have consciousness. However, not everyone agrees. It all depends, you see, if consciousness is part of the physical brain and, therefore, can be reproduced artificially, or whether it is something nonphysical. No one really knows. As expected, most scientists lean toward the physical, while the

---

*There exist too supercomputers that were introduced in the 1960s. Essentially, they have high-level computational capacity compared with general-purpose computers. Their performance is measured in floating points operations per second (FLOPS) instead of millions of instructions per seconds (MIPS). Supercomputers have thousands of processors running in parallel; the largest number so far is the forty-one thousand processors used for China's Sunway TaihuLight Supercomputer, which can do ninety-three thousand trillion calculations per second and has a ninety-three petaflops capacity (PFLOPS). As of June 2016 it is estimated that China has 167 supercomputers in the top five hundred listing, compared with the 165 in the United States. These computers are used for very specialized computations and simulations, especially in the fields of quantum physics, molecular modeling, and climate research.

philosophically, spiritually, or metaphysically inclined lean toward the nonphysical.

But what is consciousness?

Harvard biologist Stephen Jay Gould gives this semipoetic vision of consciousness: "*Homo sapiens* is one small trig (in the tree of life) . . . yet our trig, for better or for worse, has developed the most extraordinary new quality in all the history of multicellular life since the Cambrian explosion (500 million years ago). We have invented consciousness with all its sequelae from Hamlet to Hiroshima."[35]

Gould's statement is a dire warning that *Homo sapiens,* meaning us, can use our consciousness constructively or destructively. Hamlet did, however, also exclaim, "What a piece of work is a man, how noble in reason, how infinite in faculties, in form and moving, how express and admirable, in action how like an angel, in apprehension how like a god! The beauty of the world, the paragon of animals—and yet, to me, what is this quintessence of dust? Man delights not me."[36] As I read these words I am also reminded that some two thousand years earlier the same was more or less expressed in the Hermetic Texts by an unknown author who saw human beings as "*a miracle, an animal to be admired and adored,*" but also a "demon" capable of untold destruction and mayhem.[37] More optimistically, however, Kaku writes, "The more I learn about the sheer complexity of the brain, the more amazed I am that something that sits on our shoulders is the most sophisticated object we know about in the universe. As Dr. David Eagleman says: 'What a perplexing masterpiece the brain is, and how lucky we are to be in a generation that has the technology and the will to turn our attention to it. It is the most wondrous thing we have discovered in the universe, and it is us.'"[38]

Still, all this does not really enlighten us on what consciousness is. So perhaps a neuroscientist such as Christof Koch and a neuropsychiatrist such as Giulio Tononi may fair better when they attest that "consciousness is part of the natural world. It depends, we believe, only on mathematics and logic and on the imperfectly known laws of physics, chemistry, and biology; it does not arise from some magical or otherworldly quality."[39]

In a recent conference titled *The Biology of Consciousness,* Koch also affirmed that "there's nothing exceptional about the human brain" other than it is more conscious than those of other creatures. And Tononi wrote, "Everybody knows what consciousness is: it is what abandons you every night when you fall into dreamless sleep and returns the next morning when you wake up."[40]

So is consciousness really the way the neurons in the brain "reset" themselves after emerging from the unconscious state? Is that it? Koch and Tononi have performed experiments that show that human brain activity drops radically when a person is in varying states of unconscious—normal sleep, deep sleep, under anesthesia, in a coma— indicating to them that consciousness is a "mechanical function" in the brain and not something spiritual or nonphysical.[41]

If these scientists are right, and many think they are (I sincerely hope they are not!), it would mean that it is theoretically possible, once the neural network of the human brain is fully charted, to develop a computer that will replicate all the functions of the brain and also be endowed with consciousness. The idea behind this prediction is "emergence," meaning that consciousness will emerge when a complex organism develops a brain and nervous system to a great complexity, that something clicks in the brain to "upgrade" that organism into a conscious and self-aware one. So the theory is that when computers in a few decades reach that high level of "complexity" they too will behave like organisms and develop consciousness and awareness. But Stuart Hameroff is not sure that this is possible, and he argues (correctly, in my opinion) that emergence does not explain the huge diversity of experiences based on noncomputable things such as emotions, feelings, pain, and so forth. According to Hameroff, "quantum physics is the key to consciousness" and the brain looks more like a "quantum orchestra . . . with a multi-scalar vibrational resonance system, than a computer."[42]

Hameroff and his colleague Sir Roger Penrose proposed the Orch OR theory (orchestrated objective reduction), based on the belief that there are tens of thousands of microtubules within each brain neuron that "perform quantum computations [and] mediate consciousness."

More interesting, Hameroff also believes that "consciousness is present in the universe" and the brain is so structured to be able to access parts of that universal consciousness.[43]

There are many cutting-edge neuroscientists, computer experts, and AI gurus who disagree with Hameroff and Penrose and insist that supercomputers will eventually be built that will not only match the full capabilities of the human brain but also will have an "emergence of consciousness" occur in them.[44] Take, for example, Henry Markram, whom we have already met. As director of the joint government-funded Blue Brain Project and Human Brain Project, Markram believes that it is no longer a theoretical issue to create an artificial brain but rather an engineering issue limited only by the lack of ambition by the scientific community and also, mostly, from lack of funds. Makram is adamant that his joint projects will eventually create a computer that can function as the one hundred billion neurons and the one hundred trillion synapses. Makram's adamant assertions have persuaded funders such as the Swiss Federation and Future and Emerging Technologies of the European Union, and to a lesser extent some private funders, to donate 1.3 billion dollars for him to prove his claims. Indeed, many scientists are supportive of Makram's claims. But as the saying goes, it remains to be seen.[45]

Because the brain's neurons are composed of atoms, quarks, and electrons, theoretical physicists, especially particle physicists, have become deeply involved in trying to understand the workings of the human mind. One such physicist is Max Tegmark, whom we have also already encountered earlier. According to Tegmark, "Mathematics can describe not just some aspects of our world but all of them, which would imply that it could also *ultimately describe consciousness*" (italics added). He visualizes consciousness as a physical state of the brain and wonders if two mathematical matrices operators, the Hamiltonian matrix and the density matrix (which requires relativistic quantum mechanics) could

figure out everything, and understanding why we perceive ourselves as living in a three-dimensional space with this hierarchy objects. After all, I look at you and I see all my friends here, but I also see a vast number of quarks and electrons. And if I only look at these quarks and electrons, how by just looking at that picture figure out they get perceived into groups and objects, and which of these objects are conscious and so on. And my vision of this all along was, well, just give me a Hamiltonian alone. . . . What can you possibly do with just a bunch of numbers? Well, actually, a lot![46]

Tegmark gave an analogy concerning the atoms from which water is composed (i.e., two hydrogen and one oxygen; H_2O) and pointed out that the mathematical patterns of the atoms differ when in the forms of liquid, vapor, or ice. It seems to make sense, I must admit. But water does not think or feel. (Actually some people think it does, but that is another story!) At any rate, let us for a moment accept Tegmark's theory, which forces the questions Who or what *designed the human brain to function this way in the first place*? Well, it is *evolution*, is it not? Is that not just passing the buck, however? For we are also then compelled to ask who or what designed evolution and programmed it to run for billions of years to finally produce that conscious, self-aware, intelligent mushy lump of living cells that is the human brain. That is philosophy, the scientists would say, and science does go there!

At any rate, and without getting entangled in the impenetrable exotic mathematics employed by Tegmark, if I understand correctly, he is saying that when we are in a state of consciousness, the quarks and electrons in our brain are in a mathematical pattern that is different and more active than when we are in an unconscious state. If Tegmark is right, that the changing configuration of quarks and electrons in the brain when we wake up from a dreamless sleep induces consciousness, then let us try to understand how these microscopic particles behave.

Welcome to the world of quantum physics.

WEIRDER THAN WEIRD PHYSICS

All who see themselves as down-to-earth people are understandably reluctant or uncomfortable considering things that go against their rationality and logic. That attitude is commendable in our normal, daily lives, but when it comes to quantum physics, then push over, Mr. Spock, for rationality and logic fly out the window.

Before the discovery of quantum physics in the 1920s, everything could potentially be understood through reason and logic. Newtonian and Einsteinian physics served the modern world more than fine, thank you very much. Steam engines pulled trains full of goods and people across the country, and airplanes allowed people to soar like birds. But then came quantum physics, and scientists lost their cool and were forced to step out of their comfort zone. So very weird is the way that the microscopic universe behaves that many scientists wish that quantum physics had never been discovered. Indeed, one of its most prominent founders, Erwin Schrödinger, once lamented, "I don't like it, and I'm sorry I ever had anything to do with it." More recently physicist Richard C. Henry of Johns Hopkins University also complained that many "physicists shy away from the truth because the truth is too alien to everyday physics."[47] And Richard Feynman, one of the founders of quantum physics, dubbed "the greatest theoretical physicist since Einstein," also had no quibble telling his colleagues and students that "I think it is safe to say that nobody understands quantum mechanics"[48] and "anyone who claims to understand quantum mechanics is either lying or is crazy!"[49]

Brian Greene, a physicist at Cornell University, called quantum physics "microscopic weirdness" and warned that "no matter how you interpret quantum mechanics, it undeniably shows that the universe is founded on principles that, from the standpoint of our day-to-day experiences, are *bizarre*"[50] (italics added). Nobel laureate physicist Steven Weinberg of the University of Texas is a little more encouraging: "There is no principle built into the laws of Nature that says that theoretical physicists have to be happy."[51] And science writer Timothy Ferris puts it this way: "When we move our attention to areas in which we have no previous evolutionary experience—quantum mechanics, the world of the very small, say, or black holes, the world of the very dense—we find that the universe is not in accord with commonsense ideas. The universe is, of course, not obliged to conform to everyday notions on a small and obscure planet."[52]

If all these commentaries from physicists are not enough to make us wonder about quantum physics, the topic gets even more challenging to our normal commonsense awareness when we hear other physicists suggesting that because of it they are now compelled to think that the material universe is also mental and spiritual. Sir Arthur Eddington first noted this quantum dilemma when he wrote in the late 1930s that "it is difficult for the matter-of-fact physicist to accept the view that the substratum of everything is of mental character."[53] His contemporary Sir James H. Jean, professor at the University of Cambridge and gold medalist of the Royal Astronomical Society, admitted, "The stream of knowledge is heading toward a non-mechanical reality; the Universe begins to look more like a great thought than like a great machine. Mind no longer appears to be an accidental intruder into the realm of matter . . . we ought rather to hail it as the creator and governor of the realm of matter."[54]

And finally, in 2005, Henry was far more blunt with his fellow physicists by telling them to "get over it, and accept the inarguable conclusion. The universe is immaterial—mental and spiritual."[55] Such views and their implications have inevitably raised deep and troubling philosophical questions and have compelled some physicists and cosmologists to reconsider "the hand of God" or a "super intelligence behind 'all this.'" One such person was Sir John Polkinghorne, a professor of mathematics and physics at the University of Cambridge and fellow of the Royal Society. At the pinnacle of his career, in 1979, Polkinghorne left that role, and in 1982 he was ordained an Anglican priest. The meaningful side of reality, reality not as an "it" but as a "thou," says Polkinghorne, is "where truth and understanding are to be found by commitment and trusting, not by testing."[56]

Nonetheless, however weird and bizarre quantum physics is, something kept telling me that it may provide a new way of perceiving the mysteries of the past and, more specifically, of the Great Pyramid of Giza. So let us see what this intellectual and scientific fuss is all about.

DOUBLE SLIT AND ENTANGLEMENT

Quantum physics is defined as "the body of scientific principles that explains the behavior of matter and its interactions with energy on the scale of atoms and subatomic particles." Well, that doesn't sound too bad, does it? But as we shall see, that is a sugarcoated-pill definition.

A very weird (but not the weirdest!) behavior of microscopic particles is actually demonstrable with the double-slit experiment. This seemingly rather simple experiment devised in the 1950s has baffled scientists, who twist their brain to make sense of what the test reveals. The experiment entails shooting subatomic particles, for example, electrons, one at a time through a metal plate that has two narrow vertical slits and using a light-sensitive screen to record the place of impact of the particles. Contrary to what would normally be expected—which would be just two narrow bands in direct lines with the slits—the screen shows several bands, called an interference pattern, which is normally *caused by waves and not particles.* But how can a particle also be a wave? Things get even weirder when attempts are made to *observe or measure* what is happening. For when such an observation or measurement is made, the wave (also known as superposition) "collapses" and becomes a particle again! As incomprehensible as this seems, the simple act of

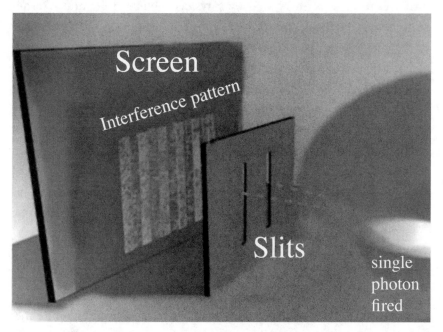

Fig. 10.14. Simple diagram of the double-slit experiment

observation or measurement will induce the electron to make a "choice" to collapse from a wave or have superposition back to a particle or having only one position. In other words, the electron seems to be *aware* that it is being observed and measured or that *consciousness is somehow involved*. No one, not even Einstein, could explain this weirdness and this totally counterintuitive behavior of subatomic particles. Einstein simply called it "spooky action."

But here is the thing: spooky and weird it may be, but physicists are nonetheless able to calculate with amazing precision where the particles will most *probably* be, thus proving that the quantum behavior is real and not some trick of nature on the mind. The mathematical equation to make these very precise calculations was devised in the mid-1920s by Schrödinger, which earned him the Nobel Prize in physics in 1933. But even though the Schrödinger equation is incredibly precise, no one, not even Schrödinger himself and least of all Einstein, could explain why it worked. It just did. It was finally accepted not to seek an explanation but to simply accept the result. This way of looking at this weirdness of quantum physics is known as the Copenhagen interpretation, a term coined by physicists Niels Bohr and Werner Heisenberg. The Copenhagen interpretation maintains that physical systems generally do not have definite properties prior to being measured, so quantum physics can only predict the probabilities that measurements will produce certain results. The act of measurement causes a set of probabilities to reduce to only one value, which is called the wave function collapse. Physicists must, at least for now, be content to calculate the probable behavior of subatomic particles and refrain from asking nagging questions as to why they behave in this weird *probabilistic* way. Physicist David Mermin came up with what seems in these circumstances the best advice for colleagues and students: "Shut up and calculate!"

Feynman, however, provided another perspective to the weirdness of the double-slit experiment that is even more baffling. For he not only endorsed the probabilistic behavior in quantum physics but also proposed that an electron may be taking different paths simultaneously, *even an infinite number of paths*. This interpretation is known as Feynman's perspective. Feynman's view on quantum physics is that it "describes nature as absurd from the point of view of common sense [but] it fully agrees with experiment. So I hope you can accept nature as she is—*absurd*"[57] (italics added).

The Double-Slit Experiment

In the double-slit experiment, what caused the wave pattern? At first it was thought that the electron had somehow become "extended" or "smeared out." Such an explanation only provoked endless debates, until the German physicist Max Born (1882–1970) showed that the wave pattern was not caused by a smeared electron or anything else so far known in classical science but rather by something even more bizarre: a "probability wave." This conclusion, and the mathematics that supported it, won Born a belated Nobel Prize for physics in 1954. In a nutshell, Born showed that the size of the wave at any location predicts the likelihood of the electron being found there. This means that a single electron could be a "jumble of possibilities." This implied that the universe and everything in it is some sort of cosmic "game of chance," to which Einstein protested that "God does not play dice" and to which Bohr said, "Stop telling God what to do." Today all scientists agree that Einstein was wrong and that "God" does indeed play dice or, to use the quantum physics jargon, that the subatomic particles from which all physical matter is made behave probabilistically. Yet in a minipoll conducted in 2011 by physicist Maximilian Schlosshauer of the University of Portland, the results showed that there is still no consensus among scientists and philosophers on what quantum physics is. In fact, there was a striking disagreement among them.[58]

The upshot of the discovery of quantum physics is that it has spawned the recent revolution in electronic technology, which has given us lasers, transistors, integrated circuits with microswitches, computers, MRI scanners, electron microscopes, color televisions, digital cameras, smartphones, iPads, and a plethora of other electronic and digital gadgets. It may one day even get us to travel instantaneously to distant stars. Understandably, scientists hail quantum physics as the most significant discovery in the history of science. There can be no denying that it has transformed, for better or for worse, the way we spend our time and how we communicate with each other.

And yet quantum physics remains profoundly enigmatic. . . .

ENTANGLED

There is one more aspect of quantum physics that I need to review before I focus my attention on the Great Pyramid. This is the "spooky action" par excellence prosaically known as *entanglement.* It is no wonder that Massachusetts Institute of Technology physicist Walter Lewin referred to the entanglement phenomenon as "the most bizarre, the most absurd, the most crazy, the most ridiculous prediction that quantum mechanics made."[59]

Entanglement was once a theoretical prediction of quantum physics that stipulated that if two subatomic particles were brought close to each other they would somehow link up and remain "entangled," no matter how far they are taken away from each other. "The most bizarre, the most absurd, the most crazy, the most ridiculous prediction" is that they will affect each other *instantaneously,* without any detectable force, field, or communication between them. So weird was this prediction that Einstein bluntly refused to accept it and called it "spooky action at a distance." He insisted that it was not reality that was weird but rather that *the math was incomplete.* The issue was still unresolved when Einstein died in 1955, but in 1967 a student at Columbia University, John Clauser, came across a scientific paper by Irish physicist John Bell (1928–1990) that inspired him to build an apparatus that could *experimentally* verify if Einstein was right about entanglement. To Clauser's utter surprise, the experiment strongly indicated that *Einstein had been wrong.* A few years later, a more sophisticated apparatus was built by French physicist Alain Aspect, who was able to actually confirm that entanglement was indeed *real.*

Entangled Particles

Austrian physicist Anton Zeilinger has been experimenting with photons and has so far succeeded in manipulating two "entangled" photon particles set 145 kilometers apart, one on the island of Las Palma and the other on the island of Tenerife. This feat earned him the 2008 inaugural Isaac Newton Medal of the Institute of Physics in the United Kingdom. Experiments performed more recently by other researchers have shown that slightly larger objects—but still on the microscopic level—behave in a quantum entangled manner. And although this is a very long way from doing the same with much larger objects, let alone human beings, the belief is that since everything is made from the same subatomic particles, then it is theoretically possible that in some distant future this may be possible when and if the superscanning technology can be developed.

There is too another, even more provocative, matter in the weirdness of quantum physics that many theoretical physicists favor. This is the *many-worlds interpretation* in which "the quantum strangeness is explained by everything having multiple existences in myriad parallel universes."[60]

The many-worlds interpretation was first proposed by American physicist Hugh Everett in 1957. According to science writer Rowan Hooper, Everett felt that "the enforced separation of the quantum world from the classical one (was) a 'monstrosity' and decided to find out what happened if the wave function did not collapse. The resulting mathematics showed that the universe would split every time a measurement is made—or in human terms, whenever we make a decision with multiple possible outcomes."[61]

While I am sitting right now in my office in Spain, writing these words, according to the many-worlds interpretation I could be having different "histories" in myriad other worlds doing other things, and in some I could even be dead or not yet born. As totally madcap as this sounds, the many-worlds interpretation has gained recognition with many theoretical physicists. According to Kaku, "In some sense, it is the simplest formulation of quantum mechanics, but also the most disturbing. There are profound consequences to this . . . approach. It means that all possible universes might exist, even ones that are bizarre and seemingly impossible."[62]

A quasi-similar concept is that of the multiverse. The basic idea is that there exists not one universe but many universes (hence, *multiverse*); in fact, an infinite number of universes floating like bubbles in an infinite space, in a never-ending cycle of creation, or multiple big bangs, with universes popping out of each other ad infinitum.[63] According to Alan Guth of the Massachusetts Institute of Technology, one of the creators of inflation theory, "in an eternally inflating universe, anything that can happen will happen; in fact it will happen an infinite number of times."[64] As completely bizarre as the multiverse notion seems to us mere mortals, there are again growing numbers of theoretical physicists who are die-hard advocates and promoters of this mind-boggling concept. This is because the mathematics that buttresses it is based on the model of inflationary cosmology, which is widely accepted. Vigorous supporters of the multiverse include many heavyweight luminaries, such as world-famous cosmologist Stephen Hawking, University of Oxford cosmologist David Deutsch, Stamford University theoretical physicist Andrei Linde, and University of California, Berkeley, particles physicist Yasunori Nomura. There are, however, an equal number of heavyweight skeptics, among them Nobel laureate theoretical physicist David Gross, Steven Weinberg, and Sir Roger Penrose. The jury, as the saying goes, is still out on this one.*

NOT JUST MANY UNIVERSES
BUT ALSO MANY DIMENSIONS

Until 1914 it was accepted that we existed in a four-dimensional universe—three spatial dimensions plus the dimension of time. No one in his right mind would have suggested that other dimensions could

---

*Recently Professor Nomura, director of the Berkeley Center of Theoretical Physics, asserted that "many cosmologists now accept the extraordinary idea that what seems to be the entire universe may actually be only a tiny part of a much larger structure called the multiverse."[65]

exist. Then, physicist Gunnar Nordstrom postulated an extra fifth dimension to explain how some of the known forces of nature could be combined. But because Nordstrom's equations did not take into account the new theory of gravity by Einstein, he was largely ignored. Then along came physicist Theodor Kaluza in 1919, who proposed a fifth dimension that *did* incorporate Einstein's theory of gravity. Still, even though Einstein was initially enthusiastic (he apparently told Kaluza "at first glance I like your idea tremendously"), he and all other scientists at the time did not think that this extra dimension was a physical reality but rather some "mathematical trick." In 1926, however, physicist Oskar Klein computed that the size of the alleged fifth dimension was incredibly tiny, in fact billions of times smaller than an atom (apparently 10^{-29}); hence, it couldn't be seen. Even so, if such an extra dimension exists, no matter how incredibly small, what does it contain?

An answer to this strange puzzle began to be gradually formulated in the 1970s. This was when physicist Leonard Susskind independently worked out mathematically that fundamental particles such as electrons and quarks are not fundamental at all but instead contain infinitesimally small "vibrating strings" of energy with no mass. It is these supertiny strings, or rather the frequency at which they vibrate, that actually produce the mass and charge of the particles. But here's the thing: for the calculations of string theory to work requires not only one extra dimension to exist but an extra six, making a total of eleven dimensions, all as incredibly minuscule as the fifth dimension calculated by Klein back in 1926![66]

At first there were some glitches with the math ("anomalies" in scientific jargon), in the equations used, which caused a serious decline in disinterest for string theory. But a few hardcore believers persisted, and eventually these glitches were sorted out by physicist John Schwarz of the California Institute of Technology, who postulated that the equations were describing the elusive *graviton* particle, which has not yet been found but is believed to transmit gravity at the quantum level. Eventually, Schwarz and a young colleague from the University of Cambridge, Michael Green, hit on the possibility that string theory was the "missing link" to a grand theory of everything. This was hot news for the international media, and string theory became the new kid on the block. Suddenly hundreds of young physicists in universities around the world who were looking for a new and exciting avenue of research declared themselves string physicists.

The math now worked beautifully, and the theory itself was such a romantic and elegant idea at the most fundamental level; namely, that everything was made of vibrating strings that were "played" by Mother Nature like a divine conductor in some cosmic orchestra, which was deeply attractive to many young physicists. One of them was Brian Greene. In his bestselling book, *The Elegant Universe,* Greene, who is also a supporter of the multiverse, enthusiastically wrote in 2000, "Can it really be that the Universe at its most fundamental level is divided, requiring one set of laws when things are large, and a different incompatible set when things are small? Superstring theory, a young upstart with the venerable edifices of quantum mechanics and general relativity, answers with a resounding 'no'. . . . According to superstring theory, the marriage of the laws of the large and the small is not only happy but inevitable."[67]

Since Greene wrote these words, however, the predicted "marriage of the laws of the large and the small" has not happened, and the protracted *fiançailles* period continues. As science writer Steve Nadis pointed out, "The novel [string] theory may never live up to the early hype."[68] But many leading string physicists—among them Greene, Kaku, and Andrew Strominger, to name but a few—remain convinced that string theory is the only way forward to solve the mystery of, well, *everything.* As already noted, Numura has seriously postulated, if not proved, that a connection may actually exist between cosmology (the world of the "big") and quantum mechanics (the world of the "small"), which he termed "the quantum universe."[69] So far, however, no one has yet come up with an experiment or an observation that could definitively verify or reject string theory. The problem is that string theory operates at such unimaginably incredibly small levels that it is practically impossible to falsify it, thus violating one of the bastions of science. As Boston University professor Sheldon Lee Glashow explains, "No experiment can ever check up on what's going on at the distances that are being studied. No observation can relate to these tiny distances of high energies. That is to say there is no experiment that could be done, nor is there any observation that could be made that would say, 'You guys are wrong!' The theory is safe, permanently safe. Is that a theory of physics or philosophy? I ask you."[70]

But who's to say that string theory may not surprise us all one day? Time will tell.

MEANWHILE, ENTER THE MATRIX

All the new findings and cutting-edge theories in physics, astrophysics, and cosmology that we have gleaned, when coupled with cutting-edge neuroscience and advances in virtual reality and AI, have led many theoretical physicists to seriously consider the most bizarre and extreme theory of all: that our universe may be a *simulation,* a sort of virtual reality created by a superadvanced alien civilization in another world.[71] Now, I must admit that this is getting a little too crazy for me. But here's the thing: apparently, it is not so crazy after all. Take the heavyweight luminary and 2006 Nobel laureate physicist George Smoot. In a TED talk, Smoot, in all seriousness, told his audience, "What I'm going to try and do is convince you [that] you are a simulation, and physics can prove it." Smoot's argument goes something like this: in the not-too-distant future, humans will have the right computer and the scanning and neuroscience technology to download a human mind into a supercomputer to operate a virtual reality of humanoids in a virtual environment. If we humans will be able to do this, so goes the argument, then it is not unlikely that some supertechnologically advanced civilization in another world may have already done it and *that we might be their simulation.*

Not surprisingly, not everyone agrees. Physicist Peter L. Kuhn, for example, believes that there is a limit to what science can do. "Some scientists say that the scientific method is the only way of knowing. If science cannot know something, these scientists say, then that 'something' is either not knowable or not worth knowing. But are there truths, real truths, beyond science? What are the limits of science? How far can it go? Are there philosophical boundaries beyond which science cannot travel?"[72]

Lately, a growing number of scientists have been forced to acknowledge that there are, indeed, real limits to science and that certain theories about the universe and about us will always remain unproved. A group of top French scientists, after being pressed to speak their minds by reporters for the popular magazine *Science & Vie,* conceded that there are ten things we will never know—things such as in which universe we exist or what an electron is or if "strings" exist at all.[73] We could, of course, also include to the list "What is life?" "What is the meaning of existence?" and "What happens to us or our consciousness after death?" The best summation comes from Princeton University physicist J. Richard Gott. "We've learned a great deal about the universe—age, structure, initial conditions, how it started, how it's developing. But a theologian might say, 'Well, have you really answered the question of why is there a universe, as opposed to no universe at all?' It's easy to imagine no universe at all. Science is not prepared to answer this question, at least not at the present time."[74]

History has shown time after time, however, that what seemed impossible at one given epoch becomes accepted fact in a later epoch. Think of the airplane, the moon landing, the Internet, and the Smartphone and you get the gist.

You may well ask at this stage, especially having gone through the intellectual rollercoaster ride of the past three chapters: What does all this have to do with the Giza pyramids? The answer is paradoxical and oxymoronic: *nothing and everything.*

Well, *nothing* if you are convinced that these monuments are just tombs, and *everything* if you are not. We cannot anymore ignore the fact that there are now several possibilities to consider, including some that appear understandably wacky at first blush but have nonetheless been put on the table in utmost seriousness by eminent scientists who should know what they are talking about. The question is no more if these possibilities exist but rather whether is it intellectually legitimate to apply these possibilities to the Giza pyramids. The answer has to be yes, for we cannot disregard this today simply because we may feel apprehensive about what Egyptologists, archaeologists, and others may think.

It is now time to return to the Great Pyramid and its mysteries and take a good look at the Giza pyramids from the new and exciting perspective of the last frontiers of science.

PLATE 1. *Where do we come from? What are we? Where are we going?*
Painting by Paul Gauguin

PLATE 2. Eagle's nest nebula showing dense clouds of dust in the galaxy

PLATE 4. Comet Hale-Bopp producing dust and becoming active beyond the orbit of Jupiter in the cold depths of space

PLATE 3. Red rain cells from Sri Lanka under an optical microscope

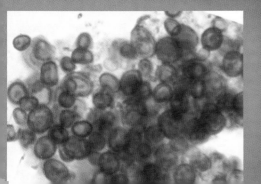

26 September 1995

PLATE 5. The Río Tinto in northern Andalusua, Spain

PLATE 6. Robert Bauval at the Río Tinto, where NASA and other space agencies have studied the microorganisms in the hostile waters rich in metallic elements.

PLATE 7. The top of the Khafre pyramid at Giza

PLATE 8. Robert Bauval examines the world's largest
Iron Meterorite in Namibia, 1999.

PLATE 9. Artist's impression of
the "astral transfiguration machine"

PLATE 10. The "water bear" tardigrade

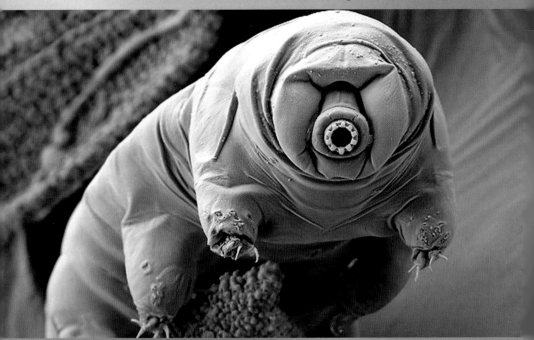

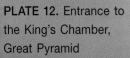

PLATE 11. The Queen's Chamber, Great Pyramid

PLATE 12. Entrance to the King's Chamber, Great Pyramid

PLATE 13. The Grand Gallery, Great Pyramid

PLATE 14. Entrance to the Queen's Chamber, Great Pyramid

PLATE 15. The Subterranean Chamber, Great Pyramid

PLATE 16. The Giza monuments in the evening

PLATE 17. The Giza Plateau from the air, looking north

11
The Archives of the Mind

Philosophy [i.e., knowledge] is written in this grand book—I mean the Universe—which stands continually open to our gaze, but it cannot be understood unless one first learns to comprehend the language and interpret the characters in which it is written. It is written in the language of mathematics, and its characters are triangles, circles, and other geometric figures, without which it is humanly impossible to understand a single word of it.

GALILEO GALILEI,
IL SAGGIATORE, 1623

Egypt is the Soul of the World.

HERMETIC TEXTS

WHERE IS EVERYBODY?

Any large-scale building project will have the same evolution. It starts when someone, somewhere—an individual, a group, or a corporation—commissions the construction of a building. The initial brief will indicate its purpose, its function, its size and dimensions, its external appearance, its internal spacial distribution and the location where it will stand. In the case of a structure like the Great Pyramid, two factors will determine if the project is feasible—assuming, of course, that material and human resources are plentiful and available. These two factors concern the *structural feasibility*.

A

B

Fig. 11.1. (A) Escarpment and the Great Pyramid, and (B) escarpment and the Great Pyramid during flood season

The Great Pyramid is estimated to have a deadweight of six million tons of stacked limestone blocks spread over an area of fifty-three thousand square meters. This produces a pressure of 113 tons per square meter on the lowest course of the building and, of course, on the soil on which it rests. The first factor that must be ascertained, therefore, is whether the lowest course of limestone blocks (these rest on a platform made of massive limestone slabs) can withstand the pressure of the whole deadweight. The second factor is whether the soil is stable and strong enough to withstand the same deadweight. This will involve physical tests and calculations allowing an adequate margin of safety. Today no structural or soil engineer would give the go-ahead for construction before being certain that these two factors are met and approved. Because the Great Pyramid is still standing with no visible settlement or subsidence, we can assume that this was the case or, less likely in my opinion, that the ancient engineers simply took the risk.

At any rate, no matter how satisfied the ancient engineers were with the strength capacity of the ground, there is another risk that no modern engineer would have taken in view of the massive scale of the monument: *the risk to place a six-million-ton structure in the proximity of an escarpment.* The Great Pyramid stands some fifty meters from an escarpment on the northeastern side of a rocky and sandy promontory known as the Giza Plateau. This plateau, although not the highest in the region, is some sixty meters above sea level and slopes gently toward the southeast. But even today can be seen the steep escarpment's edge immediately northeast of the Great Pyramid. Not surprisingly, when Sir William Matthew Flinders Petrie surveyed the Giza Plateau in 1881, he too wondered why the ancient builders placed the pyramid so close to the northeast edge of this escarpment and not farther away from it. "It may seem strange that the site chosen was not rather further from the edge of the cliff, and thus on a higher part of the rock."[1]

Strange indeed. But Petrie concluded that the ancient builders made this choice so as to have the pyramids as close as possible to the Nile so that they could be admired by the inhabitants down in the valley. But why take the risk of collapse when there was plenty of flat space a little farther west that would have been totally safe and, furthermore,

Fig. 11.2. Sir Flinders Petrie, circa 1885

afforded the same vista? In 1979, British engineer John Legon also noted the same illogical choice of location for the other two main pyramids on the Giza Plateau. These two giant pyramids partly straddled the sloping southeast side of the plateau, thus requiring extensive leveling and filling of the ground. "Why," asked Legon, "was such work undertaken when use could have been made of more level ground, further to the west?"[2] Why, indeed? And also why align them in this "anomalistic" manner, with the two larger pyramids set on a diagonal but the smaller third one offset to the east?

Egyptologists maintain that the location and alignment of the Giza pyramids were imposed by geological constraint. For example, according to Egyptologist Vivian Davies, "My own view is that the position of the pyramids had just as much, and perhaps more to do, with geology and existing topography."[3] But the topographical evidence does not support this conclusion. Professor Jean Kerisel, a seasoned Legion d'Honneur structural and soil engineer from the prestigious Ponts and Chaussées as well as president of the Franco-Egyptian Society, responded to Davies by saying, "I don't think there is any rational reason from the topographical point of view for a non-perfect alignment of the three pyramids. The line going through the center of the two first pyramids is not going through the center of the last one, the Memkaure pyramid. There is no obstacle concerning the relief. I cannot explain why there

*Fig. 11.3. Robert Bauval with Sir I. E. S. Edwards and
Professor Jean Kerisel in 1993 (left to right)*

is this anomaly. There is certainly another reason related probably to astronomy, and I think personally that the layout of the three pyramids has been designed from the very beginning by Khufu."[4] Kerisel also said, "When we consider the contour of the plateau before any human intervention, it can be seen that there are no topographic conditions that would oppose such an alignment."[5]

Kerisel favored a symbolic rather than practical motive for the placement of the pyramids, one probably related to astronomy and the cosmological ideas of the ancient builders.[6] Legon, however, proposed that the layout of the Giza pyramids was according to a geometrical and mathematical scheme of great importance to the ancient builders.[7]

We will return to the symbolic meaning of the layout of the Giza pyramids and the choice of location for the Great Pyramid when we discuss the geographical coordinates and the very controversial, admittedly, on face value impossible, suggestion of a numerical connection with the speed of light.

There are dozens of theories of how and why the Great Pyramid was

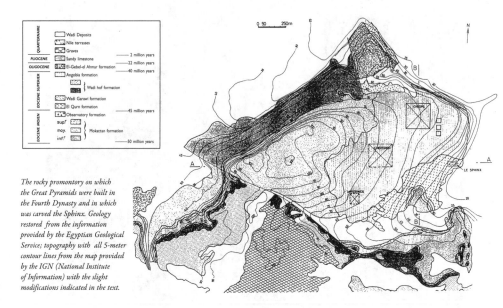

The rocky promontory on which the Great Pyramids were built in the Fourth Dynasty and in which was carved the Sphinx. Geology restored from the information provided by the Egyptian Geological Service; topography with all 5-meter contour lines from the map provided by the IGN (National Institute of Information) with the slight modifications indicated in the text.

Fig. 11.4. Topographical mapping of the Giza Plateau by Jean Kerisel

built, ranging from the totally absurd to the possible, but no consensus has been reached so far. I do not wish to embark here on an extensive review of the merits or flaws of all these theories, because when all is said and done, the simple truth is that no one really knows exactly why or how the Great Pyramid was built. As far as I am concerned, all that can be said about this special building with any degree of certainty is that today we would be hard-pressed to match this achievement without the use of mechanized cranes, special transport vehicles, and high-precision optical surveying instruments. I would much prefer to review here, among other issues, an important aspect of the design and construction phases of the project that I feel has not been adequately reviewed. This concerns the vast amount of documentation that a building project of this massive size and long duration would generate.

Today the organization and implementation of a huge project like the Great Pyramid would engender hundreds of architectural and structural drawings, detailed sketches, requisition records, transport records, storage records, labor records, and so forth. When I worked as a construction engineer on large-scale projects such as military bases and hos-

Fig. 11.5. Robert Bauval in 1977 working as a cost-control engineer on a large project in Iran

pitals in the Middle East and Africa, the amount of paperwork that was accumulated over the duration of such projects would easily fill the wall-to-wall shelves of my office. Yet here we have it: not a single papyrus, sketch, document, or inscription of any kind has been found at Giza or, for that matter, elsewhere in Egypt that relates to the Giza pyramids. I am aware, of course, that Egyptologists will argue that some inscriptions have been found inside what are known as the Relieving Chambers of the Great Pyramid (see page 245). But these are but very crude graffiti in red ochre paint left by laborers, which give absolutely no details of the design choices or methods of construction. Furthermore, there is much controversy surrounding the authenticity of these graffiti, making it very difficult to accept them as evidence without confirmation of their age by chemical or carbon-14 analysis.[8] Egyptologists, however, draw attention to a recently discovered cache of papyrus scrolls in the Red Sea area dating from the Fourth Dynasty that apparently indirectly relate to works at Giza by the pharaoh Khufu and the Great Pyramid.[9] In any case, and notwithstanding this sort of easily dismissible graffiti and vague statements in the Red Sea scrolls as evidence, it is a fact that

*Fig. 11.6. Red Sea papyrus scrolls depicting
the name of Knum-Khufu, Cairo Museum, 2016*

no *official* contemporary inscriptions have been found inside or outside the Giza pyramids.

This, to say the very least, is very odd indeed. For anyone who has visited Egypt or has strolled in one of the many museums around the world containing Egyptian collections will surely conclude that the ancient Egyptians were particularly fond of writing and inscribing walls, columns, ceilings of temples, monuments, and artifacts with hieroglyphs. Nor can it be said that there was some religious or political restriction about inscribing the inside walls of royal pyramids, for there are several near-contemporary pyramids of the Fifth and Sixth Dynasties a few kilometers from Giza at Saqqara, the internal walls of which are literally filled with the hieroglyphic inscriptions known collectively as the Pyramid Texts. So why not have the same at the Giza pyramids? This inexplicable lack of inscriptions in Fourth Dynasty pyramids should in itself raise the alarm bell that something is not quite right with the "tomb only" consensus of Egyptologists.

There is too the baffling sparsity of debris and leftover material

Fig. 11.7. The Pyramid Texts in the Pyramid of Unas, Fifth Dynasty

from the temporary works: accommodations and sanitary facilities of the workers, discarded sledges, ropes, tools, storages, roads, ramps, and remains from the daily activities of thousands of men working across several decades. So far all that has been found by Egyptologists are the pitiful remains of some human skeletons and the few ruins of the so-called workers village. But these are nowhere near what would be expected of this giant construction project, even allowing for the ravages of weather and vandalism. Like Enrico Fermi remarked when he asked about extraterrestrials in the cosmos, *Where is everybody?*

Admittedly, the same lack of documentation and leftovers also applies to all other Fourth-Dynasty pyramids located at Dahshur, Abu Ruwash, and Meydum. In this respect, the Great Pyramid does not stand alone, but is part of a scheme that includes other Fourth-Dynasty pyramids and other monuments, especially those close to the pyramids at Giza, the placement of which I have shown in many of my publications to be based on astronomical alignments and symbolism.*

The Great Pyramid, however, stands alone in its uniqueness of design, as we shall soon see. At any rate, there are two theories to consider about the placment of the Giza pyramids, which, in my opinion, are not mutually exclusive: (1) Legon's theory that the Giza pyramids were placed according to a geometrical plan, and (2) my OCT, which proposes that they were placed according to an astronomical plan.[11]

I am convinced, nevertheless, that the Great Pyramid is the centerpiece of the whole scheme, and, as such, its design should be considered separately. I am aware that Egyptologists disagree with this approach, because the Great Pyramid, they argue, is the apotheosis of an evolution in design that began a few centuries before with the simple rectangular mudbrick structures called *mastabas*. These mastabas, according to this theory, led to stepped pyramids and finally to smooth-faced pyramids. This "evolution theory," however, does not stand up to scrutiny, for the idea that such an evolution from simple rectangular mudbrick tombs to giant geometrically designed pyramids

---

*I have also shown that the Giza mound, on which stands the Great Pyramid, bears a geometrical and astronomical relationship to other mounds where Fourth Dynasty pyramids are sited.[10]

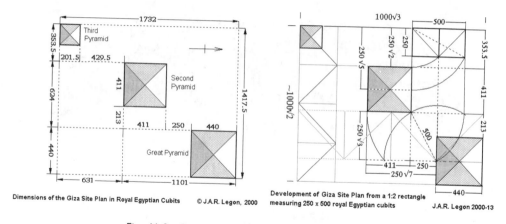

Dimensions of the Giza Site Plan in Royal Egyptian Cubits   © J.A.R. Legon, 2000

Development of Giza Site Plan from a 1:2 rectangle measuring 250 x 500 royal Egyptian cubits   J.A.R. Legon 2000-13

Fig. 11.8. Geometrical layout plans by John Legon

built with hewn limestone and granite blocks happened in little more than a century is very unlikely if not impossible. In my opinion a much longer time line is necessary, or, as may be the case, something very "special" took place that warants such a surge in design and technology that needs more serious consideration.

Fig. 11.9. Artist's impression of the sky over the Giza landscape in 10,500 BC, based on Robert Bauval's OCT

A

B

C

Fig. 11.10. (A) Typical mastaba, (B) stepped pyramid at Saqqara,
and (C) Great Pyramid of Giza

"READING" AN UNINSCRIBED PYRAMID

Faced with the lack of inscriptions on the Great Pyramid, Egyptologists remain at a loss to explain its true purpose other than to insist that it is a tomb. But when all is said and done, their "consensus" is but a collection of academic speculations based on little or no evidence. The Great Pyramid remains obstinately mute to Egyptologists. But not so to astronomers and mathematicians who can "read" its design features and alignments.

Since the late 1980s I have advocated that the only way to make good progress is to scrutinize the Pyramid Texts for clues that can be applied to the astronomical alignments and geometrical design of the Great Pyramid. Egyptologists have been reluctant in the past to use the Pyramid Texts in connection with the Giza pyramids because they regard these texts to be of a somewhat later period. They also are of the opinion that these texts are purely religious and do not contain any useful scientific information that can be applied to the pyramid structure. Today, however, there are Egyptologists who concede that the *content* of the Pyramid Texts, at least a large part of it, refers to much older events and, therefore, can and should be applied to the Giza pyramids.[12] I do not propose to review the whole corpus of the Pyramid Texts here, as I have already done so in many of my previous publications.*

Suffice it to surmise that the main purpose of these texts is to provide instructions and spells for the dead pharaoh to achieve spiritual rebirth and travel to the afterworld in the sky reserved for kingship. In other words, the reading or recitation of the texts induced a magical setting to convert the mummified corpse of the pharaoh into a star soul to be dispatched to specific regions in the starry sky. The Great Pyramid, therefore, can be thought of as a metaphysical transfiguration machine and launching pad for star souls.

The enormity of the pyramidal enterprise and the precision of the Great Pyramid's construction and alignments when coupled with the

---

*Readers wishing to know more on my take of the Pyramid Texts can consult my books *The Orion Mystery* (coauthored with Adrian Gilbert) and *Keeper of Genesis* (coauthored with Graham Hancock).

complexity of its internal system should compel us to regard this project not simply as the capricious whim of a megalomaniacal king but rather as testimony of the unflinching conviction of its creators that it could *actually* perform these functions. For no one, neither then nor now, would commission such a project of this enormous magnitude, complexity, and precision if not 100 percent convinced that it would work as planned. And although a stone structure like the Great Pyramid can hardly be regarded as a machine, let alone some futuristic apparatus to send souls to the stars, the *idea* is not as impossible as we may think. As Kaku points out, "Perhaps one day in the distant future the mind will be freed from its bodily constraints and roam among the stars, as several scientists have speculated. Centuries from now one can imagine placing our entire neural blueprint on laser beams, which will then be sent into deep space, perhaps the most convenient way for our consciousness to explore the stars."[13]

Kaku is alluding, of course, to a time when electronic technologies—computers, scanners, lasers, and such—could be developed to perform such an undertaking, provided, of course, that the massive amount of funds required for research and development are also made available. The Great Pyramid, however, is firmly set in the distant past, when such sciences, let alone technologies, were not even imagined. But what if in Egypt's distant past there had lived supergenius savants with intellects like a combination of the mathematical masterminds Newton, Einstein, and Feynman? What if they had been able to tap in to the treasure trove of knowledge of the mind and had somehow *intuited* the science required for this undertaking? *What if the Great Pyramid is not a machine as such but the three-dimensional blueprint of such a machine—one that could be used once the required science and the technology was developed in some distant future?*

Let us imagine for a moment a team of scientists ten thousand years from now, when the sciences and technologies would be as fantastic to us as ours would be to prehistoric cavemen. Let us imagine the real possibility that they have identified a potentially scientific civilization on an Earth-like planet in some distant solar system. Their assessment is that this primitive civilization will require several thousand years in order to develop the sciences and technologies to undertake astral travel. So all that can be done at this stage is to leave a manual or blueprint that will endure the ravages of time. You would be entirely justified to point out that there are a lot of "what ifs" in this scenario. But perhaps the words of Sir Martin Rees, the astronomer royal for England, may be suggestive that such a hypothesis is not so far-fetched after all. "Wormholes, extra dimensions, and quantum computers open up the speculative scenario that could transform our entire universe eventually into a 'living cosmos.' There could even be laser transmission of 'encoded' information (a kind of 'space travel' that could happen at the speed of light), which could trigger the assembly of artifacts or the 'seeding' of living organisms in propitious locations."[14]

So, if the entire universe could be transformed into a "living cosmos" by us humans in some future time, then is it not possible that a far older and more advanced civilization elsewhere in the galaxy has already done so long ago? Why not? And is it possible too that contact by them with Earth has already been attempted? I admit that hardly a few years ago I would have viewed these kinds of speculations as outrageous and only worthy of B-rated science-fiction movies. But not so today, not when I look at things from the perspective of the present frontier of science. It demands that I remain open-minded to such speculations. Fair enough, you might say. But is there any indication in the design of the Giza pyramids that justifies this type of extremely controversial speculation?

A MYSTERIOUS CONCAVITY

A priori, there is nothing very complicated to designing a regular pyramid. This holds true if the pyramid is simply four flat triangles with their base on a flat square and their apexes joined. There is, however, an unusual feature about the Great Pyramid that would have made this imposible. For, contrary to popular belief, the Great Pyramid does not have the usual four flat triangular sides but *eight sides*. This is due to a small vertical indentation, or *concavity,* that runs all along the center of each face. This feature changes the simple pyramidal base into an irregular convex octagonal shape or, alternatively, an irregular four-pointed star shape. It also impedes the monument from having a pointed top.

Although this concavity has been reported since at least the late eighteenth century, it has received but very sparse attention from Egyptologists. Seeing the huge complications and curious implications that this concavity surely caused in both the design and construction of the monument, we can be fairly certain that its inclusion not only received careful consideration but also must have had a dire importance to its creators. The question is why.

As far as I can make out, the concavity was first reported by French architect Charles-Louis Balzac (1752–1820), one of the savants who accompanied Napoleon Bonaparte to Egypt. But other than noting that the concavity could be seen running all the way down on the center of the faces of the pyramid, no measurements were taken by Balzac.[15]

Fig. 11.11. Drawing in Description de L'Egypte, *volume 18*

The next person to report on the concavity was Petrie, when he surveyed the Great Pyramid in 1881 to 1882. This is what Petrie said about it: "I continually observed that the courses of the core had dips of as much as ½° to 1° so that it is not at all certain that the courses of the casing were truly level . . . the faces of the core masonry being very distinctly hollowed. This hollowing is a striking feature; and beside the general curve of the face, each side has a sort of groove especially down the middle of the face. . . . The whole of the hollowing was estimated at 37 (inches) on the North face."[16]

After Petrie came British architect Somers Clarke and British engineer Reginald Englebach. They clearly were puzzled by the concavity when they examined it in 1930. This is how they described it: "In the Great Pyramid . . . a large depression in the packing blocks runs down the middle of each face . . . there is no satisfactory explanation of the feature."[17] Again, no measurements were taken by Clarke and Englebach as far as I can make out. In the 1960s two Italian architects-cum-engineers, Vito Maragioglio and Celeste Rinaldi, found fragments of casing blocks at the foot of the Great Pyramid that were slightly curved, implying that perhaps the concavity extended to the smooth face of the pyramid. The cladding of the pyramid was with white Tura limestone casing blocks, which has been nearly all looted by Arabs to build villas, palaces, and mosques. There are only a few casing blocks remaining on the first course of the north and west faces of the pyramid. Maragioglio and Rinaldi proposed that the concavity was meant to create an optical effect to emphasize the sharpness of the edges of the pyramid.[18] Their hypothesis seems to be supported by an aerial photograph taken in 1926 by British Royal Air Force Brigadier General P. R. C. Groves (1878–1959).[19] Groves took the photograph while flying at 1,200 meters above the Great Pyramid during sunset on the spring equinox.

In the 1930s French physicist and mathematician André Pochan (1891–1972?) measured the concavity and found it to be 0.92 meter deep, a value that is not far from Petrie's rough estimate of 37 British inches (0.94 meter). Pochan pointed out that the inclusion of a concavity would by necessity create a small "virtual space" at the top of the

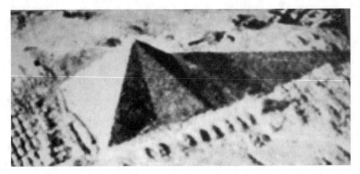

Fig. 11.12. The 1926 aerial photograph of the Great Pyramid showing the concavity

A   B

Fig. 11.13. Aerial photograph of (A) the Great Pyramid showing the concavity on the four sides, and (B) lines added to highlight the eight-sided pyramid

monument. He was the first to postulate that this virtual space had housed a metallic sphere, perhaps acting as gnomon; that is, a sundial.

The Great Pyramid was not topped, as many others, by a pyramidion of black basalt, but had a flat top from which was placed a gnomon, in my opinion a sphere, the shadow of which fell on the flooring of the northern esplanade indicating the true solar noon at different days of the year. Its maximal and minimal elongations respectively indicated the solstices of winter and summer. Furthermore, an important detail that has escaped the sagacity of Egyptologists who studied the Great Pyramid, is that the faces are not flat but have a concavity such that at the two equinoxes, at sunrise and sunset, the north and south faces are lit up only on their halves during half a minute.[20] (My translation from the original French text)

The concavity was also studied by an American sculptor and engineer, Martin Isler, in 1981. Isler was of the opinion that the concavity was not a design feature but simply an error in construction caused by the sagging of the mason's string line used for leveling the courses of core blocks. In other words, the concavity was just the result of jerry-building or "an architect's error," according to Isler.[21]

Many experienced architects I know, however, find Isler's conclusion unacceptable. And for good reason. Notwithstanding the high quality of masonry work in the Great Pyramid still evident today, even after millennia of weathering and vandalism, my architect colleagues noted that the concavity is actually seen on all four faces of the monument, making it very unlikely that an "error" was repeated four times without anyone noticing it or, worse, bothering to rectify it. Engineering precision and care was the rule rather than the exception for the builders of the Great Pyramid. If these architects are right, then in theory it should be possible to reverse engineer the Great Pyramid to deduce how it was originally designed. (See Gary Osborn's design approach in appendix 3.) Another approach, and one that I favor, would be to redesign the monument from scratch by trying to apply the same reasoning as the ancient designer and by using the royal cubit as the unit of measurement. This approach was taken by two architects: Jean-Paul Bauval and Miquel Pérez-Sánchez. Although there are some variations in their style and approach, they have arrived at the same conclusion: *the concavity forces the geometrical shape to produce a virtual space at the top of the pyramid in which was probably fitted a small spherical object.*

In reviewing the findings of Pérez-Sánchez we see that the sphere he calculated had a diameter equal to 2.7183 royal cubits and was supported on a small platform with a perimeter of 3.143 royal cubits—values that were sufficiently good approximations of the universal constants *e* and π for him to consider their appearance as a deliberation by the ancient designer. Bauval and Osborn, however, obtain other dimensions for the sphere, yet they too found that similar universal constants emerged from the design of the geometry of the virtual space. I have added appendices with their contributions for those wishing to review their reasoning and calculations (see appendices). Meanwhile, let us look more closely at how an architect would develop the design of a monument such as the Great Pyramid.

AN EARTH-COMMENSURABLE UNIT

All architects and designers, whether modern or ancient, would have to apply a linear unit of measurement in designing a structure like the Great Pyramid. They would also make use of geometrical figures—triangles, squares, rectangles, circles, polygons, cubes, and spheres—to develop the design. So what was the unit of measurement used for the Great Pyramid?

There was a time when there was much controversy regarding this issue. The story goes back to 1638, when John Greaves, a professor of astronomy from the University of Oxford, traveled to Egypt to study the Great Pyramid in the hope of finding a linear unit of measurement that might help to establish the dimensions of the planet. In other words, an *Earth-commensurable unit.*[22] Greaves published his results in 1646 in a book titled *Pyramidographia: Or a Description of the Pyramids in*

1.   Circle = SUN   2. Hexagram = PYRAMID   3. Pentagram = STAR

*Fig. 11.14. Basic geometrical shapes considered
in the design of the Great Pyramid*

Egypt. Greaves's findings eventually attracted the attention of the great Isaac Newton, who also was seeking the elusive Earth-commensurable unit. From Greaves's measurements Newton deduced that the linear unit used to design the Great Pyramid was based on *two different cubits,** one of 20.63 British inches, which he termed the "cubit of Memphis" and considered to be "profane," and another he estimated to be between 24.80 and 25.02 British inches, which he termed the "sacred cubit." Newton wrote a paper in Latin on his finding, the English title of which is "A Dissertation upon the Sacred Cubit of the Jews and the Cubits of the Several Nations; in Which, from the Dimensions of the Greatest Egyptian Pyramid, as Taken by Mr. John Greaves, the Antient Cubit of Memphis Is Determined." The paper was not published by Newton himself, but a translation in English was made in 1737 by historian Thomas Birch, secretary of the Royal Society, who included it in a compilation of John Greaves's works.[23]

Following is how Newton explained the means by which he derived the ancient unit used in the design of the Great Pyramid, which he termed the cubit of Memphis.

From the Pyramids of *Ægypt* accurately measured by Mr. John Greaves, I collect the length of the antient Cubit of Memphis in this manner. The side of the first Pyramid was 693 English feet. It is very probable, that at first the measure of it was determined by some round number of Ægyptian Cubits. Ibn Abd Alhokm, quoted by Mr. Greaves, tells us, that the measure of each side was an 100 Royal Cubits of the antient times. But it is probable, that the Ægyptians learn'd, from the Orgyiæ of the Greeks, their measure of four Cubits of Memphis, and gave it the name of the Royal Cubit. Thus the side of the Pyramid will be 400 simple Cubits, or four Arouræ; and the *Cubit* of *Memphis* will be equal to 1.732 of the English Foot. That the Pyramid was built by the Cubit of this magnitude, appears from several dimensions of it. The square passage leading into it

---

*A cubit is an ancient linear unit, about an arm's length, often used in the Bible, namely in the design of Noah's Ark and Solomon's Temple.

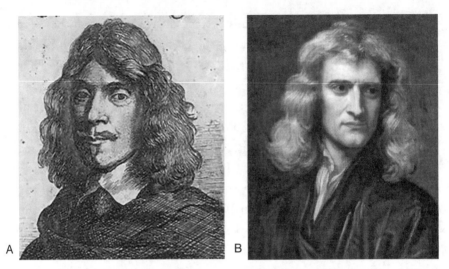

Fig. 11.15. (A) *John Greaves and* (B) *Sir Isaac Newton*

of polished marble was in breadth and height 3.463 of the English Foot, that is, two of the above-mentioned Cubits of Memphis. And of the same breadth and height were the four other galleries. In the middle of the Pyramid was a chamber most exquisitely form'd of polish'd marble, containing the monument of the king. The length of this chamber was 34.38 English Feet, and the breadth 17.19; that is, it was 20 Cubits long, and 10 Cubits broad, the Cubit being supposed to be 1.719 of the English Foot.[24] (italics added)

Newton's cubit of Memphis of 1.719 of the English foot is 20.628 British inches, a value later confirmed in 1881 by Petrie. He renamed Newton's cubit of Memphis the royal cubit and estimated it to be 20.632 +/− 0.004 British inches. The royal cubit of 20.628 British inches is universally accepted by Egyptologists as having been used for the design of the Great Pyramid.[25] As for the sacred cubit, Newton had not in fact derived it from the Great Pyramid at all but from "the Jewish historian Josephus's description of the circumference of the pillars of the Temple of Jerusalem."[26] At any rate, no one involved in Egyptology paid much attention to sacred cubit until 1859, when John Taylor, a London editor and mathematician buff and very devout

Bible reader, published a book titled *The Great Pyramid: Why Was It Built? And Who Built It?* and in 1864 also published a pamphlet titled *The Battle of the Standards (of Linear Measures): The Ancients of Four Thousand Years against the Moderns of the Last Fifty Years—the Less Perfect of the Two.* In his calculations of the slope of the Great Pyramid, Taylor used 764 British feet for the base side and 486 British feet for its total height. These measurements had been obtained by Colonel Robert William Howard-Vyse, who had explored the Giza pyramids in 1837.[27]

To Taylor's surprise, when he divided the perimeter of the base of the pyramid by twice its height, he got the number 3.144, which he deemed too close a value to the universal constant pi (π) (then known to be 3.14159) to be a coincidence. Being a keen amateur mathematician, Taylor immediately realized that the ratio of the height to the base perimeter of the Great Pyramid could be expressed as the ratio of the radius of a circle to its circumference. This convinced Taylor that the ancient designer of the Great Pyramid had *intended for the square base to also be seen as a circle*—an almost impossible mathematical puzzle known to the ancients as the "squaring of the circle." Taylor, unfortunately, was also a Bible literalist; namely, someone who believed that the holy scriptures were directly inspired by God. So he jumped to the irrational conclusion that the designer of the Great Pyramid had used the sacred cubit, which Newton had derived from the Temple of Solomon in Jerusalem, and that to the "patriarch Noah must be ascribed the original idea."

Taylor was impressed that when the base side of the pyramid was divided by 25 sacred cubits it produced a number that was a fraction more than 366, which is reminiscent of the leap year (i.e., 365 + 1 days). This further convinced Taylor that the sacred cubit of the Jews was the long-sought-after *Earth-commensurable unit* and that the reason for the captivity of the Jews in Egypt to construct the Great Pyramid was "to make a record of the measure of the Earth . . . desirous of leaving behind them a record of the circumference as correct and as imperishable as it was possible for them to construct . . . to Noah we must ascribe the original idea, the presiding mind, and the benevolent purpose. He who built the Ark was of all men the most competent to direct the building of the Great Pyramid."[28]

Taylor enthusiastically sent his publications to the Royal Society in London. Not surprisingly, no one took it seriously. But a potent mental virus, rife with evangelical fervor and soon to be labeled *pyramidology,* had been set loose on Victorian Britain. The first victim to be struck by this curious mental affliction was a highly educated but also very devout Scottish lady, Jessica Piazzi Smyth, who, as it happened, was married to one of the most prominent scientists in the United Kingdom.

PIAZZI SMYTH AND THE "PYRAMID INCH"

A massive controversy engendered in 1864 after Taylor solicited the support of the astronomer royal for Scotland, Charles Piazzi Smyth. Taylor had sent a copy of his book to Piazzi Smyth, who, at first glance, was not impressed. However, his wife, Jessica, managed to persuade him to give it his attention. Jessica was an accomplished scholar and geologist but also an ardent admirer of Taylor, with whom she shared biblical zeal, and soon her husband also fell under the spell of the Great Pyramid, and against his better judgment, he gave Taylor's theory the thumbs up with the full weight of his academic status.[29]

Piazzi Smyth quickly realized that the measurement of the base side of the pyramid was crucial for Taylor's theory. The problem, however, was that Taylor had used the measurement taken by the Howard-Vyse survey of 1837, which varied considerably from the measurement taken by Greaves in 1638. To make things even worse, these measurements varied from the one taken by French geographers in 1799 and also another taken by Egyptologist Sir Gardner Wilkinson in the 1850s.[30] So, which of the measurements could be trusted? Piazzi Smyth decided that in order to remove all doubt on this matter he would have to do the measurement himself. So in November 1864, using his own funds and resources, Piazzi Smyth and his wife, Jessica, set out for Egypt. They spent several months on the Giza Plateau diligently measuring the Great Pyramid with the latest surveying instruments available at that time. There can be little doubt that their work at Giza was scientifically

Fig. 11.16. The rubble around the base of the Great Pyramid prior to 1865

impeccable and very professional, but unfortunately there was too much rubble around the base of the pyramid, making any precise measurement impossible.

So although Piazzi Smyth did the best he could, eventually he had to fall back on the measurements taken by the French savants in 1799 and by Howard-Vyse in 1837 and average them out. Howard-Vyse's measurement was 764 British feet, and the French gave 232.747 meters, or 763.62 British feet. From these, Piazzi Smyth decided that the average of 763.81 British feet was probably correct. This decision, however, was eventually to prove fatal. Meanwhile, Piazzi Smyth refined the measurement of the vertical height of the pyramid by using the angle of the casing blocks found by Howard-Vyse in 1837 and from another casing block found by the British engineer Waynman Dixon in 1872.[31]

The angle derived by Piazzi Smyth was 51°51'14.3".

Fig. 11.17. (A) *Casing block on the north face exposed by Howard-Vyse in 1837. Note the mass of rubble.* (B) *The casing block gifted by Waynman Dixon to Piazzi Smyth in 1872.* (C) *Casing block today.*

It was then a matter of simple geometry to work out the exact height of the designed pyramid, which Piazzi Smyth concluded was 486.2567 British feet, or 148.20 meters. With these new (but erroneous!) measurements, Piazzi Smyth recalculated Taylor's estimate for π and got 3.14159 (rounded to 3.142). Piazzi Smyth then wrote, "Hence the first stage of our trials terminates itself with as eminent a confirmation as the case can possibly admit of, touching the truth of Taylor's theory, proposition, or statement . . . with this data at our command, let us return to the Taylor-Herschel analogy, which asserts that 'a band of the width of the Great Pyramid's base-breadth encircling the earth, contains 100,000,000,000 square feet.'"[32]

Piazzi Smyth took the matter even further by carrying out a variety of astronomical and geographical calculations and concluding that the "Earth-size and Sun-distance [was] monumentalized in the Great Pyramid." He wrote, "Modern astronomers are involuntarily proving that Man, unaided by supernatural Divine power, could not possibly have measured the Sun-distance accurately in the Age of the Great Pyramid, and yet it is recorded there with exceeding accuracy!"[33]

Such a statement coming from the astronomer royal for Scotland, a paragon of the scientific community, was bound to cause much controversy. And it did. The controversy, however, did not end there. Notwithstanding the other "stages of our trials" undertaken by Piazzi Smyth, which are two bulky to discuss here (they are presented in a 664-page dissertation published in 1880), there was still the nagging uncertainty over the exact length of the base side of the pyramid— the thorn in the side of Taylor's pi-pyramid theory. The matter was finally settled once and for all in 1881 and 1882 when Petrie managed to accurately make a measurement of the base side of the Great Pyramid after the rubble around the north base side of the pyramid had been completely cleared.[34] The value he obtained for the base side was 9,068.8 British inches (i.e., 755.73 British feet, or 230.34 meters), thus 8.08 British feet less than Piazzi Smyth's estimate. This was deemed enough proof to shoot down Taylor's theory. Egyptologists rejoiced in the belief that pyramidology had been given a fatal blow. Petrie was hailed as a hero by the scientific community and in later life was dubbed "the father of scientific archaeology" and received a knighthood. Of his encounter with Piazzi Smyth, Petrie was to reminisce that

> a new stir arose when one day I brought back from Smith's book-stall, in 1866, a volume by Piazzi Smyth, *Our Inheritance in the Great Pyramid*. The views, in conjunction with his old friendship for the author, strongly attracted my father, and for some years I was urged on in what seemed so enticing a field of coincidence. I little thought how, fifteen years later, I should reach the ugly little fact which killed the beautiful theory; but it was this interest which led my father to encourage me to go out and do the survey of the Great Pyramid.[35]

The very sad and unfair result of this episode is that Piazzi Smyth was labeled by Egyptologists "the great pyramidiot"—a derogatory term still used today against those who see the Great Pyramid as anything other than a tomb.[36]

In 1993, I had the good fortune to befriend the astronomer royal for Scotland, Professor Hermann Brück, and his wife, Mary. Hermann and Mary had cowritten in 1988 a biography of Piazzi Smyth, in which they showed that he had made one supremely important contribution to astronomy that alone entitles him to a place in the history of science; that is, his advocacy of "mountain astronomy."[37] Piazzi Smyth's observatory station on Tenerife is known as "the parent of all mountain observatories."[38] A leader and pioneer in spectroscopy of the late nineteenth century, Piazzi Smyth also made many other important contributions in modern astronomy. Hermann and Mary Brück were to write of this eccentric yet amazingly talented man, "The picture of Piazzi Smyth as an apostle of the mystic pyramid cult, which has persisted until the present day, has tended to obscure his real merit as a scientist . . . the other side of his personality shows a man of many talents, and outstanding observer and a gifted experimenter. . . . [Alexander] Herschel called him 'a mighty ajax in the field of science.'"[39]

To the last, Piazzi Smyth remained convinced that the Great Pyramid incorporated a message for humankind of immense importance. His meticulous and detailed approach in investigating the Great

Pyramid, even though unfortunately based on erroneous data provided by others that he ill-advisedly used, inspired many to look at this monument as something other than just a tomb. Ironically, Piazzi Smyth's belief that the Great Pyramid contained in its design an important "message" may prove to be right after all, as will become evident as we progress further into this present investigation.

DESIGNED MEASUREMENTS
VS. BUILT MEASUREMENTS

More recently, scientific measurements of the Giza monuments were taken in 1997 by American Egyptologist Mark Lehner, a scholar today deemed the foremost expert on the survey of the Giza pyramids and the Sphinx.* Consciously or unconsciously, as the case may be, both Petrie and Lehner strove to make careers in academic Egyptology that, irony of irony, were initially inspired by two of the most renowned "mystics" of pyramidology: Piazzi Smyth and Edgar Cayce! Lehner had originally gone to Egypt to confirm the claims by the mystic Cayce that people from "Atlantis" concealed their "knowledge" in a "Hall of Records" under the Great Sphinx or inside the Great Pyramid in 10,500 BC. But, also like Petrie before him, Lehner ended up doing exactly the opposite by allegedly "disproving" such claims, this especially after he joined forces with the flamboyant director general of the Giza Pyramids, Zahi Hawass.[40]

At any rate, using state-of-the-art optical instruments, Lehner obtained 230.33 meters for the base side and 146.59 meters for the height.[41] These as-built measurements (base perimeter divided by height) produced the number 3.138, which thus was too discrepant from the value of pi (π), 3.142, to be considered other than pure coincidence. *But these measurements are not the designed values,* as any architect will point out. All Egyptologists, even Lehner himself, agree that the *designed* base side of the Great Pyramid is 440 royal cubits, and its

---

*Actually another survey involving Lehner was made in 2015, see www.aeraweb.org /articles/the-2015-great-pyramid-survey.

designed height is 280 royal cubits. Taking these *designed* measurements, we now get 3.142, which is a very good value of pi (π) taken to three decimal places. So, Taylor and Piazzi Smyth had inadvertently hit on this truth, which means that the jury should still be out on the claim that the Great Pyramid was designed with an *Earth-commensurable* unit and at least one *universal constant* in mind.

GRAVITY

Egyptologists are unanimous that the slopes of Egyptian pyramids were determined by a rudimentary method known as a *seked*.[42] This method entailed choosing a horizontal displacement from a vertical drop of one royal cubit.[43]

The seked supposedly used for the Great Pyramid was 5.5, which is obtained by a vertical height of 1 royal cubit (7 palms) and a horizontal displacement of 5.5 palms (see fig. 11.18 on page 222). These values in the lowest full-number positive integers are 14 for the vertical and 11 for the horizontal displacement. In practice, the vertical drop was determined with a plumb line, and the horizontal displacement was measured along the stable water level in a trough or channel. The precision of this operation depends, of course, on the force of gravity, one of the four *universal forces of nature,* the other three being electromagnetism and the strong and weak nuclear forces. These forces, as most scientists today seem to agree, are immutable throughout the universe and have been so since the time of creation some 14.5 billion years ago.

To understand how these forces act on the physical world, several universal constants must be known, as well as the necessary knowledge of advanced mathematics. A pyramid designed with a seked of 5.5 will produce a base perimeter of 22, which, when divided by the height of 7, produces 3.142, the universal constant pi. Using the lowest full-number integers of 14 and 11, the right-angle triangle thus produced with a height of 14 and a base of 11 gives a hypotenuse of 17.80. A mathematician will quickly realize that the hypotenuse of 17.80 divided by the base of 11 will produce the value 1.618, which is the well-known universal constant phi, the golden ratio, which also applies to the Fibonacci sequence* (see appendix 1), denoted by the Greek letter ɸ.† The latter's emergent patterns and ratio can be seen in most of the shapes found in the natural world, from plants to insects to animals to humans, and even in the spiral shape of galaxies, suggesting that it is a fundamental characteristic of the universe. This is our second coincidence pigeon. We immediately get a third coincidence pigeon, however, when an equation using the numbers of the ratio 14:11 of this special triangle also produces, as if by some magic trick, the number 3.142 (π). This equation is $(4 \times 11) \div 14 = 3.142$.

Egyptologists, of course, will insist that the ancient designer of the Great Pyramid chose the seked 5.5 (i.e., $^{11}/_2$) for structural and constructional reasons and that the two universal constants, pi and phi, that are produced resulted from pure coincidence. But this is like placing the chicken before the egg. For when we reconsider the sheer size and precision of the Great Pyramid, its anonymity, its complex design, and the engineering prowess and massive amounts of resources in material and labor to actually build it, then it seems unreasonable, to say the least, to brush away the genius of its ancient designer as simply being the product of coincidence. As will become more and more obvious as we dig deeper into this conundrum, there emerge far too many "coincidences" with this particular monument to simply be, well, all coincidences!

THE ROYAL CUBIT AND THE CIRCLE

If you take any circle with a diameter of 1, its circumference will by necessity be 3.142 (i.e., pi [π]) no matter what type of measuring unit you use, be it the meter, the kilometer, the British inch, and so forth. For as long as the value of the diameter is 1, the circumference will always be 3.142. If you then divide the circumference by 6, you get the

---

*All values are rounded to the third decimal place.
†It was James Mcginnis Mark Barr (1871–1950), an American mathematician, who first suggested using the first letter (phi) of the name of ancient Greek sculptor Phidias (ca. 450 BC) to denote the golden ratio. Usually the lowercase form (ɸ or φ) is used, but the uppercase (Φ) is often used to denote the reciprocal of the golden ratio, $1/\varphi$.

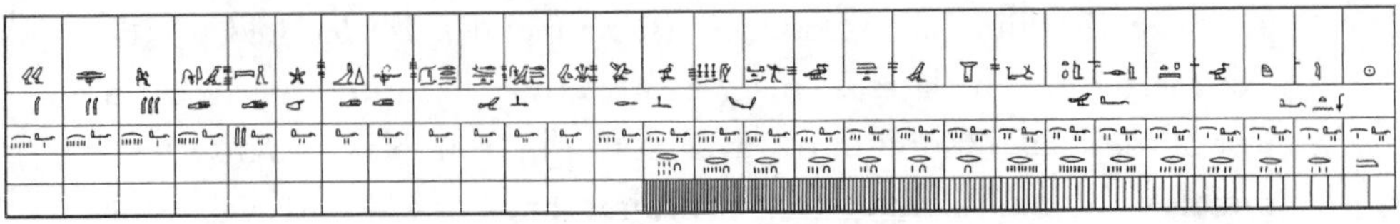

Fig. 11.18. The royal cubit and its divisions:
1 royal cubit = 7 palms = 28 fingers

number 0.5236. Now if you were to use the modern meter unit for the diameter of this circle, then the sixth part of its circumference will be 0.5236 meters, *which is exactly one royal cubit, the unit of measure used for the design of the Great Pyramid.* This shows that there is a direct relationship between the modern meter and the royal cubit when a circle is considered. We will look more closely into this strange connection later in this chapter. Meanwhile, we now have a fourth coincidence pigeon.

Wait a minute! Our staunch skeptics would surely object once more that "the modern meter unit could not have been known to anyone in antiquity, because it was determined by French geographers in 1793 by calculating the circumference of the planet!" This, we admit, is perfectly true. But it does not discount the possibility that others may have determined the circumference of the planet, and hence the meter, long before the French. Is that possible?

Let us examine the evidence.

In 1790 the Academie des Sciences in Paris created the Commission du System Métrique to determine the unit that would eventually be called the meter—a word derived from the Greek μέτρον, meaning "a measure." The mission of the commission was to determine an Earth-commensurable unit that would be one ten-millionth ($1/_{10,000,000}$) of the distance between the equator and the North Pole. The commission was headed by mathematician and physicist Jean-Charles de Borda and included illustrious members of the French academy such as mathematicians and astronomers Joseph-Louis Lagrange and Pierre-Simon Laplace, geometrician Gaspard Monge, and philosopher Nicolas de Condorcet. The idea was to accurately measure the distance between two points set on the planet's north–south (i.e., longitudinal) direction, in this case Dunkirk in France and Barcelona in Spain, roughly 1,000 kilometers apart. The actual task of measuring the arc-distance between Dunkirk and Barcelona was given to surveyor Pierre Méchain and astronomer Jean-Baptiste Delambre. Once this was achieved, and by also knowing the respective lengths of shadows cast by clock towers in each port, the arc-distance from the equator to the North Pole could be determined by simple trigonometry. The commission then took one tenmillionth of this distance and called it *le metre* (i.e., the meter). The polar circumference of Earth was then calculated to be forty million meters, or forty thousand kilometers.*

But was something similar achieved in ancient Egypt? If you accept the orthodox consensus, the answer is an emphatic no. Historians accept that the first person to measure Earth's circumference was Eratosthenes in the third century BC, two millennia *after* the Great Pyramid is thought to have been built.

Although a Greek by birth, Eratosthenes made his alleged discovery when he was chief librarian of the Great Library of Alexandria in Egypt. There are no original writings by Eratosthenes that have survived, so historians have had to rely on commentaries by other ancient Greek authors. In any case, the story goes that Eratosthenes was informed that on the day of the summer solstice at noon the sun was located directly overhead of the town of Syene in the extreme south of Egypt. This is said to have intrigued Eratosthenes, because on the same day and time in Alexandria, where he lived, the sun *was not* directly overhead but a little inclined toward the south. Eratosthenes is said to have also been informed (erroneously) that the distance between Alexandria and Syene was 5,000 *stadia*. So all he had to do was to measure the angle of the shadow cast by a tower or pole at noon on the summer solstice in Alexandria, which he determined to be 7°14', and then use simple geometry to work out

---

*The events leading to the official adoption of the so-called *mètre-étalon* was fraught with surveying difficulties and caused several remeasurements, culminating in 1799 with more accurate measurements and the official and legal definition of the meter unit in France. It eventually became obvious, however, that the meridional definition of the meter of 1799 was very slightly short of the true value of the Earth's polar circumference, but the "Official length" was retained regardless and which was declared to be in use "for all time, for all people." Today the meter is universally defined as "the length of the path traveled by light in a vacuum during a time interval of $1/299,792,458$ of a second.

that the arc-distance between Alexandria and Syene was one-fiftieth of full circumference of the planet. A simple multiplication then gave him 250,000 stadia for Earth's circumference. There is much doubt among scholars which stadium Eratosthenes used, but assuming that it was the Olympic Stadium (of 176.4 meters), then his measurement for Earth's circumference comes to 44,100 kilometers, making it some 10 percent greater than the actual value of 40,075 kilometers at the equator. The data that Eratosthenes used were clearly not very accurate, but the method he used was not very different from the one used by the French of 1793. The true distance from Alexandria to Syene is in fact 4,744 stadia (837 kilometers), and those two cities are not exactly on the same longitude: Alexandria is 29°52′ E, whereas Syene is 32°53′ E. Furthermore, due to a phenomenon known as the obliquity of the ecliptic, Syene was not exactly on the Tropic of Cancer in the third century BC, but some twenty-three kilometers to the north of it, so that the noon sun at summer solstice was not exactly directly overhead (i.e., at zenith). This had occurred in the distant past, roughly around 3000 BC.[44]

Could it be that Eratosthenes simply used data kept in the archives of the Great Library of Alexandria? And could the Greek commentators have allocated the discovery of Earth's spherical shape and size to Eratosthenes to glorify one of their own? Is it possible that we have here a historical case of plagiarism?

One of the first modern scholars to suggest this was Edme-François Jomard, the eminent geographer who had been with Napoleon Bonaparte during the 1798–1801 Egypt expedition. Jomard had been hugely impressed with the architecture and art of the ancient Egyptians, and especially their advanced knowledge of land surveying and geodesy, and he became convinced that the Egyptians had known of the curvature of Earth and had also accurately calculated its circumference long before Eratosthenes. This is what Jomard wrote on this issue:

> Let us consider the Greeks in the era of Thales and Pythagoras, still plunged in an almost gross ignorance and suddenly proud to be in possession of the sciences with which until then they had been unfamiliar. The Egyptians, on the contrary, a people isolated and

ancient, worn by long prosperity, communicating with reserve a small part of their knowledge to studious visitors. . . . The petty thefts by the Greeks could not have been discovered in their own country; in Egypt these thefts were neither presumed nor prevented. How wonderfully Greek historians have concealed almost all the sources which they had drawn![45]

During his stay in Egypt, Jomard had the opportunity to measure ancient roads, which he then compared with the records found in the works of classical authors such as Diodorus and Herodotus who sojourned in Egypt. To his surprise, Jomard found them to be "very exact." He challenged his colleagues by asking them to explain "how else these measurements reported by Diodorus and Herodotus could be as accurate as they are if the Egyptians had not possessed, as Clement of Alexandria reports, a detailed chorography, [or] if they did not have maps on which the distances were figured exactly? The distances one finds in these authors' works are not of the traveled routes; rather they are straight-line measurements [and] they would have had to measure from bird's eye view. How could the Egyptians have known these without the help of either maps or trigonometric observations?"[46]

The same conclusions as Jomard's were also reached by Laplace, who, after studying the various commentaries by Greek authors on

Fig. 11.19.
Edme-François Jomard

Fig. 11.20.
R. A. Schwaller de Lubicz

Eratosthenes, concluded, "It would lead us to believe that this astronomer (Eratosthenes) had only reproduced an ancient measure of the Earth that had been executed with great skill and whose origin has been lost."[47]

The same was also pointed out in 1957 by mathematician and symbolist R. A. Schwaller de Lubicz (1887–1961), who wrote, "The majority of scholars who have studied the subject think that since Eratosthenes was the director of the Library of Alexandria, he was able to look at all sorts of documents and thus had used measurements established before him, in view of the perfection of the Egyptian cadastral survey."[48]

According to Peter Tompkins, author of the *Secrets of the Great Pyramid*, "Jomard found that several Greek authors reported that the perimeter of the base of the [Great] Pyramid was intended to measure half a minute of longitude."[49]

Not being someone to take comments like this on face value, I decided to consult the works of Jomard to find out what he had written about classical authors who had referenced the Great Pyramid. I found this:

> It results from all that precedes [of classical authors] that the perimeter of the Great Pyramid is half-a-minute of the terrestrial degree, by that I mean the actual degree of Egypt . . . [also] on the one hand,

there is the testimony of a Greek author claiming that the Egyptians were the first to measure the Earth, and on the other hand two other authorities irrecusably, and that nothing can alter, seem aware of this fact; that is, the absolute value of the terrestrial degree and the principal dimensions of the Great Pyramid.[50]

Jomard was a very meticulous scholar and a very accomplished geographer. Like many erudite scholars of his epoch, he was conversant with classic authors—Greek, Roman, and Arab—especially those who had written on geography and geodesy in relation to the Great Pyramid. The excellent work Jomard had undertaken in Egypt had so impressed his colleagues at the Academie Française that they appointed him as one of the main collaborators for the multivolume *Description de l'Egypte,* to which Jomard contributed 157 memoires and articles. Jomard was also the founder of the Société de Geographie and the Société d'Ethnographie Américaine et Orientale and held the title of *académicien exemplaire.* He also had been president of the prestigious Académie des Inscriptions et Belles-Lettres in 1838 and in 1853.[51]

In other words, Jomard knew what he was talking about when it came to geography and geodesy. Yet his studies on the Great Pyramid have been largely ignored by modern Egyptologists.

Let us take a closer look at all this.

Fig. 11.21.
Peter Tompkins;
photo courtesy of
Arianna Mendo

A REVIEW

As we have seen earlier, it is generally agreed that the unit of measurement used by the designer of the Great Pyramid was the royal cubit, originally derived by Newton as equivalent to 1.719 British feet, or 20.628 British inches. This value converts to 0.5236 meter. Egyptologists ascertained that the royal cubit was divided into seven palms, or twenty-eight fingers, and that the royal cubit itself was derived from the approximate measure of the part of the human arm measured from the tip of the fingers to the elbow.

It is a mathematical fact that a circle with a diameter of one unit produces a circumference of six equal arcs of 0.5236 (3.14159 ÷ 6). It is also a fact that if the diameter is taken as one meter, each of the six arcs will be 0.5236 meter, thus exactly one royal cubit.

The implication, as impossible as it may seem *historically,* is that there is a direct relationship between the royal cubit, the circle, the hexagon, and the modern meter. As I have noted earlier, to know these relationships the designer of the Great Pyramid would, by necessity, have been aware of the meter unit, derived from a precise knowledge of the circumference of Earth measured at the equator! However, the

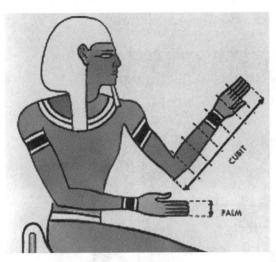

*Fig. 11.22. The relationship between the palm and the cubit
in ancient Egyptian measurement*

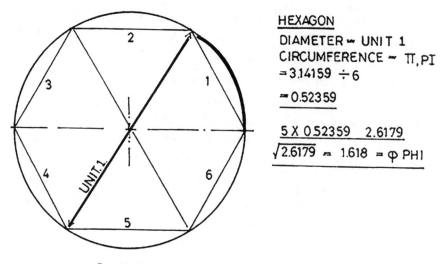

HEXAGON

DIAMETER ~ UNIT 1

CIRCUMFERENCE ~ π, PI

$= 3.14159 \div 6$

$= 0.52359$

$\dfrac{5 \times 0.52359 \quad 2.6179}{\sqrt{2.6179} \approx 1.618 = \varphi \text{ PHI}}$

Fig. 11.23. Circle with a diameter of one meter;
circumference divided by six equal arcs is one royal cubit

meter unit, as we have already seen, was obtained millennia later by French geographers in 1793 who accurately measured the arc-distance from the equator to the North Pole and then divided this distance by ten million.

The controversial claim that the ancient Egyptian knew the shape and dimensions of the planet is not new. We have already seen that it had been postulated in 1799 by Jomard and Laplace, both of whom were also convinced that the Egyptians had known of these geodetic facts long before Eratosthenes. Jomard estimated that the arc-length of a geographical degree at the mean latitude of Egypt, 27°40' N, was 110,828 meters. This meant that one minute of arc was 1,847.13 meters (110,828 ÷ 60 = 1,847.13). Jomard was aware that certain Greek scholars had been informed by ancient Egyptian priests that the height of the Great pyramid was one stadium, thought to be $^{1}/_{600}$ of a geographical degree. So Jomard simply divided 110,828 meters by 600 to get 184.713 meters. To his surprise, this value was almost exactly the length of the apothem of the Great Pyramid, which he had calculated to be 184.722 meters.[52]

Jomard then measured the base side of the pyramid and found it to be 230.902 meters, which gave a perimeter for the square base of 923.60 meters (230.902 × 4). He quickly realized that twice this value (923.6 × 2) was 1,847.2 meters, thus uncannily similar to the value he had obtained for one minute of arc at the latitude of 27°40' N. He thus felt compelled to conclude that whoever it was who had designed the Great Pyramid must have known the dimensions of the planet.[53]

Unfortunately, Jomard, like Piazzi Smyth a century or so after him, had used measurements of the Great Pyramid that were in error. The 1881 survey by Petrie proved conclusively that the designed base side of the Great Pyramid was exactly 440 royal cubits (i.e., 230.379 meters; 440 × 0.52359), which gives a perimeter for the square base of 921.518 meters.[54]

Jomard's value for the apothem of the Great Pyramid of 184.722 meters was also wrong. The exact value is, in fact, 186.50 meters. Nevertheless, Jomard, like Piazza Smyth after him, remained convinced throughout his life that that the Great Pyramid incorporated geodetic measurements. And although the measurements used were misleading, *his strong hunch was, in fact, correct.*

Let us see why.

Modern geographers have established that one degree measured at the equator is 110,574.27 meters. Thus, one minute of arc at the equator is 1,842.90 kilometers (which is slightly different from Jomard's calculation of 1,847.13 meters).[55]

Twice the base perimeter of the Great Pyramid is 1,843.06 meters (2 × 921.53), and thus almost exactly one minute of arc at the equator. The value of 1,843.06 meters, oddly enough, also bears a direct relationship to the nautical mile at the equator. The nautical mile is defined as follows: "The nautical mile is the length of one minute of arc of the meridian, in the latitude where the ship is. The length of the minute of arc varies within certain limits according to the latitude."[56]

Also, by definition, the old (admiralty) nautical mile is 1,000 fathoms. One fathom is 6 British feet, and 1 British foot is 0.3048 meter, thus giving an old (admiralty) nautical mile of 1,828.80 meters. But, as I have noted, the length of one minute of arc varies according to the latitude where it is measured. It has been calculated that one arc minute at the equator will increase by a factor of about 1.0077 as we move down the latitudes from pole to equator, thus giving a value of 1,842.90 meters. This value is extremely close indeed to 1,843.06 meters, which is twice the base perimeter of the Great Pyramid—the difference being only 0.000086 percent! To put it another way, *half of one minute of arc measured at the latitude of the equator is virtually the same as the perimeter of the base of the Great Pyramid.* The perimeter of the base is 1,760 royal cubits, so that the circumference of Earth at the equator would be 2 × 1,760 × 60 × 360 = 76,032,000 royal cubits = 39,810,355 meters—a value than is only 0.006 percent less than the actual measure of 40,075,000 meters!

I must at this stage emphasize that any relationship among the principal dimensions of the Great Pyramid, one minute of arc measured at the equator, the British fathom, the nautical mile, and finally the modern meter are, to put it bluntly, historical aberrations. The Great Pyramid is traditionally dated to circa 2500 BC, the invention of the geographical coordinates is traditionally attributed to Eratosthenes circa 250 BC, the British units of fathom and nautical mile were established in 1617, and the modern meter was derived by the French in 1793! As the old saying goes, all those twains do not meet! And yet we are confronted with these units emerging from the geometrical design and size of the Great Pyramid.

Let us carefully compare the units involved.

1 royal cubit = 0.52359 meter = 1.7178 feet.
1 meter = 3.2894 feet = 1.9098 royal cubits.
Oddly, 1.7178 ÷ 3.2894 = 0.5222.
This is 99.7 percent the numeric of the royal cubit (i.e., 0.52359).
1 foot + 1 royal cubit + 1 meter = 1 + 1.7178 + 3.2894 = 6.00 feet.

And 6 feet are, of course, 1 British fathom! How is it remotely possible that by mixing 1 British foot, 1 royal cubit and 1 meter—effectively mixing *apples, oranges, and pears!*—we get exactly 6 British feet? And how is it possible that when 1 fathom, which is 6 feet, *is taken at the equator,* thus 1,843 meters +/− 0.006 percent (as one minute of arc taken at the equator), we then get twice the base perimeter of the Great Pyramid? "Impossible!" will say historians. But there you have it in numbers that do not lie.

The uncanny interrelationship between these units defies coincidence. Skeptics, of course, will say that this is just playing with numbers and means nothing. Others, less skeptical, will nonetheless point out that the geographical "degree" used by Jomard is based on the *sexagesimal* system (i.e., using base 60 for calculations, whereas the ancient Egyptians used the decimal, a base 10 system). Jomard, however, argued convincingly that the sexagesimal system was actually known and used in ancient Egypt and that only later was it imported into Europe by the Romans.[57]

Jomard correctly showed that from earliest times the Egyptians had used a calendar of twelve months of thirty days, giving a year of 360 divisions (to which they added five epagomenal days). Furthermore, they had also divided the sky landscape into 36 "decans" (6 × 6) equivalent to stellar asterisms or constellations, which strongly implies, if not proves, that they indeed used sexagesimal computations.[58] Do we have a fifth coincidence pigeon here? Reluctantly, yes, I think so. And a very controversial one at that. . . .

Just for measure, let me throw in a very wild card at this stage. I am doing this because there is something about the number 1,843 in all this that has nagged me for a long time. According to Laurence Eaves, the number 1,840 (very close to our mysterious 1,843), or one very close to it, would be a favored one to transmit a message to an alien civilization in the cosmos, because it is close to "the ratio of the mass of the proton to the electron. . . . So if you send . . . 1,840, then the alien civilization would say, right, these people understand science and technology, understand quantum mechanics, so it would really be a nice number to send out to them."[59]

And although the ratio of the mass of the proton to the electron is precisely 1:1,836.152767389, the closeness to the positive integers ratio 1:1,840 is obvious, and this would quickly indicate that the signal originated from a scientific and technologically capable civilization.

Well 1,843, when considered in subatomic size, is also close to 1,836, is it not?

I can now imagine Egyptologists either throwing this book in the rubbish bin in disgust or, as often is the case, resorting to authoritative intimidation and name-calling. Let us take a pause from our investigation and review some examples of this attitude.

DEALING WITH
EGYPTOLOGICAL INTIMIDATION

In 1975 renowned geodesist Irene Fischer, after reviewing Eratosthenes's calculations, concluded that "Eratosthenes determined the size of the Earth" using "Egyptian surveying." But she also added that he used "Greek astronomy."[60]

Fischer, like most other scholars, accepted without really questioning the consensus of Egyptologists that the ancient Egyptians "did not contribute to the history of mathematical astronomy"[61] and that they had "borrowed their knowledge of the signs of the Zodiac, together with much else, from the Greeks."[62] Yet, most ironically, this Egyptological consensus is contradicted by the ancient Greeks themselves! There are a plethora of classical writers and philosophers who adamantly affirm that it was the Greeks who obtained their astronomical knowledge from the ancient Egyptians, and not the other way around! Herodotus (484–425 BC), who spent much time in Egypt, declared, "The Egyptians were the first to discover the solar year. . . . The Egyptians . . . first brought into use the names of the twelve gods [or constellations], which the Greeks adopted from them."[63] The great Plato (ca. 429–347 BC), who studied under the Egyptian priests of Heliopolis, wrote that the Egyptians had observed and studied the stars "for ten thousand years, or so to speak for an infinite time,"[64] and Diodorus of Sicily (90–30 BC) acknowledged that "the disposition of the stars as well as their movements have always been the subject of careful observation among the Egyptian."[65]

There is too the testimony of the high priest of Heliopolis, Manetho of Sebennytos (ca. 250 BC), who informed his Greek patron "that we would be universal scientists if it were given to us to inhabit the sacred land of Egypt."[66] And this is to name but a few.

Yet any student in Egyptology who suggests that the Egyptians practiced astronomy long before the Greeks will be shunned by his peers. Going against consensus in this field of study is seen as high treason! The same, of course, goes for any student deviating from the "tomb, and tomb only" consensus for the Great Pyramid. And no wonder.

Following is a selection of quotes that are warnings for the nonconformist.

EGYPTOLOGIST **Sir William Matthews Flinders Petrie:** "The fantastic theories [about the Great Pyramid], however, are still poured out, and the theorists still assert that the facts correspond to their requirements. It is useless to state the real truth of the matter, as it has no effect on those who are subject to this type of hallucination. They can be but left with the flat earth believers and other such people to whom a theory is dearer than a fact."[67]

EGYPTOLOGIST **Jean Capart (1877–1947):** "With the help of mathematicians—and often mingling with them—mystics have invented what might be called the 'religion of the pyramids.'"[68]

EGYPTOLOGIST **Barbara Mertz:** "Even in modern times when people, one would think, should know better, the Great Pyramid of Giza has proved a fertile field for fantasy. The people who do not know better are the Pyramid mystics, who believe that the Great Pyramid is a gigantic prophecy in stone, built by a group of ancient adepts in magic. Egyptologists sometimes uncharitably refer to this group as 'Pyramidiots,' but the school continues to flourish despite scholarly anathemas."[69]

EGYPTOLOGIST **Vivian Davies:** "The Great Pyramid has this power over people, and in my view it has the power to destroy common sense."[70]

There are also the many angry and insulting outbursts from Zahi Hawass, the former minister of Egyptian antiquities. I only quote one, my favorite, as example: "A group of people [Robert Bauval, Graham Hancock, and John Anthony West] are making an organized campaign. There are some people [Israel] pushing them . . . waging a war against us! . . . I was laughing at their views two years ago. . . . I am writing this article in response to many great authors who wanted me to respond to the Jews' claims and lies that it was they who built the pyramid. Recently they have used the image of the three Giza pyramids [as] a symbol for one Israeli TV station!"[71]

With such intolerance and misinformation (not to say outright lies!), few, if any, within the scholarly community will risk defying the established consensus, especially so with talk about possible extraterrestrial contact. It would be academic suicide. Yet history has shown that many of the important advances occur when someone *does* take the risk and think outside the box. One such person was Schwaller de Lubicz, whom we have already encountered briefly earlier in this chapter.

THE SYMBOLIST MATHEMATICIAN

The son of an eminent pharmacist in Strasbourg, Schwaller de Lubicz was groomed early in the hard sciences of chemistry, physics, and mathematics. He was also much influenced by the then recent scientific discoveries of Max Planck and Albert Einstein and by the then new discoveries in quantum physics, much talked about in the 1920s and 1930s. Schwaller de Lubicz was of the opinion that these discoveries in physics concurred with the cosmological ideologies of the ancients rather than the "mechanisitic" physics of Newton, which saw the universe as some giant complex clockwork. He also developed a deep understanding of symbolism and of harmonics while he was being mentored by modernist painter Emile Matisse. This potent blend of cutting-edge science and art would turn Schwaller de Lubicz into the ideal scholar to understand the multifarious layers of meanings in the art and architecture of the ancient Egyptians.

In 1926, Schwaller de Lubicz married Jeanne Germain, an artist from Normandy who had a deep passion for Eastern theologies and mysticism, especially those of ancient Egypt. Twice married before (with *armateur* George Lamy and with Louis Allainguillaume), Germain, who had adopted the name Isha, was a stunningly beautiful woman of forty-one when she married Schwaller de Lubicz, two years younger. Deeply mystical and articulate, Isha inspired Schwaller de Lubicz to go to Egypt in 1936, taking along with them Isha's two children, Jean Lamy and Lucie Lamy.*

There they set up home at the Winter Palace Hotel in Luxor, where they devoted the next fifteen years to diligently studying the art and architecture of ancient monuments, with particular focus on the temple of Luxor. The result was a booklet by Schwaller de Lubicz, published in 1949, *Le Temple Dans L'Homme* (The Temple in Man), and in 1957 a three-volume opus, *Le Temple de L'Homme* (The Temple of Man). Anyone who has been able to sift through this rather complicated but fascinating thesis will acknowledge that Schwaller de Lubicz had an uncanny ability to extract the deeper layers of symbolism in Egyptian architecture and art and to explain them in the mathematical "language" of nature.[72] While in Egypt, Schwaller de Lubicz formed a group of kindred spirits, which included eminent Egyptologist Alexandre Varille.[73] Together with Varille, Schwaller de Lubicz created the "symbolist approach" to Egyptology. Not unexpectedly, they were hotly opposed by orthodox Egyptologists, especially by the director of the Egyptian Services des Antiquitiés in Cairo, Etiene Drioton, a sturdy Catholic abbot dubbed "one of the most famous Egyptologists of the twentieth century."†

At any rate, in his review of the mathematical design of the Great Pyramid, Schwaller de Lubicz used the royal cubit of 0.5236 meter and soon became convinced, as Jomard and others had before him, that *"the ancient Egyptians were perfectly well acquainted with the meter"*[75] (italics added). Schwaller de Lubicz was also of the opinion that the royal cubit "is the measure that reduces the curve of a circle into a

---

*It is not certain that Isha's son, Jean Lamy, went to Egypt with Schwaller de Lubicz, as I have not be able to confirm this.
†Today the Services des Antiquitiés is known as the Supreme Council of Antiquities and is under the Egyptian Ministry of Antiquities.[74]

straight line," which would much explain why the so-called squaring of the circle was chosen for the base of the Great Pyramid.[76] According to Schwaller de Lubicz:

> It so happens that the Ancients knew the actual meter, which is only slightly different from our first international meter. They arrived at this by a special method. As for the equatorial circumference of the Earth (which we accept today as 40 million meters) they measured it by the *fathom*, which we find to be the basis of the measurement for the temple of Luxor. The fathom is the measure of circumference. It has a numerical relationship with the (royal) cubit. . . . *The royal cubit implies a measure of the meter, and the fathom, which is a geodetic measure, implies knowledge of the circumference of the globe.*[77] (italics added)

We have already reviewed the uncanny connection among the nautical mile, the fathom, and the royal cubit and how their application in the design of the Great Pyramid "implies knowledge of the circumference of the globe." We have also seen how one minute of arc at the equator is 1,842.9 meters. But here is something else even more intriguing: my brother, Jean-Paul, noted a connection with the mysterious concavity of the Great Pyramid: 1,842.9 meters divided by 1,000 is 1.8429 meters (i.e. one fathom at the equator, which can be expressed as 2 × 0.92145 meter).

Now, 0.92145 meter is, as we have previously seen, practically the same as the depth of the concavity of 0.92 meter as measured by Pochan in the 1930s! In consideration of how the inclusion of such a concavity would have complicated the design and construction of the monument, Jean-Paul had a hunch that it signaled something very profound in the overall scheme. But what? His architectural instincts, gained from years of design experience, told him that something was amiss, a "secret in plain sight," so to speak.

"I kept looking at the Great Pyramid," he hinted, "and I felt sure that there was something that was there in plain sight and yet, paradoxically, couldn't be seen."

I had no idea what he meant. I had visited the Great Pyramid hundreds of times; I had watched it day and night for three years from the window of my office;* I had climb to its top on several occasions and had even spent some time alone inside it. I knew this monument inside out. What was there in plain sight that couldn't be seen?

THE VIRTUAL SPACE AT
THE TOP OF THE PYRAMID

Early in 2016, Jean-Paul came to visit me in my office. We live in the same housing compound in southern Spain. He has been here since 1966, and I moved here permanently in 2008, although I have been coming to visit him since 1968. Today, judging from the expression on his face, I could tell he had something exciting to tell me. He pulled up a chair facing my writing desk.

"What if I could show you that on the Great Pyramid is a globe that has a diameter of *one meter accurate to three decimal points*?" Jean-Paul asked.

"And where is this globe?" I returned the question. "I've explored the Great Pyramid dozens of times, and I have never seen such a globe!"

"You cannot see it. No one can. This is because this globe cannot be seen with the eyes; it can only be *seen* with the mind," he replied, then added sarcastically with a grin, "the same way you 'see' subatomic particles when you look at things!"

To any experienced architect, it was obvious that the designer of the Great Pyramid had made use of geometrical figures such as right-angle triangles, circles, and polygons. Using such basic figures, Jean-Paul explained how he had applied them to work out the *designed* depth for the mysterious concavity, which, as we have seen earlier, was 0.9215 meter, extremely close to Pochan's 0.92 meter. Using this designed depth, Jean-Paul then reverse-engineered the exterior shape of the pyramid, which resulted in a *truncated pyramid with a virtual space at the top*.

---

*I lived on the fourth floor of an apartment block opposite the Great Pyramid from 2005 to 2008.

Fig. 11.24. Truncated top of the Great Pyramid

Remembering the ideas of Pochan and Pérez-Sánchez—and also of Osborn (see appendix 3)—that the Great Pyramid had a sphere at the top, Jean-Paul wondered if such a sphere or globe could be fitted into the virtual space he had calculated. He solicited the expertise of colleagues who could work out the very complex geometry using specialized design software. The result was a sphere with a diameter of 1.911 royal cubits. Jean-Paul then converted this value into meter units (1.911 × 0.523598) and obtained precisely the length of one meter, *accurate to three decimal places*! (See appendix 1.) I must confess that I was stunned! For we now had, I strongly sensed, the sixth coincidence pigeon, and what a fat pigeon it was! I now wondered how many more there still were to discover.

CORRIDORS, GALLERY, CHAMBERS, AND SHAFTS

So far we have dealt with the external design of the Great Pyramid. But much of its mystery is locked in the design of its interior.

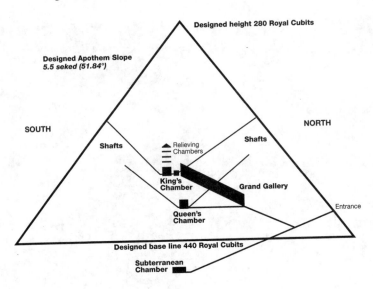

Fig. 11.25. The interior of the Great Pyramid

The Great Pyramid has a complex internal system of corridors and chambers that is unique among all other pyramids in Egypt or, for that matter, in the whole world. The main entrance is in the north face, a design feature clearly intended to direct visitors upward toward the south. This entrance is about 16.97 meters above the base level and offset from the north–south centerline of the pyramid by 7.29 meters.*

From the entrance starts the low rectangular Descending Passage of 1.2 × 1.05 meters and angled at about 26.5°. The Descending Passage cuts at one point through the living rock and runs for some 105 meters with gun-barrel precision to reach the Subterranean Chamber some 30 meters below the baseline of the pyramid. The Subterranean Chamber is roughly carved out of the living rock; it is about 8.5 meters long, 14 meters wide, and 3.9 meters high.

At some 28 meters from the main entrance of the pyramid is a "closed" access on the ceiling of the Descending Passage that is blocked by three granite plugs that total 10 meters in length.

---

*All measurements given here are taken from Petrie's 1881 survey.

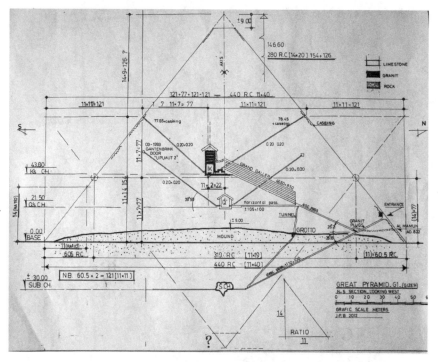

Fig. 11.26. Jean-Paul Bauval's preliminary "blueprint" of the Great Pyramid, 2012

*Fig. 11.27.
Photographer
Joanne Cunningham
at the original
entrance of the
Great Pyramid,
2007*

Fig. 11.28. The Descending Passage, Great Pyramid

A

B

Fig. 11.29. (A) Granite plugs at the bottom of the Descending Passage of the Great Pyramid, circa 1930 and (B) modern view of granite plugs

From all accounts, the main entrance of the Great Pyramid was hidden by casing blocks until the ninth century AD, when the Abbasid caliph Al Ma'mun (AD 786–833) had his workers cut a tunnel from the centerline of the north face of the monument. The Arab workers fortuitously swerved the tunnel eastward and hit upon the Ascending Passage just above the granite plugs. It was thus that the internal system of the pyramid was first discovered. From the inside of the granite plugs is considered the start the Ascending Passage. It is also rectangular in its cross section, measuring 1.09 × 1.0 meters, and is sloped upward at about 26.5°. It is 39.3 meters long and culminates at the foot of the Grand Gallery.

The Grand Gallery has corbeled side walls 8.7 meters high and continues upward at 26.5° for 47.8 meters. At the lower level of the Grand Gallery starts the Horizontal Passage, which runs southward some 39 meters to reach what is known as the Queen's Chamber. The (rather rough) floor of this chamber is 21.7 meters above the base of the pyramid and measures 5.23 × 5.75 meters (10 × 11 royal cubits). The chamber has a pitched ceiling whose pointed apex is 6.18 meters above the floor. It also has a curious high corbeled niche cut into the east wall, thought to have perhaps housed a statue. At the top end of the Grand Gallery starts a short horizontal passage leading into an antechamber and finally into what is known as the King's Chamber, the holy of holies of all ancient monuments in the world.

Unlike everything else of the Great Pyramid, which is made from limestone blocks obtained from local quarries,* the King's Chamber is made entirely from red-gray granite blocks brought from Aswan, some 700 kilometers south of Giza. The chamber floor is a rectangle 5.24 × 10.47 meters (10 × 20 royal cubits), and its flat ceiling is 5.85 meters high. The blocks of the floor and walls are on average 30 tons each, and the nine massive monolithic granite beams that make up the ceiling are on average 70 tons each. As if that was not impressive enough, above the King's Chamber are low rectangular cavities called

---

*The core blocks of the monument are limestone taken from adjacent quarries in the Giza necropolis, whereas the casing stones were of harder limestone taken from the Tura hill quarries on the east side of the Nile.

A

B

Fig. 11.30. (A) *The Queen's Chamber and* (B) *the King's Chamber*

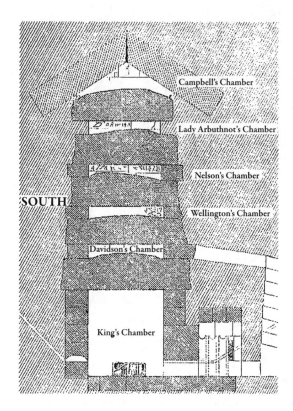

*Fig. 11.31. The
Relieving Chambers
discovered by
Howard-Vyse in
1837*

the Relieving Chambers, the floors of which are also made from massive monolithic granite beams, totaling forty-three with the nine of the King's Chamber ceiling.

The Relieving Chambers were completely hermetically sealed even before the pyramid was fully completed. They were only reopened in 1837 by Howard-Vyse, who used gunpowder to blast his way into them one by one. The floors and ceilings of the first four Relieving Chambers are made of massive granite beams, kept rough for the floor but ground flat for the ceiling. The fifth Relieving Chamber has a rough granite floor, but the ceiling is gable-shaped with massive limestone rafters. Actually, the term *relieving chamber* is a misnomer, since no one knows the real purpose of these mysterious empty spaces or, for that matter, the whole internal system of the Great Pyramid. I have already mentioned that in the last four of the Relieving Chambers was found graffiti crudely painted in red ochre. There are, of course, numerous theories to consider, but none have produced a consensus, even among Egyptologists.

Every small detail in the design of the Great Pyramid is, of course, extremely important. But I have refrained from discussing too many here so as to keep the investigation focused on the main issues. However, readers who do wish to review these small details can refer to Petrie's survey, available online.[78] My intention is to concentrate on the King's Chamber and Queen's Chamber, especially the recent explorations of the star shafts that emanate from them.

Reaching the King's Chamber after the long and arduous climb up the Ascending Passage and the Grand Gallery will engender a mixed sense of relief, awe, marvel, and, most of all, otherworldliness. You have now reached the epicenter of the occult and mystical world. This is the place where it was once believed that physical matter became unphysical spirit and where souls of the dead were sent to the stars. No matter how controlled and sensible you try to be in here, it is impossible not to feel your mind shifting from rational mode to metaphysical mode. Because in here you are in the presence of the unknown and the mysterious personified. Here your normal sense of reality withers away, and you are enveloped in the fantastic, the strange, the completely unfamiliar. For a brief moment—or an eternity, it seems to some—everything stops, even the beat of your heart. There is no "time" in here, no sense of life or death, for such mundane thoughts and perceptions have no meaning in this darkened and unversed ambiance. You might even feel in another dimension of existence. And yet too there is a comforting feeling of belonging. For here your soul, although somewhat shaken and bewildered by the mysterious, also feels . . . at home.

The walls and ceiling of the King's Chamber are completely bare, bereft of decorations or inscriptions. The only features that cut the starkness of this chamber are two small rectangular cuts on the north and south walls and the empty granite coffer at the west side of the chamber. "The King's Chamber," wrote Petrie, "was more completely measured than any other part of the Pyramid; the distances of the walls apart, their verticality in each corner, the course heights, and the levels were completely observed."[79]

Petrie found the rectangular floor to be exactly 206.29 × 412.11 British inches (5.24 × 10.47 meters). As for the height of the ceiling, he obtained a value of 230.09 inches (i.e., 5.844 meters). When these measurements are converted into royal cubits, the result is as follows:

Length of chamber (east–west) = 20 royal cubits
Width of chamber (north–south) = 10 royal cubits
Height of chamber = 11.16 royal cubits.

We may wonder why the height of the chamber is not a whole number in royal cubits. The answer again seems to be in the clever geometrical design. For the diagonal lines linking the bottom corners with the top corners of the chamber measure exactly 25 royal cubits and thus create a 3:4:5 right-angle triangle. This type of triangle, where all sides are sequential integers, is known as a Pythagorian triple.

The coffer is the only loose artifact found in the chamber and, indeed, inside the whole pyramid. Not surprisingly, it has been the subject of much speculation and intrigue. As far as can be ascertained, it was found completely empty, with absolutely no trace of anything

Fig. 11.32. The empty coffer in the King's Chamber

ever having been in it. It has no inscriptions or decorations, except for small grooves and three small holes on the upper edge, indicating that it might have had a lid, although no fragments of a lid have been found. Its upper-southeast corner is badly damaged due to modern visitors who disrespectfully chipped pieces to take away as souvenirs. It is unsure whether the coffer served as a coffin or whether it had another function. In any case, here is how Petrie described it:

> The coffer in the King's Chamber is of the usual form of the earliest Egyptian sarcophagi, an approximately flat-sided box of red granite. It has the usual under-cut groove to hold the edge of a lid along the inside of the N., E., and S. sides; the W. side being cut away as low as the groove for the lid to slide over it; and having three pinholes cut in it for the pins to fall out of similar holes in the lid, when the lid was put on. It is not finely wrought, and cannot in this respect rival the coffer in the Second Pyramid.[80]

- The outer dimensions of the coffer are: length, 2.28 meters; width, 0.98 meter; height, 1.05 meters.
- The inside dimensions of the coffer are: length, 1.98 meters; width, 0.677 meter; depth, 0.88 meters.*

The coffer was certainly placed in the King's Chamber before the ceiling was closed with the giant monolithic granite beams; this is known because its width is a fraction larger than the entrance of the chamber, and thus it could not have come through the internal system of passages. Modern machinists have often remarked how difficult it would have been to make this coffer out of a monolithic block of granite with rudimentary copper tools. Petrie suggested that a "jeweled bronze saw . . . nine feet long" and also a diamond-tipped drill were used. However, in 1984, Christopher Dunn, an American machinist

---

*My friend Alan Green, the British musician and author, believes that there is a mathematical relationship between the volume of the coffer and that of the King's Chamber, which, oddly, produces a numerical value that is very close to the reciprocal of the fine-structure constant 137.03. Green intends to publish his findings soon.

and toolmaker with extensive experience in stonecutting, published an article in which he convincingly argued that the speed of rotation needed to fashion a monolithic chunk of granite in the form of a coffer would not be possible by hand tools and would require a machine-operated drill![81]

Originally from Manchester, England, Dunn was recruited in 1969 by an aerospace manufacturing company in the United States, where he has lived and worked ever since. For forty years Dunn worked at every level of high-tech manufacturing, from machinist, toolmaker, programmer, and operator of high-power industrial lasers to project engineer and laser operations manager. He also was a human resources director for a Midwest aerospace manufacturer. Over the years Dunn has investigated many ancient sites in Egypt and also around the world, and he has become convinced that advanced machine-operated tools for cutting hard stones such as granite were used in Egypt and elsewhere in ancient times.[82] Dunn has published several books on this topic, including one in 1998 in which he postulated that the Great Pyramid was an acoustical "power plant" to generate clean energy.[83] As to be expected, much controversy surrounds such claims, and Dunn suffered the inevitable deleterious treatment from Egyptologists and archaeologists. Although I do not subscribe to Dunn's notion of a "power plant," many of his findings concerning the possible use of advanced technology in ancient Egypt are definitely worthy of serious consideration.

But no matter how the monolithic granite blocks were cut and fashioned or, indeed, how the whole Great Pyramid was built, the undeniable fact that it is still there and almost intact after more than four millennia, and perhaps even much longer, is in itself confirmation of the resolute determination of its creators to ensure that it would survive the ravages of time and vandalism so that it would reach . . . who? Us? Why? How can we understand this strange "book in stone"?

PRIME NUMBERS

In the course of the years 1992 and 1993, Rudolf Gantenbrink employed state-of-the-art robotic technology to undertake a daring exploration of the shafts of the King's and Queen's Chambers in the Great Pyramid. Using his own resources and finances, Gantenbrink constructed a small mechanized vehicle, which he called Upuaut II ("Opener of the Way" in ancient Egyptian), and equipped it with a laser that could very accurately measure angles and distances. The crowning moment of the exploration, however, was the unexpected discovery of a small "door" at the end of the southern shaft of the Queen's Chamber.

In early March 1993, a few weeks before Gantenbrink made his historic discovery on the twenty-second day of that month, an introduction had been arranged for me by Sir I. E. S. Edwards to see Rainer Stadelmann, Ph.D., the director of the German Archaeological Institute in Cairo, under whose aegis Gantenbrink was working in the Great Pyramid. Stadelmann seemed at first reluctant for me to see Gantenbrink, claiming that the latter was away in Germany and would not be back for three days. I nonetheless insisted, and a meeting was arranged at the Movenpick Hotel for March 6.[84] Being that I was the

Fig. 11.33. Robert Bauval and Rudolf Gantenbrink in Munich, 1993

discoverer of the stellar alignment of the shafts of the Queen's Chamber in 1990,[85] it was inevitable that our lives would become entangled with the immensely controversial politics that usually follow such important archaeological discoveries.*

Having almost unlimited access to the Great Pyramid for nearly two years, Gantenbrink was able to use his sophisticated equipment "to re-survey certain important basic points within the corridor chamber system" because, as he was to write later, he had noticed that several measurements that he "required to produce a digital computer model were incomplete or wrong and a re-survey was therefore required." His resurvey was thus "a complete scientific report about the investigation of what are called air shafts inside the Great Pyramid of Cheops, and all related additional information. It includes a set of 4 extremely detailed CAD drawings, 27 explanatory graphics and 61 original photos."[86]

Gantenbrink made available online a three-dimensional model of the Great Pyramid on the AUTO-CAD system. In this design he had incorporated data from Petrie's 1881–1882 survey, the 1924 survey of Morton Edgar and John Edgar, the 1965 survey of Maragioglio and Rinaldi, and also his own resurvey of 1992–1993, which he deemed "the best and most exact." Gantenbrink explained his design approach as follows:

> It is interesting that the shifting of the lower construction point of the [King's Chamber] shafts from the pyramid axis amounts to exactly 22 cubits, i.e., 2 × 11 cubits. This shift resulted in quite substantial problems during execution of the works, because the exit points clearly had to lie at equal height. For this, not only had two angles to be determined but so had the ratio of the two angles to each other and to the axis of the pyramid, in order for them to be precisely executed structurally. A grid of 11 × 11 cubits was placed above the pyramid. The grid therefore corresponds to a scale of 1:40 referred to the pyramid base. This grid is irrelevant to the height of

---

*Readers wanting to know more about these events are invited to refer to chapter 11 of my book *Secret Chamber Revisited*.

the pyramid. In actual fact, the Cheops grid, as I ascertained during my ongoing work, is not square but rectangular, in a ratio of 7 to 11 cubits, i.e., one 40th of the height to one 40th of the base. We are using the square grid here only to clarify the design process more effectively. The right northern shaft is clearly designed in a ratio of 11:7 grid points and the left southern one in a square ratio of 7:7 grid points. By reversing the ratio of 11:7 to 7:11, I obtained the counter-angle in the diagonal, which lies at 90° to the northern shaft. The angle, the counter-angle and the square counter-ratio can therefore be geometrically determined.

The above approach enabled Gantenbrink to prove that the ancient designer of the Great Pyramid had established the various junction points in the design of the interior system at multiples of 11 and also of 7 royal cubits. The numbers 11 and 7 are prime numbers, the fourth and fifth in the sequence. The number 5 is also a prime number, the

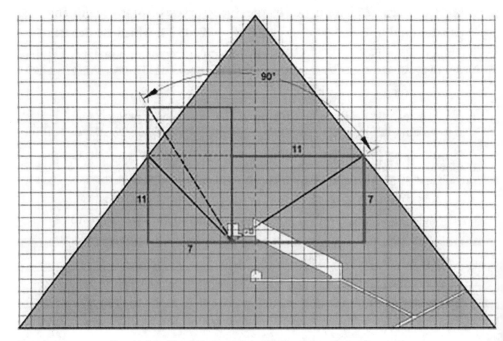

Fig. 11.34. The "Gantenbrink Grid" of the Great Pyramid; courtesy of R. Gantenbrink

third in the sequence. The number 3 is also a prime number, the second in the sequence. Finally, 2 is the first prime number. Clearly there is here an invitation to consider prime numbers, especially 7 and 11. Why?

BLUEPRINT

In a blueprint* of the pyramid using a square grid of 11 × 11 royal cubits, Gantenbrink also demonstrated that "the upper air shafts mark the commencement of [the] interior design." The "upper air shafts" are those of the King's Chamber. When these are "projected" below the floor of the King's Chamber, they will intersect at a point on the grid 22 royal cubits from the central axis of the pyramid and 77 royal cubits above the baseline. It does not take much to realize that 22 is a prime factorization, 11 × 2, and 77 is a prime factorization, 11 × 7. Furthermore, $2 \times 7/11 = 2 \times 0.6363636363 \ldots = 1.272727272727 \ldots$, which is the tangent of the angle 51.84°, *the apothem angle of the Great Pyramid.* I have already said that Egyptologists believe that this angle was derived by the ancient designers using the seked method. The seked in this case being 5.5 seked, which, in palms, is $28/22 = (2 \times 7)/11 = 2 \times 0.63636363 \ldots = 1.27272727 \ldots$ Oddly, in these calculations we get decimal fractions with two numbers that are running in sequence to infinity, such as $0.2727272727 \ldots$ and $0.6363636363 \ldots$ In fact, if you divide *any* number by 11 (except those full numbers that are multiples of 11), you get the same curious result of the decimal fraction showing two numbers that are repeated ad infinitum. For example, $23 \div 11 = 2.0909090909 \ldots$, $47 \div 11 = 4.27272727272 \ldots$, $857 \div 11 = 77.9090909090909 \ldots$, $1843 \div 11 = 167.545454545454 \ldots$, and so on.

Again, I am not sure what to make of this, but the impression I distinctly get is that there seems to be some sort of coded "message" in this mathematical design that has to do mostly with the prime number 11. My hunch is that the prime factorization of the designed base side of

---

*The term *blueprint* comes from the blue paper once used by architects to make copies of their drawings on large sheets of photographic paper. The term is generically used to signify a plan.

440 royal cubits has a coded meaning associated with the number 11. For example, the prime factorization of 440 is 2 × 2 × 2 × 5 × **11**. Another appearance of the number 11 is in the Queen's Chamber's floor plan, which is **11** × 10 royal cubits. There are also three markings in red ochre on the floor of the small space behind the "Gantenbrink door" at the end of the southern shaft of the Queen's Chamber, which, according to Luca Miatello, who is a specialist in ancient Egyptian mathematics, are 1, 20, and 100, thus totaling 121 = **11** × **11**.[87]

The integer 121 "prime factorizes" to 11 × 11 and is thus similar to the 11 × 11 grid that Gantenbrink superimposed on the Great Pyramid to mark the nodes of the interior system. So whoever designed the Great Pyramid was expressing himself, herself, or itself with prime numbers, with prime 11 clearly being the favored one.

Let us now look more closely at the shafts shooting out from the King's Chamber. According to Gantenbrink, "In our measuring campaigns in 1992, I attached particular value to measuring the exit points of the upper airshafts. . . . I could already clearly see that these exit points lay at the same height."[88]

The points of exit of these shafts are on the 103rd course of masonry of the Great Pyramid, and 103 is a prime number, the twenty-sixth in the prime sequence. The exit is 154 royal cubits above ground level. The integer 154, when divided by prime 11, gives 14, and "prime factorizes" as 2 × 7 × 11. Also, 154 divided by prime 7 gives 22, which in turn "prime factorizes" as 2 × 11. Furthermore, 14 × 3.142 (π) = 43.99, a fraction away from 44, which is 4 × 11. And 44 × 10 = 440, which is numerically the same as the base side of the Great Pyramid expressed in royal cubits. A question surely wants to be asked: Did the ancient designer use a coding system based on prime numbers, their position in the prime sequence, and prime factorization?

If so, then what for? . . .

CONTACT?

In the 1997 movie *Contact,* based on Carl Sagan's 1985 eponymous novel, a radio message from an extraterrestrial source is received in the frequency 4.4623 gigahertz. SETI scientist Eleanor Arroway immediately realizes that this number is "hydrogen times pi." She also deduces that the "message" was emitted from the star Vega in the constellation Lyra. The use of frequency 4.4623 gigahertz in the movie was, in fact, borrowed from Australian physicist David Blair, who devised for Parkes Radio Observatory what is known as the "magic frequency" by taking the product of two universally known constants, the hydrogen line frequency of 1420.40575 megahertz multiplied by 3.14159 (π), giving a frequency of 4.464132 gigahertz, very slightly different from 4.4623 gigahertz used in the movie.[89]

We have seen how the Kepler spacecraft's photometer telescope is directed at the Cygnus-Lyra region, although this telescope was not yet in operation when the movie was made. At any rate, also in the movie, Arroway realized that the signal is initially in a sequence of prime numbers starting with the first prime, 2, and abruptly ending with the twenty-seventh prime, 101, confirming that the signal must be artificial and intelligent. In Sagan's book, however, the sequence of primes stops at prime 261. Also in the book, Arroway is prompted by the extraterrestrials to devise a computer program to calculate the decimal digits of pi (π) to record lengths and in different bases. She then finds that when base 11 is used, a special pattern of zeros and ones emerges when the decimal digit reaches 10^{20} (10 to the power of 20). Furthermore, this special pattern of zeros and ones is a long string that "factorizes" with eleven prime numbers. Interestingly, the abrupt stopping of the message at prime 101 in the movie is synchronistically curious if we think of the Great Pyramid, because it is known that 101 is what is known as a *chen prime* with prime 103.* If we divide prime 103 by prime 101, we get the curious sequential decimal series 1.0198019801980. . . . In this respect we recall how prime 103 is defined by the point of exit of the shafts. I am definitely not suggesting, of course, that there is a connection between these shafts and the movie *Contact* but merely pointing out the bizarre synchronicities involved.

---

*A prime number is considered a chen prime if adding 2 to it gives another prime number. For example, prime 5 is a chen prime because 5 + 2 = 7.

STAR SHAFTS

Because Gantenbrink discovered that the shafts of the King's Chamber "mark the commencement of [the] interior design" of the pyramid, then it follows that the location of the chamber was also determined by these shafts and the angles at which they rise toward the outside of the monument. It can be seen at a glance that the King's Chamber is *not* positioned in the axial center of the pyramid but rather displaced southward. This displacement is 21 royal cubits from the centerline of the pyramid. Now, 21 royal cubits is the product of two primes: 3 and 7. The prime 5 is between 3 and 7. Is it then a coincidence that 21 royal cubits converts to 11 meters, *the fifth prime in the series?* Twenty-one royal cubits are precisely 10.99 meters, which is almost exactly 11.[90]

There has been much debate among Egyptologists about the function of these mysterious shafts. It was once thought that they were for ventilation, but this idea has long been abandoned in favor of a symbolic function that is explained in the desired astral ascension for the soul of the king, as specified in the ancient Pyramid Texts.

Egyptologists agree that the Pyramid Texts present us with both a solar and a stellar cosmology. The most recent translation and interpretation of the Pyramid Texts is by James P. Allen, who notes that "echoes of this stellar destiny appear throughout the Pyramid Texts."[91] Allen further explains that "the Pyramid Texts are largely concerned with the deceased's relationship to two gods, Osiris and the sun. Egyptologists once considered these two themes as independent views of the afterlife that had become fused in the Pyramid Texts, but more recent research has shown that both belong to a single concept of the deceased's existence after death—a view of the afterlife that remained remarkably consistent throughout ancient Egyptian history. . . . In these texts the deceased is addressed not only by name *but as Osiris himself*"[92] (italics added).

It is well established that in the cosmology of the ancient Egyptians, Osiris is identified with the constellation of Orion or specifically Orion's belt. This identification is indeed vividly described in the Pyramid Texts. Following are some examples.

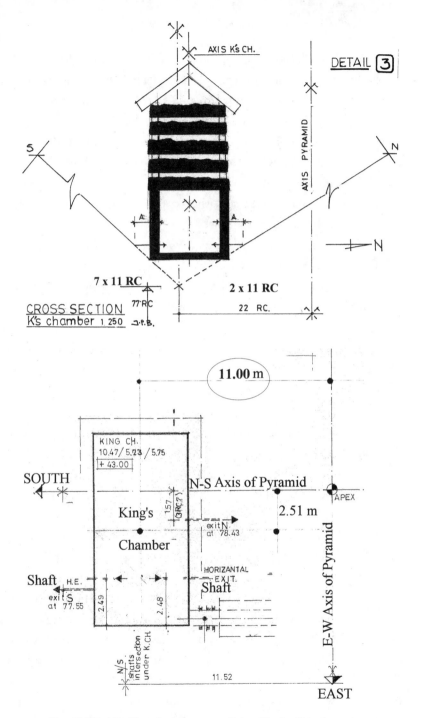

Fig. 11.35. (A) The displacement of the King's Chamber and the point of intersection of the two shafts below the chamber; (B) the displacement on the plan

O King, the sky conceived you with Orion, the dawn-light bears you with Orion . . . you will regularly ascend with Orion from the eastern region of the sky, you will regularly descend with Orion in the western region of the sky. (Pyramid Texts, line 820)

O King, you are this great star, the companion of Orion, who traverses the sky with Orion, who navigates the Duat [the sky underworld] with Osiris; you ascend from the East of the sky, being renewed at your due season, the sky has borne you with Orion. (Pyramid Texts, utterance 466)

The Netherworld has grasped your hand in the place where Orion is. (Pyramid Texts, line 802)

This [dead] king is Osiris, this pyramid of the king is Osiris, this construction of his is Osiris. (Pyramid Texts, line 1657)

The circumpolar stars, known as the Ihemu-Seku, meaning "Imperishables," were also seen as a favorable stellar destiny for the afterlife.

You shall set me to be a magistrate among the spirits, the Imperishable Stars in the north of the sky. (Pyramid Texts, line 1220)

I will cross to that side of the sky on which are the Imperishable Stars, that I may be among them. (Pyramid Texts, line 1222)

In 1881, Petrie measured the angles of the shafts of the King's Chamber and found them to be 45°14' for the south one and 31°33' for the north one. He also measured the angle of the shafts of the Queen's Chamber and found them to be 38°28' for the south one and 37°28' for the north one. In 1964 astronomer Virginia Trimble and Egyptologist-cum-architect Alexander Badawy used these measurements to show that the King's Chamber's shafts had symbolic functions compatible with the ideologies of the ancient builders; namely, to direct the "soul" of the deceased toward Orion's belt in the south and the circumpolar stars in the north.[93] Trimble and Badawy did not bother with the shafts of the Queen's Chamber, because Egyptologists had concluded (wrongly) that this chamber had been abandoned in favor of the King's Chamber. In

1987, however, I discovered that the shafts in the Queen's Chamber, referred to by Gantenbrink as the "lower shafts," were also aimed at stars, the southern shaft at the star Sirius (associated with the goddess Isis, who was the sister-consort of Osiris), and the northern shaft at the star Kochab in the circumpolar region.[94]

In 1992 to 1993, Gantenbrink remeasured the slopes of the shafts with very accurate instruments. For the King's Chamber's shafts he obtained 45°00' for the south one and 32°36' for the north one. But even with this slight disagreement with Petrie's measurements, a computerized reconstruction of the sky around 2500 BC (the date generally ascribed for the construction of the Great Pyramid) shows that the southern shaft would have targeted Orion's belt and the northern shaft the circumpolar stars. The conclusion is inescapable: the shafts were deliberately intended to be aimed at specific star systems and were regarded as passageways for the soul, or the archaic equivalent of cosmic wormholes to travel to specific destinations in our galaxy.

Since Gantenbrink's exploration of 1992–1993, the Egyptian authorities have conducted two more explorations, one in 2002 with a team from the National Geographic Society, who drilled a small hole in the Gantenbrink "door," only to find another "door" or "block" some fifty centimeters farther up the shaft. The National Geographic team also found a similar "door" at the end of the northern shaft of the Queen's Chamber. The other exploration was in 2010 with a team from the University of Leeds, who managed to get digital images of red ochre markings in the small space behind the Gantenbrink door. We have seen earlier that these markings are thought to be three numbers, 1, 20, and 100, totaling 121 (11 × 11). No further exploration of these shafts has been allowed to date.

The Pyramid Texts leave no doubt that Orion, and more specifically Orion's belt, was regarded as the place where the star souls are born. This, in the minds of the ancients, was a special stellar region

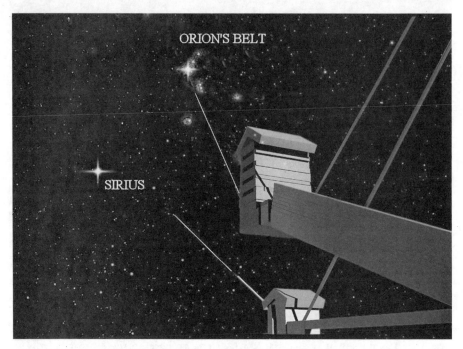

Fig. 11.36. Artist's impression of the star shafts
with the core masonry removed

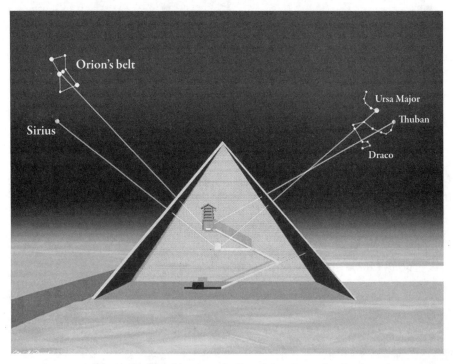

Fig. 11.37. The four star shafts of the Great Pyramid

where select humans could be sent to rejoin their ancestral creator, Osiris, the mythical founder of the Egyptian civilization and, in this context, the male creator of the human race with his consort, Isis. We are confronted here with what seems to be amazing *intuitive* knowledge of cosmology, because, as it turns out, several astronomers and astrobiologists today think that this stellar region, and more specifically the nebula located just below Orion's belt, is a kind of "star nursery" where stars are literally "born." The nebula is within our own Milky Way galaxy some 1,300 light-years away, practically in our backyard in terms of cosmic distances. It has a diameter of some thirty light-years; thus, it is a huge cosmic space in which thousands of stars are being given birth on a regular basis. Recently astrobiologists have also come to suspect that elements spewed out from this stellar region could be the source of life on our planet. An international team of astronomers headed by Tsubasa Fukue and Motohide Tamura of the National Astronomical Observatory of Japan believe that the Orion nebula may have had a part in the origins of life on Earth by "delivering" materials that are inductive to life via comet or meteorites.[95]

We have now reached the seventh coincidence pigeon.

The eighth and last coincidence pigeon that I will examine in this book (and there are many more!) is the most controversial of all and the most difficult to come to terms with. But it is also the most fascinating if there is even the slightest possibility that it may not be coincidence. . . .

A PLANETARY GPS?

How and why was the location of the Great Pyramid chosen? It would be logical to assume that this choice would have been of paramount importance and thus given the utmost consideration. Egyptologists have always supposed that the location of the Giza Plateau was chosen because it was a high point that could be viewed from the Nile Valley below. But that hypothesis does not hold to scrutiny. This is because there exists a much higher and better location for this purpose: the high plateau at Abu Ruwash, located only eight kilometers to the northwest of Giza. It was there that the pharaoh Djedefre, the son of Khufu (the alleged owner of the Great Pyramid), erected his own pyramid. The Giza Plateau is only 60 meters above sea level, whereas the Abu Ruwash Plateau is 150 meters above sea level. Furthermore, Abu Ruwash is also much nearer to Heliopolis, the center of cult worship in the pyramid age,[96] clearly making this site a much better choice than Giza if, as Egyptologists imply, impressive visibility was the motive.

So why had Khufu not taken this more commanding location? A more likely reason for placing the Great Pyramid on the Giza Plateau is that it was imperative to whoever commissioned this monument that it should sit on a small mound that existed there. Today this mound is totally engulfed by the pyramid, but parts of it are still visible from inside the Descending Corridor. It is estimated to be 12 meters high with a rough diameter of about 200 meters. The geographical coordinates of this mound are 29°58'44" N, 31°08'03" E. It is therefore extremely close, but not exactly on, to the thirtieth parallel, north latitude. Indeed, many have suggested that this was the reason for choosing this location.

But if this was indeed the reason, then why did the ancient surveyor-architect not choose the *precise* latitude of 30° N, which is only 2.3 kilometers as the crow flies farther north? As it turns out, there is a flat rocky region in the vicinity of the thirtieth parallel that would have been ideal. This region is some 90 meters above sea level, thus much higher than the Giza Plateau, and only 5.5 kilometers to the northwest of the Giza Plateau, thus closer to Heliopolis. It also has a stratum of suitable limestone that would have been plentiful for construction works. So why was the Great Pyramid not placed there?

It has been suggested that the slight displacement of the Great Pyramid, which is about 1'26" of arc south of the thirtieth parallel, is due to an optical error caused by the refraction of the atmosphere, which made the pole of the sky appear 0.0208° lower than it really is, thus tricking, as it were, the ancient surveyors to place the monument at 29°58'44" instead of the desired 30°00'00".[97] Another much more controversial reason, however, has also been suggested. But this other reason is so outrageous that even though I had heard about it years ago, I rejected it outright. But now, after having updated myself on the cutting-edge advances in science, my resistance has gradually softened, and I want to follow the argument regardless of how uncomfortable I feel about it. I am encouraged by the words of poet and visionary Kahlil Gibran: *"Perplexity is the beginning of knowledge."* [98]

So what is this "outrageous other reason" for placing the Great Pyramid over the Giza mound?

THE SPEED OF LIGHT?

Today geographical coordinates are generally given not in the sexagesimal system but rather in a decimal arrangement. Using a high-precision Global Positioning System (GPS) tool such as the U.S. Geological Survey's EarthExplorer, coupled with the latest computer technology, it can be ascertained with much accuracy that the summit of the Great Pyramid is located at 29.9792° N. [99] It has often been noticed by pyramid researchers that if the decimal point of this value is moved forward by four digits it will give the number 299,792, which is, as weird as this may sound, precisely the speed of light in a vacuum measured in kilometers per second.

The Speed of Light

Prior to the seventeenth century it was assumed that light was instantaneous. The first person to measure the speed of light within a fair approximation was Danish astronomer Ole Christensen Roemer in 1676, using the position of Jupiter relative to Earth and the sun, and the eclipses of the moons of Jupiter. Roemer noticed that there was up to one thousand seconds difference between the *predicted times* of the eclipses and the *actual times* they were observed, and he concluded that this was the time it took for light to travel from Jupiter to Earth. He calculated a value of 214,000 kilometers per second, which, considering the low-tech method he used, was pretty good. After James Maxwell published his theory of electromagnetism, the speed of light was calculated with much more accuracy. When the laser was developed in the 1970s, as well as superaccurate clocks, the accuracy was determined within 1 meter per second. Today the speed of light in a vacuum (which is assumed to be the same for any observer anywhere in the universe) is considered to be a fixed value: 299,792.458 kilometers per second.*

---

*In recent years, some experiments with photons have suggested that the speed of light may not, in fact, be a constant, but may have varied slightly over great periods of time.

Let me be very clear on this. To consider anything other than coincidence for the numeral 299,792 to be the same for the location of the Great Pyramid and the speed of light will fling out the window everything we know—or think we know—about ancient history and about who or what we are. And yet this number is there, fixed on the ground by a six-million-ton pyramid, like some giant nagging question that cannot be removed or ignored. Should I behave like the unflinching prosecutors of the papal Inquisition who forced Galileo to recant his

Fig. 11.38. The GPS-determined coordinates of the apex of the Great Pyramid

"outrageous" claims, or am I to listen to those researchers who meekly mutter, as Galileo did in saying, "Eppur si muove" (And yet it moves"), "But the number 299,792 is there"? My classical approach urges me to behave like the former, but my new quantum approach urges me to brave the ridicule barrier and be at least open to the possibility that coincidence is not at play here! But it is impossible, I nonetheless tell myself, for an ancient people to know the speed of light in a vacuum! It is completely irrational, for sure, to think in this way. Well, impossible and irrational, that is, if I stay rooted in the classic physics of Newton and Einstein. But I can no longer do that, not after learning about the quantum world and its counterintuitive realities. For my defense I can only quote the words of science writer Michael Brooks, "Whatever the true answer is, it will be weird, and will certainly confuse us further. Welcome to quantum reality!"[100]

Triangles, squares, rectangles, circles, polygons, and other exotic shapes, all forming myriad patterns and shapes of living and nonliving matter, all controlled by four finely tuned forces, forever dancing to a symphony of strings composed fifteen billion years ago by . . . who or what? I cannot anymore think of the Great Pyramid without wondering if it might hold part of the answer. Do I ignore this? *Can I ignore this?* There are too many coincidence pigeons involved, and my mind struggles to replace the word *coincidences* with something else. But with what else? The truth for now is that there is no answer, there are only *possibilities.**

POSSIBILITY 1: The coincidence pigeons are just coincidences. The Great Pyramid is a "tomb and nothing but a tomb." But I discounted this one long ago.

POSSIBILITY 2: Supergenius savant. Could it be that a supergenius savant has accessed, consciously or unconscious, that part of the brain where these computations are made? How? A lost system of initiation?

---

*As I write these words, an international high-tech team of researchers using the latest state-of-the-art scanners is trying to find hidden chambers or passages in the Great Pyramid. Known as the Scan Pyramids Mission, they are working under the aegis of the government of Egypt and the Ministry of Antiquities. The results so far are inconclusive.[101]

An anecdotal story told by Leon M. Lederman in his book *The God Particle: If the Universe Is the Answer, What Is the Question?* comes to mind. Lederman imagined himself having a dialogue with Democritus of Abdera, a fifth-century-BC Greek philosopher who is reputed to be the first to formulate an atomic theory of the universe. At the end of the dialogue Lederman made this interesting comment: "Imagine then the focus and integrity of a mind that could ignore the popular beliefs of the age and come up with concepts harmonious with quarks and quantum theory. In ancient Greece, as now, progress was an accident of genius—with individuals with a vision of creativity."[102] Was the ancient designer of the Great Pyramid such a man?

POSSIBILITY 3: Cosmic archives. Is the universe "mental"? Is there a universal consciousness where all knowledge is stored, a sort of cosmic "archives of the mind," accessible only to some gifted individuals or perhaps through a special form of initiation or gnosis? The phrase "archives of the mind" was coined by Archibald Roy, Ph.D., a longtime emeritus professor of astronomy at the University of Glasgow. In the 1960s Roy had been a consultant for NASA's Apollo Projects, and he even had asteroid 5806 named in his honor.* In one of his better known books, *The Archives of the Mind,* Roy proposed that there existed a sort of multidimensional web akin to Jung's collective unconscious, onto which all human minds were somehow connected. He described it as a "treasure of knowledge, experiences, solutions to problems, and so on gathered by countless human beings now gone," which could be accessed by gifted individuals under the right conditions. Roy regarded paranormal phenomena such as synchronicity, telepathy, and super-ESP as manifestations of the "archives of the mind."[103] He once told me that he saw no reasons why there could not have been supergeniuses in ancient times of the intellectual caliber of Newton, Einstein, or Heisenberg, who also might have found a way to tap in to a universal treasure trove of knowledge, an "archives of the mind," if you prefer, or Jung's "collective unconscious."

---

*I had the good fortune of knowing Roy for many years. He gallantly defended my OCT during the BBC *Horizon* scandal in 1999, and we remained friends until his death in 2012.

Could the designer of the Great Pyramid have had access to such high knowledge?

POSSIBILITY 4: Contact. I am compelled to seriously consider the possibility of contact with a "higher intelligence." But a higher intelligence from where? A forgotten civilization whose traces are lost? Or a contact with an extraterrestrial civilization? One of the obstacles (and there are many!) was that the distances between star systems are so great that interstellar communication would take too long, even at the speed of light. However, an experiment conducted in 2008 by physicist Nicolas Gisin and his colleagues at the University of Geneva showed that "if reality and free will hold . . . the speed of transfer of quantum states between entangled photons held in two villages 18 kilometers apart was somewhere above 10 million times the speed of light."[104] There is also the (albeit theoretical) possibility to have a two-way instantaneous communication between parts of the galaxy via these wormholes that are theorized to be inside black holes.*[105]

Did a "contact" already take place in the pyramid age of Egypt? Well, why not?

POSSIBILITY 5: Simulated world. We reviewed earlier the very bizarre possibility that we are a simulation of a higher intelligence. We have seen how, even more bizarrely, this possibility is gaining support with many top theoretical physicists and cosmologists today. A keen advocate of this hypothesis, although not a scientist himself, is South African–born billionaire and supermagnate Elon Musk, who is funding research in many fields of cutting-edge science, including a project to set up a colony on Mars. At a conference in California in June 2016, Musk reminded the audience that "forty years ago we had Pong—two rectangles and a dot. That's where we were. Now forty years later, we have photorealistic, 3-D simulations with millions of people playing

---

*Oddly, the idea of something akin to a cosmic wormhole first came to a mathematics professor at Christ Church, University of Oxford. Lewis Dodgson, better known by his pen name, Lewis Carroll, published *Alice's Adventures in Wonderland* in 1865, in which a young girl enters another world by falling through a rabbit hole. Presumably, Dodgson chose to write under a pen name to avoid ridicule from his peers.

simultaneously and it's getting better every year. And soon we'll have virtual reality, we'll have augmented reality. If you assume any rate of improvement at all, then the games will become indistinguishable from reality."[106]

If the argument is that if we humans will develop games that will become indistinguishable from reality after only a century or so of electronic revolution, then imagine what civilizations elsewhere in the cosmos that are thousands or millions of years ahead of us may have as games? Could there be a mega-super computer geek whose game is our planet Earth? Rich Terrile, director of the Center for Evolutionary Computation and Automated Design at NASA's Jet Propulsion Laboratory and also an enthusiastic supporter of the simulation hypothesis, even thinks it possible that this mega-super computer geek could be someone in our future, and he speculates that a super-technologically advanced version of us living, say, ten thousand years in the future may have simulated their own ancestors (us!). According to Terrile:

> If we believe that there is nothing supernatural about what causes consciousness and it's merely the product of a very complex architecture in the human brain, we'll be able to reproduce it. Soon there will be nothing technical standing in the way to making machines that have their own consciousness. . . . If one progresses at the current rate of technology a few decades into the future, very quickly we will be a society where there are artificial entities living in simulations that are much more abundant than human beings. If in the future there are more digital people living in simulated environments than there are today, then what is to say we are not part of that already?[107]

Not unexpectedly, there is stiff opposition to the simulation hypothesis, even though it is within the ethos of scientific logic. According to Max Tegmark, "Is it logically possible that we are in a simulation? Yes. Are we probably in a simulation? I would say no. . . . In order to make the argument in the first place, we need to know what the fundamental laws of physics are where the simulations are being made. And if we are in a simulation then we have no clue what the laws of physics are. What I teach at MIT would be the simulated laws of physics."[108]

Still, Terrile feels that the reluctance of many scientists to embrace the notion that we are in a simulation is comparable to the pre-Copernicus era when the notion of a heliocentric system "was such a profound idea that it wasn't even thought of as an assumption," yet once it was accepted "everything else became much simpler to understand." Terrile points out that the simulation hypothesis can explain the "observer" problem in quantum physics. "For decades it's been a problem. Scientists have bent over backward to eliminate the idea that we need a conscious observer. Maybe the real solution is you do need a conscious entity like a conscious player of a video game." Tegmark, however, rejects this seemingly "Occam's razor" explanation. "We have a lot of problems in physics and we can't blame our failure to solve them on simulation." But no matter how very wacky and provocative the simulation hypothesis is, everyone admits that the possibility, however faint, cannot be excluded: Could the pyramids of Egypt be "simulations" of a super-advanced civilization?

MY TAKE

There is no telling the leaps and bounds of technology that may take place in a few decades from now or a few centuries from now, let alone a few millennia from now. In less than two centuries we have moved from the horse and carriage to the jumbo jet, from the Pony Express to emails and Skype. The technological adventure has barely begun on this planet, and provided that we do not blow ourselves out of existence in a nuclear holocaust, traveling among the stars in our galaxy may one day be as common as taking a flight from New York to London. Indeed, we may not even need starships to move about in the galaxy, for we may find ways to teleport our bodies or our consciousnesses using supersophisticated quantum scanners or cosmic wormholes. And if we humans will be able to do such things—and many scientists are convinced we will, given enough time and resources—then there is no reason why a much older and much more advanced civilization elsewhere in the cosmos might not have done them long ago.

There is only 1 percent in the genetic DNA code that separates us from chimpanzees, and as Neil DeGrasse Tyson cogently pointed out, this mere 1 percent has allowed us to land human beings on the moon, put the Hubble Space Telescope into Earth's orbit, and provide millions of us with electronic gadgets that would have seemed like magic hardly a century ago (and still do to me!). So if only 1 percent makes us so amazingly more technologically advanced than the common ape, then imagine if there were intelligent beings elsewhere in the cosmos who had 1 percent more genetic DNA than us or even 2 percent more? Let me quote the passionate statement from Tyson when asked the proverbial question, Are we alone in the universe?

We're made of the most common ingredients there are! And our chemistry is based on carbon. Carbon is the most chemically active ingredient in the entire periodic table. If you were to find a chemistry on which to base something really complex called "life," you would base it on carbon. Carbon is like the fourth most abundant ingredient in the universe. It's not rare! You can make more molecules out of carbon than you can make of all other kinds of molecules combined. So if we ask ourselves are we alone in the universe, it would be—in spite of my diatribe about UFOs—I tell you in the same breath that it would be inexcusably egocentric to suggest that we are alone in the cosmos! The chemistry is too rich to declare that! The universe is too vast! There are more stars in the universe than grains of sand in all the beaches of the world! To say we're alone in the universe . . . well no, we haven't found life outside of Earth yet. We're looking, but we haven't looked very far yet. The galaxy's this big [Tyson stretches out his arms] and we looked about that far [Tyson points to one of his fingernails]. But we're looking. . . . So it may be given that information, given the right ingredients, which are everywhere, life may be inevitable. An inevitable consequence of complex chemistry.[109]

To be sure, there are many "maybes'" and "ifs" in Tyson's statement. But he is making *intelligent speculation based on what we know today of the cosmos, of biology, of neurology, of physics, of technology.*

Regarding the Great Pyramid of Giza, we can now say, hand on heart, that we have examined objectively an anonymous, empty, undated, pyramidal assembly of 2.6 million blocks built with baffling engineering skill, aligned with astronomical precision to cardinal directions and star systems, and designed according to a complex mathematic scheme of prime numbers and universal constants. The question, therefore, must be posed: Are we dealing with a three-dimensional message in stone written in the language of the universe or just a very big tomb for a megalomaniacal Egyptian king?

Egyptologists and archaeologists may scoff at such extreme speculations applied to the Giza pyramids and brand them as "crazy ideas." Perhaps the words of Peter Millican, professor of philosophy and computer science at the University of Oxford, will provide an opposing scholarly view. "It's healthy to have some crazy ideas. You don't want to censor ideas according to whether they seem sensible or not because sometimes important new advances will seem crazy to start with. You never know when good ideas may come from thinking outside the box."[110]

Forecasting the Future

By Chandra Wickramasinghe

When early humans had evolved to adopt an upright posture, possibly four million years ago, their hands were freed to make tools and to carry food. With later evolutionary developments that led to a dramatic increase in brain size, intelligence and cognitive abilities also increased dramatically. The scene was now set for the dawn of human history. Further progress was linked to the discovery of metal smelting, which heralded the Bronze Age and Iron Age civilizations and eventually the industrial revolution of the eighteenth and nineteenth centuries, leading up to the modern high-tech age.

As our capacity to exploit the environment advanced over time, the world population soared dramatically, from one million to six thousand million over a period of ten thousand years—from 8000 BC to the present era.

Forecasting the future is always a tricky affair. This is particularly true for the future of humanity. The state of our human society cannot be characterized by a set of independent parameters that vary in a continuous or predictable way. Human societies differ markedly in this regard compared with nonliving physical systems or even simple biological systems. The competition for limited food resources, which straddles a wide spectrum of life at the lower end of the scale of complexity, leads to more or less predictable outcomes. In the human case, the same type of competition extends to ideologies and political philosophies, and the more basic survival instincts are relegated to a secondary role. Struggles to assert the superiority and dominance of one's particular ideologies often bring out the worst in human nature. Pride of one's nation, race, or clan, as noble as it may sound, gives expression for the basest of human attributes—guile, mendacity, and the ruthless conduct of wars. Such modes of conduct have remained unchanged over centuries and millennia.

What distinguishes the present era from past history is the bewildering range of technological developments that have been taken in recent years. From fundamental particle physics, space science, nanotechnology, biotechnology, and robotics to communication technology, the scale of the advances seen in the past few years could not have been remotely guessed as recently as two decades ago. Rapid progress in information science and computer technology gives a hope for connecting human beings ever more closely than before. Advances in medical science over the past century have led to diminished suffering from disease, as well as a significant increase in the average length of life.

Despite all these positive achievements, *Homo sapiens* as a species have not been able to overcome or sublimate its most savage instincts. The desire for tribal, cultural, religious, or national supremacy still plagues the world and causes much suffering and distress. The threat of terrorism and wars hangs over us as an ever-present curse with which to contend. In parallel with the advances in science and technology, military techniques have also evolved. The levels of sophistication and destructive power associated with modern weapons have a frightening doomsday aspect. It remains true that the nuclear arsenals around the world have a total explosive power capable of annihilating human life altogether.

Concurrent with the rapid advances of technology, the total human population is still on the rise (now standing at six thousand million). As a result, the energy and food resources needed to maintain our population are stretched to the limit. With emphasis shifting to renewable energy sources as well as improved methods of agriculture, these problems may be alleviated in the foreseeable future, although not, of course, indefinitely. Before the easily accessible energy sources run out, it is conceivable that space exploration could develop to the point that we could contemplate migrating to another planetary body in the solar system, exploiting resources of a neighboring planet, or developing space technologies that might enable us to intercept and use a larger fraction of the sun's energy output.

Besides all the existential hazards we have already discussed, there is also the ever-present threat of an asteroid or comet impact, which cannot be ignored. I referred earlier to comet-fragment impacts that almost certainly have punctuated our history for tens of thousands of years. But the risk of a direct hit by a large comet or asteroid one kilometer or greater in size is real, though unpredictable.

Over the past two decades, a concerted effort has been made to use a network of small telescopes to detect near-Earth objects that are in potentially dangerous orbits. There are also ongoing discussions about mitigation strategies in the event of a real threat being discovered. These include physically nudging the object into a noncollision course or even using a nuclear weapon to explode the object in space. The most serious hazard in my view is not from known near-Earth objects but from a population of extremely dark (nonreflecting) cometary bodies that are difficult if not impossible to observe using optical telescopes. Estimates of the probability of an impending collision vary from one in a few thousand years to one in many millions of years. But the stochastic nature of these predictions leaves the situation wide open. What is certain is that while the sun will continue to shine for a comfortable two or three billion years into the future, there are other hazards that may intervene on a much shorter timescale and spell the end of human history.

Epilogue

CHANDRA WICKRAMASINGHE

In part 1 of this book I have presented an overwhelming body of evidence that points inexorably to our cosmic origins. Nearly 4,200 million years ago microbial life was introduced to the Earth by comets and slowly came to be established on the planets. Comets have been shown to be the repositories, incubators, and distributors of all life in the universe. From the moment of its first inoculation onto the Earth the further evolution of life from single-celled organisms to the magnificent panorama of the living world required a continuing connection with comets—the injection of new genes in the form of bacteria and viruses. The Darwinian process of natural selection is then left to only a limited role of fine-tuning—involving the selection of the best possibilities that ensure survival in a given niche or environment

Recent studies by several groups of investigators have confirmed the presence of microorganisms from comets in the stratosphere at heights of 40 kilometers, and even entirely outside the atmosphere at a height of 400 kilometers on the surface of the International Space Station. All these facts combined with the discovery that inactivated viruses (retroviruses) lie buried in our DNA show that the ideas discussed in earlier chapters are no longer speculation but fact. Our cosmic origin and genetic ancestry is now beyond dispute, although its acceptance by the wider community is fraught with problems mainly of a sociological nature. These ideas imply also that intelligence of the type with which we are well acquainted is part and parcel of our cosmic genetic legacy. Such intelligence must show up not only on our planet but also on a large fraction of the hundred billion or more Earth-like planets that have been estimated to exist in the Milky Way. It is inconceivable that humans represent the end of the road in the development and evolution of intelligence. The odds must be high for levels of intelligence far higher than we are accustomed. This opens the door to super-intelligent alien beings and even the possibility of alien invasions in the very distant past.

ROBERT BAUVAL

In part 2 of this book I have pushed the investigation into the mysteries of the Giza pyramids, especially the Great Pyramid, to a very different level than I am normally accustomed—or had previously been willing—to undertake. To be sure, being open to the possibility of super-intelligent beings that might have made "contact" with humans in the past and that their "fingerprints" might be detected in the geometrical design of the Great Pyramid is the stuff of heady controversy, to say the very least. But I will admit that it is a step that I have long wanted to take and yet, I also admit, for fear of ridicule by the orthodox establishment and the skeptical public, I refrained from doing so . . . until now. As I have stated elsewhere in this book, what spurred me to take this bold step was getting "updated" to the frontiers of modern science and cutting-edge ideas on the cosmos and the human brain. It would thus be hypocritical of me, and indeed of anyone who is similarly "updated," to deny the strong possibility of the existence of super-intelligent beings outside our planetary system and the attempt they might have made in the past to communicate with us. No matter how uncomfortable such investigation may be to Egyptologists and other experts on ancient Egypt, and no matter the ridicule or scorn that such an investigation may bring, I feel fully justified to have taken this step. Indeed, I believe that future generations will wonder why serious researchers have waited so long to do so in view of the many unexplained and anomalistic aspects of the Great Pyramid. The speculations expressed in this book are based on verifiable evidence or, at the very least, on hypotheses currently entertained by scientists and futurists. Whether these will eventually prove to be valid in the long run remains to be seen. But it is part of the collective quest that humanity has been allocated and, consequently, must pursue regardless of the outcome. Perhaps the intention is not to actually find the "Holy Grail" but rather to never stop seeking it. For on this road of self-discovery we may finally understand and accept that we are not mere physical creatures enduring a short life on a small planet we call Earth—"a poor player that struts and frets his hour upon the stage, and then is heard no more" to quote the English bard—but that we also, and mostly, are endowed with a soul whose immaterial and eternal nature is part and parcel of the never-ending process of Creation. The Great Pyramid may be the visiting card of those who already knew this truth.

The Concavity of the Great Pyramid: A Design Feature?

Did the Designer Know the Meter Unit?

By Jean-Paul Bauval

Abstract: *The objective of this exercise is to demonstrate that the concavity of the faces of the Great Pyramid could be a designed feature and not, as is assumed by Egyptologists, a construction error. Furthermore, I intend to demonstrate that the geometry generated by the concavity on the overall shape of the monument shows a clear relationship, whether intended or by accident, between the Egyptian royal cubit and the meter unit. Finally, this geometrical design has the peculiarity of creating a virtual space at the top of the monument on which might have been placed a spherical object.*

THE CONCAVITY

The Great Pyramid of Giza is believed by Egyptologists to have belonged to the Fourth Dynasty pharaoh Khufu (ca. 2500 BC). It is probably the most studied monument in the world. Over the past two centuries there have been a plethora of theories about its purpose and the method of construction, none of which has achieved any consensus. My intention is not

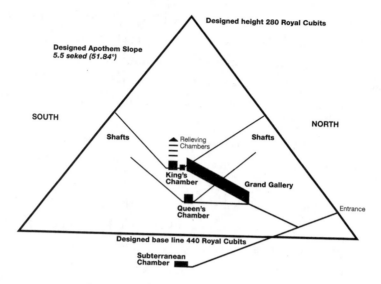

Fig. A1.1. Interior design of the Great Pyramid

to propose a new theory but to simply bring to attention a peculiarity about this pyramid that, in my opinion, deserves more careful attention. The shape and interior design of the Great Pyramid have been described in countless books and articles, making it unnecessary here for me to repeat this exercise. Readers can refer to figure A1.1 as a refresher.

My approach to this problem as an architect is that no matter what may be thought of the Great Pyramid, ultimately it is a building and, more precisely, a designed building. A priori, there is nothing complicated in drawing a regular square-based pyramid. But the Great Pyramid has an unusual feature that is almost unnoticeable from the ground and often ignored and that makes the construction of this particular structure very complex and, if planned, ingenious. For contrary to popular belief, the Great Pyramid is not four-sided but eight-sided. This peculiarity is due to an indention, or concavity, that runs along the apothem of each face, and although this oddity has been known since at least the late eighteenth century, little attention has been given to it by Egyptologists, who generally assumed it to be a construction error. As far as I can make out, the concavity was first recorded in a drawing by French architect Charles-Louis Balzac (1752–1820), who was one of the sixty-seven savants who accompanied Napoleon to Egypt in 1798 to 1801. This is what Balzac said about it: "The clear part marked as 10, just under the summit, represents the breaking of stones, which is more pronounced along the apothem than anywhere else because of the direction that the stones, which get loose at the Summit, take during their fall."[1]

In 1881, Sir William Mathew Flinders Petrie carefully examined the concavity of the Great Pyramid and reported thus:

> I continually observed that the courses of the core had dips of as much as ½° to 1° so that it is not at all certain that the courses of the casing were truly level . . . the faces of the core masonry being very distinctly *hollowed*. This hollowing is a striking feature; and beside the general curve of the face, each side has a sort of groove especially down the middle of the face, showing that there must have been a sudden increase of the casing thickness down the midline. The whole of the hollowing was estimated at 37 [inches] on the North face.[2] (brackets and italics added)

In 1930, British architect Somers Clarke and British engineer Reginald Englebach were clearly puzzled by the concavity when they wrote, "Most pyramids have individual peculiarities which are as yet difficult to explain. For instance, in the Great Pyramid, as possibly in certain others, a large depression in the packing-blocks runs down the middle of each face, implying a line of extra-thick facing there. Though there is no special difficulty in arranging the blocks of a course in such a manner that they increase in size at the middle, there is no satisfactory explanation of the feature."[3]

In 1947, Sir I. E. S. Edwards, the leading expert on Egyptian pyramids in the twentieth century, described the concavity of the Great Pyramid and believed it to be unique among all other pyramids of Egypt. This may not be quite correct, for Italian architects Vito Maragioglio and Celeste Rinaldi reported a similar concavity in the Third Pyramid at Giza (Menkaure, Fourth Dynasty), and Polish Egyptologist Miroslav Verner also reported a concavity in the Red Pyramid at Dashour (Snefru,

Fig. AI.2. The first aerial photograph taken of the Great Pyramid showing the concavity was taken in 1926 by Brigadier General P. R. C. Groves of the Royal Air Force at sunset at the spring equinox.

Fourth Dynasty). They all believed that the concavity was meant to "increase the stability" of the casing stones. At any rate, according to Edwards, "The packing blocks were laid in such a way that they sloped slightly inwards towards the center of each course with the result that a noticeable depression runs down the middle of each face, a peculiarity, as far as I know, shared by no other pyramid."[4]

In 1971 the French physicist and mathematician André Pochan, measured the concavity of the Great Pyramid, giving an average value of 0.92 meter, which is very close to that given by Petrie. Pochan then proposed the hypothesis that the designer intended to have a platform at the top of the monument (rather than an apex) so as to create a small virtual space for a spherical object. "The Great Pyramid was not topped, as most others, by a pyramidion [small pyramid] of black basalt, but had a platform in the center of which rose a gnomon, in my opinion spherical."[5]

Now, many other researchers have discussed the concavity of the Great Pyramid, giving their own views, ranging from it being a construction error to a designed element. There is one view that requires

Fig. AI.3. A recent aerial photograph shows, albeit faintly,
the concavity on all four sides.

special mention, which is that of Martin Isler given in 1983 in the
Journal of the American Research Center in Egypt, for it reflects the pre-
ferred prosaic conclusions often congenial to the Egyptological community. At any rate, according to Isler the concavity on the four faces of the
Great Pyramid was simply caused by the sagging of the mason's string
line over long horizontal distances, and it is therefore "an architect's
error." In other words the concavity was not part of the initial design.[6]
Many experienced architects, most recent among them architect Miquel
Pérez-Sánchez, Ph.D., of the Polytechnic University of Catalunya, have
rejected this explanation and have instead argued that the concavity was
an original feature of the design. Let us see why.[7]

THE PYRAMID GEOMETRY
FROM FIRST PRINCIPLES

In my opinion, to understand how and why the designer of the Great
Pyramid included the concavity in the original plan, it is necessary

to work the geometry from first principles, starting with the main features of a pyramidal design: the designed height and base, and the slope derived thereof. It is widely accepted that the Great Pyramid was intended to have a square base of 440 royal cubits per side and a vertical height of 280 royal cubits. It is also accepted that the ancient Egyptians' measuring unit was 1 royal cubit, which was equal to 7 palms, or 28 fingers. From the study of various measuring rods dating from later epochs, it has been concluded that 1 royal cubit = 0.52359 meter (usually rounded to 0.5236 meter).

Egyptologists are unanimous that the pyramid designers used a measurement method known as the *seked* to define the slope of a pyramid. This idea was first proposed in 1948 by French architect Jean-Philippe Lauer (1902–2001).[8] Corrina Rossi, an Egyptologist with a Ph.D. in mathematics, is best qualified to explain the seked, as follows: "The Egyptians measured the slope (of pyramids), which was called seked, as the horizontal displacement of the sloping face for a vertical drop of one (royal) cubit. That is they measured the number of cubits, palms and fingers from which the sloping side had 'moved' from a vertical line of one cubit. Basically the Egyptians constructed a right-angle triangle."[9]

One of the rules for the slope of pyramids was that the seked should be of integers (whole numbers) of Egyptian units, meaning that no fraction of the finger unit was used. It should be perhaps emphasized that a perfectly vertical line and a perfectly horizontal line, which are the basis of the seked method in creating a right angle, are universal in the sense that they depend on the force of gravity. The seked could be said to be a *universal variable unit.*

STEP 1

The seked for the Great Pyramid is 5½ (5 palms, 2 fingers). This is derived from the height-to-half-base-side ratio of the pyramid (i.e., 280:220 royal cubits) and can be taken to the lowest two integers of 14:11, as shown in figure A1.4. This produces a triangle with base 11 (*B*), height 14 (*H*), and hypotenuse 17.80 (*HY*). It can be easily calculated that the slope of the hypotenuse is 51.84°, equivalent to

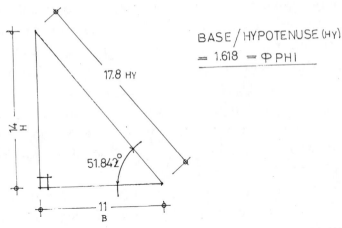

BASE / HYPOTENUSE (HY)
= 1.618 = Φ PHI

17.8 HY

H

51.842°

11
B

Fig. AI.4. Triangle showing the ratio of the base to hypotenuse is 1:1.61818, the universal dimensionless constant φ (phi), popularly known as the golden number

seked 5½. It also follows that the ratio of base to hypotenuse of this triangle is 1:1.61818, the universal dimensionless constant φ (phi), popularly known as the golden number. A formula can also be constructed with the dimensions of this triangle that produces another universal dimensionless constant, π (pi), as follows: $8 \times b/2 \times h = 88/28 = 3.142$.

Figure A1.4, seen mathematically, invites the possibility that the designer intended the square base of the Great Pyramid to be also imagined as a circle. This idea, of course, has been known since the mid-nineteenth century, when it was first proposed by John Taylor.[10] But this revelation has generated so many nonsensical theories that Egyptologists understandably cringe at any theory that deals with this possibility and simply consider the inclusion of constants such as φ (phi) and π (pi) in the design of the Great Pyramid as purely coincidental.

STEP 2

Let us, however, for a moment accept that the designer intended a circle to be considered. Taking a circle having a diameter of 1 unit (any unit will do), the circumference of that circle will be, of course, π or 3.14159. Using the radius (half diameter) of the circle, it is then possible to draw six adja-

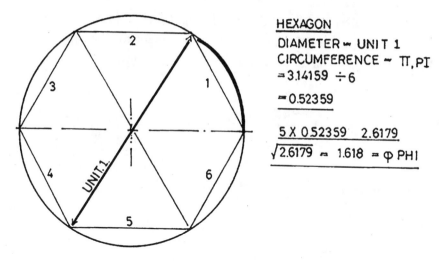

HEXAGON

DIAMETER ~ UNIT 1
CIRCUMFERENCE ~ π, PI
= 3.14159 ÷ 6

= 0.52359

5 X 0.52359 2.6179
√2.6179 ~ 1.618 = φ PHI

Fig. AI.5. Six adjacent equilateral triangles will produce a perfect hexagon.

cent equilateral triangles that will produce a perfect hexagon, as shown in figure A1.5. It must be admitted that the peculiarity of this construct strongly suggests, but does not prove, a numerical relationship between the royal cubit and the meter unit. What would be more convincing, of course, would be a similar construct where both units are expressed.

I believe that there is. Let us see how.

STEP 3

Let us now consider another polygon: the pentagon. It is well known that a perfect pentagon will produce a five-pointed star that when fitted within a circle generates the constant φ (phi), as can be seen in figure A1.6 on page 286.

Now, if we take the actual base perimeter of the Great Pyramid (440 × 4 = 1,760 royal cubits) and create a circle having the same circumference of 1,760 royal cubits and fit a five-pointed star/pentagon in it, it will produce five arcs of 352 royal cubits, as shown in figure A1.7 on page 286.

Here is the curious thing: divide 352 royal cubits by 100 (i.e., move the decimal point back by two digits to give 3.52 royal cubits), convert this into meters (3.52 × 0.5236), giving 1.843 meters, then divide by 2, which gives 0.9215 meter—the measurement for the concavity by Pochan (i.e., 0.92 meter to within 0.99 percent; figure A1.8).

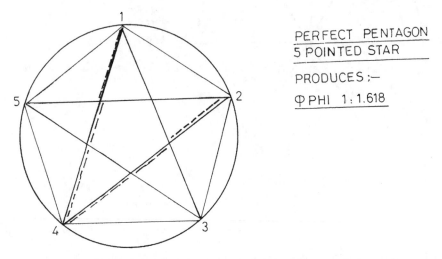

PERFECT PENTAGON
5 POINTED STAR

PRODUCES :—

φ PHI   1 : 1.618

Fig. AI.6. A five-pointed star fitted within a circle generates the constant φ (phi).

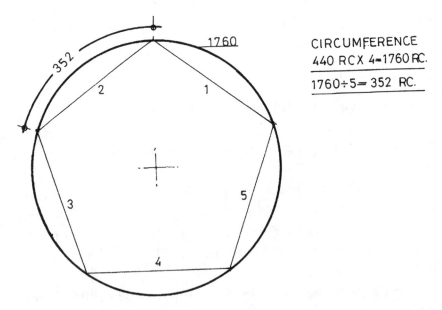

CIRCUMFERENCE
440 RC X 4 = 1760 RC.

1760 ÷ 5 = 352 RC.

Fig. AI.7. Five arcs of 352 royal cubits

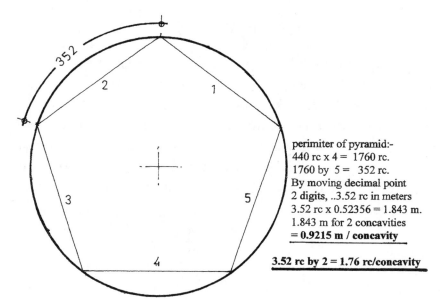

perimiter of pyramid:-
440 rc x 4 = 1760 rc.
1760 by 5 = 352 rc.
By moving decimal point
2 digits, ..3.52 rc in meters
3.52 rc x 0.52356 = 1.843 m.
1.843 m for 2 concavities
= 0.9215 m / concavity

3.52 rc by 2 = 1.76 rc/concavity

Fig. AI.8. The measurement for the concavity by Pochan:
0.9215 meter.

In my view, it is not far-fetched to assume that the designer of the Great Pyramid used the same approach to calculate the concavity. If this is correct, then it follows that the designer cleverly integrated several important symbols related to the known ideologies prevalent in the pyramid age and expounded in the Pyramid Texts that associate the pyramidal edifice with both the solar disc and the five-pointed star.

Hexagon = two inverted pyramids
Pentagon = five-pointed star
Circle = sun disc

All of the above require, by necessity, a knowledge of ɸ (phi) and π (pi).

Now, we have seen how Step 1 produced an uncanny connection between the royal cubit and the meter in a nondimensional manner (i.e., without units). I will now demonstrate that another circle can be derived from the geometry of the Great Pyramid, this time *with a royal cubit measurement that converts to one meter accurate to three decimal places.*

THE VIRTUAL SPACE

Taking the calculated value of the concavity, 0.9215 meter, we now get a measurement for the central axis of the monument, 436.48 royal cubits; (that is, 440 − (2 × 1.76). Keeping the original slope of 51.84°, it can be calculated that the height of the Great Pyramid is 277.758 royal cubits, against a theoretical height of 280 royal cubits. *This creates a virtual space of two interlocked triangles,* each with a height of 2.242 royal cubits (280 − 277.758) and a base of 4.9778 royal cubits, as shown in figure A1.9.

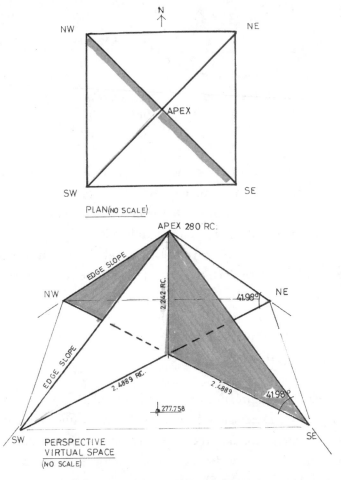

Fig. A1.9. The virtual space of two interlocked triangles in the geometry of the Great Pyramid

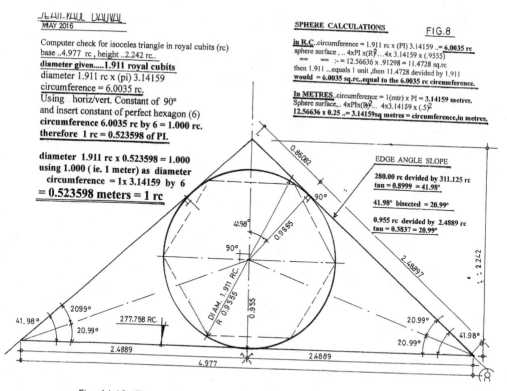

Fig. AI.10. The royal cubits diameter of a circle inside the pyramid equals 1 meter.

In any of the two virtual triangles can be fitted a circle. Precise computer calculations give a diameter of 1.911 royal cubits for this circle. This in itself does not mean anything until we convert it into the meter unit, as shown in figure A1.10.

1.911 royal cubits × 0.523598 = 1.000 meter.

With such precision involved, the possibility that we are dealing with more coincidences is highly reduced.

A SPHERE AT THE TOP?

Could there have been a sphere at the top of the Great Pyramid? The reply must remain theoretical. The idea that a sphere crowned the Great

Pyramid is, of course, not new. Pochan, as we have seen, suggested it in 1971 and, more recently, so did intuitive mathematician Gary Osborn, as well as Pérez-Sánchez in 2014. In the case of Pérez-Sánchez, the sphere he has calculated had a diameter of 2.7183 royal cubits, which he equates to the constant *e*, known also as Euler's number. He also finds it significant that this value is $^1/_{103}$ the height of the designed Great Pyramid and that 103 is the twenty-eighth prime, which is one-tenth of 280. Pérez-Sánchez also strongly suspects that the designer of the Great Pyramid knew the meter unit, and he points as evidence to the various dimensions of the King's Chamber, which produce integers of the meter, such as the level of the floor above baseline being 43 meters, the diagonal of the east–west wall being 12 meters, and the volume of the chamber being 321 cubic meters.[11]

Other researchers have also suspected the use of the meter unit in the design of the Great Pyramid, but I do not wish to embark on a detailed discussion on this complex issue here. However, the implications of a sphere or circle with a diameter of 1 meter on the Great Pyramid, if correct, is momentous, because this would mean that the Egyptians of the pyramid age, or at least the designer, knew the spherical shape and size of the planet. Many will argue with justification that there is no historical evidence to support this. But science dictates that absence of evidence is not evidence of absence. At any rate, this is a matter for historians of science and geographers to resolve.

The Location of the King's Chamber in the Great Pyramid

Modified article submitted on April 20, 2016, to academia.com by Jean-Paul Bauval

Abstract: *The Great Pyramid of Giza has spawned many theories as to how, when, and why it was constructed: its immense size, its location near the thirtieth parallel. Its angle of slope, height, and square perimeter produces the (almost precise) mathematical constant pi, its intriguing units of measurement and its various dimensions, and most of all its mysterious internal system of tunnels and chambers have puzzled generations of researchers. From scientists to historians, from experts to laypersons, from engineers and architects to armchair amateurs, from geniuses to cranks, all have had a go at solving the "mystery of the pyramids." In this brief and preliminary paper, architect Jean-Paul Bauval looks at the most intriguing component of the Great Pyramid, the noncentral location of the King's Chamber, and provides a possible answer to why it is offset from the central axes of the pyramid.*

Note: *All measurements are taken from the 1992–1993 survey and calculations of Rudolf Gantenbrink.[1] All measurements are given in meters unless otherwise stated. For measurements given in royal cubits, 1 royal cubit = 0.5236 meter.*

THE KING'S CHAMBER

The Great Pyramid is generally said to contain three main chambers known as the Subterranean Chamber, the Queen's Chamber, and the King's Chamber. But this is not quite correct, because since 1836 this monument is known to also contain five so-called Relieving Chambers, located directly above the King's Chamber.[2] These bear the names allocated to them by their discoverer, British colonel Robert William Howard-Vyse: Davison's Chamber, Wellington's Chamber, Nelson's Chamber, Lady Arbuthnot's Chamber, and Campbell's Chamber (see fig. A2.1). I shall only focus on the King's Chamber (KC) and, more particularly, on its location relative to the main axes of the pyramid (figs. A2.2 and A2.3).

The floor level of the KC rests on the fiftieth course of the core masonry of the pyramid, at a height of 43 meters above ground level. The KC is a two-by-one rectangular space having a floor dimension of 10.47 meters × 5.23 meters, and a height of 5.75 meters. Unlike the

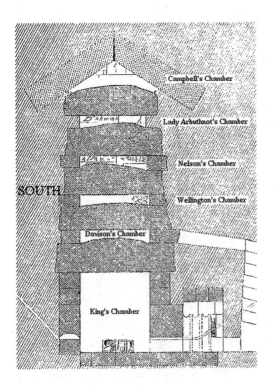

Fig. A2.1. The five so-called Relieving Chambers, located directly above the King's Chamber, named for those who discovered them

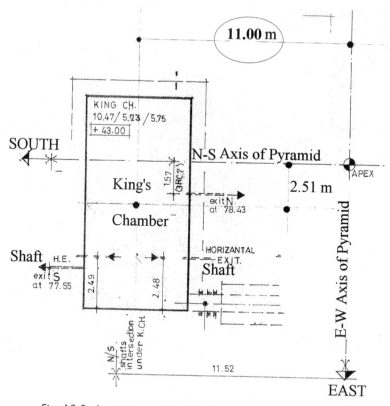

Fig. A2.2. Aerial view of the King's Chamber in relation to the main axes of the pyramid

rest of the pyramid, which is made of local limestone blocks, the KC's floor, walls, and ceiling are constructed with massive *granite* blocks, some weighing more than sixty tons, and they are perfectly dry-jointed together. Intriguingly, the KC is totally bare and bereft of inscriptions except for an empty granite box or sarcophagus, also itself without inscriptions. It is estimated that the total mass of cut granite used for the KC is about three thousand metric tons. Granite, as it is well known, does not occur naturally locally, but had to be imported from Aswan, which is some seven hundred kilometers south of Giza.

In consideration of the immense importance of the KC, many researchers have puzzled over its spatial location. This is because the KC is offset from the main axes of the pyramid, such that its north–south

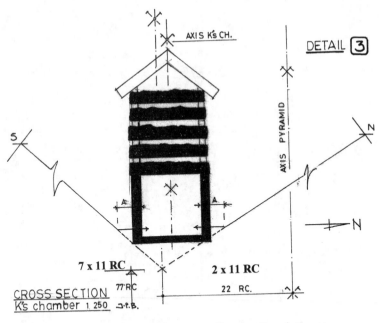

Fig. A2.3. Cross section of the King's Chamber in relation to the main axes of the pyramid

axis is 2.51 meters east of that of the pyramid, and its east–west axis is 10.99 meters south of that of the pyramid (fig. A2.1). It has been previously theorized that the location was determined as a mathematical function of the base area of the pyramid.[3] This may be so, but an equally and probably more significant explanation seems to be related to the highly symbolic shafts that emanate from the north and south walls of the KC. The most accepted view regarding these shafts is that they were deliberately aligned to stars that were important to the ideologies of the ancient builders.[4]

THE STAR SHAFTS

Since 1964 it has been known that the small inclined tunnels, or "shafts," that emanate from the north and south walls of the KC were aligned to stars. The southern shaft to Orion's belt and the northern shaft to Thuban, the pole star at the epoch of the ancient pyramid builders, circa 2500 BC.[5] In 1992 to 1993, German engineer Rudolf Gantenbrink had the opportunity to explore these shafts internally and externally. He deduced that the levels at which these shafts exit the pyramid are roughly the same, with the south shaft exiting at 77.55 meters and the north shaft exiting at 78.43 meters. At the lower level the inclined shafts (note that the inclinations are not the same) take a horizontal direction to enter the KC such that their mouths are directly opposite each other and are also located at the same height above the floor line and the same distance from the east wall of the KC (figs. A2.2 and A2.3). When the inclined trajectory of the two shafts is extended downward, they intersect at a height of 77 royal cubits, measured from the base of the pyramid, and at 22 royal cubits south of the east-west axis of the pyramid (figs. A2.2 and A2.3). The reason for this is that the short horizontal parts of the two shafts had to turn upward to continue their ascent at the required angles in order to reach their corresponding exit points on the outside face of the pyramid. This may explain why the east–west axis of the KC had to be shifted 10.99 meters south of the main east–west axis of the pyramid.

CONCLUSION

We may thus logically conclude that the location of the KC is a direct result of the specific design of the two star shafts. This implies a deliberate and important motive for this specific location of the KC by the ancient designers of the Great Pyramid that may have to do with the stellar symbolism of the shafts.

Note: The position of the intersection of the extended shaft underneath the floor of the KC provides the numbers 77 and 22. It is intriguing to note that $22 \div 77/11 = 3.142$, which is the value of the mathematical constant pi, which is used to work out the circumference of a circle. It is well known that the height-to-base-perimeter (circumference) ratio of the Great Pyramid as measured in royal cubits also provides the value of pi; namely, $(4 \times 440) \div (2 \times 280) = 3.142$.

The Great Pyramid of Giza

New Facts, Discoveries, and Theories

By Gary Osborn

It can now be reasonably established that the Great Pyramid of Giza was constructed to a royal cubit length of 0.5236 meter, as first proposed in 1956 by French archaeologist and mathematician Charles Funck-Hellet,[1] who suggested that the ancient Egyptian royal cubit was simply derived by dividing 3.1416—a close approximation of π (*pi*)—by 6.[2]

There have been many estimates given for the ancient Egyptian royal cubit, but none work so well to produce the precise and superlative data we see encapsulated within the Great Pyramid, as that of 0.5236 meter ($\pi/6$), which is 20.6142 inches (1.717845 feet—virtually 1.718 feet, which expresses the constant e-1).

Some mention should also be given to the fact that in 1816 the book *Lilawati: or, A treatise on arithmetic and geometry* by Bhāskara Āchārya (AD 1114–ca. AD 1185), the leading mathematician of the twelfth century, was translated from Sanskrit to English and published in India by none other than the pyramidologist John Taylor (1781–1864).

In the book, we find a) the ratio of 22/7, which of course is the same base-to-height ratio of the Great Pyramid of Giza and produces the same 99.96 percent *pi* approximation of 3.1428571428571429, and b) the calculation of 3927/1250 = 3.1416 (which is as accurate as 99.9997 percent compared to *pi* at fifteen decimal places).

It is said that the mathematics in the books *Lilavati* and *Vija-Ganita*—both written by Bhāskara Āchārya, and which contain problems dealing with determinate and indeterminate linear and quadratic equations, and Pythagorean triangles—*were evidently derived from earlier Hindu sources.*

Also interesting is the fact that 3.1416 divided by 8 = 0.3927, divided by 0.1250 = 3.1416.

It is largely accepted that the Great Pyramid was constructed to a height of exactly 280 royal cubits. The royal cubit length of 0.5236 meter × 280 gives a height of 146.608 meters, which converts to 480.9973753 feet—virtually 481 ft.

As for the base, it is generally assumed that the four bases of the Great Pyramid, complete with its casing stones, each reflected a length of exactly 440 royal cubits, as was intended by its architect/designer(s). However, the fact of the matter is that none of the four base lengths of the completed pyramid was an exact 440 royal cubits. . . .

FOUR DIFFERENT BASE LENGTHS

Between 1880 and 1882, Egyptologist William Matthew Flinders Petrie found that all four base lengths of the Great Pyramid varied slightly from each other. Measurements taken of the few limestone casing stones that still exist at the base of the north side of the pyramid indicated that the length of each of the four bases—including the limestone casing—*would have all varied slightly, no two sides being identical.* This also means that the base-to-height ratio for each side and the side angles produced would have all been slightly different in the completed pyramid, making the whole construct slightly skewed and twisted from its intended "precise" alignment to the four cardinal points.*

---

*The deviation from the 90-degree angles of the four corners: 0°00'02" (northwest), 0°03'02" (northeast), 0°3'33" (southeast) and 0°3'33" (southwest).

In 1925 surveyor J. H. Cole tried to determine once and for all what the exact dimensions of the Great Pyramid would have been, complete with its mantle of white limestone casing and its capstone. The measurements of the four base lengths as per Cole's survey were given in meters and are the estimates often quoted. However, as recently as 2015, a new survey of the Great Pyramid was conducted by the U.S.-based Glen Dash Research Foundation and the Ancient Egypt Research Associates (AERA), from which a slightly different set of base length estimates were published.

From these surveys the range of base length estimates for each of the four sides of the pyramid were determined without any predisposition to even a fleeting awareness of what the base lengths might have conveyed in terms of mathematical data. They are just objectively arrived at estimates of what the four base lengths might have been in the completed pyramid.

However, to someone having some knowledge of the mathematics involved, and also blessed with both their rational and intuitive senses in balance (see box below) the possibility would certainly be entertained that the four bases of the pyramid were *deliberately* constructed to different specific lengths *and in respect of the height* to both preserve and convey not only significant mathematical data relating to the measure of the Earth and the universal constants, *pi, Phi, e,* and even *c* (the speed of light constant), but that these mathematical elements all share a close relationship, encapsulated as they are in this pyramid-shaped construct and its very location. As we shall see, this is exactly what we find.

According to the *Myers-Briggs* psychological types developed from the work of psychiatrist Carl G. Jung, I am an INTJ. However, I would attribute my *intuitive* mathematical ability, my research discoveries, and my insights into the Great Pyramid of Giza to the extraordinary life-changing experience I personally underwent on November 10, 1993, which I later discovered was associated with the universal phenomenon known as *Kuṇḍalinī*—an ancient Hindu term.

This "awakening" experience was spontaneous and without any prior instruction or knowledge of what this phenomenon was or what had happened to me. This experience is what the late paranormal investigator and author John Keel referred to as Cosmic Illumination.

Since that experience, and having studied the ancient Egyptian Pyramid Texts, I have long entertained the idea that the Great Pyramid was used as a kind of shamanic initiation chamber for the pharaoh to access the "hypnagogic trance state," initiate shamanic "astral flight" and experience an NDE (near-death experience)—a theory first pioneered by author William R. Fix and now presented by scholar Jeremy Naydler. In effect, the king would learn how to die and possibly long before his physical demise. However, the ultimate aim, which is also the aim of the yogi but not essentially required, was for the initiate to "awaken the kuṇḍalinī serpent within" and undergo the enlightenment experience; *become as an akh* (enlightened soul). It was through these initiations taking place inside the pyramid, and during the Heb Sed festivals, that the king was tested to see if he was fit (enlightened) enough to rule.

The base lengths listed below, which are all extremely close to 440 royal cubits, each fall within only 2.7 centimeters (1.063 inches) of the range of estimates given in the surveys mentioned above, and the base-to-height ratios extracted from these base lengths do indeed convey mathematical data—in fact, *highly advanced mathematical data in the forms just mentioned,* as I will reveal in this summary of my work.

North Side Base Length:
439.76 royal cubits . . . 230.2577 meters (755.439 feet).

East Side Base Length:
439.96 royal cubits . . . 230.3649 meters (755.79 feet).

South Side Base Length:
440.13 royal cubits . . . 230.452 meters (756.076115 feet).

West Side Base Length:
439.99 (virtually 440) royal cubits . . . 230.3806 meters. (755.84186352 feet).

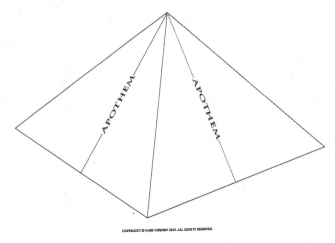

Fig. A3.1.

Since the four base lengths in the completed pyramid would have each varied slightly, this also means that the base-to-height ratios of the Great Pyramid's north–south and east–west cross sections would also have been slightly different.

Before I reveal the dimensions of the two cross sections, I should mention that the *apothem* of a pyramid is the abstract vertical line at the center of each of the four faces. The length of the apothem on each side is measured from where the line of the apothem begins at the center of the pyramid's base to where it ends at the tip of its apex.

Understandably, the lengths and angles of the four apothems of the Great Pyramid are determined by calculating the base-to-height ratio of its *north–south* and *east–west cross sections*. Although the height of the completed pyramid would have remained the same at 280 royal cubits, the two cross sections would have expressed *two different base lengths* in royal cubits and two different side angles, as determined by the different base lengths of the north, south, east, and west sides of the Great Pyramid.

GROUND PLAN

Could the marked difference in the four base lengths and the two cross sections have been intentional? According to William R. Fix, "It seems obvious that given the precision with which the Pyramid was built, the builders could have made the sides within a fraction of an inch of being equal if they had so desired. The differing lengths of the sides are likely not errors but the result of intentional design. Possibly these differences refer to subtle configurations in the shape of the earth."[3]

Indeed, the superlative mathematical data we can derive from the Great Pyramid indicates that the designer/architect(s) had set out to construct a pyramid that encapsulated the following properties.

1. The size of the pyramid would be at the scale of 1:43,200 in respect to the Northern Hemisphere of the Earth (as first discovered in 1977 by William. R. Fix).[4]
2. The base-to-height ratio of the pyramid's east–west cross section, with its height of 280 royal cubits and base length of 439.824 royal cubits—expressing an exact 140 × 3.1416 π (*pi*)— would provide the "mean" measure of the Earth.
3. The base-to-height ratio of the pyramid's north–south cross section, with its height of 280 royal cubits and base length of 440 royal cubits, would provide the *combined* "mean" measures of both the Earth and Moon.

To achieve all this and more, it could be conjectured that the architect(s) simply began by instructing the surveyors to mark a circle at a specified location on the Giza Plateau,* within which the pyramid would be constructed and which had the following properties.

Radius: 280 royal cubits × 2 = Diameter: 560 royal cubits.

A circle with a diameter of 560 royal cubits (× 3.1416 *pi*) produces a circumference of precisely 1,759.296 royal cubits.

The first important task was aligning the pyramid with true North.[5] The architect would have instructed the surveyors to measure a

---

*Evidence suggests that the Great Pyramid was built over a preexisting mound of bedrock, which some say was formerly worshipped as the "Primordial Mound." It is likely that this mound provided a stable foundation for the pyramid.

N–S line at EXACTLY 440 royal cubits (0.5236 meter each) in length, which would define the *north–south cross section* of the pyramid. As we shall see, this is the only instance in which the base would have been an exact 440 royal cubits in length.*

The measurements associated with the north–south cross section of the Great Pyramid—whether measuring in royal cubits or meters—produces the *Prime Number Factors*, 2, 5, 7, 11, and 17.

For example, height of 280 rc = 2 × 2 × 2 × 5 × 7.

Base length of 440 rc = 2 × 2 × 2 × 5 × 11.

Height of 146.608 meters, without the decimal point:

146608 = 2 × 2 × 2 × 2 × 7 × 7 × 11 × 17.

Base length of 230.384 meters, without the decimal point:

230384 = 2 × 2 × 2 × 2 × 7 × 11 × 11 × 17.

These meter measurements are derived from the royal cubit of 0.5236 meter ($\pi/6$) × 280 and 440: 5236 = 2 × 2 × 7 × 11 × 17.

The east–west cross section would have been slightly shorter at precisely 439.824 royal cubits.

Naturally, one would ask, *If all this was intended then why be so meticulous about this particular length?* Well, not only does this length express an exact 140 × *pi* (3.1416 π), but also the base-to-height ratio of the east–west cross section produces the "mean" measure of the Earth, as I will reveal later.

As to how the base length of 439.824 royal cubits was derived so precisely, a logical answer would be that the 1,759.296–royal cubit circumference of the circle was simply divided by 4, resulting in an "arc length" of 439.824 royal cubits. Being exactly one-fourth of the

---

*Along with the height of 280 royal cubits, it could be said that the north–south cross section provides a kind of primer, or "Rosetta Stone," for the length of the royal cubit employed in the pyramid's construction, so that anyone studying the dimensions of the pyramid would be able to use the royal cubit (0.5236 meter in length) like a "key" to unlock the advanced, mathematical properties that had been encoded and preserved within the pyramid, and this includes the four different base lengths.

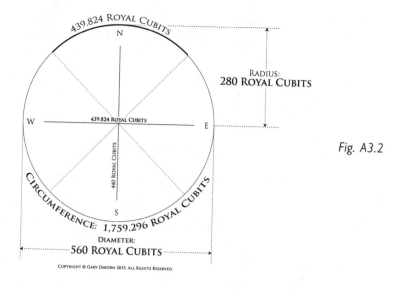

Fig. A3.2

circumference of the circle, this arc length section was measured and marked by a rope, which was then straightened out and applied to the straight horizontal line marked out on the ground for the pyramid's east–west cross-section baseline.

Next, the four sides of the pyramid would have been measured to enclose the north–south and east–west cross sections in a square—thus "squaring the circle."

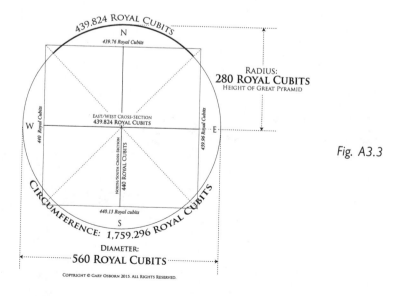

Fig. A3.3

The significant point here is that the lengths of the four bases would have both *determined* and been *determined in turn* by the Great Pyramid's north–south cross section base length of 440 royal cubits, and its east–west cross section of 439.824 royal cubits—everything having been already worked out on the initial drawing board.

NORTH–SOUTH CROSS SECTION

- The Great Pyramid's north–south cross section apothem of 186.44866 meters, when divided by a royal cubit length of 0.5236 meter is 356.08987 . . . royal cubits, which rounds off to 356 royal cubits. However, the precise length of 356.08987 royal cubits approximates the number *e* (2.7182) × 131. Compared to 356.0842 being the result of *e* (2.7182) × 131, this is an accuracy of 99.998 percent.

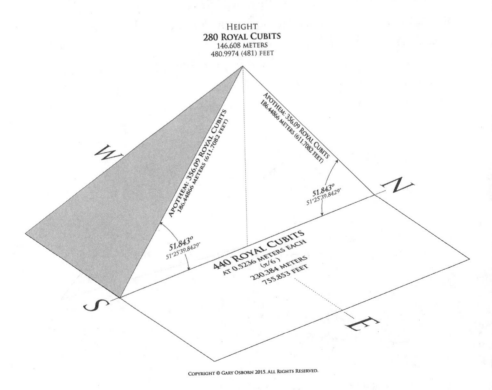

Fig. A3.4

- As listed in my own written work, the north–south cross-section base-to-height ratio dimensions also give reference to the constants *pi; Phi* and its reciprocal, *phi;* and the *mi/s* "speed of light" figure. The accuracy of these results compared to the true figures of these constants range between 99.94 and 99.996 percent.

EAST–WEST CROSS SECTION

- As mentioned, the Great Pyramid's east–west cross-section base length of 439.824 royal cubits is exactly 140 x π (*pi*).
- The east–west cross-section base length of 439.824 royal cubits, divided by the half-height of 140 royal cubits (280 ÷ 2) = 3.1416 π (*pi*).

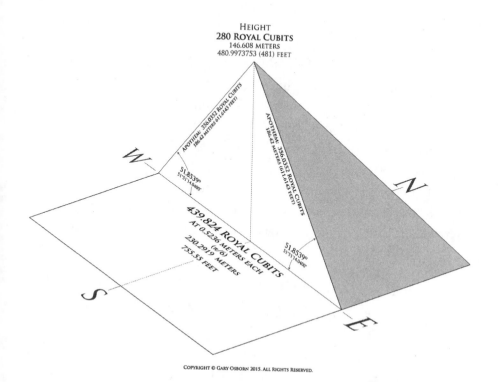

Fig. A3.5

- The east–west cross-section base length in royal cubits also reflects $e \times \Phi$ (the golden ratio, known as *Phi*). 2.7182818284590452 $e \times$ 1.6180339887498948 Φ = 4.398272389448—rounded off to 4.39827, $\times$ 100 = 439.827. Compared to the east–west cross-section base length of 439.824 royal cubits, this is an accuracy of 99.999 percent.
- The base-to-height ratio of the Great Pyramid's east–west cross-section dimensions—i.e., base length of 439.824 royal cubits $\times$ 0.5236 meters = 230.2919 meters, divided by 2 = a base apothem (half-base) of 115.146 meters.

Great Pyramid height of 146.608 meters, divided by the base apothem of 115.146 meters = 1.273236 meters, which is virtually the same result as 4 ÷ 3.1416 π (4 divided by *pi* . . . expressed mathematically as $4/\pi$). This is also the same result when dividing the 560 royal cubits "ground plan" circle by the base length of 439.824 royal cubits, and/or the Great Pyramid height of 280 royal cubits by the half-base length of 219.912 royal cubits.

Now converted to meters, this simple calculation of dividing the height of the Great Pyramid by half its base length immediately transforms (or *reduces*) the east–west cross-section dimensions of the Great Pyramid to a height of only 1.273236 meters and an "apothem base" length of ONE METER! (See left box in fig. A 3.6.)

The last result is understandable, as $4/\pi$ is the same constant from which the meter unit seems to have been originally derived and which provides us with the "mean diameter" of the Earth, as I will now reveal.

EAST–WEST CROSS-SECTION DIMENSIONS OF THE GREAT PYRAMID

(Pi and the Measure of the Earth)

As many of us will know, due to the equatorial bulge caused by the Earth's rotation, the Earth is not a perfect sphere . . . it is an *oblate*

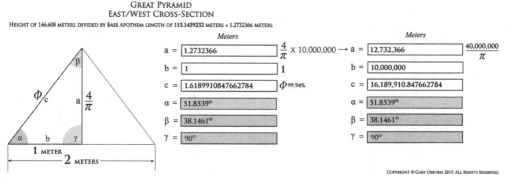

Fig. A3.6

spheroid/ellipsoid. This means that the circumference of the Earth is slightly wider around the horizontal equator than around the vertical poles. As per recent estimates, the 12,713.5046-kilometer polar diameter of the Earth is precisely *0.3352812 percent* shorter than the Earth's equatorial diameter of 12,756.274 kilometers.

It now follows, that if we take the number 1.273236 (4/π), which is 4 ÷ 3.1416 *pi,* as extrapolated from the base-to-height ratio of the Great pyramid's east–west cross section, and multiply 1.273236 by 10,000,000 (ten million), the result is 12,732,360, *which provides us with the mean diameter of the Earth in meters.*

As per today's estimates, the mean diameter of the Earth is 12,734,000 meters. Some sources give the mean diameter as 12,730,000 meters—being the same figure as obtained in 240 BC by the Greek philosopher and mathematician Eratosthenes. This is interesting, as the figure of 12,732,360 meters falls roughly between both these estimates.

Above are the same results using a right-angle triangle calculator.

Note that this ratio produces the east–west cross-section side angle of 51.8539°, which is 51°51'14.0400" in degrees, arc minutes and seconds. The angle in degrees rounds off to 51.854°.

Earlier I presented my theory of the 560-royal-cubit-diameter circle "ground plan," and that the Great Pyramid's east–west cross-section

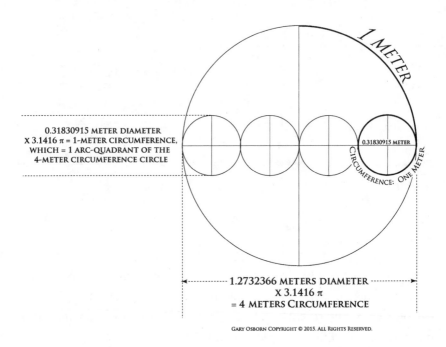

0.31830915 METER DIAMETER
X 3.1416 π = 1-METER CIRCUMFERENCE,
WHICH = 1 ARC-QUADRANT OF THE
4-METER CIRCUMFERENCE CIRCLE

0.31830915 METER

CIRCUMFERENCE: ONE METER

1 METER

1.2732366 METERS DIAMETER
X 3.1416 π
= 4 METERS CIRCUMFERENCE

Fig. A3.7

base line of 439.824 royal cubits was taken from one-fourth the "arc length" of the 1,759.296–royal cubit circumference of the circle.

In the same way, the 0.31831-meter diameter of one of the four smaller circles that fit together inside and along the diameter of the larger circle in the graphic below, is *one-fourth* the 1.273236-meter diameter of the large circle. Therefore, the 1 meter circumference of each of the four small circles is also *one-fourth* (one arc-quadrant) the 4-meter circumference of the large circle.

In other words, 1.273236 meters divided by 4 = 0.31831 meter, multiplied by 3.1416 π = 1 meter.

Again, in the same way, 12,732,360 meters (mean diameter of the Earth) divided by 4 = 3,183,100 multiplied by 3.1416 π = 10,000,000 . . . meters.

So, 10,000,000 of these meters = one arc-quadrant of the Earth— *which would be the distance between the equator and the North Pole along a meridian.* . . .

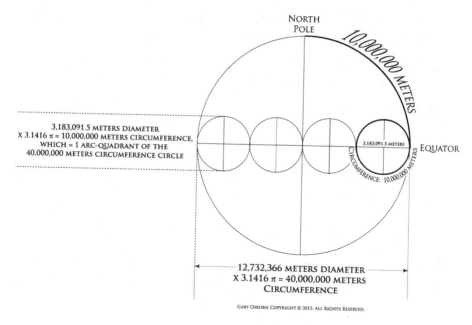

NORTH POLE

10,000,000 METERS

3,183,091.5 METERS DIAMETER
X 3.1416 π = 10,000,000 METERS CIRCUMFERENCE,
WHICH = 1 ARC-QUADRANT OF THE
40,000,000 METERS CIRCUMFERENCE CIRCLE

3,183,091.5 METERS

EQUATOR

CIRCUMFERENCE: 10,000,000 METERS

------ 12,732,366 METERS DIAMETER ------
X 3.1416 π = 40,000,000 METERS
CIRCUMFERENCE

Fig. A3.8

The results above, as extrapolated from the east–west cross section of the Great Pyramid, are interesting as the metric measuring system is said to have first originated in 1789, in Paris, France.

On March 30, 1791, the French National Assembly accepted the proposal of a new definition for the meter by the French Academy of Sciences . . . *that it be one-ten-millionth* ($^1/_{10,000,000}$) *the distance between the equator and the North Pole, as measured along the meridian through Paris at sea level.*

Today the meter is generally viewed as being *theoretically* one-ten-millionth this distance. This is due to our modern-day, GPS satellite technology, which first became operational during the 1990s, and through which it was discovered that the distance between the equator and the North Pole is not 10,000 kilometers, as was supposedly believed to be the case when the meter was first introduced, *but is actually 10,001.97 kilometers.* Naturally, this has led some to argue that the meter, having been established as being one-ten-millionth this distance, should in fact be 1.0001970 (39.378 inches).

However, those who argue that the meter should express the value 1.0001970 have overlooked the obvious: *that the meter unit was based on the MEAN measure of the Earth* . . . and no one appears to have realized that the meter had already been seemingly "encoded" within the Great Pyramid, as derived from 4/π — i.e., 4 ÷ 3.1416 = 1.273236* (again, see fig. A3.6).

NORTH–SOUTH CROSS-SECTION DIMENSIONS OF THE GREAT PYRAMID

(The Measure of the Earth and Moon)

By examining the casing stone blocks found at the base of the north side of the Great Pyramid and that of another casing stone that had been found in the rubble at the base and which now resides in Scotland,[6] it was determined that the slope angle of the Great Pyramid would have been around 51°50'40" (51°51') in arc minutes and seconds, which is 51.84° in degrees.

We can easily check the *hypotenuse* and angle properties of the base-to-height ratio of the Great Pyramid accurately and to many decimal places by simply using an online "right-angle triangle" calculator. To see how accurate the information is, which has been encapsulated within the Great Pyramid, I set the values to fourteen decimal places.

As mentioned, the *intended* base length of the Great Pyramid's north–south cross-section dimensions was evidently 440 royal cubits. The meter value can be determined by simply multiplying 0.5236 meter (π/6) by 440 royal cubits, which results in a base length of 230.384 meters (755.853 feet).

Again, using trigonometry, or an online right-angle triangle calculator set to fourteen decimal places, the base-to-height ratio of the

---

*Researcher Scott Onstott agreed with me that whoever devised the meter unit in ancient times must have been aware of this slight variance but had decided to ignore it in favor of the all-round figure. Compared to the true figure, this "mean" figure is an accuracy of 99.98 percent, which is close enough.

NORTH/SOUTH CROSS-SECTION DIMENSIONS OF THE GREAT PYRAMID OF GIZA

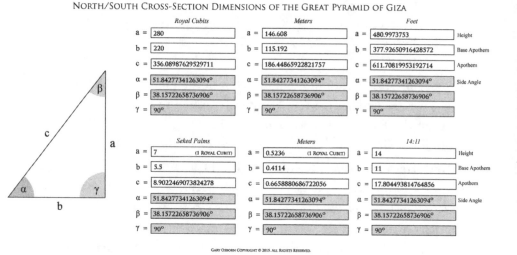

	Royal Cubits		Meters		Feet	
a =	280	a =	146.608	a =	480.9973753	Height
b =	220	b =	115.192	b =	377.92650916428572	Base Apothem
c =	356.08987629529711	c =	186.44865922821757	c =	611.70819953192714	Apothem
α =	51.84277341263094°	α =	51.84277341263094°	α =	51.84277341263094°	Side Angle
β =	38.15722658736906°	β =	38.15722658736906°	β =	38.15722658736906°	
γ =	90°	γ =	90°	γ =	90°	

	Seked Palms		Meters		14:11	
a =	7 (1 ROYAL CUBIT)	a =	0.5236 (1 ROYAL CUBIT)	a =	14	Height
b =	5.5	b =	0.4114	b =	11	Base Apothem
c =	8.9022469073824278	c =	0.6658880686722056	c =	17.804493814764856	Apothem
α =	51.84277341263094°	α =	51.84277341263094°	α =	51.84277341263094°	Side Angle
β =	38.15722658736906°	β =	38.15722658736906°	β =	38.15722658736906°	
γ =	90°	γ =	90°	γ =	90°	

Fig. A3.9

Great Pyramid's north–south cross-section dimensions—i.e., half-base length of 220 royal cubits, or 115.192 meters (230.384 ÷ 2), and height of 280 royal cubits (146.608 meters)—produces the precise side angle value of 51.84277341263094°, which rounds off to 51.843°, or 51.84°.

Converted into arc minutes and seconds, the angle of 51.84277341263094° is 51°50'33.9843".

It is also a fact that a right-angle triangle at the base-to-height ratio of 7/5.5 palms (*seked*) produces the same hypotenuse angle of 51.84277341263094°.

Also, a right-angle triangle at the base-to-height ratio of 1 royal cubit at 0.5236 meter/0.4114 meter, again, produces the same angle of 51.84277341263094°.

This side angle is the same precise side angle value as that produced by the base-to-height ratio of 14/11. In fact, it has been known since the late nineteenth century that the Great Pyramid was constructed to the base-to-height ratio of 14/11—i.e., the profile of a 14 rise on an 11 base; however, this would have only been evident in the pyramid's north–south cross section.[7]

The illustration on page 311 illustrates the different measurements at the same ratio, which produces the same precise angle to fourteen decimal places of 51.84277341263094°.

More importantly, the base-to-height ratio of 14/11, which should in fact be expressed as 140/110, is not only related to the combined radiuses of the Earth and moon *but also the "mean average" DISTANCE between the Earth and moon.* As far as I know, this is the first time this information has been presented, and I am sure it would also surprise people to know that this knowledge was again, originally derived from 4/π . . . *the same constant from which the meter unit can easily be derived,* as demonstrated earlier.

The fact that the ancients knew both the size of the Earth and the size of the moon is not as incredible or absurd as it might first appear. It is a fact that the ancient Greeks already knew the diameter of the Earth. By observing the moon carefully during a solar eclipse and seeing how the Earth's shadow fell on it, the Greek mathematicians found that the diameter of the Earth's conical shadow at the distance of the moon was about two-and-a-half times the moon's own diameter. They realized that on mean average, *the moon is 30 "Earth diameters" and 110 "moon diameters" distant from the Earth,* and so from this, they could calculate the moon's "mean diameter."

However, when studying the dimensions of the Great Pyramid of Giza it soon becomes apparent that its architect(s) had already determined the mean diameter of the Earth and moon long before the ancient Greeks, and most likely using the same method, which is why the height of the pyramid was constructed to exactly 280 royal cubits (2 × 140), and the north–south cross-section base length to exactly 440 royal cubits (4 × 110).

Note that 140 − 30 = 110.

It also becomes apparent that the architect(s) had also achieved this via *prior knowledge* of the meter unit, again based on the constant 4/π, (1.273236). However, here we will work with the true value of 4/π to sixteen decimal places, which is 4 ÷ 3.1415926535897932 π = 1.2732395447351627.

1.2732395447351627 multiplied by 10,000,000 is 12,732,395.447351627 being the "mean diameter" of the Earth, as we know it today *in meters*.

From this, and knowing that the moon is on average 30 "Earth mean diameters" and 110 "moon mean diameters" distant from the Earth, the mean radius of the moon could then be easily determined and in the most precise figures . . . *by first simply multiplying the constant of 4/π by 10,000,000, multiplying the result by 30, and then dividing that result by 110 . . .*

4/π (1.2732395447351627) × 10,000,000 = 12,732,395.447351627 meters.

Earth's mean diameter of 12,732,395.447351627 meters × 30 (Earth mean diameters) = 381,971,863.42054881 . . . the "mean" average distance between the Earth and moon in meters.

381,971,863.42054881 meters divided by 110 (moon mean diameters) = 3.472.471.48564135282 meters (mean radius of moon).

From just these simple calculations, we are then provided with the following data regarding the dimensions of the Earth and moon, again in meters.

Earth's mean diameter: 12,732,395.447351627 meters, ÷ 2 =

Earth's mean radius: 6,366,197.7236758135 meters.

Earth's mean circumference: 40,000,000 meters.

Moon's mean diameter: 3,472,471.4856413526 meters, ÷ 2 =

Moon's mean radius: 1,736,235.7428206763 meters.

Moon's mean circumference: 10,909,091 meters.

Granted, these are long numbers, but the fact is these numbers relate to the same precise side angle to fourteen decimal places of 51.84277431263094°, which would have been naturally achieved anyway via the *seked* ratio of 7/5.5 (again, see A3.9).

Also, today we would measure the Earth and moon and the distance between them in kilometers. To convert all these figures to kilometers,

Meters

a = 8102433.4664964898   'MEAN' RADIUSES OF THE EARTH AND MOON COMBINED

b = 6366197.7236758135 $\dfrac{20,000,000}{\pi}$ 100%

c = 10304266.181341466   379*e* x 1000   99.98%

α = 51.84277341263094°

β = 38.15722658736906°

γ = 90°

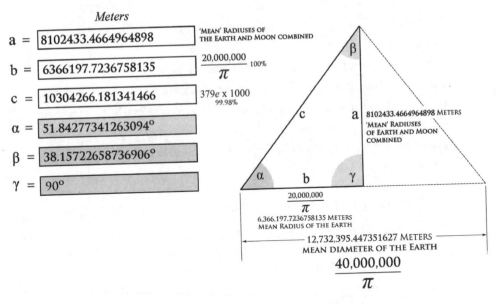

ARTWORK BY GARY OSBORN. COPYRIGHT © 2016. ALL RIGHTS RESERVED.

Fig. A3.10

all we need do is simply divide each number by 1,000 to move the decimal point back three places. (The results above cross-reference with fig. A3.11 and fig. A3.16).

Returning to the ground plan, we see that the height of the Great Pyramid relates to its four base lengths, just as a circle's radius relates to its circumference. In other words, the perimeter of the base equals the circumference of a circle whose radius is equal to the height of the pyramid, and so it could be said that the Great Pyramid *"squares the circle."*[*]

The graphic below should be studied closely to see the beauty in both the math and geometry and how it ties together much that has been encapsulated within the Great Pyramid of Giza.

---

*The deeper symbolic meaning of the "squaring of the circle" is that it represents the *marriage, union,* and *fusion* of the male and female opposites, as is required to produce a child. However, the merged square (male) and circle (female) was perceived—if not, merely symbolically—as a portal or gateway between worlds and in the context of *rebirth* and *resurrection.*

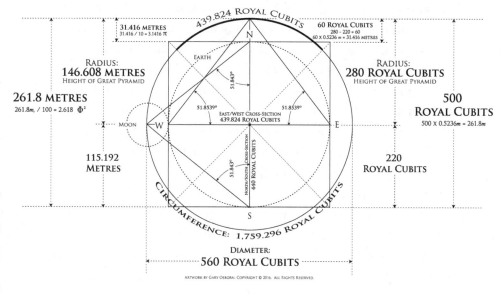

Fig. A3.11

The diameter of the 560 royal cubits circle, subtract the north/south cross-section base length of 440 royal cubits = 120, divided by 2 = 60 royal cubits × 0.5236 meter = 31.416 meters, / 10 = 3.1416 π (*pi*).

500 royal cubits × 0.5236 meter – 261.8 meters, / 100 = 2.618 Φ^2 (*Phi* squared).

Because π (*pi*) was discovered in 1882 to be a *transcendental* number rather than an *algebraic, irrational number* and therefore cannot be exactly measured because it spirals off into infinity, the problem of "squaring the circle" was proved mathematically impossible. This, and the fact that it has been believed for a long time now that the Great Pyramid will only produce *pi* to an accuracy of 99.96 percent, then it's no wonder that any reference to "the fact" that the Great Pyramid of Giza "squares the circle" is often met with disdain by Egyptologists and the mainstream in general.

However, when you "square the circle" in relation to the perimeter of the Great Pyramid with its "two cross-section planes" and four different base lengths—with the different base-to-height ratios of each producing the combined "mean radius" proportions of the Earth and moon at

3:11 ratio . . . also π (*pi*), Φ (*Phi*), φ (*phi*), and $\sqrt{\Phi}$ (the square root of *Phi*), and all to an accuracy of 99.9998 percent compared to these same constants at sixteen decimal places as I have now discovered—*then you come about as close as you can get to the solution.*

All this, as well as the mean diameter of the Earth based on $4/\pi$; approximations of the constant *e;* the *m/s* speed of light constant *c* and its equivalent in *mi/s*—and even the *fine-structure constant*—can all be derived from the royal cubit and meter measurements of the Great Pyramid of Giza as I have now determined and which are very close to the estimates presented from the surveys conducted by Petrie (1880–1882), J. H. Cole (1925), and the GDFAE (Glen Dash Foundation for Archaeological Research; February 2015).

These discoveries also reveal that the meter unit and the royal cubit are related, in that the royal cubit of 0.5236 meter ($\pi/6$) was derived from the meter unit—i.e., *one-sixth* of a one-meter-diameter circle, which appears to have been already familiar to the architect(s), having been originally derived from $4/\pi$. Also, the volume of a sphere with a diameter of 1 meter, is 0.5236 meter—again the length of the royal cubit.*

It would perhaps surprise people to know that the north latitude location of the Great Pyramid is also related to the royal cubit of 0.5236 meter and the constant $4/\pi$. . . .

NORTH LATITUDE LOCATION

The Great Pyramid of Giza is 2,300 meters and 1.43 miles from an exact 30° N latitude—which is *one-sixth* the circumference of the Earth from the North Pole and *one-twelfth* the circumference of the Earth from the equator. *one-sixth* of the π (*pi*) circumference of a

---

*A sphere with a diameter of 1 meter and a volume of 0.5236 meter (1 royal cubit) will fit exactly inside a cube with twelve 1-meter-length edges and a volume of 1 cubic meter. However, a sphere with a diameter of 1 meter and a volume of 0.5236 meter, divided by a cube with the volume of 1 cubic meter = 0.5236 meter.

Therefore, the length of the royal cubit at 0.5236 meter, which was used to construct the Great Pyramid, reflects not only the volume of a 1-meter-diameter sphere, but also the volume of a 1-meter sphere divided by a cube with a volume of 1 cubic meter. This is yet more evidence that the royal cubit is related to the meter unit and was derived from it.

circle is 0.5236 (which in meters is the length of the royal cubit). *one-twelfth* is 2.618 (φ^2).

It is a fact that the Great Pyramid of Giza is centered on the north latitude, "degree" coordinates 29.9792° N. In fact, using the accurate, online *USGS Earth Explorer* mapping program, we find that the coordinates of 29.9792458°N, 31.1341965°E, which contain the full nine-digit *m/s* speed of light figure in its latitude coordinates, will target a point approximately less than only 1 meter south of the apex-center of the Great Pyramid.

This is way beyond coincidence (see box below). If we can remove the staunchly held view that the Great Pyramid was constructed by simple, ancient people with no knowledge of advanced mathematics, then perhaps we can move forward in our understanding. . . .

As regards this particular connection between the speed of light and the Great Pyramid of Giza (although there are numerous other references to the speed of light in its dimensions, as has been presented in this appendix), several pseudosceptics who are in denial and would prefer that we all remain ignorant of this or equally in denial, had already made attempts to "debunk" the earlier claim by nit-picking the numbers of the coordinates and questioning the placement of the decimal point—stating that 29.9792 IS NOT 299,792 meters or 299,792 kilometers. Directly under the coordinates given on the first page that comes up when we Google *"Great Pyramid coordinates,"* the reader will find the most popular and regularly quoted blog article used by the skeptics, which was initially written and published to debunk any notion that the significance of these coordinates is more than just a mere coincidence.

However, no matter how we view it, it is nevertheless a fact *that the nine numbers of the degree latitude coordinates upon which the Great Pyramid is centered are the same nine numbers in both the meters and kilometers per-second speed of light figure* . . . "making this striking similarity difficult to accept as a coincidence," writes author Robert Bauval, and that's the important point here.

When we simply see it this way, the argument against this fact regarding the placement of the decimal point *to make the point* that any correlation these degree latitude coordinates have with the speed of light figure is "flawed" and "therefore doesn't mean anything," *is in fact irrelevant* and shows just how pedantic and censorious people can be when they are confronted with factual details that reveal an obvious correlation, even when the odds against a significant nine-digit sequence of numbers that already exists coming up so randomly and especially in something that is seen to have no connection whatsoever, *can actually be compared to winning the National Lottery.*

For example, all one need do is divide the meters-per-second speed of light figure 299,792,458 by 10,000,000 (the meter being one-ten-millionth of the distance between the equator and the North Pole), which converts the meters-per-second "light speed" figure to the latitude coordinates 29.9792458° N. This is mathematically expressed as $c/10^{-7}$ (c being the m/s speed of light constant).

In any case, it is truly remarkable that the fine latitude line on the Earth that precisely corresponds to the same nine-digit value given to the m/s "speed of light" figure *just happens to pass through the center of the most enigmatic and astounding structure that exists on this planet. . . .*

A royal cubit length of 0.5236 meters, when multiplied by the number 1.273236 ($4/\pi$), generates a number that when rounded off to the nearest ten-thousandth, is 0.6667—approximating the result of 2/3 to an accuracy of 99.995 percent.

0.6667 multiplied by 2.7182818284590452 (e to sixteen decimal places) results in the value 1.8122784950336455 (which is 2/3e to 99.995 percent).

When 1.8122784950336455 is placed with the number 3.1415926535897932 π (*pi* to sixteen decimal places) in a right-angle triangle calculator to create the ratio $\pi/{\sim}2/3e$, the result is the hypotenuse ("degree" side angle) of 29.979192643°, which rounds off to 29.9792°.

One can then use the degree angle of 29.9792° to determine a lati-

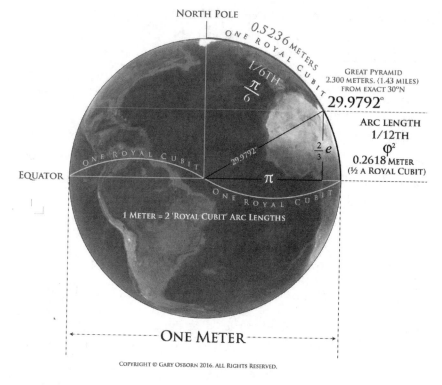

NORTH POLE

0.5236 METERS
ONE ROYAL CUBIT

1/6TH
$\frac{\pi}{6}$

GREAT PYRAMID
2,300 METERS, (1.43 MILES)
FROM EXACT 30°N

29.9792°

ARC LENGTH
1/12TH
φ^2
0.2618 METER
(½ A ROYAL CUBIT)

ONE ROYAL CUBIT

29.9792°

$\frac{2}{3}e$

EQUATOR

π

ONE ROYAL CUBIT

1 METER = 2 'ROYAL CUBIT' ARC LENGTHS

ONE METER

Fig. A3.12

tude location on the Earth by simply converting it to degree coordinates, as in 29.9792° N, which are the same latitude coordinates on which the Great Pyramid is centered. The graphic above of the Earth reduced to a diameter of one meter, encapsulates all the above.

Furthermore . . .

If the Earth's mean circumference of 40,000,000 meters was reduced to a circumference of exactly 31,416,000 meters (10,000,000 × *pi*), which would automatically reduce the Earth's "mean diameter" of 12,732,360 meters to a diameter of exactly 10,000,000 meters, then Giza would be situated at a distance of 10,000,000 royal cubits from the North Pole. Again, this reveals a close relationship between the meter unit and the royal cubit. However, the above is not surprising really when we realize the possibility that the ancient Egyptian royal cubit of 0.5236 meter was actually derived from a perfect circle with a diameter of 1 meter and a circumference of 3.1416 (π) meter . . . *divided by 6.*

And here's another interesting fact about the coordinates of the Great Pyramid:

The numbers in the Great Pyramid's latitude coordinates (29.9792) multiplied by the numbers in the Great Pyramid's longitude coordinates (31.134177) = 933.3777191184.

933.3777191184 divided by 18 = 51.8543177288—the first five digits providing us with the Great Pyramid's east–west cross-section side angle of 51.854° . . . an accuracy of 99.999 percent. It would appear, that the coordinates on which the Great Pyramid is centered also provide us with a *checksum* for its east–west cross-section side angles.*

THE FOUR SIDES AND THE EXTRAORDINARY MATHEMATICAL DATA THEY EACH PRODUCE

Again, along with the height of the Great Pyramid, each of the four different base lengths that enclose the two cross sections when measured in both royal cubits and meters, produce more mathematical data in terms of the constants *pi, Phi, e* . . . even the meters-per-second speed of light in a vacuum constant (*c*) and its equivalent in miles-per-second, which provides a logical-enough reason as to why each of the four bases would have varied in length. Following are just a few examples of the extraordinary data produced by the base-to-height ratio of the four sides.

First of all, it should be noted and emphasized that the base-to-height ratios of the four sides relate to the height of 146.514312 meters (480.69) feet—a height estimate that exists on public record since Petrie first published his survey of the Great Pyramid in 1883. Theoretically, the height of 146.514312 meters would have been one of FOUR different heights expressed in the completed pyramid relating to the dimensions of a sphere that was designed to be placed on top of the apex—a

---

*1.273236 × 73.304 (half height of Great Pyramid in meters) = 93.333291744 (which is ~280 ÷ 3).

93.333291744 × 10 = 933.33291744, ÷ 18 = 51.85182874666667 . . . the first four digits again providing us with the Great Pyramid's east–west cross-section side angle of 51.85°.

conclusion I was forced to accept while studying the dimensions of the Great Pyramid.

It should be emphasized, that aside from its overall height of 280 royal cubits (146.608 meters), there are in addition three other heights to consider—especially concerning the base-to-height ratios these different heights would have produced with each of the four different base lengths and both the north–south and east–west cross sections.

Why would the Great Pyramid have expressed four different heights?

Recent independent studies by André Pochan in 1971, the Spanish architect Miguel Pérez-Sánchez in 2014, and most recently Jean-Paul Bauval (brother of Robert) in 2016 have led to the same theory, that a capstone did indeed crown the Great Pyramid but that it was itself truncated, and that an object—most likely a sphere—was designed to be placed on top of the capstone/apex. From closely studying the dimensions of the Great Pyramid, I too had also arrived at this same conclusion. However, each of our theories differ on the actual size of this sphere, which I say was around 0.23622 meter (0.775 foot) in diameter—about the size of an average basketball—and for reasons I have yet to reveal.

This would mean that aside from the primary height of 146.608 meters (280 royal cubits—virtually 481 feet), the Great Pyramid would have

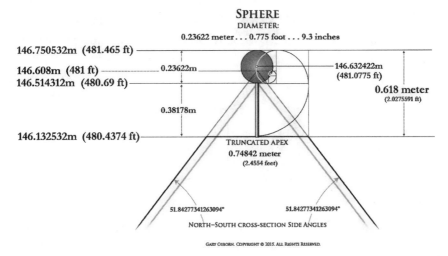

Fig. A3.13

expressed, in addition, three other heights related to this sphere: one to the base of the sphere (146.514312 meters), one to the center of the sphere (146.632422 meters), and one to the top of the sphere (146.750532 meters), and all designed around the proportions of the *Phi* ratio.

Compare the graphic above with the ancient Egyptian hieroglyph below, which was apparently included in inscriptions around Saqqara, Egypt, and recorded by Gaston Maspero between 1880 and 1886.

Sir Gaston Maspero, director of the Department of Antiquities of the Cairo Museum found a curious hieroglyph in inscriptions around Saqqara for which he could find no explanation: an obelisk atop a truncated pyramid, with a solar disk balanced on top of it. For Cotsworth, he kindly made a drawing of it. To Cotsworth, the similarity of Maes-Howe, the Silbury Hill Maypole and obelisk atop a mastaba or unfinished pyramid was inescapable. Only how did this fit with the Pyramid of Cheops?[8]

I came upon the above information about the hieroglyph long after the insights I had about the sphere and its design, as illustrated in figure A3.13.

I personally regard this sphere as being symbolic of the "source-center of creation" from which everything is made manifest in the material world—i.e., representing zero-point, which the apex of the

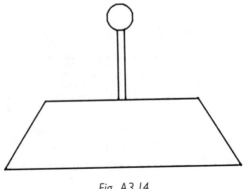

Fig. A3.14

Great Pyramid also represents. As for any practical purpose, it may have had, one would immediately compare it to the elevated, "top-load" sphere (sometimes torus or doughnut-shaped) that surmounts a *Tesla Coil,* named after the Serbian American electrical engineer, inventor, and genius, Nikola Tesla (1856—1943).

Also, related to the overall Great Pyramid height of 146.750532 meters, which is level with the top of the sphere placed on the apex, is this extraordinary result when we add together the constants *phi* (φ), *Phi* (Φ – added twice), *e*, and *pi* (π), and each at a practicable and measurable number of decimal places.

0.618 (φ) meter, + 1.618 (Φ) meters, + 1.618 (Φ) meters, + 2.718 (*e*) meters, + 3.1416 (π) meters = 9.7136 meters.

Height of 146.750532 meters (to the top of the Sphere), subtract the result of 9.7136 meters = 137.036932 meters.

The number 137.036932 again gives reference to the most mystifying number known to physicists, which has an approximate value of 137.036. When this number is divided from 1, as in 1/137.036, it generates the *fine-structure constant* (0.007297352 . . .), denoted as α (*alpha*), and originally known as *Sommerfeld's constant*—a *dimensionless* constant in physics. Compared to 137.035999139 (the most recent estimate for the reciprocal value of the *fine-structure constant* according to CODATA) . . . the result is an accuracy of 99.9993 percent.

It is also interesting that today and excluding a large portion of its apex, the Great Pyramid stands at a height of 137 meters.

North Side

According to the 2015 GDRF/AERA survey, the north side base length of the Great Pyramid at minimum is given as 230.256 meters. This is a difference of only 1.7 mm from my estimate of 230.2577 meters for the north side base length.

The reader may ask, *Why should we choose the "minimum" estimate over the "mean" and "maximum" base length estimates also given from this survey?*

Answer: my estimate of 230.2577 meters is also supported by the meter estimate given for the north side base length by J. H. Cole in 1925 of 230.253 meters—a difference of only 4.7 mm.

- 1.618033988749 Φ (*Phi*), to twelve decimal places, multiplied by the Great Pyramid's north side, base apothem length of 115.12885 meters, and the result multiplied by 1,000, results in a number that begins with the first eight digits of the *miles-per-second* speed of light in a vacuum figure, 186,282.3970512. *Accuracy: 99.999997 percent.*

South Side

For the south side of the Great Pyramid, J. H. Cole estimated a length of 230.454 meters. However, by slightly reducing Cole's base length of 230.454 meters down to 230.452 meters—*a difference of only 2 millimeters!*—produces the following mathematical results.

- A south-side base-to-height ratio of 115.226 meters (half-base) × 146.514312 meters (height), set to fifteen decimal places, produces a side angle of 51.816763126497227°. 51.816763126497227 multiplied TWICE by the number 59.9584916, which is 2 × 29.9792458 (being the north latitude number on which the Great Pyramid is centered, and which is the *c*, [speed of light] constant 299,792,458 divided by 10,000,000), will result in a number, which begins with the same first seven digits of the precise miles-per-second, speed of light in a vacuum figure, 186,282.3970512. *Accuracy: 99.99997 percent.*
- The Great Pyramid south side base length of 440.13 royal cubits (230.4519 meters) is 0.14319617186 miles, which rounds off to 0.1432 mile. 0.1432 × 1000 = 143.2 miles.

This gives reference to the Nile Delta Triangle, which is exactly 1,000 times the size of the Great Pyramid of Giza. 143.2 miles divided by 2 = 71.6 miles. 71.6 × 360 = 25,776, which is the exact number of years given to the *precessional cycle* by today's estimates. 71.6 miles also brings us to the *halfway-point center* of the Nile Delta Triangle, which reflects the *halfway-point center* of the Great Pyramid (see fig. A3.16 on p. 336).

East Side (Phi)

The east side base length of 230.3649 meters, which I have now determined based on the remarkable mathematical data this length produces, is only 2.61 cm longer than J. H. Cole's estimate of 230.391 meters (1925), and only 8.1 mm shorter than the GDRF/AERA maximum estimate (2015) of 230.373 meters.

- The base-to-height ratio of the Great Pyramid's east side dimensions (height: 146.514312 meters x half base: 115.18245 meters) produces a side angle of 51.8273°, which is the *Phi* (Φ) proportion angle—the same precise angle produced by the ratio of 1.27202/1, which is an approximation of the square root of *Phi* ($\sqrt{\Phi}$) divided by 1). *Accuracy: 99.99997 percent.*
- The "east side" side angle of 51.8273° is a close approximation of the *hypotenuse* angle 51.827292372987752° produced by the ratio of Φ / $\sqrt{\Phi}$ (1.6180339887498948 *Phi* divided by the square root of *Phi*—1.2720196495140689453, both to sixteen decimal places). *Accuracy 99.999985 percent.*
- Here's the fine-structure constant, accurate to seven decimal places:

Great Pyramid's east side Base length of 230.3649 meters, divided by 73.304 (half height of Great Pyramid of 146.608 meters) = 3.1425965840881807 ($\sim\pi$ *pi*).

3.1425965840881807 divided by 100 = 0.031425965840881807, $\times e$ = 0.08542463188704369535, when squared = 0.007297367733037, which is the reciprocal of 1 ÷ 137.035714326519 . . .

This result is 99.9998 percent accurate when compared to 0.007297352566355, being the reciprocal of 1 ÷ 137.035999139 . . . the *fine-structure constant*. This is the most mystifying number known to physicists, denoted as *α* (*alpha*), and originally known as *Sommerfeld's constant*—a *dimensionless* constant in physics.

We can also approach this in reverse, which gives a more accurate result . . .

1 ÷ 137.035999139 = 0.007297352566355 (*fine-structure constant*).*

The square root of 0.007297352566355 is 0.0854245431146986, divided by *e* = 0.0314259331833611018, × 100 = 3.14259331833611018 (~π *pi*), x 73.304 (half height of Great Pyramid) = 230.36466 meters, which is accurate to 99.99996 percent compared to the Great Pyramid's east side base length of 230.3649 meters.

West Side

For the west side of the Great Pyramid, the base length estimate (including the casing stones) provided by J. H. Cole suggest a length of 230.357 meters. Cole's estimates suggest that the west side base length is slightly shorter than the east side base length.

However, according to the U.S.-based Glen Dash Research Foundation (GDRF) and the Ancient Egypt Research Associates (AERA) survey conducted in 2015, *it is the east side base length which was slightly shorter than the west side base length,* and seeing as this is the most recent survey to date, I would consider this to have been a most likely fact.

The GDRF/AERA survey presents an estimate of between a minimum of 230.378 meters and a maximum of 230.436 meters for the west side base length.

I discovered that the west side base length, which provides us with a reference to the meters-per-second speed of light in a vacuum figure, as well as the reciprocal of *phi* (*φ*), and which is close to both J. H. Cole's estimate and to the GDRF/AERA minimum estimate, is a base length of 230.3806 meters. This is a difference of only 2.36 cm

---

*The *fine-structure constant* was named after the German theoretical physicist Arnold Johannes Wilhelm Sommerfeld (1868–1951), who introduced it in 1916 to account for the splitting of atomic spectral lines.

over Cole's estimate and within 2.6 mm from the GDRF/AERA minimum estimate.

> The circumferences of two circles—i.e., 1023.554 meters and 723.762 meters—can be derived from a square perimeter of all four sides of the Great Pyramid set to the west side base length of 230.3806 meters.
>
> 230.3806 meters x π (*pi*) = 723.762 meters . . . the circumference of the small circle.
>
> The ratio of 230.3806 meters x 230.3806 meters produces a *hypotenuse* of 325.80736902765106 meters.
>
> 325.80736902765106 x π (*pi*) = 1023.554 meters . . . the circumference of the large circle.
>
> 1023.554 subtract 723.762 = 299,792—the first six digits of the *c* (*m/s* speed of light) constant.

PERIMETER OF THE GREAT PYRAMID IN METERS

West side base length of 230.3806 meters + north side base length of 230.2577 meters + east side base length of 230.3649 meters + south side base length of 230.4519 meters, results in a perimeter of 921.4551 meters, which is ~339 × *e*.

In other words, if we take the number 339 as a length in meters, × 2.7182818284590452 meters (expressing true *e*), the result is 921.49754 meters.

Compared to the 921.4551-meters perimeter figure . . . *an accuracy of 99.995 percent.*

Also, twice the base perimeter of 921.4551 meters = 1,842.9102 meters, *which is virtually 1 fathom, 1 nautical mile, and 1 minute of arc at the equator!*

As first discovered by the author W. R. Fix, the Great Pyramid is virtually a mathematical "scale model" of the Northern Hemisphere of the Earth at the scale of **1:43,200**.

Let's say that YOU as the architect are already familiar with the meter unit and you want to construct a pyramid at a specific size in respect to the measure of the Earth. You imagine that the sum length of the base perimeter of this pyramid could be matched to one "half arc minute" of latitude at the equator, making sure that the corresponding ratio of its height is in reference to the polar radius of the Earth. This would make the size of the pyramid the scale of 1:43,200 in respect to the Earth's polar radius and the Earth's equatorial circumference, *which would be just at the right size—not too large, not too small.*

However, although the meter is a "divine unit" of measurement relating to the measurement of the Earth, you had already found that when you worked out the base-to-height ratio to determine the height, the length of the four bases, and the base perimeter *at this size,* all of which were expressed in METERS—*they did not work out to "whole number" lengths.* For example, the height works out to 460.608 meters and the base to 230.384 meters. You realize that for there to be no ambiguity or doubt about this having been intended, you would then need to *invent* a new unit of measurement that would express these same lengths in *"whole number" integer values.*

You then set about deriving this new unit from the sacred meter.

You find that if you mark out a one-meter-diameter circle and divide it by six, it results in a "sacred arc" length of 0.5236 meter, which is equal to 7 palms (an expression of π/6). You then create a template consisting of a triangle—the *seked*—which has a rise of 0.5236 meter (7 palms) on a base of 5½ palms, thereby fixing a base-to-height ratio of 7/5.5. You know that measuring out the base length of your pyramid, 88 times the 5.5 base of your triangle, will result in a length of exactly 440 × 0.5236 meter. You also know that if you also measure the height of your pyramid to 280 times the 0.5236-meter height of your triangle, the size of your pyramid will then be at the scale of 1:43,200 in respect to the measure of the Earth. At the same time, the pyramid will also be at the same base-to-height ratio as the combined "mean" radiuses of the Earth and moon—i.e., 140/110—and that this same ratio will also encode the "mean" distance between the Earth and the moon of 30 Earth diameters and 110 moon diameters . . . 140 − 30 = 110.

To make sure this new unit of 0.5236 in meters (π/6) would be familiar to those in the future who would measure your pyramid, you also introduce this new measurement to the surrounding culture, showing them how it can be derived from the width of 7 palms or 28 fingers. You do this so that this new unit becomes a common unit measurement used daily and in other constructions. This would ensure that it would then be known on record, having been passed down through the centuries. *This new unit is what became the ancient Egyptian royal cubit (meh niswt)* ⸢₋₋⸣.

- The 146.608-meter (280 royal cubits) height of the Great Pyramid + the height of its pavement/platform of 0.5236 meter (1 royal cubit) = 147.1316 meters (281 royal cubits), multiplied by **43,200** = 6,356,085.12 meters, *which references the 6,356,752.3-meter polar radius of the Earth to an accuracy of 99.99 percent.* (Inspired by W. R. Fix, 1978.)
- The 921.4551-meter "base perimeter" of the Great Pyramid multiplied by **43,200** = 39.806.860.32, divided by 360 results in 110,574.612 meters, which references one degree of *LATITUDE* at the equator of 110,574.3 meters—*being the distance from the equator to one-degree north* . . . accuracy 99.999 percent.*
- The 927.71976-meter perimeter of the Great Pyramid at the extent of each of the four corner sockets, again multiplied by **43,200** = 40,077,493.632, divided by 360 results in 111,326.3712 meters, which is close to one degree of *LONGITUDE* at the equator of 111,319.49 meters (W. R. Fix, 1978). This is an accuracy of 99.99 percent.

---

*(Base perimeter measurements inspired by the findings made by W. R. Fix who attributed the knowledge of this to the ancient Greek historians [namely, Agatharchides of Cnidus] who suggested that the Great Pyramid incorporates a fraction of a geographical degree.)

- The 927.71976 "base perimeter" of the Great Pyramid at the extent of each of the four corner sockets in inches, divided by 100 = 365.244, *the precise number of days in a year.*

CONCAVITIES

As I will reveal in more detail in my own written work (in progress), the exact all-round, seven-digit figure for the speed of light in *miles*-per-second in a vacuum is referenced in the length of the Great Pyramid's apothem *inside the concavities* in meters, × 1000 (186,282.39). At the same time, the depth of the concavities in meters gives reference to the speed of light in *meters*-per-second in a vacuum × 10,000,000 (299,792,4).

These meaningful, concavity measurements are also supported by the fact that the differences between a) the square base perimeter of the Great Pyramid of 921.4551 meters; b) the square base perimeter of the pavement/platform on which the Great Pyramid stands of 923.1471 meters; and c) the square base perimeter of 920.338 meters, as a result of the depth within the concavities (which are likely to have been visible in the mantle, and from a point above the base), each express the same proportional differences between the *mean circumference,* the *equatorial circumference,* and the *polar circumference* of the Earth, respectively.

1. The square base perimeter of the Great Pyramid of Giza:
    The mean circumference of the Earth on which the meter unit was based is 40,000,000 meters, 40,000 kilometers, and **24,854.8477** miles.
    A circumference of 40,000,000 meters divided by 4 (which expresses the distance between the North Pole and the equator) = 10,000,000 meters.
    The square base perimeter of the Great Pyramid (all four base lengths added together) is a total of 921.4551 meters.
    921.4551 meters divided by 4 = 230.363775 meters.
    10,000,000 meters divided by 230.363775 meters = 43,409.6030 meters.

921.4551 meters divided by 1609.344 meters (which equals one statute mile) = 0.572565654 meter.

0.572565654 x 43,409.6030 (the number presented above in meters) = **24,854.8477**, which is the same number given to the *mean circumference* of the Earth in miles . . . 99.9999999 percent accuracy.

2. The square base perimeter of the pavement/platform on which the Great Pyramid stands:

   The equatorial circumference of the Earth is precisely 40,075,016.7 meters, 40,075.0167 kilometers, and **24,901.461** miles.

   The level pavement/platform upon which the Great Pyramid rests is said to extend outward from the edge of the outer casing of the Great Pyramid by an average of 42.3 cm (0.423 meter) on each side.[9]

   This makes the square base perimeter of the pavement/platform exactly 923.1471 meters.

   923.1471 meters divided by 1609.344 meters (which equals 1 statute mile) = 0.5736170141374374 meter, × 43,409.6030 = **24,900.4868**.

   Compared to the precise equatorial circumference of the Earth figure of 24,901.461 miles, *this is an accuracy of 99.996 percent.*

3. The square base perimeter determined by the depth of the *concavities* on each side:

   The polar circumference of the Earth is precisely 39,940,652.65 meters, 39,940.65265 kilometers, and **24,817.971** miles.

   The square base perimeter that is determined by the depth of the *concavities* on each side is 920.338 meters.

   920.338 meters divided by 1609.344 meters (which equals 1 statute mile) = 0.571871521 meter.

   0.571871521 × 43,409.6030 = **24,824.7157**.

   Compared to the precise polar circumference of the Earth figure of 24,817.971 miles, *this is an accuracy of 99.97 percent.*

MYSTERY OF 103

Again, it is accepted that the Great Pyramid was constructed to a height of 280 royal cubits.

280 divided by the number *e* (2.718) = 103.0169242089772.

If we divide 103.0169242089772 by 2, the result is 51.5084 . . . which can be rounded off to 51.51. This result converted to "degrees and arc minutes"—as in 51°51'—again, provides us with the side angle of the Great Pyramid, which in degrees is 51.84°. It is interesting that the result of dividing 280 by *e,* and then the result divided by 2, results in 51.5084 . . . which contains the numbers of the side angle in both "arc minutes" and "degrees." Also, 51.51 × *e* (2.718) = 140.0186969839254201, which rounds off to 140 and is, again, half the Great Pyramid height of 280 royal cubits.

Furthermore, 1.618033988749 (*Φ Phi*), divided by 3.1415926535897932 (*π pi*) = 0.5150360270374413985 × 100 = 51.50360270374413985—again, the side angle in degrees and arc minutes is 51°51'. Also, 51.50360270374413985 × 2 = 103.0072054074882797, × 2.7182818284590452 (*e*) = 280.0026146595236926816, which rounds off to 280.

As many of us would know, the number 33 is a significant number in Freemasonry, being the highest "Degree" level that can be attained. As discovered by pyramid researcher Ibrahim Ibrahim, 33 × *π* (*pi*), also provides us with the side angle of 51.84°.

33 × 3.1415926535897932 (π) = 103.6725575684631756,
divided by 2 = 51.8362787842315878, which rounds off to 51.84°.

In fact, all three constants of *e, pi,* and *Phi* can be used to attain the slope angle of the Great Pyramid's sides via the number 103, which is the tewnty-seventh prime number.

Height 280 divided by 2.7182818284590452 (e) = 103 . . .

$$33 \times 3.1415926535897932 \ (\pi) = 103 \ldots$$

$$1.618 \ (\Phi \ phi), \ \text{divided by} \ 3.141 \ (\pi) = 0.5151225724291627 \times 100$$
$$= 51.51225724291627, \times 2 = 103 \ldots$$

$$103 \ \text{divided by} \ 2 = 51.5.$$

There is also another way we can arrive at the number 103, and this time in degrees—as in 103°. And to do this we simply add together the angles of the shafts of the King's Chamber.

King's Chamber Southern Shaft = 45° . . . 45.2° (mean).
King's Chamber Northern Shaft = varies from 30.716° to 32.67° . . . 31.7° (mean).[10]

31.7° indicates the meaningful *Phi* ratio angle of 31.718°. That this was the intended angle would be logical, seeing as the *Phi* golden ratio is evident throughout the Great Pyramid. If so, then it follows that the intended angle for the KC southern shaft could have been 45.282°, as the mean value implies.*

$$45.282° + 31.718° = 77°.$$

$$180° - 77° = 103°.$$

However, we would get the same result if we simply rounded off the angles of the shafts to 45° and 32°.

$$45° + 32° = 77°.$$

$$180° - 77° = 103°.$$

---

*I am inclined to accept these specific angle values as being the intended angles of the designer/architect for the two King's Chamber shafts. In my own work, I present both possibilities: that although they may indeed have had a practical function as "star shafts"—i.e., pointing to specific stars—that at the same time, the shafts were also meant to correspond *aesthetically* with the *Phi ratio* geometry of the Great Pyramid.

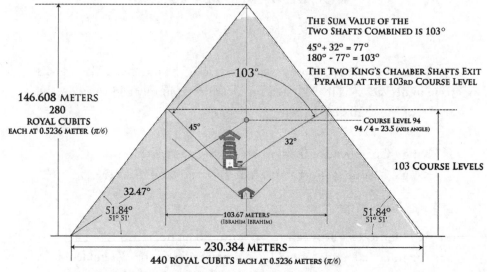

Fig. A3.15

So then, the angles of the two King's Chamber shafts amount to 103°. And, the evidence implies that both the King's Chamber shafts were meant to exit the Great Pyramid at around the 103rd Course Level.[11] Above is a graphic of the north–south cross-section dimensions of the Great Pyramid showing its internal features.

In the ground plan (see A3.11, p. 315), the 31.416-meters portion of the apex converts to 103.070866 feet. It can be concluded then, that the Great Pyramid encodes or expresses the prime number 103 in *Meters,*

Feet, Inches, and *Degree Angles,* and also in its number of *Course Levels.*

But, there are more remarkable results with the chamber shafts.

King's Chamber Shafts: 45° + 32° = 77°.
Queen's Chamber Shafts: 38.5° + 38.5° = 77°.
Great Pyramid side angle of 51.5° × 4 (four sides) = 206°.
77° + 77° + 206° = 360°, which gives reference to the 360° circle and the *360-degree measuring system.*

SECRET CHAMBER?

To appreciate WHY the architect had the north–south cross section of the Great Pyramid constructed to the 14/11 or 140/110 base-to-height ratio dimensions, which also produces a precise side angle to fourteen decimal places of 51.84277341263094°, *we must view it all graphically by doing what the author John Michell first did.*[12]

One simply superimposes a cross-section diagram of the Great Pyramid over an image of the Earth along with the moon—with both placed in such a way that both the 6,366,197.7236758135-meters "mean radius" of the Earth and the 1,736,235.7428206763-meters "mean radius" of the moon are *tangentially joined* together to give a combined total of 8,102,433.4664964898 meters.

(Again, these are long numbers, but these numbers are the result of setting the right-angle triangle calculator to 14 decimal places, which gives us the precise side angle of 51.84277341263094°, and which I use here to demonstrate how accurate this data is, based on the north–south cross-section side angles of the Great Pyramid derived simply from a 7/5.5 *seked* ratio).

We also make sure that the base of the Great Pyramid aligns with the equator and that the Giza meridian (once believed to be the world's Zero Prime Meridian in ancient times) is its centerline. When we do this, we immediately grasp what we were meant to see . . . that the location of the Great Pyramid at Giza on the Earth is positioned right at the heart center of the image of the Great Pyramid superimposed over

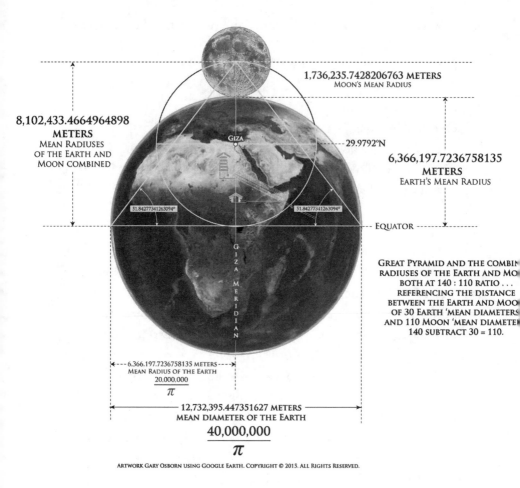

1,736,235.7428206763 METERS
MOON'S MEAN RADIUS

8,102,433.4664964898
METERS
MEAN RADIUSES
OF THE EARTH AND
MOON COMBINED

GIZA

29.9792°N

6,366,197.7236758135
METERS
EARTH'S MEAN RADIUS

51.84277341263094°

51.84277341263094°

EQUATOR

G
I
Z
A

M
E
R
I
D
I
A
N

GREAT PYRAMID AND THE COMBIN
RADIUSES OF THE EARTH AND MO
BOTH AT 140 : 110 RATIO . . .
REFERENCING THE DISTANCE
BETWEEN THE EARTH AND MOO
OF 30 EARTH 'MEAN DIAMETERS
AND 110 MOON 'MEAN DIAMETE
140 SUBTRACT 30 = 110.

6,366,197.7236758135 METERS
MEAN RADIUS OF THE EARTH

$$\frac{20,000,000}{\pi}$$

12,732,395.447351627 METERS
MEAN DIAMETER OF THE EARTH

$$\frac{40,000,000}{\pi}$$

ARTWORK GARY OSBORN USING GOOGLE EARTH. COPYRIGHT © 2015. ALL RIGHTS RESERVED.

Fig. A3.16

the Earth, and exactly where the Great Pyramid is located on the Earth at the meters-per-second speed-of-light-related latitude coordinates of 29.9792° N. During the Great Pyramid's inception phase, and to preserve the information encoded within it, it appears to have been decided that both the external and internal dimensions of the pyramid be drawn up to the combined proportions of the Earth and moon. However, the purpose was not just to preserve information and knowledge like an encyclopedia or almanac in stone. . . .

As I had revealed in the book *The Giza Prophecy* (2012, coauthored with Scott Creighton), when a diagram of the north–south cross section of the Great Pyramid, showing all its internal features is superimposed over a graphic of the Earth, the apex of the Great Pyramid points toward its own location on the Earth via the geophysical/geodetic-related angles within its angle geometry.

One of many spooky facts emerging from the geometry is that the Great Pyramid perfectly encodes its own exact position on Earth's surface. This achievement cannot be a coincidence and is far beyond the science of ancient Egypt as it is understood by Egyptologists.[13]

The result can be read like a map, just like the "map" above, which is pointing to a specific location within the Great Pyramid—namely, its *core heart center.*

What could be more accurate and as long-lasting and self-preserving than a "map" that has been encoded within a stone-made mountain— especially a "map" based on the combined proportions of the Earth and moon?

Could this central point in the Great Pyramid be the location of another chamber? And if so, what would it contain?

It may interest people to know that the "heart-center" of the Great Pyramid of Giza was also targeted by the seven coordinates found in the *Rendlesham Binary Code* that Jim Penniston (USAF ret.) claims he received while investigating an unidentified triangular craft in Rendlesham Forest on Boxing Day morning, 1980.

Because of my work on deciphering symbols and codes, and my discovery that the Earth's axis angle of 23.5 degrees had been encoded in numerous sources throughout history—especially paintings from the seventeenth century—I was commissioned by Jim Penniston to work on these coordinates in February 2011. In the first few weeks of working on the seven coordinates, I was amazed to find reflected in what emerged from them my own research and findings concerning the Great Pyramid of Giza, made since 2001. This was unexpected, as I had received the coordinates from Jim Penniston the very same week that the final draft of the manuscript for the book *The Giza Prophecy* (the first book to feature my research and discoveries about the Great Pyramid) had been sent to the publishers. In fact, some of the new revelations outlined in this summary concerning the Great Pyramid, are the result—or rather the "inspiration"—of what I had initially discovered during my five-year study of the seven coordinates found in the Rendlesham Binary Code.

The seven coordinates are themselves a code that must be approached in a certain way to retrieve another level of information. The initial information that emerges could be described as "homogeneous" in that the parts (coordinates) all fit together via the same key to produce a "bigger picture." This "picture" is unmistakably familiar to many of us and does not require interpretation. It is there, it is obvious, and is as factual as $2 \times 2 = 4$, which proves the results were intentional and not something that we are just seeing because we want to see it, like "faces in clouds" (*pareidolia* or *apophenia*) and certainly not projected or cherry-picked data.

Also, the deeper we go into studying this "picture," we find things that are more ambiguous, and this is where interpretation does indeed come into it. However, the information is so cleverly devised, we also find that it is multileveled in respect to the further meanings and associations we can derive from it—all of which can be seen to correlate with the initial information that emerges and is pointing to something specific.

The initial information formed by the coordinates remains invisible until one knows the "key." One is reminded of the scene in the movie *Contact* (1997), based on the book by Carl Sagan, where the pages of primary numbers were totally transformed into a 3-dimensional cube when the cipher to unlock the code was given to Ellie Arroway by S. R. Hadden. It was the only way the code could be read properly.

Jim Penniston and I are currently completing a series of books together on the results of this study.

The center point of the Great Pyramid is on the Great Pyramid's *94th Course Level,* and it is interesting that 94 divided by 4 = 23.5, which is the all-round figure given to the obliquity (tilt angle) of the Earth's axis . . . 23.5°—an angle that is also evident within the north–south cross-section geometry of the Great Pyramid as I had discovered in 2002.

LAST NOTES

What I have revealed above is a relatively short summary of the new data now fast accumulating about the Great Pyramid of Giza—most of it based on my own fifteen-year study of its dimensions and measurements. Among the many primary sources consulted was the data gathered by Sir William Mathew Flinders Petrie, as published in *The Pyramids and Temples of Giza* (1883); also, the measuring survey made on the Great Pyramid by J. H. Cole and published in his book, *Determination of the Exact Size and Orientation of the Great Pyramid of Giza* (1925); as well as the most recent survey conducted in 2015 by the U.S.-based Glen Dash Research Foundation and the Ancient Egypt Research Associates (AERA).

The superlative mathematical/geometric information encapsulated within the Great Pyramid is complicated to unravel and difficult at times to present and explain—especially in an appendix. Not everything could be included here. For example, I have had to exclude several other instances of the numerous references to the constants *pi, Phi, e,* and *c* (the speed of light constant) that I discovered in the dimensions of the Great Pyramid, including how I was able to determine the remarkable data relating to the concavities, the different base-to-height ratios relating to a *spherical object* that I and others have now concluded was once designed to be placed on the apex-capstone of the Great Pyramid, but instead could have been secreted away inside it; the fascinating mathematical data that emerges when we apply various circumcircles to the dimensions of the Great Pyramid; the chamber shafts; the geophysical/geodetic-related angles in its cross-section angle geometry and which relate to the Pythagorean theorem; the fact that the Great Pyramid was constructed on the apex of the Nile Delta Triangle, which is *exactly 1,000 times the size of the Great Pyramid;* and the mathematical relationship that the Great Pyramid has with the true Geographical Center of the Earth, some 775 miles distant, near Ankara, Turkey, as discovered by Holger Isenberg in 2003.

However, in this rather condensed summary of just some of my discoveries, I hope I have gone some way in defining the measurements relating to some of the pyramid's features, while at the same time demonstrating how these measurements work to produce the most remarkable, mathematical data yet seen to emerge from the Great Pyramid of Giza. I could just as well have approached all this as if I were the architect myself, designing a pyramid that encapsulates the knowledge and understanding we have today concerning the measure of the Earth, the combined proportions of the Earth and moon, the mathematical, universal constants *pi, Phi,* and *e,* including the *c* (speed of light) constant, and even the *fine-structure constant,* and so forth. Once completed, then regarding the mathematical data and properties that I have factored into my designed pyramid, I could then take each of its features and compare the data each provides with the data provided by the Great Pyramid of Giza, and I would wager that the comparisons between what I have designed and what was constructed at Giza and on the apex of the Nile Delta—which, although in a dilapidated state still provides us with a close indication of what was drawn up in the initial phase— would be as accurate as 99.999 percent.

I would like to extend my gratitude and thanks to Robert Bauval and Professor Chandra Wickramsinghe for granting me the opportunity to include here some of the results of my own extensive and detailed work.

Notes

CHAPTER 1.
DEFINITE KNOWLEDGE VS. SPECULATION

1. Walker and C. Wickramasinghe, *Big Bang and God.*
2. Bell et al. "Potentially Biogenic Carbon."
3. Hoyle and N. C. Wickramasinghe, *Lifecloud;* Hoyle and C. Wickramasinghe, *Diseases from Space;* Hoyle and C. Wickramasinghe, *Evolution from Space;* Hoyle and C. Wickramasinghe, "Proofs that Life is Cosmic"; Hoyle and N. C. Wickramasinghe, *Living Comets;* Hoyle and N. C. Wickramasinghe, "Case for Life," 509–11; and Hoyle and N. C. Wickramasinghe, *Astronomical Origins of Life.*
4. Walker and C. Wickramasinghe, *Big Bang and God.*
5. Hoyle and C. Wickramasinghe, *Evolution from Space.*
6. Crick and Orgel, "Directed Panspermia," 341.
7. Joseph and N. C. Wickramasinghe, "Genetics Indicates Extra-Terrestrial Origins"; and Keeling and Palmer, "Horizontal Gene Transfer."

CHAPTER 2.
UNRAVELING OF A CONTROVERSY

1. C. Wickramasinghe, *Where Did We Come From?*
2. C. Wickramasinghe, *Journey with Fred Hoyle.*
3. Hoyle and N. C. Wickramasinghe, *Theory of Cosmic Grains;* N. C. Wickramasinghe, *Interstellar Grains.*
4. N. C. Wickramasinghe, "Formaldehyde Polymers in Interstellar Space," 462.
5. Hoyle, and N. C. Wickramasinghe, "Identification of the 2200Å

Interstellar Absorption Feature"; Hoyle and N. C. Wickramasinghe, "Biochemical Chromophores."

6. Hoyle and N. C. Wickramasinghe, *Lifecloud.*
7. Hoyle and N. C. Wickramasinghe, "Biochemical Chromophores."
8. Hoyle et al., "Infrared Spectroscopy"; and Hoyle and N. C. Wickramasinghe, "Case for Life."
9. Hoyle, and N. C. Wickramasinghe, "The Case for Life," 509–11.
10. Bowen, "Unorthodox View of the Weather," 1121.
11. Hoyle and C. Wickramasinghe, *Diseases from Space.*
12. N. C. Wickramasinghe, "DNA Sequencing and Predictions."
13. Hoyle and C. Wickramasinghe, "Some Predictions."
14. *The Times,* March 12, 1986.
15. D. T. Wickramasinghe and Allen, "Discovery of Organic Grains."
16. *IUA Circular,* 1986. No. 4305.
17. Claus and Nagy, "Microbiological Examination"; and Claus, Nagy, and Europa, "Further Observations," 580.
18. Pflug, "Ultrafine Structure."
19. McCafferty, "Bloody Rain Again!"
20. Louis and Kumar, "Red Rain Phenomenon."
21. Rauf, Kani. Ph.D. diss. Cardiff University; Nori Miyake, Ph.D. diss. Cardiff University; Rajkumar Gangappa. Ph.D. diss. Glamorgan University.
22. Wickramarathne and N. C. Wickramasinghe, "Red Rain Cells."
23. Rauf and Miyake, Ph.D. dissertation.
24. J. Wallis et al., "Polonnaruwa Meteorite."

CHAPTER 3. HISTORY OF PANSPERMIA

1. Helmholtz and Wertheim, *Handbuch der Theoretische Physik.*
2. Arrhenius, *Worlds in the Making.*
3. Miller and Urey, "Organic Compound Synthesis."
4. C. Wickramasinghe, *Search for Our Cosmic Ancestry.*
5. Capaccione, Coradini, and Filacchione, "Organic-Rich Surface of Comet 67P/Churyumov-Gerasimenko"; Altwegg et al., "Prebiotic Chemical"; and M. K. Wallis and N. C. Wickramasinghe. "Rosetta Images of Comet 67P/Churyumov-Gerasimenko."

CHAPTER 4. COSMIC COINCIDENCES, GOD, CREATIONISM, AND CONSCIOUSNESS

1. Paley, *View of the Evidence of Christianity.*
2. Wald, "Innovation in Biology."
3. Dyson, *Disturbing the Universe.*
4. Darwin, *On the Origin of Species.*
5. Hoyle and C. Wickramasinghe, *Evolution from Space.*
6. Hameroff and Penrose, "Consciousness in the Universe."

CHAPTER 5. BACTERIA ENTERING EARTH

1. V. W. Greene et al., NASA Report N65-23980, 1962–65.
2. Imshenetsky, Lysenko, and Lach, "Microorganisms of the Upper Layer."
3. D. T. Wickramasinghe, N. C. Wickramasinghe, and Napier, *Comets and the Origin of Life.*
4. Bigg, "Particles in the Upper Atmosphere."
5. Bowen, "Unorthodox View of the Weather," 1121.
6. Harris et al., "Detection of Living Cells"; and Wainwright et al., "Microorganisms Cultured from Stratospheric Air Samples," 161.
7. Shivaji et al., "*Janibacter hoylei* sp. nov."
8. Wainwright et al, 2015. "Biological entities isolated from two stratosphere launches—continued evidence for a space origin," 3:2. www.omicsonline .org/open-access/biological-entities-isolated-from-two-stratosphere -launchescontinuedevidence (accessed July 12, 2017).
9. "Russia Looks for Traces of Extra-Terrestrial Life Forms on ISS Surface," http://tass.com/science/947789 (accessed July 12, 2017).
10. Wainwright et al., "Microorganisms Cultured from Stratospheric Air Samples," 161; and Shivaji et al., "*Janibacter hoylei* sp. nov."
11. Albertin et al., "Octopus Genome."

CHAPTER 6. ALIEN PLANETS AND ALIEN INTELLIGENCE

1. Bruno, *De l'infinito universo e mondi,* 26–28.

CHAPTER 7. EARTH'S
CONTINUALLY CHANGING CONDITIONS

1. Hoyle and N. C. Wickramasinghe, "Comets, Ice Ages and Ecological Catastrophes."
2. Gibbon, *Decline and Fall of the Roman Empire,* chap. 43.

PART II. PROLOGUE

1. Budge, *Mummy,* 406.
2. Bauval, "Master Plan for the Three Pyramids."
3. BBC, *Great Pyramid.*
4. BBC, *Horizon, Atlantis Reborn.*
5. Orofino and Paulo, "Archaeoastronomical Study of the Main Pyramids."

CHAPTER 8.
THE "COINCIDENCE PIGEONS"

1. Hardy, *Ramanujan,* chap. 1.
2. Pickover, *Passion for Numbers,* 2.
3. Aron, "Mathematical Proof Reveals Magic."
4. Kaku, *Future of the Mind.*
5. Tammet, *Born on a Blue Day,* 10–11. See also TED Conference, Long Beach, California, March 2011.
6. Tammet, *Born on a Blue Day,* 140–42.
7. Teffert, "Accidental Genius."
8. Stephen Wiltshire Official Site. www.stephenwiltshire.co.uk/ (accessed March 30, 2017).
9. Wikipedia. "Kim Peek." https://en.wikipedia.org/wiki/Kim_Peek (accessed March 30, 2017).
10. Bauval and Gilbert, *Orion Mystery,* 114–16; see also Bauval and Hohenzollern, *Vatican Heresy,* 248–49.
11. Kaku, *Future of the Mind.*
12. Lederman, *God Particle,* 28.
13. "Why 137?" *Secrets in Plain Sight.* www.secretsinplainsight.com/2015/12/08/why-137 (accessed July 12, 2017).
14. "Why 137?" *Secrets in Plain Sight.* www.secretsinplainsight.com/2015/12/08/why-137 (accessed July 12, 2017).

15. A. Miller, *Deciphering the Cosmic Number.*
16. Read more at Zyga, "Variations in Fine-Structure Constant."
17. Zabriskie, "Jung and Pauli."
18. Primäs, "Synchronicité et Hasard."
19. Feynman, *QED: Strange Theory of Light and Matter,* 129.
20. Lederman, *God Particle,* 28–29.
21. Genesis 25:17; Exodus 6:16, and Exodus 6:20.
22. Lehner, Mark. *Complete Pyramids,* 12; see also Bayuk, "Guardian's Egypt."
23. Bauval and Hancock, *Keeper of Genesis,* 69, 75; for the full story of the Edgar Cayce Foundation and its involvement at Giza, see also Bauval, *Secret Chamber Revisited.*

CHAPTER 9.
PHYSICS AND SYNCHRONICITY

1. Pérez-Sánchez, *La Gran Pirámide.*
2. Bauval, R., "Investigation on the Origins," 5–17.
3. Schaaf, *Nature and History of Pi.*
4. Palmer, "Pi Record Smashed."
5. Mansoori, *Principles of Nanotechnology.*
6. See Pickover, "We Are in Digits of Pi."
7. Maor, *e: The Story of a Number,* 3.

CHAPTER 10.
THE NEXT FRONTIER OF KNOWLEDGE

1. "Neil Tyson Tired of God." YouTube. www.youtube.com/watch?v=BRHefbIgKxk (accessed March 30, 2017).
2. Sagan, *Demon-Haunted World,* 237.
3. Tegmark, "Consciousness as a State of Matter."
4. See Piazza et al. "Simultaneous Observation of the Quantization."
5. Chow, "Top 4 Bonkers Things."
6. See *Scientific American,* vol. 316, no. 6, June 2017, p.34.
7. Jäger, "Hubblecast 96."
8. NASA, "Exoplanets 101."
9. Phillips, "Discovery of 'Arsenic-Bug.'"
10. www.nasa.gov/kepler/discoveries (accessed July 12, 2017).

11. Anthony, "Astronomers Estimate 100 Billion."
12. Kaku, *Future of the Mind*, 300.
13. "Prof. Says Beings from Outer Space Have Visited Earth" *Stars & Stripes*, November 26, 1962, p. 6.
14. Cain, "Dr. Seth Shostak Answers Your Questions."
15. Howell, "Kepler-22b."
16. Kaku, *Future of the Mind*, 302.
17. Bruno, *De l'infinito universo e mondi*, 26–28.
18. Bauval and Hohenzollern, *Vatican Heresy*, 129.
19. Descartes, *Meditations on First Philosophy*, www.marxists.org/reference/archive/descartes/1639/meditations.htm (accessed July 12, 2017); see also Ariew, *Philosophical Essays and Correspondence*, 119.
20. Sagan, *Cosmos*, 318.
21. CERN, "The Early Universe."
22. Sánchez-Andrea, "Microbial Diversity in Anaerobic Sediments."
23. Sagan, *Cosmos*, 318.
24. Henderson, "Intel Claims that by 2026."
25. Bromer et al., "Memory Capacity of Brain."
26. Castelvecchi, "Quantum Computers Ready to Leap."
27. Kaku, *Future of the Mind*, 7–8, 282.
28. Blue Brain Project FAQ 2004 and, for more, see the Blue Brain Project's website: http://bluebrain.epfl.ch (accessed March 31, 2017).
29. Fildes, "Artificial Brain '10 Years Away.'"
30. https://blog.frontiersin.org/2017/06/12/blue-brain-team-discovers-a-multi-dimensional-universe-in-brain-networks.
31. Woollaston, "We'll Be Uploading Our Entire MINDS."
32. Kaku, *Future of the Mind*, 216–17.
33. Kaku, *Future of the Mind*, 217.
34. Kaku, *Future of the Mind*, 214.
35. Quoted in Kaku, *Future of the Mind*, 326.
36. Shakespeare, *Hamlet*, act 2, scene 2.
37. Yates, *Giordano Bruno and the Hermetic Tradition*, 282–83.
38. Kaku, *Future of the Mind*, 327.
39. Koch and Tononi, "Can Machines Be Conscious?"
40. Tononi, Giulio, "Everybody Knows What Consciousness Is," 216.
41. Koch and Tononi, "Physics of Information."
42. Hameroff, "Is Your Brain Really a Computer?" See also Hameroff's

Quantum Consciousness website: www.quantumconsciousness.org (accessed March 31, 2017).

43. Hameroff, "Quantum Consciousness & Mind over Matter."

44. Marcus, "Face It, Your Brain Is a Computer."

45. Keats, Jonathan. "$1.3B Quest."

46. Tegmark, "Consciousness as a State of Matter."

47. Henry, "Mental Universe."

48. Feynman, *Character of Physical Law*, 129.

49. Feynman, quoted in Moskowitz, "Physicists Disagree over Meaning."

50. B. Greene, *Elegant Universe*, 85, 108.

51. *NOVA*, "Fabric of the Cosmos."

52. Ferris, *Red Limit*, 12.

53. Eddington, quoted in Chandler, *Android Myth*, 288.

54. Jean, quoted in Henry, "Mental Universe."

55. Henry, "Mental Universe."

56. UCSD-TV, *Friendship of Science and Religion;* see also Discovery Channel, "Is there a Creator?"

57. Feynman, *QED: Strange Theory of Light and Matter.*

58. See Moskowitz, "Physicists Disagree over Meaning."

59. *NOVA,* "Fabric of the Cosmos."

60. Brooks, "Matter of Interpretation."

61. Hooper, "Multiverse and Me."

62. Kaku, *Future of the Mind*, 335.

63. Kaku, "Multiverse Theory."

64. *Scientific American,* June 2017, vol. 316, no. 6, p. 30.

65. See *Scientific American,* June 2017, vol. 316, no. 6, p. 30.

66. Hewett, "Hidden Dimensions and String Theory."

67. B. Greene, *Elegant Universe*, 4.

68. Nadis, "Fall and Rise of String Theory."

69. *Scientific American,* June 2017, vol. 316, no. 6, p. 29.

70. www.weedvideos.com/video.mason/The-Universe-Science-TV-Series (accessed July 12, 2017).

71. See American Museum of Natural History, "Isaac Asimov Annual Memorial Debate."

72. Kuhn, "Testing the Multiverse."

73. Monnier et al., "Pourquoi on ne saura Jamais."

74. Gott, quoted in Kuhn, "Testing the Multiverse."

CHAPTER 11. THE ARCHIVES OF THE MIND

1. Petrie, *Pyramids and Temples of Gizeh,* 1990, 80–81.
2. Legon, "Plan of the Giza Pyramids."
3. BBC, *Great Pyramid: Gateway to the Stars.*
4. BBC, *Great Pyramid: Gateway to the Stars.*
5. Kerisel, *Khéops,* 227.
6. Bauval and Gilbert, *Orion Mystery,* app. 9.
7. Legon, "Ground Plan at Giza," 33–40; Legon, and "Giza Ground Plan and Sphinx," 53–60. See John A. R. Legon, "The Plan of the Giza Pyramids," www.legon.demon.co.uk/gizaplan.htm (accessed April 3, 2017).
8. Creighton, *Great Pyramid Hoax.*
9. Stille, "World's Oldest Papyrus."
10. See Bauval and Brophy, *Imhotep the African,* 24–27.
11. Bauval, *Orion Mystery;* Bauval and Hancock, *Keeper of Genesis;* and Bauval and Brophy, *Imhotep the African.*
12. Allen, *Ancient Egyptian Pyramid Texts* (2005), 8.
13. Kaku, *Future of the Mind,* 7–8.
14. Rees, *Our Final Hour,* 181–82.
15. Lane, "Explications des Planches."
16. Petrie, *Pyramids and Temples at Gizeh,* 43–44.
17. Clarke and Englebach, *Ancient Egyptian Construction and Architecture,* 128.
18. Maragioglio and Rinaldi, *L'Architettura delle Pitamidi Memfite,* 104.
19. The aerial photograph of the Giza pyramids by P. R. C. Groves was published in Groves and McCrindle, "Flying over Egypt, Sinai and Palestine."
20. Pochan, *L'Enigme de la Grande Pyramide,* 134.
21. Isler, "Concerning the Concave Faces," 27–32.
22. Tompkins, *Secrets of the Great Pyramid,* 21. See also Shalev, "Measurer of All Things."
23. Birch, *Miscellaneous Works of Mr. John Greaves,* 405–33.
24. See Newton, "Dissertation upon the Sacred Cubit."
25. Petrie, *Pyramids and Temples of Gizeh,* 81. See also items 51 & 52 from the book at www.ronaldbirdsall.com/gizeh/petrie/c7.html#51 (accessed April 3, 2017).
26. Tompkins, *Secrets of the Great Pyramid,* 31.
27. Piazzi Smyth, *Great Pyramid,* 27.
28. Quoted in Bonwick, *Great Pyramid of Giza,* 71–72.

29. Brück and Brück, *Peripatetic Astronomer,* 97–98. See also Piazzi Smyth, *Great Pyramid,* ix–x.
30. Piazzi Smyth, *Great Pyramid,* 19.
31. Piazzi Smyth, *Great Pyramid,* 29. The casing block brought by Waynman Dixon is now displayed at the National Museum of Scotland. See Lightbody, "Edinburgh Casing Stone."
32. Piazzi Smyth, *Great Pyramid,* 27, 55.
33. Piazzi Smyth, *Great Pyramid,* 61.
34. Piazzi Smyth, *Great Pyramid,* 29.
35. Petrie, *Seventy Years in Archaeology.*
36. Cottrell, *Mountains of Pharaoh,* 164.
37. Brück and Brück, *Peripatetic Astronomer,* ix.
38. Brück and Brück, *Peripatetic Astronomer,* 258.
39. Brück and Brück, *Peripatetic Astronomer,* 256.
40. Bauval, *Secret Chamber Revisited,* chap. 9.
41. Lehner, *Complete Pyramids,* 12.
42. Lauer, *Le problème des pyramides d'Egypte;* also Lauer, "Sur le choix de l'angle." See also Robbins and Shute, "Mathematical Base."
43. Rossi, "Note on the Pyramidion."
44. Jacobs, "Temporal Epoch Calculations." See also Newton, "Source of Eratosthenes' Measurement."
45. Jomard, Edme-François. "Memoire sur le systeme metrique," 723–28. See original text in French in Jomard, "Exposition due système metrique," 440–41.
46. Jomard, Edme-François. "Memoire sur le systeme metrique," 723–28. See original text in French in Jomard, "Exposition due système metrique," 440–41.
47. Laplace, *Exposition du système du monde,* chap. 2, 411–12.
48. Schwaller de Lubicz, *Temple of Man,* 305.
49. Tompkins, *Secrets of the Great Pyramid,* 1971, 46–47.
50. Jomard, "Remarques sur les signes numériques," 204.
51. Lassus and Jomard, *Le dernier Egyptien.*
52. Jomard, "Hauteur du triangle des face," 36–38
53. Jomard, "Remarques et recherches," 163–80.
54. Cole, *Determination of the Exact Size and Orientation.*
55. CSG Network, "Length of a Degree."
56. Buchanan, *Comptes Rendus,* 466.
57. Jomard, "Exposition due système metrique," chap. XII, 18, 435.
58. Jomard, "Exposition due système metrique," chap. XII, 23–24.

59. Secrets in Plain Sight, "Why 137?"

60. Fischer, "Another Look," 152.

61. Neugebauer, "History of Ancient Astronomy," 24.

62. Wallis-Budge, *Gods of the Egyptians,* 132.

63. Herodotus. *Histories II,* 4.

64. Bauval, *Egypt Code,* 112–16; see also Antoniadi, *L'Astronomie Egyptienne,* 3–4.

65. Diodorus of Sicily. *Bibliotheca Historica,* book V, 57, and book I, 81.

66. Schwaller de Lubicz, *Sacred Science,* 280.

67. Petrie, *Seventy Years in Archaeology* (1931), 35.

68. Capart and Werbrouck, *Memphis à l'ombre des pyramides.*

69. Mertz, *Temples, Tombs, and Hieroglyphs.*

70. BBC. *The Great Pyramid: Gateway to the Stars.*

71. Bauval, *Secret Chamber Revisited,* 32–32, 225–29.

72. Schwaller de Lubicz, *Temple of Man,* 281.

73. Ibid., xviii.

74. Cheak, *Alchemical Tradition,* 466.

75. Schwaller de Lubicz, *The Temple of Man,* 281, n. 9.

76. Ibid.

77. Ibid., 281, 283.

78. For an online version of Petrie's *Pyramids and Temples of Gizeh,* see www
.ronaldbirdsall.com/gizeh (accessed April 5, 2017).

79. Petrie, *Seventy Years in Archaeology,* 1931, sect. 51.

80. Petrie, *Seventy Years in Archaeology,* 1931, sect. 57.

81. Dunn, "Advanced Machining in Ancient Egypt?" See also Dunn, "Advanced Machining in Ancient Egypt."

82. Dunn, *Lost Technologies of Ancient Egypt.*

83. Dunn, *Giza Power Plant.*

84. Bauval, *Secret Chamber Revisited,* 352–53.

85. Bauval, "Seeding of the Star Gods."

86. Gantenbrink, "Upuaut Report."

87. Miatello, "Reading of the Graffito."

88. Gantenbrink, "Upuaut Report."

89. Dr. Seti. "What Is the Hydrogen Line?"

90. See Purplemath. "How Can 0.999 . . . = 1?"

91. Allen, *Ancient Egyptian Pyramid Texts,* 2nd ed., 12.

92. Ibid., 7, 12.

93. Badawy, "Stellar Destiny of Pharaoh"; and Trimble, "Astronomical Investigations."
94. Bauval, "Seeding of the Star-Gods," 21–25.
95. Space Daily. "Orion Nebula Gives Clues."
96. Lehner, *Complete Pyramids,* 120.
97. Piazzi Smyth, *Great Pyramid,* 80.
98. Gibran, *Voice of the Master.*
99. See the U.S. Geological Survey's EarthExplorer page at http://earth explorer.usgs.gov/. "Great Pyramid of Giza" (accessed April 6, 2017). See also GEOHACK of World Geodetic System 1984 (WGS84), which gives 29.979175° N, 31.134358° E. For the uncertainty level for WGS84 datum see Nearby.org.uk, "Precision and Uncertainty of Latitude Longitude Coordinates." www.nearby.org.uk/precision-ll.cgi?lat=29.9792&long =31.1342 (accessed April 28, 2017).
100. Brooks, Michael. "Seven Wonders of the Quantum World."
101. For more about the Scan Pyramids Mission, see the Arab Republic of Egypt Ministry of Antiquities' Scan Pyramids Mission website: www.scan pyramids.org (accessed April 6, 2017).
102. Lederman, *God Particle,* 58.
103. Roy, *Archives of the Mind,* 362. See www.telegraph.co.uk/news/obituaries /9946847/Professor-Archie-Roy.html (accessed April 6, 2017).
104. Brooks, "Spooky Action at a Distance."
105. Mullins, "Quantum Time Machine."
106. Musk, "Full Interview: Code Conference 2016."
107. Solon, "Is Our World a Simulation?" The newspaper's online article includes a short video statement from Elon Musk.
108. Solon, "Is Our World a Simulation?" The newspaper's online article includes a short video statement from Elon Musk.
109. Tyson, Neil DeGrasse, "Best Explanation Ever!"
110. Kinder, "Do We Live in the Matrix?"

APPENDIX I.
THE CONCAVITY OF THE GREAT PYRAMID

1. Lane, "Explications des planches."
2. Petrie, *Pyramids and Temples at Gizeh,* 43–44.
3. Clarke and Englebach, *Ancient Egyptian Construction and Architecture,* 128.

4. Edwards, *Pyramids of Egypt,* 222.

5. Pochan, *L'Enigme de la Grande Pyramide,* 134.

6. Isler, "Concerning the Concave Faces."

7. Pérez-Sánchez, *La Gran Pirámide,* 94–95.

8. Lauer, *Le problème des pyramides d'Egypte.* Also Lauer, "Sur le choix de l'angle."

9. Rossi, "Note on the Pyramidion."

10. Taylor, *Great Pyramid.*

11. Pérez-Sánchez, *La Gran Pirámide,* 162.

APPENDIX 2. THE LOCATION OF
THE KING'S CHAMBER IN THE GREAT PYRAMID

1. See Gantenbrink, "Upuaut Report."

2. Howard-Vyse, *Operation Carried Out at Gizeh,* 205.

3. Legon, "Design of the Pyramid of Khufu"; and Legon, "Geometry of the Great Pyramid."

4. Lehner, *Complete Pyramids,* 112–13. A few researchers, however, discount the stellar meaning of the shafts and attribute to them a geometrical meaning relative to the position of the King's Chamber (see Legon, "Geometry of the Air-Shafts").

5. Trimble, Virginia. "Astronomical Investigations," heft 2/3.

APPENDIX 3.
THE GREAT PYRAMID OF GIZA

1. Funck-Hellet, *La Bible et la Grande Pyramide d'Egypte* (*The Bible and the Great Pyramid of Egypt*).

2. See Boyer and Merzbach, *A History of Mathematics.*

3. Fix, *Pyramid Odyssey.*

4. Fix, *Pyramid Odyssey.*

5. See Dash, "How the Great Pyramids May Have Found Their True North," 8–14.

6. The small section of one of the Great Pyramid's casing stones resides in the National Museum of Scotland at Edinburgh. See, Lightbody, *Biography of a Great Pyramid Casing Stone.*

7. Taylor, who in 1859 published his book, *The Great Pyramid: Why Was*

It Built? And Who Built it? was the first person to notice the very simple 14:11 ratio intrinsic in the basic proportions of the Great Pyramid, and who also revealed both *pi* and *Phi* to an unexpected degree of accuracy.

8. Tompkins, *Secrets of the Great Pyramid,* 146.
9. Dash, "New Angles on the Great Pyramid," 9.
10. Petrie, *The Pyramids and Temples of Gizeh,* 83.
11. Petrie, *The Pyramids and Temples of Gizeh,* 17.
12. Michell, *City of Revelation.*
13. Hancock, from the foreword of *The Giza Prophecy* by Gary Osborn and Scott Creighton.

Bibliography

Albertin, Caroline B., Oleg Simakov, Therese Mitros, Z. Yan Wang, Judit R. Pungor, Eric Edsinger-Gonzales, Sydney Brenner, Clifton W. Ragsdale, and Daniel S. Rokhsar. "The Octopus Genome and the Evolution of Cephalopod Neural and Morphological Novelties." *Nature* 524 (2015): 220–24.

Allen, James P. *The Ancient Egyptian Pyramid Texts.* Atlanta, Ga.: Society of Biblical Studies, 2005.

———. *The Ancient Egyptian Pyramid Texts.* 2nd ed. Atlanta, Ga.: SBL Press, 2015.

Altwegg, Kathrin, Hans Balsiger, Akiva Bar-Nun, Jean-Jacques Berthelier, Andre Bieler, Peter Bochsler, Christelle Briois, et al. "Prebiotic Chemical— Amino Acid and Phosphorus in the Coma of Comet 67P/Churyumov-Gerasimenko." *Science Advances* 2, no. 5 (2016): 2.

American Museum of Natural History. "Isaac Asimov Annual Memorial Debate: Is the Universe a Simulation?" YouTube. www.youtube.com /watch?v=wgSZA3NPpBs (accessed March 31, 2017).

Anthony, Sebastian. "Astronomers Estimate 100 Billion Habitable Earth-Like Planets in the Milky Way, 50 Sextillion in the Universe." ExtremeTech. www.extremetech.com/extreme/152573-astronomers-estimate-100-billion -habitable-earth-like-planets-in-the-milky-way-50-sextillion-in-the-universe (accessed March 30, 2017).

Antoniadi, M. *L'Astronomie Egyptienne.* Paris: Gauthier-Villars, 1934.

Ariew, R. *Philosophical Essays and Correspondence by René Descartes.* Cambridge, Mass.: Hackett Publishing Co., 2000.

Aron, Jacob. "Mathematical Proof Reveals Magic of Ramanujan's Genius." *New Scientist,* November 10, 2012.

Arrhenius, S. *Worlds in the Making.* London: Harper, 1908.

BBC. *The Great Pyramid: Gateway to the Stars.* February 7, 1994.

BBC *Horizon. Atlantis Reborn.* November 4, 1999.

Badawy, A. "The Stellar Destiny of Pharaoh and the So-Called Air-Shafts of Cheops's Pyramid." *Mitteilungen der Instituts fur Orientforschung* (Akademie der Wissenschaften zu Berlin) Band 10 (1964): 189–206.

Bauval, Robert. *The Egypt Code.* London: Century Books, 2006.

———. "Investigation on the Origins of the Benben Stone: Was It an Iron Meteorite?" *Discussions in Egyptology* 14 (1989): 5–17.

———. "A Master Plan for the Three Pyramids of Giza Based on the Configuration of the Three Stars of the Belt of Orion." *Discussions in Egyptology* 13 (1989): 7–19.

———. *Secret Chamber Revisited: The Quest for the Lost Knowledge of Ancient Egypt.* Rochester, Vt.: Bear & Company, 2014.

———. "The Seeding of the Star Gods: A Fertility Ritual inside the Great Pyramid." *Discussions in Egyptology* 16 (1990): 21–29.

Bauval, Robert, and Thomas Brophy. *Imhotep the African: Architect of the Cosmos.* New York: Disinformation Books Inc., 2013.

Bauval, Robert, and Adrian Gilbert. *The Orion Mystery: Unlocking the Secrets of the Pyramids.* London: William Heinemann, 1994.

Bauval, Robert, and Graham Hancock. *Keeper of Genesis: A Quest for the Hidden Legacy of Mankind.* London: William Heinemann, 1996.

Bauval, Robert, and Chiara Hohenzollern. *The Vatican Heresy: Bernini and the Building of the Hermetic Temple of the Sun.* Rochester, Vt.: Inner Traditions, 2013.

Bayuk, Andrew. "Guardian's Egypt." Guardians.net. www.guardians.net/egypt /pyramids/Khafre/KhafrePyramid.htm (accessed March 30, 2017).

Bell, Elizabeth A., Patrick Boehnke, T. Mark Harrison, and Wendy L. Mao. "Potentially Biogenic Carbon Preserved in a 4.1 Billion-Year-Old Zircon." *PNAS* 112, no. 47 (2015): 14518–21. www.pnas.org/cgi/doi/10.1073 /pnas.1517557112 (accessed April 25, 2017).

Bigg, E. K. "Particles in the Upper Atmostphere." In *Fundamental Studies and the Future of Science,* edited by Chandra Wickramasinghe. Cardiff: University College Cardiff Press, 1984.

Birch, Thomas. *Miscellaneous Works of Mr. John Greaves, Professor of Astronomy in the University of Oxford.* Vol. 2. London: J. Hughes, 1737.

Bonwick, James. *The Great Pyramid of Giza: History and Speculation.* New York: Dover, 2002.

Bowen, E. G. "An Unorthodox View of the Weather." *Nature* 117 (1956): 1121–23.

Boyer, Carl B., and Uta C. Merzbac. *A History of Mathematics*. San Francisco: Jossey Bass, 2011.

Bromer, Cailey, Justin Kinney, Michael A. Chirillo, and Jennifer N. Bourne. "Memory Capacity of Brain Is 10 Times More than Previously Thought." Salk News. www.salk.edu/news-release/memory-capacity-of-brain-is -10-times-more-than-previously-thought (accessed March 31, 2017).

Brooks, Michael. "Matter of Interpretation." *New Scientist: The Quantum World* 3, no. 3 (2016): 16.

———. "Seven Wonders of the Quantum World." *New Scientist: The Quantum World*. www.newscientist.com/article/mg20627596-000-seven-wonders-of -the-quantum-world (accessed April 6, 2017).

———. "Spooky Action at a Distance." *New Scientist: The Quantum World*. www.newscientist.com/article/mg23030710-500-thats-odd-quantum -entanglement-mangles-space-and-time.

Brown, James, James J. Hurtak, and Desiree Hurtak. *Ancient Egypt's Electrical Power and Gas Generating Systems*. Los Gatos, Calif.: Academy for Future Science, 2012.

Brück, Mary, and Hermann Brück. *The Peripatetic Astronomer: The Life of Charles Piazzi Smyth*. Bristol, England: Adam Hilger Publishers, 1988.

Bruno, Giordano. *De l'infinito universo e mondi*. Venice, Italy: Edizione Acrobat a Cura di Patrizio Sanasi, 1584.

Buchanan, John Young. *Comptes Rendus of Observations and Reasoning*. Cambridge: Cambridge University Press, 1917.

Budge, Ernest Alfred Wallis. *The Mummy*. Cambridge: Cambridge University Press, 1925.

Cain, Fraser. "Dr. Seth Shostak Answers Your Questions about SETI." Universe Today: Space and Astronomy News. www.universetoday.com/10229/dr -seth-shostak-answers-your-questions-about-seti (accessed March 30, 2017).

Capaccione, F., A. Coradini, and G. Filacchione. "The Organic-Rich Surface of Comet 67P/Churyumov-Gerasimenko as Seen by VIRTIS/Rosetta." *Science* 347 (2015): 6220.

Capart, Jean, and Marcel Werbrouck. *Memphis à l'ombre des pyramides*. Brussels: Vromant, 1930.

Castelvecchi, Davide. "Quantum Computers Ready to Leap Out of the Lab in 2017."

Nature. www.nature.com/news/quantum-computers-ready-to-leap-out-of -the-lab-in-2017-1.21239 (accessed March 31, 2017).

CERN. "The Early Universe." http://home.cern/about/physics/early-universe (accessed March 30, 2017).

Chandler, Keith. *The Android Myth: How Humans Think, and Why Computers Can't.* New York: Writer's Showcase, 2002.

Cheak, Aaron, ed. *Alchemical Tradition: From Antiquity to the Avant-Garde.* Melbourne, Australia: Numen Books, 2013.

Chow, Marcus. "Top 4 Bonkers Things about the Universe." Physics.org. www .physics.org/featuredetail.asp?id=41 (accessed March 30, 2017).

Clarke, Somers, and R. Englebach. *Ancient Egyptian Construction and Architecture.* Oxford: Oxford University Press, 1930.

Claus, George, and Bartholomew Nagy. "A Microbiological Examination of Some Carbonaceous Chondrites." *Nature* 192 (1961): 594.

Claus, George, Bartholomew Nagy, and D. L. Europa. "Further Observations on the Properties of the 'Organized Elements' in Carbonaceous Chondrites." *Annals of the New York Academy of Science* 108 (1963), 580–605.

Cole, J. H. *Determination of the Exact Size and Orientation of the Great Pyramid of Giza.* Cairo: Government Press, 1925.

Cottrell, Leonard. *The Mountains of Pharaoh.* London: Book Club Associates, 1975.

Creighton, Scott. *The Great Pyramid Hoax.* Rochester, Vt.: Bear & Company, 2017.

Crick, Francis Harry Compton, and Leslie Eleazer Orgel. "Directed Panspermia." *Icarus* 19 (1973): 341–46.

CSG Network. "Length of a Degree Of Latitude and Longitude Calculator." www.csgnetwork.com/degreelenllavcalc.html (accessed April 4, 2017).

Darwin, Charles F. *On the Origins of Species by Means of Natural Selection.* London: John Murray, 1859.

Dash, Glen. "How the Pyramid Builders May Have Found Their True North." *AERAGRAM* 14, no. 1 (Spring 2013): 8–14.

"New Angles on the Great Pyramid." *AERAGRAM* 13, no. 2 (Fall 2012): 10–19.

Descartes, René. *Meditations on First Philosophy.* www.marxists.org/reference /archive/descartes/1639/meditations.htm (accessed July 12, 2017).

Diodorus of Sicily. *Bibliotheca Historica.*

Discovery Channel. "Is There a Creator?" *Through the Wormhole,* 2014.

Dr. Seti. "What Is the Hydrogen Line?" SETI League. www.setileague.org /askdr/hydrogen.htm (accessed April 5, 2017).

Dunn, Christopher. "Advanced Machining in Ancient Egypt." Giza Power. www.gizapower.com/Advanced/Advanced%20Machining.html (accessed April 5, 2017).

———. "Advanced Machining in Ancient Egypt?" *Analog Magazine,* August 1984.

———. *The Giza Power Plant.* Rochester, Vt.: Bear and Company, 1998.

———. *Lost Technologies of Ancient Egypt.* Rochester, Vt.: Bear and Company, 2010.

Dyson, Freeman. *Disturbing the Universe.* New York: Harper & Row, 1979.

Edwards, I. E. S. *The Pyramids of Egypt.* London: Penguin Books, 1946.

Ferris, Timothy. *The Red Limit: The Search for the Edge of the Universe.* London: Corgi Books, 1979.

Feynman, Richard. *The Character of Physical Law.* Cambridge, Mass.: MIT Press, 1965.

———. *QED: The Strange Theory of Light and Matter.* Princeton, N.J.: Princeton University Press, 2006.

Fildes, Jonathan, "Artificial Brain '10 Years Away.'" BBC News. http://news.bbc .co.uk/2/hi/8164060.stm (accessed March 31, 2017).

Fischer, Irene. "Another Look at Eratosthenes' and Posidonius' Determinations of the Earth's Circumference." *Quarterly Journal of the Royal Astronomical Society* 16 (1975): 152.

Fix, William R. *Pyramid Odyssey.* New York: Smithmark, 1978.

Funck-Hellet, Charles. *La Bible et la Grande Pyramide d'Egypte: Temoignages authentiques du metre et de pi* (The Bible and the Great Pyramid of Egypt: Genuine Testimonies of the Meter and Pi). Paris: Editions Vincent, Freal and Co., 1956.

Gantenbrink, Rudolf. "The Upuaut Report." Cheops.org. www.cheops.org (accessed April 5, 2017).

Gibbon, Edward. *Decline and Fall of the Roman Empire.* New York: Fred de Fau and Co., 1906.

Gibran, Kahlil. *The Voice of the Master.* New York: Citadel Press, 1958.

Greene, Brian. *The Elegant Universe.* London: Vintage, 2000.

Greene, V. W., P. D. Pederson, D. A. Lundgren, C. A. Hagberg, and G. A. Soffen. NASA Report N65-23980, 1962–65.

Groves, P. R. C., and Major J. R. McCrindle. "Flying over Egypt, Sinai and Palestine." *National Geographic* 50, no. 3 (September 1926): 313–55.

"Halley's Comet." *The Times,* March 12, 1986.

Hameroff, Stuart. "Quantum Consciousness & Mind over Matter." YouTube. www.youtube.com/watch?v=5_w39gHqF3Q (accessed March 31, 2017).

———. "Is Your Brain Really a Computer, or is It a Quantum Orchestra?" *Huffington Post,* July 8, 2016.

Hameroff, Stuart, and Roger Penrose. "Consciousness in the Universe: A Review of the 'Orch OR' Theory." *Physics of Life Reviews* 11, no. 1 (2014): 39–78.

Hancock, Graham. In Osborn, Gary, and Scott Creighton. *The Giza Prophecy.* Rochester, Vt.: Bear & Company, 2012.

Hardy, G. H. *Ramanujan.* London: Cambridge University Press, 1940.

Harris, Melanie J., Nalin Chandra Wickramasinghe, David Lloyd, J. V. Narlikar, P. Rajaratnam, Michael P. Turner, Shirwan Al-Mufti, Max K. Wallis, S. Ramadurai, and Fred Hoyle. "Detection of Living Cells in Stratospheric Samples." 2002. *SPIE Proceedings* 4495 (2002): 192.

Helmholtz, Hermann, and G. Wertheim, trans. *Handbuch der Theoretische Physik.* Vol. 1. Paris: G. Masson, 1874.

Henderson, Rik. "Intel Claims that by 2026 Processors Will Have as Many Transistors as There Are Neurons in a Brain" Pocket-Lint. www.pocket-lint .com/news/126289-intel-claims-that-by-2026-processors-will-have -as-many-transistors-as-there-are-neurons-in-a-brain (accessed March 31, 2017).

Henry, Richard C. "The Mental Universe." *Nature* 436 (July 7, 2005).

Herodotus. *The Histories II.* classics.mit.edu/Herodotus/history.2.ii.html (accessed July 12, 2017).

Hewett, Joanne. "Hidden Dimensions and String Theory." YouTube. www .youtube.com/watch?v=92Ov7foW0iA (accessed March 31, 2017).

Hooper, Rowan. "The Multiverse and Me." *The Quantum World* 3: 24. www.newscientist.com/article/mg22329880-400-multiverse-me-should-i-care -about-my-other-selves (accessed July 12, 2017).

Howard-Vyse, Richard William. *Operation Carried Out at Gizeh.* Vol. 1. London: James Fraser, 1840. archives.org (accessed July 12, 2017).

Howell, Elizabeth. "Kepler-22b: Facts about Exoplanet in Habitable Zone." Space .com. www.space.com/24128-kepler-22b.html (accessed March 30, 2017).

Hoyle, Fred, and Chandra Wickramasinghe. *Diseases from Space.* London: J. M. Dent, 1979.

———. *Evolution from Space.* London: J. M. Dent, 1980.

———. *Proofs that Life Is Cosmic: Memoirs of the Institute of Fundamental Studies, Sri Lanka.* Sri Lanka: Institute of Fundamental Studies, 1982.

————. "Some Predictions on the Nature of Comet Halley." *Earth, Moon, and Planets* 36 (1968): 288–93.

Hoyle, Fred, and Nalin Chandra Wickramasinghe. *Astronomical Origins of Life: Steps towards Panspermia*. Dordrecht, the Netherlands: Kluwer Academic Press, 2000.

————. "Biochemical Chromophores and the Interstellar Extinction at Ultraviolet Wavelengths." *Astrophysics and Space Science* 65, no. 1 (1979): 241–44.

————. "The Case for Life as a Cosmic Phenomenon," *Nature* 322 (1986): 509–11.

————. "Comets, Ice Ages and Ecological Catastrophes." *Astrophysics and Space Science* 53 (1978): 523–26.

————. "Identification of the 2200Å Interstellar Absorption Feature." *Nature* 270 (1977): 323.

————. *Lifecloud*. London: J. M. Dent & Sons, 1978.

————. *Living Comets*. Cardiff: University College Cardiff Press, 1985.

————. *The Theory of Cosmic Grains*. Dordrecht, the Netherlands: Kluwer, 1991.

Hoyle, Fred, Nalin Chandra Wickramasinghe, S. Al-Mufti, A. H. Olavesen, and D. T. Wickramasinghe. "Infrared Spectroscopy over the 2.9–3.9 Micron Waveband in Biochemistry and Astronomy." *Astrophysics and Space Science* 83 (1982): 405.

Imshenetsky, A. A., S. V. Lysenko, and S. P. Lach. "Microorganisms of the Upper Layer of the Atmosphere and the Protective Role of Their Cell Pigments." *Life Sciences in Space Research* 17 (1979): 105–10.

Isler, Martin. "Concerning the Concave Faces of the Great Pyramid." *Journal of the American Research Center in Egypt (JARCE)* 20 (1983): 27–32.

IUA Circular. No. 4305, 1986.

Jacobs, James Q. "Temporal Epoch Calculations." www.jqjacobs.net/astro /epoch_2000.html (accessed April 28, 2017).

Jäger, Mathias. "Hubblecast 96: How Many Galaxies Are There?" Hubble Space Telescope. www.spacetelescope.org/announcements/ann1615 (accessed March 30, 2017).

Jomard, Edme-François. "Exposition due système metrique des anciens Égyptiens." In *Description de L'Egypte*. Tome 7. Paris: C.L.F. Panckoucke, 1822.

————. "Hauteur du triangle des face, c'est-a-dire apotheme ou hauteur oblique de la pyramide." In *Memoire sur le systeme metrique des anciens Égyptiens*. Paris: Imprimerie Royale, 1817.

———. "Memoire sur le systeme metrique des anciens Égyptiens." In *Description de L'Egypte*. Translation into English by Deborah and Robert Lawlor. Paris: (1808–1828), 1:723–28.

———. "Remarques et Recherches sur les Pyramides D'Egypte." *Description de L'Egypte*. Paris: C.L.F. Panckoucke, 1822.

———. "Remarques sur les signes numériques des Anciens Égyptiens, fragment d'un ouvrage ayant pour titre: observations et recherches nouvelles . . ." *Description de L'Egypte,* Paris: (1808–1828): C.L.F. Panckoucke, 1822.

Joseph, R., and Nalin Chandra Wickramasinghe. "Genetics Indicates Extra-Terrestrial Origins for Life: The First Gene: Did Life Begin Following the Big Bang?" *Journal of Cosmology* 16 (2011): 6832–61.

Kaku, Michio. *The Future of the Mind*. New York: Penguin Books, 2014.

———. "Multiverse Theory." YouTube. www.youtube.com/watch?v=nZiRO WO6iVs (accessed March 31, 2017).

Keats, Jonathan. "The $1.3B Quest to Build a Supercomputer Replica of a Human Brain." Wired. www.wired.com/2013/05/neurologist-markam -human-brain (accessed March 31, 2017).

Keeling, Patrick J., and Jeffrey D. Palmer. "Horizontal Gene Transfer in Eukaryotic Evolution." *Nature Reviews Genetics* 9 (2008): 605–18.

Kerisel, Jean. *Khéops: Genie e démusure d'un pharaon*. Paris: Stock, 1996.

Kinder, Lucy. "Do We Live in the Matrix? Scientists Believe They May Have Answered the Question." *Telegraph,* November 20, 2013.

Koch, C., and G. Tononi. "Can Machines Be Conscious?" *IEEE Spectrum* 45, no. 6 (2008): 55. doi: 10.1109/MSPEC.2008.4531463.

———. "The Physics of Information." Foundation Questions Institute FQXi Fourth International Conference, Vieques Island, Puerto Rico, January 5–10, 2014. www.youtube.com/watch?v=1cO4R_H4Kww (accessed March 31, 2017).

Kuhn, Robert L. "Testing the Multiverse: Beyond the Limits of Science?" April 1, 2016. Space.com. www.space.com/32452-can-science-explain-the -multiverse.html (accessed March 31, 2017).

Lane, Edward William. "Explications des Planches." In *Description de L'Egypte*. Tome V, planche 8, no. 10. Paris: Imprimerie de C. L. Panckoucke, 1809–1829.

Laplace, Pierre-Simon. *Exposition du système du monde*. Vol. 6. Book 5. Paris: Bachelier, 1884.

Lassus, Yves. *Jomard, Le dernier Egyptien*. Paris: Fayard, 2004.

Lauer, Jean-Philippe. *Le problème des pyramides d'Egypte*. Paris: Payot, Bibliothèque Historique, 1948.

————. "Sur le choix de l'angle de pente dans les pyramides d'Egypte." *Bulletin de l'Institut d'Egypte* XXXVII (1955): 57–67.

Lederman, Leon M. *The God Particle: If the Universe Is the Answer, What Is the Question?* Boston, Mass.: Houghton Mifflin Harcourt, 1993. Reprint, New York: Mariner Books, 2006.

Legon, John. "The Design of the Pyramid of Khufu." *Discussions in Egyptology* 12 (1988): 41–48.

————. "The Geometry of the Air-Shafts." www.legon.demon.co.uk/geomgp .htm (accessed April 6, 2017).

————. "The Geometry of the Great Pyramid." *Göttinger Miszellen* 108 (1989): 57–64.

————. "The Giza Ground Plan and Sphinx." *Discussions in Egyptology* 14 (1989): 53–60. www.legon.demon.co.uk/gizaplan.htm (accessed April 3, 2017).

————. "A Ground Plan at Giza." *Discussions in Egyptology* 10 (1988): 33–40.

————. "The Plan of the Giza Pyramids." *Archaeological Reports* 10, no. 1 (May 1979). The Archaeology Society of Staten Island and the Staten Island Society, Archaeological Institute of America.

Lehner, Mark. *The Complete Pyramid*. London: Thames & Hudson, 1997.

Lightbody, David. "The Edinburgh Casing Stone: A Piece of Giza at the National Museum of Scotland." National Museums Scotland. http://blog .nms.ac.uk/2013/07/15/the-edinburgh-casing-stone-a-piece-of-giza-at-the -national-museum-of-scotland (accessed April 3, 2017).

Lightbody, David Ian. "Biography of a Great Pyramid Casing Stone." *The Journal of Ancient Egyptian Architecture* 1 (2016): 39–56.

Louis, Godfrey, and A. Santhosh Kumar. "The Red Rain Phenomenon of Kerala and Its Possible Extraterrestrial Origin." *Astrophysics and Space Science* 302 (2006): 175–87.

Mansoori, G. Ali. *Principles of Nanotechnology*. Singapore: World Scientific Publishing Co. Ltd., 2005.

Maor, Eli. *e: The Story of a Number*. Princeton, N.J.: Princeton University Press, 1994.

Maragioglio, Vito, and Celeste Rinaldi. *L'Architettura delle Pitamidi Memfite.* Part 4. Rome: Tavole, 1965.

Marcus, Gary. "Face It, Your Brain Is a Computer." New York Times Sunday Review, June 27, 2015. www.nytimes.com/2015/06/28/opinion/sunday /face-it-your-brain-is-a-computer.html?_r=2 (accessed March 31, 2017).

Mazur, Joseph. *Fluke: The Maths and Myths of Coincidences.* London: One World Publications, 2016.

McCafferty, Patrick. "Bloody Rain Again! Red Rain in Meteors in History and Myth." *International Journal of Astrobiology* 7, no. 1 (2008): 9–15.

Meier, C. A., ed. *Atoms and Archetypes: The Pauli/Jung Letters 1932–1958.* Princeton, N.J.: Princeton University Press, 2014.

Mertz, Barbara. *Temples, Tombs, and Hieroglyphs: A Popular History of Ancient Egypt.* London: Constable and Robinson, 2010.

Miatello, Luca. "Reading of the Graffito at the End of the QC's Southern Shaft in the Pyramid of Khufu as Hieratic Numerals." www.academia .edu/10975606/Reading_of_the_graffito_at_the_end_of_the_QC_s _southern_shaft_in_the_pyramid_of_Khufu_as_hieratic_numerals (accessed April 5, 2017).

Michell, John. *City of Revelation: On the Proportions and Symbolic Numbers of the Cosmic Temple.* London: Garnstone Press, 1972.

Miller, Arthur. *Deciphering the Cosmic Number: The Strange Friendship of Wolfgang Pauli and Carl Jung.* New York: W. W. Norton & Co., 2009.

Miller, Stanley L., and Harold C. Urey. "Organic Compound Synthesis on the Primitive Earth." *Science* 130 (1959): 245.

Monnier, Emmanuel, Thomas Cavillé-Fol, Mathieu Grousson, Roman Ikonicoff, Emilie Rauscher, and Benoît Rey. "Pourquoi on ne saura Jamais" (Why We Will Never Know). *Science & Vie,* July 2016, 71.

Moskowitz, Clara. "Physicists Disagree over Meaning of Quantum Mechanics, Poll Shows." *Live Science,* January 21, 2013.

Mullins, Justin. "The Quantum Time Machine." *New Scientist: The Quantum World* 208, no. 2787 (November 2010): 114.

Musk, Elon. "Full Interview: Code Conference 2016." www.youtube.com /watch?v=wsixsRI-Sz4 (accessed April 7, 2017).

Nadis, Steve. "The Fall and Rise of String Theory." *Discover,* June 2016, pp. 18–19.

NASA. "Exoplanets 101." NASA: Exoplanet Exploration. https://exoplanets .nasa.gov/the-search-for-life/exoplanets-101 (accessed March 30, 2017).

Neugebauer, Otto. "The History of Ancient Astronomy." *Journal of Near Eastern Studies* IV (1945): 24.

Newton, Isaac. "A Dissertation upon the Sacred Cubit of the Jews and the Cubits of the Several Nations." The Newton Project. www.newtonproject .sussex.ac.uk/view/texts/normalized/THEM00276 (accessed April 3, 2017).

Newton, Robert R. "The Source of Eratosthenes' Measurement of the Earth." *Journal of the Royal Astronomical Society* 21 (1980): 379–87. http://adsabs .harvard.edu/full/1980QJRAS..21..379N (accessed April 3, 2017).

NOVA. "The Fabric of the Cosmos: Quantum Leap." PBS-TV. November 16, 2011.

Orofino, Vincenzo, and Bernardini Paulo. "Archaeoastronomical Study of the Main Pyramids of Giza, Egypt: Possible Correlation with the Star?" *Archeological Discovery* 4 (January 2016): 1–10.

Osborn, Gary, and Scott Creighton. *The Giza Prophecy.* Rochester, Vt.: Bear and Company, 2012.

Paley, W. *A View of the Evidence of Christianity.* Dublin: Exshaw White, 1794.

Palmer, Jason. "Pi Record Smashed as Team Finds Two-Quadrillionth Digit." BBC News. www.bbc.com/news/technology-11313194 (accessed March 30, 2017).

Pérez-Sánchez, Miquel. *La Gran Pirámide, clave secreta del pasado.* Seville, Spain: Casa de la Ciencia, 2015.

Petrie, Sir William Mathew Flinders. *The Pyramids and Temples at Gizeh.* London: 1883. New and revised edition, London: Histories & Mysteries of Man Ltd., 1990.

———. *Seventy Years in Archaeology.* London: Sampson Low, Marston & Co. 1931. Also New York: Holt and Co., 1932.

Pflug, Hermann D. "Ultrafine Structure of the Organic Matter in Meteorites." In *Fundamental Studies and the Future of Science,* edited by Chandra Wickramasinghe, 24–37. Cardiff: University College Cardiff Press, 1984.

Piazza, L., T. T. A. Lummen, E. Quiñonez, Y. Murooka, B. W. Reed, B. Barwick, and F. Carbone. "Simultaneous Observation of the Quantization and the Interference Pattern of a Plasmonic Near-Field." *Nature Communications,* March 2, 2015. doi: 10.1038 /ncomms7407.

Piazzi Smyth, Charles. *The Great Pyramid: Its Secrets and Mysteries Revealed.* New York: Bell Publications 1990.

Phillips, Tony, ed. "Discovery of 'Arsenic-Bug' Expands Definition of Life." NASA Science Beta. https://science.nasa.gov/science-news/science-at -nasa/2010/02dec_monolake (accessed March 30, 2017).

Pickover, Cliff. "We Are in Digits of Pi and Live Forever." Sprott's Gateway. http://sprott.physics.wisc.edu/pickover/pimatrix.html (accessed March 30, 2017).

Pickover, Clifford A. *A Passion for Numbers.* Hoboken, N.J.: John Wiley & Sons Inc., 2005.

Pochan, André. *L'Enigme de la Grande Pyramide.* Paris: Robert Laffont, 1971.

Primäs, Hans. "Synchronicité et Hasard." Metaphysique.org. www.metapsychique .org/synchronicite-et-hasard.html (accessed March 30, 2017).

"Prof. Says Beings from Outer Space Have Visited Earth." *Stars & Stripes,* November 26, 1962, p. 6.

Purplemath. "How Can 0.999 . . . = 1?" www.purplemath.com/modules /howcan1.htm (accessed April 5, 2017).

Rauf, K. Ph.D. *Stratospheric Dust—Relevance to the theory of Cometary Panspermia.* Dissertation. Cardiff University, 2010.

Rauscher, Elizabeth, and Richard Amoroso. *Orbiting the Moons of Pluto.* London: World Scientific, 2011.

Rees, Sir Martin. *Our Final Hour: A Scientist's Warning.* New York: Basic Books, 2003.

Robbins, G., and C. Shute. "Mathematical Base of Ancient Egyptian Architecture and Graphic Art." *Historia Mathematica* 12 (1985): 107–22.

Rossi, Corinna. "Note on the Pyramidion Found at Dashour." *The Journal of Egyptian Archaeology* 85 (1999): 219–22.

Roy, Archibald E. *The Archives of the Mind.* Essex, England: NSU Publications, 1996.

"Russia Looks for Traces of Extra-Terrestrial Life Forms on ISS Surface," *Science & Space* May 26, 2017. http://tass.com/science/947789 (accessed July 12, 2017).

Sagan, Carl. *Cosmos.* New York: Book Club Associates, 1981.

———. The *Demon-Haunted World.* London: Headline Books, 1996.

Sánchez-Andrea, Irene, Nuria Rodríguez, Ricardo Amils, and José Luis Sanz. "Microbial Diversity in Anaerobic Sediments at Río Tinto, a Naturally Acidic Environment with a High Heavy Metal Content." American Society for Microbiology: Applied and Environmental Biology. http://aem.asm.org /content/77/17/6085.full (accessed March 30, 2017).

Schaaf, William Leonard. *Nature and History of Pi*. School Mathematics Study Group, 1967.

Schwaller de Lubicz, R. A. *Sacred Science: The King of Pharaonic Theocracy*. Rochester, Vt.: Inner Traditions, 1982.

———. *The Temple of Man*. Rochester, Vt.: Inner Traditions, 1998.

Scientific American 316, no. 6, June 2017, p. 34.

Secrets in Plain Sight. "Why 137?" www.secretsinplainsight.com/2015/12/08/why-137 (accessed March 30, 2017).

Shalev, Zur. "Measurer of All Things: John Greaves (1602–1652), the Great Pyramid, and Early Modern Metrology." *Journal of the History of Ideas* 63, no. 4 (October 2002): 555–75.

Shivaji, S., Preeti Chaturvedi, Zareena Begum, Pavan Kumar Pindi, R. Manorama, D. Ananth Padmanaban, Yogesh S. Shouche, et al. "*Janibacter hoylei* sp. nov., *Bacillus isronensis* sp. nov. and *Bacillus aryabhattai* sp. nov. Isolated from Cryotubes Used for Collecting Air from the Upper Atmosphere." *International Journal Of Systematic and Evolutionary Microbiology* 59 (2009): 2977–86.

Solon, Olivia. "Is Our World a Simulation? Why Some Scientists Say It's More Likely than Not." *The Guardian,* October 11, 2016. www.theguardian.com/technology/2016/oct/11/simulated-world-elon-musk-the-matrix (accessed April 6, 2017).

Space Daily. "Orion Nebula Gives Clues to Origin of Life on Earth." www.spacedaily.com/reports/Orion_Nebula_Gives_Clues_To_Origin_Of_Life_On_Earth_999.html (accessed April 6, 2017).

Stille, Alexander, "The World's Oldest Papyrus and What It Can Tell Us About the Great Pyramids." *Smithsonian Magazine*. www.smithsonianmag.com/history/ancient-egypt-shipping-mining-farming-economy-pyramids-180956619 (accessed April 3, 2017).

Tammet, Daniel. *Born on a Blue Day*. London: Hodder and Staughton, 2007.

Taylor, John. *The Great Pyramid: Why Was It Built? And Who Built It?* London: Longman, Green, Longman, and Roberts, 1859.

Teffert, Darold. "Accidental Genius." *Scientific American,* August 2014.

Tegmark, Max. "Consciousness as a State of Matter." Foundation Questions Institute FQXi Fourth International Conference, Vieques Island, Puerto Rico, January 5–10, 2014.

Tesla, Nikola. "Cloudborn Electric Wavelets to Encircle the Globe." *New York Times,* March 27, 1904.

———. *Nikola Tesla on His Work.* Edited by Leland Anderson. Breckenridge, Colo.: 21st Century Books, 2002.

Tompkins, Peter. *Secrets of the Great Pyramid.* New York: Harper & Row, 1971.

———. *Secrets of the Great Pyramid: Two Thousand Years of Adventures and Discoveries Surrounding the Mysteries of the Great Pyramid of Cheops.* New York: BBS Publishing Corporation, 1997.

Tononi, Giulio. "Everybody Knows What Consciousness Is." *Biological Bulletin* 215, no. 3 (December 2008): 216.

Trimble, V. "Astronomical Investigations Concerning the So-Called Air-Shafts of Cheops's Pyramid." *Mitteilungen der Instituts fur Orientforschung* (Akademie der Wissenschaften zu Berlin) Band 10 (1964): 183–87.

Tyson, Neil DeGrasse. "Best Explanation Ever! To A Fascinatingly Disturbing Thought!" YouTube. www.youtube.com/watch?v=aTZyVZBtP70 (accessed April 6, 2017).

UCSD-TV. *The Friendship of Science and Religion—An Afternoon with John Polkinghorne.* University of California Television. November 14, 2010. www.youtube.com/watch?v=nFrYXr8JYgU (accessed March 31, 2017).

Wainwright, M., C. E. Rose, A. J. Baker, Nalin Chandra Wickramasinghe, and T. Omairi. "Biological Entities Isolated from Two Stratosphere Launches—Continued Evidence for a Space Origin." *Astrobiology & Outreach* (2015): 3:2. www.omicsonline.org/open-access/biological-entities-isolated-from-two-stratosphere-launchescontinuedevidence (accessed July 12, 2017).

Wainwright, M., Nalin Chandra Wickramasinghe, J. V. Narlikar, and P. Rajaratnam. "Microorganisms Cultured from Stratospheric Air Samples Obtained at 41 km." *FEMS Microbiology Letters* 218 (2003): 161–65.

Wald, G. "Innovation in Biology." *Scientific American* 199 (1958): 100–115.

Walker, Theo, Jr., and Chandra Wickramasinghe. *The Big Bang and God: An Astrotheology.* Basingstoke, England: Palgrave-Macmillan, 2015.

Wallis, Jamie, Nori Miyake, Richard B. Hoover, Andrew Oldroyd, Daryl H. Wallis, Anil Samaranayake, K. Wickramarathne, et al. "The Polonnaruwa Meteorite: Oxygen Isotope, Crystalline and Biological Composition," *Journal of Cosmology* 22, no. 2 (2013): 21.

Wallis, M. K., and Nalin Chandra Wickramasinghe. "Rosetta Images of Comet 67P/Churyumov-Gerasimenko: Inferences from Its Terrain and Structure." *Journal of Astrobiology & Outreach* 3 (2015): 12.

Wallis-Budge, E. A. *The Gods of the Egyptians.* Vol. 2. New York: Dover Publications, 1969.

"Why 137?" *Secrets in Plain Sight.* www.secretsinplainsight.com/2015/12/08/why-137 (accessed July 12, 2017).

Wickramarathne, K., and Nalin Chandra Wickramasinghe. "Red Rain Cells Recovered from Interior of the Polonnaruwa Meteorite." *Journal of Cosmology* 22, no. 5 (2013): 10076–79.

Wickramasinghe, Chandra. *Fundamental Studies and the Future of Science.* Cardiff: University College Cardiff Press, 1984.

———. *A Journey with Fred Hoyle.* 2nd ed. Singapore: World Scientific Publishing, 2014.

———. *The Search for Our Cosmic Ancestry.* Singapore: World Scientific Publishing, 2015.

———. *Where Did We Come From? Life of an Astrobiologist.* Singapore: World Scientific Publishing, 2015.

Wickramasinghe, D. T., and D. A. Allen. "Discovery of Organic Grains in Comet Halley." *Nature* 323 (1986): 44–46.

Wickramasinghe, D. T., Nalin Chandra Wickramasinghe, and W. M. Napier. *Comets and the Origin of Life.* Singapore: World Scientific Publishing, 2010.

Wickramasinghe, Nalin Chandra. "DNA Sequencing and Predictions of the Cosmic Theory of Life." *Astrophysics and Space Science* 343, no. 1 (2012). doi: 10.1007/s10509-012-1227-y; open access at http://arxiv.org/ftp/arxiv/papers/1208/1208.5035.pdf (accessed April 26, 2017).

———. "Formaldehyde Polymers in Interstellar Space." *Nature* 252 (1974): 462.

———. *Interstellar Grains.* London: Chapman & Hall, 1967.

Wickramasinghe, Nalin Chandra, and E. J. Steele. "Dangers of Adhering to an Obsolete Paradigm: Could Zika Virus Lead to a Reversal of Human Evolution?" *Journal of Astrobiology & Outreach* 4, no. 1: (2016). doi: https://doi.org/10.4172/2332-2519.1000147.

Wikipedia. "Kim Peek." https://en.wikipedia.org/wiki/Kim_Peek (accessed March 30, 2017).

Woollaston, Victoria. "We'll Be Uploading Our Entire MINDS to Computers by 2045 and Our Bodies Will Be Replaced by Machines within 90 Years, Google Expert Claims." *Daily Mail.* www.dailymail.co.uk/sciencetech/article-2344398/Google-futurist-claims-uploading-entire-MINDS-computers-2045-bodies-replaced-machines-90-years.html (accessed March 31, 2017).

Yates, Frances. *Giordano Bruno and the Hermetic Tradition.* Oxon, England: Routledge, 1964.

Zabriskie, Beverley. "Jung and Pauli: A Meeting of Rare Minds." In *Atoms and Archetypes: The Pauli/Jung Letters 1932–1958,* edited by C. A. Meier, xxviii. N.J.: Princeton University Press, 2014.

Zyga, Lisa, "Variations in Fine-Structure Constant Suggest Laws of Physics Not the Same Everywhere." Phys.org. http://phys.org/news/2010-09-variations -fine-structure-constant-laws-physics.html#jCp (accessed March 30, 2017).

Index

Page numbers in *italics* indicate illustrations.
Numbers in *italics* preceeded by *pl.* indicate color insert plate numbers.

BOOKS OF RELATED INTEREST

Origins of the Sphinx
Celestial Guardian of Pre-Pharaonic Civilization
by Robert M. Schoch, Ph.D., and Robert Bauval

Forgotten Civilization
The Role of Solar Outbursts in Our Past and Future
by Robert M. Schoch, Ph.D.

Black Genesis
The Prehistoric Origins of Ancient Egypt
Restoring the Spiritual Engine of the World
by Robert Bauval and Thomas Brophy, Ph.D.

Secret Chamber Revisited
The Quest for the Lost Knowledge of Ancient Egypt
by Robert Bauval

Breaking the Mirror of Heaven
The Conspiracy to Suppress the Voice of Ancient Egypt
by Robert Bauval and Ahmed Osman

Lost Knowledge of the Ancients
A Graham Hancock Reader
Edited by Glenn Kreisberg

The Great Pyramid Hoax
The Conspiracy to Conceal the True History of Ancient Egypt
by Scott Creighton
Foreword by Laird Scranton

Forbidden History
Prehistoric Technologies, Extraterrestrial Intervention, and
the Suppressed Origins of Civilization
Edited by J. Douglas Kenyon

INNER TRADITIONS BEAR & COMPANY
P.O. Box 388
Rochester, VT 05767
1-800-246-8648
www.innertraditions.com

Or contact your local bookseller